DEER

PRATT

The Wildlife Series

Deer

Edited by
Duane Gerlach, Sally Atwater, and Judith Schnell

STACKPOLE
BOOKS

Copyright © 1994 by Stackpole Books

Published by
STACKPOLE BOOKS
5067 Ritter Road
Mechanicsburg, PA 17055

Printed in Hong Kong

First Edition

10 9 8 7 6 5 4 3 2 1

Cover photo by Leonard Lee Rue III
Cover design by Caroline M. Miller
Interior layout by Marcia Lee Dobbs
With special thanks to Valerius Geist for his editorial
assistance

Library of Congress Cataloging-in-Publication Data

Deer / edited by Duane Gerlach, Sally Atwater, and
Judith Schnell.
  1st ed.
      p.   cm. – (The Wildlife series)
   Includes bibliographical references (p.   ) and
index.
   ISBN 0-8117-0433-5
   1. Deer. I. Gerlach, Duane. II. Atwater, Sally.
III. Schnell, Judith.   IV. Series: Wildlife series
(Harrisburg, Pa.)
QL737.U55D3935   1994   94-9642
599.73'57 – dc20   CIP

1/95

Contents

———————

Evolution and taxonomy

Inside the animal

White-tailed deer

MULE AND BLACK-TAILED DEER

THE FUTURE

Contributors

ROBERT D. BROWN is professor and head of the Department of Wildlife and Fisheries Sciences at Texas A&M University. His research interests include comparative wildlife nutrition, venison farming, and antler physiology.

GEORGE A. BUBENIK is an associate professor in the Department of Zoology, University of Guelph, Ontario. His main interests are in the mechanisms of antler growth, environmental endocrinology of deer species, and regulation of seasonality.

WILLIAM KENT CHAPMAN, a member of the adjunct faculty of the Utica College of Syracuse University, specializes in unique plant and animal populations. His research interests include orchids, sambar, sika, and ghost deer.

GARY L. DUSEK, a research biologist with the Montana Department of Fish, Wildlife and Parks, has conducted field research on deer in several areas of the northern Rocky Mountains and Great Plains.

DANIEL B. FAGRE, with the newly created National Biological Survey, continues as the global charge research coordinator and research ecologist at the Glacier National Park field unit where he also serves as unit leader. Past research on predators and ungulates has expanded to ecosystems.

VALERIUS GEIST is a professor and program director of Environmental Science at the University of Calgary, Alberta. He has studied the deer family for more than thirty-five years, focusing on behavior, ecology, and evolution.

DAVID C. GUYNN, JR., is a professor of forest resources at Clemson University. His primary interests are population dynamics of white-tailed deer and wildlife management on private lands.

R. JOSEPH HAMILTON is an assistant regional wildlife biologist with the South Carolina Department of Natural Resources. He resides in the deer-rich Lowcountry, serves on the Advisory Board of the Quality Deer Management Association, and is technical editor of the QDMA quarterly journal *Quality Whitetails*.

RICHARD F. HARLOW is a research wildlife biologist retired from the USDA Forest Service, Southeastern Forest Experiment Station. His primary studies include the habitat requirements of white-tailed deer and the red-cockaded woodpecker.

DAVID H. HIRTH is an associate professor of wildlife biology at the University of Vermont. His primary interest is the behavioral ecology of deer and other large animals.

HARRY A. JACOBSON, professor of wildlife management in the Department of Wildlife and Fisheries at Mississippi State University, has spent his career researching all aspects of white-tailed deer behavior, biology, and ecology.

PAUL R. KRAUSMAN is a professor of wildlife and fisheries science at the University of Arizona, Tucson. He researches and teaches wildlife management, large terrestrial mammals in arid ecosystems, and international wildlife management issues.

JAMES C. KROLL founded the Institute for White-tailed Deer Management and Research at Stephen F. Austin State University's College of Forestry. He has written more than 250 scientific and popular articles as well as a reference book on deer. In addition to whitetails, his research interests have included insectivorous birds and endangered species.

ROLAND C. KUFELD is a wildlife researcher with the Colorado Division of Wildlife in Fort Collins. His primary interests are deer and moose research.

SUSAN LINGLE, a Ph.D. student at the University of Cambridge, is investigating antipredator and reproductive behavior of white-tailed and mule deer. Previously, as a research associate at the University of Calgary, she did extensive research on deer escape gaits.

RICHARD J. MACKIE, professor of wildlife management at Montana State University, has participated in studies of deer population ecology and habitat relationships in the northern Great Plains and Rocky Mountains for more than thirty years.

MARTIN B. MAIN is a Welder Wildlife Fellow and doctoral candidate at Oregon State University. His research focuses on sexual segregation among mule deer from Oregon's high desert and white-tailed deer in south Texas.

R. LARRY MARCHINTON, professor of wildlife biology at the University of Georgia, has studied white-tailed deer for more than thirty years. With his students and colleagues, he has authored nearly two hundred papers on deer behavior and management.

CLIFFORD J. MARTINKA, senior scientist with the National Biological Survey and affiliate faculty member at the University of Montana, has spent nearly three decades designing, conducting, and administering wildlife and other ecological research in Glacier National Park.

KARL V. MILLER is a research scientist and instructor in wildlife biology at the Warnell School of Forest Resources at the University of Georgia. His research interests include the physiology, behavioral ecology, and habitat requirements of white-tailed deer.

AARON N. MOEN is professor of wildlife ecology at Cornell University. He has studied white-tailed deer energetics, physiology, nutrition, behavior, and population dynamics for more than thirty years. He is now preparing electronic information systems on white-tailed deer biology and management.

DIETLAND MÜLLER-SCHWARZE, professor of environmental biology at the SUNY College of Environmental Science and Forestry in Syracuse, has studied chemical communication of caribou, reindeer, and black-tailed, white-tailed, and red deer. Currently, he works on the ecology and conservation of the South American pampas deer.

JOHN J. OZOGA is a former research biologist for the Michigan Department of Natural Resources. He spent nearly thirty years conducting deer research at the Cusino Wildlife Research Station in upper Michigan.

KATHERINE L. PARKER is an assistant professor in the Department of Zoology and Physiology at the University of Wyoming, Laramie. Her primary interests are bioenergetics and nutritional ecology.

OLIN E. RHODES, JR., is an assistant research ecologist at the University of Georgia's Savannah River Ecology Laboratory and serves as an adjunct graduate faculty member at both Texas Tech University and Clemson University.

DAVID E. SAMUEL is professor of wildlife biology and the program coordinator in wildlife and fisheries at West Virginia University. His research focuses on deer management, including the impacts of hunting on deer, and indexing deer numbers in West Virginia.

WILLIAM M. SAMUEL, professor of zoology at the University of Alberta, has studied infectious agents of wildlife with special emphasis on parasites of North American members of the deer family.

MICHAEL H. SMITH is the director of the Savannah River Ecology Laboratory and a professor in the departments of Genetics and Zoology, the Institute of Ecology, and the School of Forest Research at the University of Georgia.

ALAN K. WOOD, wildlife program specialist for the Montana Department of State Lands, has studied habitat and population management of white-tailed and mule deer and other wild and domestic ungulates.

Photographers and artists

STEPHEN B. ANTUS, JR.
THOMAS R. AUBREY
ROBERT E. BARBER
ERWIN & PEGGY BAUER
DAVID BESENGER
MIKE BIGGS
JOHN BINDERNAGEL
MARV BINEGAR
DOMINIQUE BRAUD/
  DEMBINSKY PHOTO
ALAN D. BRIERE
DENVER A. BRYAN
GAY BUMGARNER
KELSEY CAIN
GARY W. CARTER
WILLIAM KENT CHAPMAN
AL CORNELL
ALISSA CRANDALL
SHARON CUMMINGS/
  DEMBINSKY PHOTO
ROBERT B. DAVIES
JEANNE DRAKE
DAVID DVORAK, JR.
LINDA ESCHER
ROY DAVID FARRIS
MICHAEL H. FRANCIS
D. ROBERT FRANZ
VALERIUS GEIST
STEPHEN J. GETTLE
SCOTT WILLIAM HANRAHAN
JESSIE M. HARRIS
HEINER C. HERTLING
KEN HUNTER
GERRY R. JOHNSON
DONALD M. JONES

BILL KINNEY
STEPHEN KIRKPATRICK
DAVID K. LANGFORD
LON E. LAUBER
WILLIAM S. LEA
GERARD LEMMO
SUSAN LINGLE
ANN G. LITTLEJOHN
TINA LLOYD
DOUG LOCKE
JAMES McFALLS
MARTIN B. MAIN
BILL MARCHEL
DAVE MASLOWSKI
DICK MERMON
CHARLES R. MILLER
JAMES C. MILLER
RON MORREIM
BROOKE MORRISON
GERALD L. NAGLE
ARNOLD OLSEN
DAN POLIN
DAVID A. PONTON
ROBERT PRATT
MARGO J. PYBUS
JON RACHAEL
PAUL REZENDES
JEFFREY RICH
GEORGE E. ROBBINS
LEN RUE, JR.
LEONARD LEE RUE III
WILLIAM M. SAMUEL
GREGORY K. SCOTT
JOHN SERRAO
RICHARD P. SMITH

CHICA STRACENER
TOM TIETZ
JOHN TROUT, JR.
MARK F. WALLNER
MARK S. WERNER
ELIZABETH S. WILLIAMS
JIM YUSKAVITCH
DONNA H. ZIEGENFUSS

Publisher's note

---

*I*n a book I was recently reading, a paperback mystery having nothing to do with wildlife, deer were described, in passing, as "gentle."

The book was a good read, but deer, contrary to much popular belief and sentiment, are not gentle. They may do gentle things, or appear gentle, but deer are not gentle.

Little that goes on in the natural world is.

Certain schools insist on seeing the natural world as peaceful and pure. Oddly these same schools refuse to take animals in their natural habitat seriously as legitimate subjects for high art. Art—"serious" art—depicting many varieties of human violence is often praised, while an oil of a weasel killing a chicken would be in effect censored.

Deer, like virtually all wild creatures, lead lives filled with violence. Other animals hurt deer. Deer hurt each other. They get damaged, maimed, cut—they walk around on three legs. They savagely ravage the plant world, as the owner of an apple orchard near deep forest will learn. Winter weather and a diversity of ugly diseases kill deer horribly, as may humans: bad hunters as well as well-meaning ignorants who try to help the animal by improperly feeding or relocating it or otherwise tampering with the natural cycle.

Swift, aggressive, and adaptable, deer are one of the most appreciated and biologically scrutinized animals on the face of the earth. The complexity of their nature fascinates. Their resourcefulness and resiliency are a source of wonder for all who are drawn to study them. Their strength, their handsome bearing and fugitive cunning, not to mention the loveliness of their habitat, make deer a symbol, as well as a prime scientific example, of the majesty of the wild.

Following *Ruffed Grouse* and *Trout* in Stackpole's Wildlife Series, this book is an attempt to provide the latest biological information about the animal and a picture—an evocation—of the deer's life in its world.

There is much new information in the pages that follow, notably exciting data on the deer's senses, appearing for the first time in English, and heretofore unpublished discoveries about deer communication.

You will get the why as well as the how of deer behavior. Photo sequences of the rut, of courtship and copulation, of scraping and rubbing, and of buck-to-buck interaction such as sparring and fighting in earnest show in unprecedented detail the beauty (if we could only get notions of "gentleness" out of our heads) of this amazing creature's days in the reality of its environment.

In the spirit of believing that the planet will never change for the better unless we take as our starting point how things are (as opposed to how we hope they will become), you are invited to turn the pages of *Deer* and step into the beautiful mystery of the real life of a natural creature in its natural world.

M. David Detweiler
President
Stackpole Books

WERNER

Evolution and
taxonomy

Origin of the species

_I_t was excellent habitat for deer: great stretches of magnificent forest, hardwoods like walnut and oak, conifers like spruce and pine, with an understory of hawthorn and honeysuckle. This was not the Green Mountains of Vermont, however; it was north of the Arctic Circle, and the time was 6 million years ago. Such vegetation would easily have supported populations of various deer species, rabbits, squirrels, and other herbivores. Yet there are no bones to be found: a pair of mammalian skulls embedded in wood have been uncovered, but little else. The same acidic conditions that so favored plant preservation—even memorializing beaver dams whose poles still bear the tooth marks of a small, ancient species of beaver—dissolved the bones soon after the animals' death.

Nevertheless, it is likely that ancient deer browsed through the hardwood forests of the high Arctic. As the climate cooled and glaciers formed, the deer and their environment were pushed south on the continent. Four million years ago, the deer reached the unglaciated latitudes of what is now the continental United States. Most of the fossil record from which scientists could reconstruct their forms was pulverized under the crushing glaciers that repeatedly scoured the continent and the Arctic. Just two species of ancient deer can be inferred from the few fragmented bones that have been recovered. _Bretzia pseudalces_ was as large as a modern mule deer and carried palmated antlers, like a moose. _Odocoileus_ was the primitive form of the modern whitetail. Probably, like today's deer, it was an edge species, for its remains have been recovered from fen deposits.

Once having moved south, this ancestral whitetail roamed in the deciduous forests amid moderate or warm temperatures. Other New World deer, those with special ability to deal with cold climates, appeared later beyond the glacial margins: the ancestral moose appeared 2.6 million years ago, and the caribou and roe deer appeared about a million years ago, in the middle of the major glaciations.

There were other members of the deer family as well. A mule-deer-sized, short-legged deer, _Navahoceros,_ took up a mountain habitat. A large moose from Siberia evolved into the American stag-moose _Cervalaces scotti._ Fossil evidence suggests that a large deer reminiscent of caribou lived in eastern Canada, and that another species similar to the large South American marsh deer inhabited the marshes of Florida. True caribou remained in the far north and appear to have moved south into the continental United States only when pushed by the last glacial advance. The elk appeared south of Alaska for the first time in a brief respite of warm temperatures about 40,000 years ago, but failed to establish itself.

None of these deer were abundant—at least not during the Pleistocene. The black-tailed deer, which seem to have first appeared about a million years ago, were also

rare. For more than 2 million years, deer survived in the shadow of the many ecological specialists that grazed and browsed in the savannah, seeking refuge in the scattered clumps of trees that punctuated the landscape. The various genera of deer fit in between the niches of specialized species—camels, elephants, mastodons, ground sloths, six species of native horses—that had cleared the land and moved on (just as today's deer take advantage of the natural succession of plant species after a wildfire or logging clearcut or farm abandonment).

Giant carnivores preyed on these animals. Huge bears with short bulldog faces attacked young elephants, mastodons, and giant bison. Saber-toothed tigers leapt on young pachyderms. A large species of true lion—a veritable emperor compared with today's smaller king of beasts—feasted on horses, llamas, and ground sloths. Large wolves and pumas made eastern whitetails and a western species of deer their prey. A large, fleet cheetahlike cat chased pronghorns.

All these animals had diversified and specialized, each evolving to fill and exploit an ecological niche, during the Ice Ages. They are called the Rancholabrean fauna, after the Rancho La Brea in Los Angeles, where rich bone deposits were recovered from tar seeps, but they ranged across the continent—and beyond, for with so much water locked in glaciers the sea level had fallen, and the animals stepped onto the continental shelf.

Then, some 11,000 years ago—just after man crossed the Bering land bridge from Asia into the American continent—the mammoths, horses, camels, and sloths began to disappear, along with their huge predators, the ancient forms of lions, tigers, and wolves. The best hypothesis to explain their extinction includes a series of pivotal events: an increase in temperature (a major cold wave had ended about 1,500 years earlier), the extinction of the giant, predacious bear, and the entry of man into North America. Most of the large herbivores could not adjust to this new threat. As their populations dwindled, the large predators could no longer find their staple food. Each of them, like their prey, was too dependent on one source of sustenance.

The North American species of deer evolved in the forests that once grew within the Arctic Circle, then moved south as the climate changed.

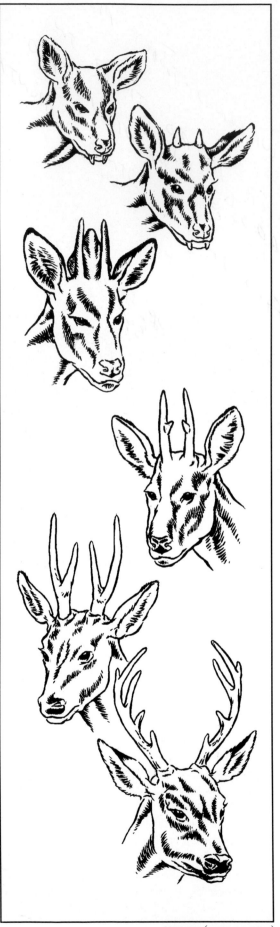

BESENGER (AFTER KAMINSKI)

Once some of the huge predators—against whom a spear had been no defense—had disappeared, human beings could expand into the continent. Omniverous man, after killing off the mammoth, turned to a large species of bison to kill and eat, and thus prompted an evolutionary change: this big bison had been aggressive and able to fend off the huge predators of old, but only the smallest, fleetest, most wary bison in a herd could escape the spears of hunters. (Today's bison are these smaller animals' descendants, and their speed and timidity served them well until firearms aimed by expansion-minded settlers replaced the spears and arrows of subsistence hunters.)

In the deer family, the stag-moose, mountain deer, and marsh deer died out, but the white-tailed and western black-tailed deer survived the mass extinction, as did their distant relatives the pronghorn and the peccary. It is reasonable to attribute the survival of *Odocoileus* to the genus's adaptability: as an edge species, it made use of both open and dense habitat, and as for food, it selected as broad an array as an herbivore can. When the climate and vegetation changed, it simply changed its diet. Of major predators, the only natives to survive were the mountain lion, the coyote, and the black bear, an early immigrant from Asia. The timber wolf and the grizzly bear, both Siberians, came to North America with man and other large mammals.

The extinction of megafauna was massive in scope and profound in its effect. Large herbivorous mammals were so scarce in the latter part of the Pleistocene that there is no evidence of fungi commonly associated with the dung of such animals for several millennia. Freed from the intense competition and fearsome predation of the specialized Ran-

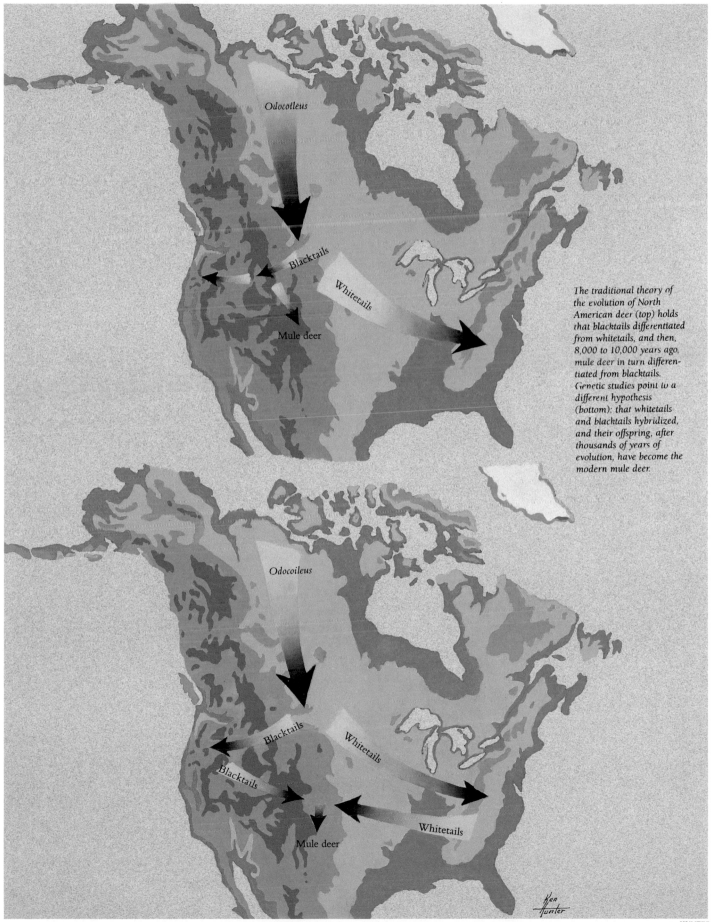

The traditional theory of the evolution of North American deer (top) holds that blacktails differentiated from whitetails, and then, 8,000 to 10,000 years ago, mule deer in turn differentiated from blacktails. Genetic studies point to a different hypothesis (bottom): that whitetails and blacktails hybridized, and their offspring, after thousands of years of evolution, have become the modern mule deer.

HUNTER

cholabrean fauna, the surviving herbivores extended their ranges. The western deer—let's say for now it was a black-tailed deer—and white-tailed deer from the Southeast presumably met and hybridized. The result, after some 8,000 to 10,000 years of evolution, is the modern mule deer.

That is the theory, at least: that mule deer resulted from the interspecific cross between white-tailed does and black-tailed bucks. It is a relatively new theory, and it challenges the long-held supposition that black-tailed deer are the sole ancestors of mule deer.

The more traditional theory also acknowledges the distance—geological and geographical—between ancient black-tailed deer and ancient white-tailed deer. In fact, it places even greater emphasis upon this separation, holding that the two species have not hybridized. According to this scenario, as black-tailed deer expanded into new areas, they encountered different, but still tenable, habitat and climate. Over several millennia, evolutionary responses to these different conditions resulted in the modern mule deer.

BODIES OF EVIDENCE

Each theory has its strong points and weak, its proponents and detractors. Let us start with the points of agreement:

• That there is one genus of North American deer, *Odocoileus,* comprising three major forms—whitetail, blacktail, and mule deer.

• That white-tailed deer are the ancestral form. It follows, then, that certain characteristics of whitetail anatomy, social markings (like tail coloration and antler formation), and possibly behavior can be called primitive.

• That each of the three major forms has its special adaptations for escaping predators. The whitetail bounds away at high speed, outrunning the threat; the mule deer stotts uphill and over obstacles, confounding the predator on broken terrain; the secretive blacktail hides in cover or stotts away as the situation demands.

It's the interpretation of those points of agreement, when taken with certain pieces of evidence, that leads to different conclusions about how the forms of deer came into being.

Genes in the genus. Following the old theory, that whitetails played no role in the differentiation of mule deer from blacktails, genus *Odocoileus* has traditionally been divided into two species, *virginianus* (whitetail) and *hemionus* (blacktail and mule deer). Pioneering genetic research by Cronin and Carr, however, demands that taxonomists take a second look. The astounding discovery: in terms of their mitochondrial DNA, mule deer are genetically closer to whitetails—a different species—than they are to their *hemionus* relatives the blacktails.

Cronin was studying mitochondrial genes (mtDNA) among deer in Montana, and Carr was doing the same in Texas, where mule deer and whitetail ranges overlap. Yet the correspondence of the genetic material in Montana was apparently not attributable to any interbreeding: the mtDNA, which is inheritable only from the mother, of Cronin's Montana mule deer resembled not the mtDNA of Montana whitetails, but the mtDNA of white-tailed deer in the Southeast, half a continent away. There was, then, very little—if any—gene flow between the two Montana populations, and therefore the connection between the two forms must go far back in time. Carr's data in Texas, however, suggested some recent crossings as well.

Blacktails' mtDNA is considerably different from both whitetails' and mule deer's. Those with the most distinct mtDNA are found along the Pacific Coast from north of Los Angeles to Alaska. Now Alaska is home to the most primitive of the black-tailed deer, the Sitka deer *(Odocoileus hemionus sitkensis).* These animals, presumably closest to the ancestral form of blacktails, bear certain resemblances to whitetails, which are presumably the ancestral form of all North American deer. The shape and color of the tail and the small metatarsal gland are more whitetail-like than not. Yet these deer have the pronounced facial masks typical of other blacktails and of mule deer.

In southern California there are deer that, to look at them, you would almost think were blacktails. They have short metatarsal glands, small rump patches, and black stripes running down their tails. But genetic testing reveals them to be mule deer: their

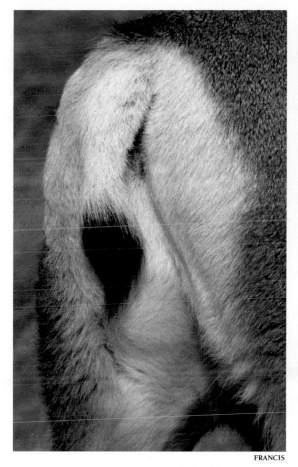

FRANCIS

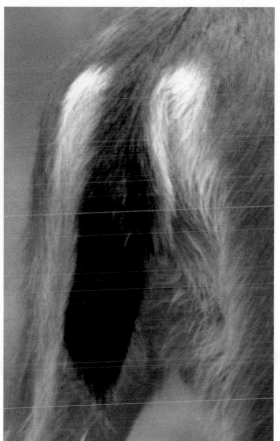

BAUER

The mule deer's large, bright rump patch (left) is a more advanced social marking, suggesting that the blacktail is the primitive, ancestral form of Odocoileus hemionus and more closely related to the whitetail progenitor.

mtDNA, like that of other mule deer, is akin to whitetail mtDNA. How far south whitetail-like mtDNA extends into Central America is not yet known. That information, along with genetic data on the apparently aberrant blacktail deer of Cedros Island off the coast of Mexico, would help determine whether mule deer arose from whitetails that moved outward from small populations in the Southeast, or whether whitetails in Central America were involved in mule deer speciation.

Family resemblance. Consider a scenario in which Mexican whitetails and coastal blacktails met and bred, with mule deer their offspring. Simple geography would suggest that mule deer subspecies in southern California are the primitive forms, the direct descendants of such a union, and that Rocky Mountain and desert mule deer are the advanced forms. The changes we see—larger size, larger rump patch, longer metatarsal glands, lack of dark stripe down the tail—evolved as the animals differentiated in the process of spreading east and crossing the Rockies and deserts.

The problem with such a scenario is that the cross of a blacktail and a whitetail doesn't look anything like a mule deer, nor does a cross of a whitetail and a mule deer. The researchers' first-generation hybrids do not have the mule deer's forked antlers, facial markings, rump patch, or small tail. They look, in fact, much like whitetails, although their yellow metatarsal glands, twice as large as those of whitetails, identify them as hybrids.

If mule deer arose as a hybrid species, then, they must have been subjected to severe environmental pressures that selected for mule deer traits. The mtDNA research strongly suggests that mule deer arose recently; was 10,000 years enough time for the hybrids to evolve into modern mule deer? The changes in physical appearance could have occurred not only as an adaptation to drier, colder climates with more seasonal variation, but rather as a response to the dispersal itself. That is, when dispersing populations of deer—or any other large mammal for that matter—expand rapidly to colonize available land, they escape, tempo-

LAUBER

LEA

rarily, the normal regime of natural selection. Food in the new territory is so abundant that there is no need to compete for it. Freed from that concern, males compete all the more ferociously for females: aggressiveness and courtship prowess are at a premium. During the brief period of colonization, the successful males are those that grow and flaunt the most luxurious ornamental organs, develop the greatest physical power, and foster traits that lead to greater reproduction. In the tumult of adult males vying for dominance and female attention, social organs become increasingly important socially and sexually. With the genes of the dominant males, ensuing generations develop larger and more complex social organs and markings, showier courtships, and larger bodies.

Body size today says little about a subspecies' genetic potential to grow large, however: it is so sensitive to nutrition that only experiments that control for food quality and quantity could determine, say, whether Rocky Mountain mule deer are *genetically* larger than California mule deer.

On the eastern side of the Sierra Nevada, mule deer do not differ much in markings. Even desert mule deer differ little from Rocky Mountain mule deer. Regional differences in body size appear to reflect the relative richness of resources of local environments.

Solving the puzzle of speciation is not just a question of physical characteristics, how-

ever. There is a behavioral component as well.

Escape and evasion. Each species has its strategies for escaping from predators.

Whitetails. In flight, a white-tailed deer aims for speed, putting distance between itself and the predators. The greater the distance, the more time there is for the deer's scent to evaporate, confusing and slowing its pursuer. To maximize speed, the deer must minimize indecision. It therefore uses the well-known trails through its range, since they assure safe passage around such obstacles as boulders and impenetrable brush. The deer may also run downhill, using gravity to good advantage; or run through shallow water, where its scent cannot be picked up; or cross other deer trails, to throw the predator off on the wrong track.

This antipredator behavior is the product of life in the Ice Ages, when deer had to flee from many diverse predators. The deer's niche as an edge species had much to do with its strategy. A deer feeding along the edge of a wood could slip into a thicket and hide if the threat was distant; it could break cover and outrun its pursuer across the adjacent meadow if the threat came close. Most of the predators—the large lions, saber-toothed tigers, and dire wolves—are now extinct, but this inherited behavior lives on and is still effective because the animal still occupies the same ecological niche.

Modern wolves nevertheless can reduce the number of whitetails significantly in the

center of a pack's range. Deer may survive in greater numbers along pack boundaries, where avoidance of the rival pack reduces hunting by all the wolves.

Mule deer. The mule deer's strategy is the opposite of the whitetail's. Instead of running swiftly past a downed tree or large bush, it actually seeks out such obstacles to put between itself and its pursuer. Its gait is the stott, a very specialized form of locomotion just a bit slower than a gallop. These stylized, precise bounds allow the mule deer to put long distances between its tracks, to ascend steep hills straight on like a jackrabbit, and to jump unpredictably over boulders and ditches.

This flight strategy is especially effective in broken terrain. Ernest Thompson Seton, in trying to course mule deer with greyhounds, discovered that though the dogs could close on the deer in the open, they lost the race once their quarry reached rocky ground. Here the deer could flee with virtually undiminished speed. At the turn of the century, deer in the California chaparral were hunted with dogs; the deer could easily outrun packs on the steep, rocky, often densely vegetated ridges. One buck that was spooked repeatedly took a different escape route each time—so unlike the whitetail strategy of fleeing by familiar trails.

Mule deer are much more likely than whitetails to stop and look at their pursuers. They can afford to take the time to make an evaluation: if need be, they can get away from even a close-by predator by jumping unpredictably yet precisely over a boulder that the pursuer must then circle. Nevertheless, the mule deer tries to identify and evaluate potential dangers before they get too close. Taking advantage of the open landscape, the mule deer uses its large ears and keen eyes to detect danger at long distance, then moves to a secure area. Mule deer are masters in the art of hiding in sparse cover and withdrawing silently. When detected, they get up and leave quietly at a walk; they do not have the explosive getaway of whitetails.

Where wolf packs are common, mule deer are virtually invisible, even though tracks and sign in the snow may betray their presence. Mule deer are the preferred prey for wolves in western Canada, and the best strategy for survival appears to be keeping out of sight.

Coyotes are less formidable—mule deer, alone or with other members of the herd, may attack or mob them—but, well, more wily. Adult mule deer are rarely taken, but these predators have learned how to trap young deer. In winter, for example, coyotes may drive fawns from steep hillsides onto frozen lakes, where they lose their footing and are quickly caught and killed. The mule deer in one study area countered with avoidance: they began to disperse and hide, some of them climbing steep slopes through a deep blanket of snow to the very edge of timberline. On occasion each of several groups under observation cleared out by swimming across an open stretch of water. Similar behavior was recorded from radio-collared mule deer when a cougar entered their range.

Blacktails. The coastal black-tailed deer is specialized at hiding. This secretive animal waits until dusk to become active, and on a clear night around a full moon it may not become visible at all, even when the population is at high density and the observer is keen-eyed and quiet. Dark nights bring these deer out of the dense forests and shrub thickets where they move silently about. The observer must learn to recognize the audible signs: the chewing of food, a gentle rumbling of the rumen, the plucking of leaves and shoots, the sound of a hard hoof

Each species' behavior matches its habitat. Although the black-tail can stott to safety, it prefers to take advantage of its dense cover and hide from predators. The mule deer stotts unpredictably to keep the boulders and bushes of its open, rocky habitat between itself and its pursuer. The whitetail speeds away along its known trails through the forest, sometimes following or crossing a stream to throw the predator off the scent.

HUNTER

The whitetail's gallop is faster than the mule deer's stott, but each is effective in the animal's habitat.

scraping a dry twig, the rustling of leaves as the deer brushes by, perhaps a soft bleat or an occasional sneeze.

A predator would have to move with incredible stealth not to be detected in the dense vegetation preferred by these deer. But when raindrops are falling and water drips from the wet branches and leaves, the deer may become nervous and restless as they seek to distinguish safe noises from dangerous. But because they are more accustomed to rain, blacktails appear less nervous than do mule deer and whitetails during a rain storm.

Blacktails tend to inspect potential danger up close, while they are still within cover; they are no more likely to run than are whitetails. This may be a consequence of the many little noises made by frequent rain showers and the proximity of other deer: they choose to wait out the predator as the background noise continues. At the turn of the century, T. S. van Dyke, an exceptionally keen naturalist who had hunted all three forms of deer for more than three decades, observed that black-tailed deer frequently hid and lay low in cover, allowing him to pass close by. But for his pointer's keen nose, he would not have known the deer were there. Most chose not to run.

When surprised into flight, the blacktail stotts over fallen trees, rocks, and bushes in high bounds similar to those of a mule deer. It may stop to look back. Blacktails, like mule deer, use random, unpredictable movement, which works to good advantage in the precipitous country they prefer. They navigate rocks expertly.

They also navigate water. Excellent swimmers, they readily take to water and cross miles of ocean between coastal islands, some of which are predator-free havens. The Sitka form of the blacktail, in fact, is found almost entirely on islands, because in the coastal rainforests it is very vulnerable to wolf predation: when the rain turns to snow, the deer are pushed into narrow strips between the ocean and the forest, with little place to escape.

Blacktails may also attack predators. In research done with dogs, individual bucks sometimes charged their adversaries with lowered antlers. There is no evidence, however, that they gang up on predators as mule deer do.

Hybrid confusion. Crosses of whitetails and mule deer occasionally occur where their ranges overlap, and such hybrids have also been bred and studied in researchers' pens.

The salient aspect of the mule deer's strategy for escaping from predators is the stott. The genetics of the stott are so specialized that a deer must be 100 percent mule deer to do it; in tests, even a deer only one-eighth whitetail fails to stott and instead runs in a clumsy bound. This hybrid has difficulty jumping obstacles and often neither runs from nor attacks predators. Its scrambled, nonfunctional set of antipredator tactics would doom it in the wild. How could crosses of whitetails and blacktails—which according to theory resulted in the mule deer species—have survived with confused, malfunctioning escape behaviors? They have been bred in captivity, and there was a population of hybrids after some blacktails were released in Tennessee. They died out, presumably because of their inadequate antipredator strategies: the instinct of how to

LINGLE

evade danger successfully is a genetic trait, not a learned behavior, and hybridization destroys it.

The offspring of such interspecific unions are confused, and their escape behavior is scrambled. A comparison of the locomotion patterns shows just how ineffective the hybrids are. In one experiment, Lingle confronted deer with obstacles: whitetails fled under, around, or over; mule deer stotted over in great bounds, even clearing an eight-foot fence with what appeared to be great enthusiasm. The whitetail-muley hybrids, however, hesitated. When they did jump, they invariably hit the obstacles.

When the deer were confronted with a large dog on leash, the whitetails fled; the mule deer assembled and attacked, stotting around and over the snapping dog. The hybrids approached the dog at a walk, stopped, looked, turned, looked over their shoulders, and acted confused.

In the wild, such animals would be quickly killed by predators. But most hybrids are observed within groups of mule deer, whose behavior they adopt. If predators are few and far between, the hybrid does may survive to breeding age, as long as they stick close to the matriarchal group. The hybrid bucks are not fertile.

Limited observations of lone hybrids indicate that they are surprisingly tame and approachable. They react to nearby danger the same way a mule deer does to a distant threat: trying to walk away unobserved.

Hybrids, the offspring of whitetail bucks and mule deer does, are fertile, but because their escape behavior is confused, they are not likely to survive long enough to breed in the wild when predators are present.

Interpreting the strategies. All three forms of deer—whitetail, mule deer, and blacktail—eat similar foods, but their preferred habitats are different because of their radically different strategies for dealing with predators.

The whitetail is an opportunist that exploits the early stages of plant communities after wildfires and floods (or, today, reversion of cropland). It does not scramble or contest for resources; instead, it moves on, avoiding competitions. This explains why white-tailed deer transplanted to New Zealand and Europe have not done well: they cannot compete with the native deer. In New Zealand whitetails have been reduced to two populations, one of which is not expected to last. In Finland, where whitetails have established themselves, they thrive on agricultural land, but only in the absence of roe deer. Even whitetails in their native North America have competed poorly against escaped sika deer and other exotics.

The whitetail inhabits field-forest edges where it can feed while having the option, should a threat appear, of slipping into the forest or bursting across the field at full tilt. The mule deer's antipredator strategy likewise determines its habitat: because it can stay concealed in bushes while the predator approaches and hold off on the decision to flee or intimidate until it has evaluated the threat, the mule deer prefers broken, hilly terrain. The blacktail must remain in thickets because its antipredator strategy depends on concealment; it flees as a last resort, preferring, like a mule deer, to stott across rough, steep terrain.

It appears, then, that the deer family has split along the lines of behavior—specifically escape behavior—rather than according to food niche.

THE FLOW OF GENES

Under natural conditions, the meeting of mule deer and white-tailed deer does not often result in hybridization. A courting mule deer buck wouldn't run after a fleet white-tailed doe, let alone catch up with her, because the mule deer expects his mate to lead him on in a 5-foot circle, not a quarter-mile chase. He would not recognize her be-

Whitetails south of the border

In the vast sweep of geologic time, the Strait of Panama has not always linked North and South America. But when, about 2 million years ago, the strait rose from the sea, an ancient form of white-tailed deer was there with other North American animals, waiting to cross to the south.

The deer spread south and diversified, adapting themselves to the different climate and terrain of this new territory. There were the rabbit-sized hiders that lived in dense shrubs, like the modern *Pudu,* the smallest deer in the world. There was a now-extinct pampas species in Argentina as large as a small elk, with massive antlers. There was the rock-climbing deer, the huemal *(Hippocamelus),* a few of which still inhabit the Andes and rocky coast of southern Chile. Most of that early radiation died out, probably after the mass extinctions that eliminated the horses, mastodons, ground sloths, and their predators. Two of the remaining species, the pampas deer *(Ozotoceros)* and the swamp deer *(Blastocerus),* are now rare and threatened with extinction. Still widely distributed are three *Mazamas* species—small, territorial hiders in forests.

All South American deer today are closely related to *Odocoileus,* the North American deer genus. The tremendous radiation occurred because the ancestral whitetails were highly adaptable, developing different sizes, shapes, and behaviors as the animals adjusted to the diversity of habitats on the American continent.

The modern white-tailed deer itself appears to have crossed into South America later than the ancestral *Odocoileus* deer that gave rise to the first radiation. It spread into the tropics, across the equator, and colonized as far as 18 degrees south latitude, in Peru. East from there its territory wavers northward a bit, to 10 degrees south in Brazil. Since in North America whitetails have pushed beyond the 60th parallel, close to the Arctic Circle in Canada, their range covers an astonishing 78 degrees of latitude and encompasses steamy tropic and frozen forest and every climate in between.

No matter where found, however, whitetails look basically alike. There are differences in overall size—whitetails grow large in northern latitudes and in fertile agricultural areas, small in southern latitudes and on islands. South American whitetails are especially small, with modest antlers. Antlers and tails tend to be larger in deer of open landscapes, such as the savannah of Venezuela, than in deer of the forests, like those of Columbia.

There are differences in pelage, too, depending on climate. In some tropical races the summer coat is worn year-round, and the winter hair appears only sparsely on head, neck, and back. In some Andean populations living at high altitude, it is the winter coat that is worn year-round.

The more or less equal periods of daylight and darkness in the tropics apparently affect reproductive seasons. Some tropical races have extended ruts, and though most fawns are born during favorable seasons, newborns may appear throughout the year. Consequently, the antler cycle is not so closely synchronized with season as in North America.

There are other differences as well—in some tropical races there is no discernible metatarsal gland, for example—that might indicate subspecies. Definitions of subspecies have in fact been suggested, based on such differences in morphometric features. But comparative morphometry cannot determine whether a particular feature is truly the result of genetics. Features such as size and proportion are greatly affected by environmental factors. Is the year-round winter pelage of an Andean whitetail a response to cold, for example, and if that deer were plucked from its mountain and transported to the tropics, would it exchange its winter coat for light summer pelage? Or is its pelage an inherited characteristic?

The genetic differences among white-tailed deer are not readily detectable. It has been discovered that whitetails from North America may differ genetically more from whitetails in South America than they do from North American *black*tails. Yet, externally, white-tailed deer differ little from one another, be they from North or South America.

— *Valerius Geist*

RUE III

havior; confused, he would stop. For that reason, the cross invariably takes place between a white-tailed buck and a mule deer doe.

Even that union is problematic. An amorous white-tailed buck would have a tough time competing with a large, pugnacious mule deer buck protecting a doe in estrus. But if the biggest, most formidable bucks of a mule deer herd have been killed off by hunters, the whitetail buck may find and breed an undefended doe. Once successful, this may become a habit for the whitetail buck.

Because the hybrid fawns are not likely to survive once they are on their own and no longer copying the escape behavior of their dams, this one-way hybridization could reduce reproduction by mule deer: the does would produce not viable, fertile offspring but confused, sterile males and susceptible females. It has probably led to a severe decline in the number of mule deer where the ranges overlap. The two species are, however, compatible—even under severe hunting pressure—in the steep territory that favors mule deer. Does near estrus can stott straight up a sand dune, canyon wall, coulee, or badland dike, leaving the whitetail buck panting in the dust.

A very conservative species, white-tailed deer have changed little in nearly 4 million years and are not expected to do so in the near future. Likewise, black-tailed deer should continue, physically and behaviorally, much as they are today. Mule deer, though, face a less certain future, threatened with extinction where whitetail range overlaps their own.

—Valerius Geist

DEER

Taxonomy of white-tailed deer and mule deer

*T*o even the most casual observer, the differences between a white-tailed deer and a mule deer are obvious. Watch the one animal flag its broad white tail as it bounds away into the brush, and you immediately know you've just glimpsed a whitetail. When the other flicks its large, eponymous ears, you think, "Muley." Other, more subtle differences exist, but in distinguishing the two species, the layman instinctively turns to the visible signs that have been used by taxonomists since the time of Linnaeus.

In the system of classification devised in the eighteenth century by the Swedish botanist, plants and animals were categorized according to their physical characteristics. Comparative anatomy was the tool: broad tail that's white underneath vs. slender, black-tipped tail; large, mulelike ears vs. smaller ears; and so forth.

Today, with advances in knowledge of ecology, biochemistry, hybridization, immunology, and karyotyping and genetics, researchers have added new criteria in their efforts to sort out species and subspecies, family relationships, and evolutionary order. For North American deer, dominance behavior can be just as important as body size and antler configuration. According to some researchers, hair color is one of the most important criteria in classification. And even though a mule deer's leg musculature differs not at all from a whitetail's, its signature stotting gait is now evidence that the two animals are different species.

Anatomical differences, then, are no longer the sole criteria when it comes to classifying deer. But since comparative anatomy was the starting point in the history of taxonomy, it remains a good place to begin.

Based on anatomical similarities, white-tailed and mule deer both belong to order Artiodactyla. Members of this order are very adaptable, and deer are no exception, as evidenced by their wide distribution throughout the Americas. All artiodactyls share characteristics outlined by Gilbert in 1978. They are generally even-toed and hooved, which Nowak and Paradiso call the principal distinguishing feature of the order. The first digit is found only in certain fossil forms; the main axis of the foot is between the third and fourth toes. The second and fifth toes usually form dew hooves or dewclaws.

Other characteristics include a generally herbivorous diet and the lack of an os-penis, or penis bone. Also canine teeth and upper incisors are reduced or absent. Molars are more complex than premolars and are low-crowned with cusps in the suborder Suina but high-crowned with cressents, or high ridges, in the suborders Tylopoda and Ruminantia. Artiodactyls have two-, three-, or four-chambered stomachs.

North American ruminants share these additional characteristics: a complex four-chambered stomach; cud chewing (they re-

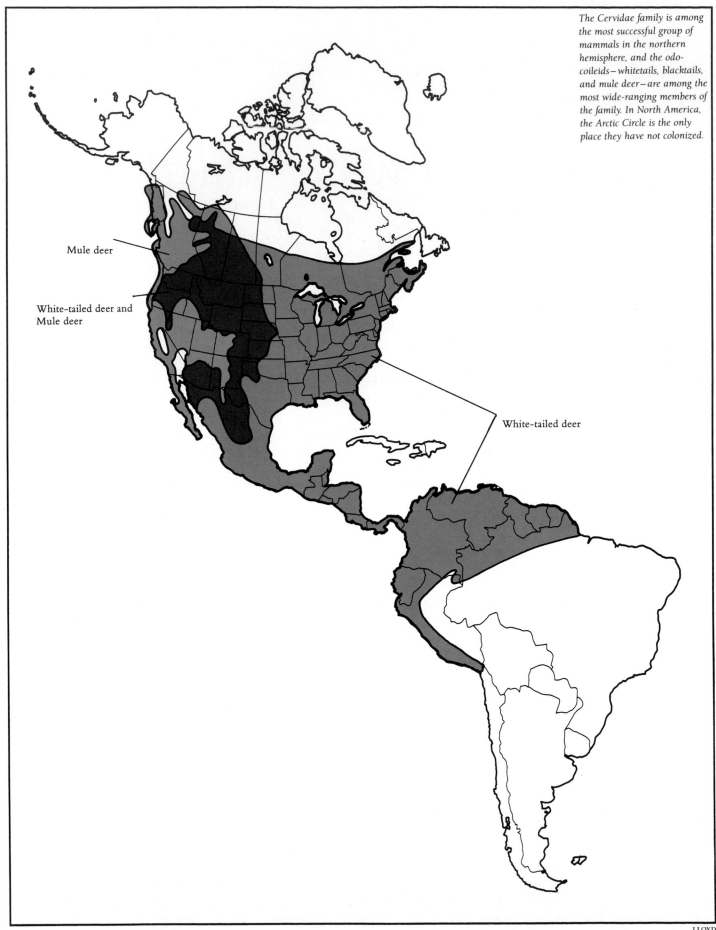

Mule deer

White-tailed deer and
Mule deer

White-tailed deer

The Cervidae family is among
the most successful group of
mammals in the northern
hemisphere, and the odo-
coileids—whitetails, blacktails,
and mule deer—are among the
most wide-ranging members of
the family. In North America,
the Arctic Circle is the only
place they have not colonized.

LLOYD

DEER

gurgitate food more than once before the final swallowing); metacarpals and metatarsals fused into a cannon bone; horns or antlers in males; and a general lack of incisors and canines in the upper jaw. Depending on the presence or absence of upper canines, they have thirty-two or thirty-four teeth. Also, ruminants have brittle, hollow hair and shed twice a year.

Deer belong to the *Cervidae* family, which has five identifying characteristics: only mature males have antlers (except *Rangifer*, in which both sexes have them); there is no gallbladder; dew hooves show, so the feet are four-toed; there is a lachrymal depression in front of each eye; and, except for *Cervus* and *Rangifer*, there are thirty-two teeth—three premolars and three molars on each side of the maxillary (upper jaw) and three incisors, one canine, three premolars, and three molars on each side of the mandible (lower jaw).

Dama is the correct taxonomic name for deer because it is the oldest, but *Odocoileus* is more common. Although white-tailed and mule deer are both classified as members of the genus *Odocoileus*, there are pronounced differences between the species, including the tail, ear length, metatarsal gland, antlers, gait, behavior, and face coloration. In general, the white-tailed deer *(Odocoileus virginianus)* has a large, broad tail that is white underneath. When erect, the white tail is exposed like a flag. The mule deer has a shorter, ropelike tail that is white outside with a black tip. Whitetails have short ears compared with the mule deer, which is named for its long, mulelike ears.

Metatarsal glands on the lower hind legs are smaller on whitetails (25 to 50 millimeters or 1 to 2 inches) than on mule deer (up to 175 millimeters or 6.8 inches). The points of a whitetail's antlers grow from a forward-curving main beam; in a mule deer, the points grow from both branches of a more upright, forked main beam.

When fleeing danger, whitetails run with long, graceful strides. Mule deer can run in a similar, though somewhat slower, manner, but are more likely to take off with a peculiar bouncing gait. Habitat may explain the difference. Whitetails prefer dense vegetation; mule deer usually live in hillier, broken

areas. The bouncing gait may provide mule deer with better visibility over obstacles—rocks, brush, downed trees—as they rapidly leave danger behind. Finally, mule deer have more black on the face and whitetails more white on the face and underbody.

Still, there is tremendous individual variation among North American deer. In 1956, Kellogg warned, "No salient single character considered alone . . . seems entirely trustworthy" in identifying deer. In 1990, Geist proposed that subspecies classification be based on social markings—face, body, and tail marks and colorations that play a role in social interactions—because they are the best available criteria. Regardless of classification problems, authors such as Hall recognize thirty subspecies of white-tailed deer in North and Central America and eight in South America. There are at least nine subspecies of mule deer in western North America. Cowan classified eleven mule deer subspecies in 1956, but two may not be valid.

Whitetails range from the Atlantic to the Pacific and from Hudson Bay to Panama. The ranges of many of the subspecies overlap and intergradation is widespread, according to Whitehead. There also has been widespread translocation of various subspecies into the geographic ranges of others. Still, the larger white-tailed deer live in northern climates and smaller ones in the southern. The largest inhabit the northern United States and southern Canada—the northern woodland, Dakota, and northwest whitetailed deer. These deer stand about 102 centimeters (40 inches) at the shoulder and can weigh up to 181 kilograms (400 pounds). At the southern extension of their range, whitetails such as *O. v. margaritae* weigh less than 18 kilograms (40 pounds).

Mule deer also have an extensive range, but it is limited to western North America from central Mexico to just south of the arctic tundra. Cowan described the range as "extending from Great Slave Lake in the north to Tiburon Island and Cape San Lucas in the south; and from western North Dakota, South Dakota, and Nebraska west to the Pacific Coast and adjacent islands." Mule deer do not vary in size as much as whitetails, but like their white-tailed cous-

PRATT

ins, the larger mule deer inhabit the northern portions of the range and the smaller ones the southern. The largest, Rocky Mountain mule deer, stand about 106 centimeters (42 inches) at the shoulder and weigh as much as 111 kilograms (245 pounds). Desert mule deer, on the other hand, stand about 100 centimeters (39 inches) and weigh about 80 kilograms (176 pounds).

Subspecies classification is undoubtedly clearer on paper than it is in the field. In 1981, Wallmo suggested that the deer classification system may be arbitrary. Subspecies arise because of genetic isolation from the main species and from the genetic selection imposed by different environments. It follows, Wallmo argued, that "a subspecies is better adapted to its own habitat and less well equipped to exist in the habitat of other subspecies." Both mule deer and whitetails have been transplanted successfully to the habitats of other subspecies, though, so biologists cannot simply assume that deer are unique genotypic or phenotypic products of specific habitats. When Harrington in 1978 addressed the issue of anatomical classification, he concluded that there was little else available for establishing the relationships among deer. Recent advances in genetics and electrophoretic studies have helped establish new degrees of relatedness, however, and one day may clarify relationships among the ungulate genera.

– Paul R. Krausman

DRAKE

Inside the animal

Internal anatomy

*T*o understand deer, consider the world in which these animals evolved. Although they now exploit a wide variety of habitats, deer evolved in the forest. Every anatomical adaptation is focused on coping with the problems of feeding, surviving, and reproducing in the dense woods that once covered the continent.

In a dense forest, for example, and with the low population densities of prehistoric times, how do individuals communicate with each other? Visibility is limited; sounds are muffled. Scent communication evolved as the answer. The glands of deer produce chemicals that communicate information about sex, sexual readiness, status, and possibly other data of which we are, as yet, unaware.

The production of these chemicals would be in vain if deer, like humans, had a poor sense of smell. But their olfactory adaptations are specialized for reading other deer's messages, as well as for tracking food and water and keeping track of predators. With their elongated muzzles and well-developed nasal conchae, deer can intercept and interpret chemicals at the molecular level—well beyond the ability of humans.

And because deer serve as a prey base for a wide variety of predators, their eyes have evolved to function at low light levels and detect danger even in a dark wood. The tapetum lucidum—the reflective layer behind the retina that gives the animal a double exposure of nighttime images—is one such adaptation. That a deer can perceive light waves in the ultraviolet range a million times better than humans, and thus see as well at night as we do in broad daylight, is another.

The antlers of deer evolved to meet many needs, from combat to scent communication, but their particular form was influenced by the forested habitat. Despite a wide variety of shapes and sizes, deer antlers are generally shaped to allow movement through thick vegetation.

Those are some of the more visible manifestations of the odocoileids' adaptation to the North American forests where they arose. The internal anatomical structures, too, are strongly related to function.

THE VEGETARIAN LIFESTYLE

Deer have adapted to obtain the nutrients they need for growth, reproduction, and survival from vegetation. Viewed from above, the deer's muzzle is much more pointed than in other ruminant species, such as cattle and sheep. The pointed snout allows deer to be specific in foraging. Cattle, in contrast, are referred to as forage generalists, but deer are considered forage concentrators. They walk from plant to plant, selecting the best parts of the best plant species to satisfy their physiological needs. Unless forced by starvation to eat highly fibrous plants, deer seem to select only those foods with low cell-wall content. As a result, they do not have—or need—the diversity of ru-

As concentrate feeders, deer select and consume the most nutritious and digestible plant parts. Once eaten, the food is rapidly fermented in the animal's rumen; regurgitation and rumination speed the digestive process.

LEA

men microorganisms of the bovines, which graze on grasses.

The digestive system is designed to help deer, an attractive prey species, limit exposure to predators: the deer eats rapidly, not taking time to chew its food, then retires to protective cover to digest what it has consumed. The anatomy of deer thus requires a large storage facility, the rumen—hence the general terms for such animals, ruminants. Whereas the monogastric human stomach can hold only about a pound of food, the rumen of a deer has a capacity of 10 pounds or more.

The ruminant digestive system holds the food for a long time to allow the digestive microflora and microfauna to break down fibrous plant foods. The long retention time is a function of the shape of things: Because the rumen's exit is located very near its entrance, the incoming and outgoing boluses of food are caught in a "traffic jam," increasing the time they remain in the rumen. But even this is not enough to make the food nutrients available for absorption by the body. The bites of food, which were swallowed nearly whole, need to be mechanically broken down.

A complex assortment of voluntary and involuntary muscles allow the deer to move the food bolus back up the esophagus for mastication, or cudding. Bedded down in a secure spot, the deer brings a ball of food up, chews it slowly, then swallows it again.

The absence of a collarbone allows a deer a wide range of motion. Flexibility and speed have their drawbacks, however; the leg bones are fragile.

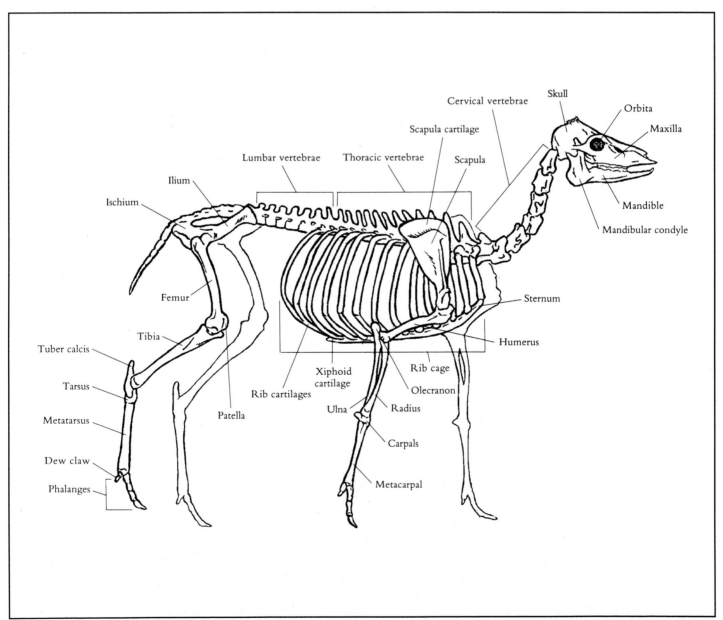

DEER

Back in the rumen, the food is again mixed with cellulose-digesting microorganisms. By repeating the chewing, swallowing, and regurgitating of their food for yet another session of cudding, deer are eventually able to degrade fibrous plant materials. Less fibrous, more digestible foods require little chewing; more fibrous items must be chewed many times.

From the rumen, the food and its microorganisms move into the reticulum, which is primarily a fermentation tank. As in the rumen, there is a long retention time in the reticulum to allow the initial breakdown of cellulose and other plant fibers into smaller molecules of digestible carbohydrates and by-products. The primary energy products produced are volatile fatty acids, which are then absorbed through the wall of the chamber.

The partially digested mass then moves into the omasum and abomasum, where the process of digestion is similar to that in non-ruminant animals. Here the microorganisms are killed by the high acidity of what amounts to the deer's true stomach. In this process, the more easily digested bodies of the microorganisms are broken down in the same way as foods in the human stomach. Because microbial organisms have the ability to break down the large cellulose and fiber molecules of plants, ruminants nurture these organisms, eventually feeding on them and their by-products.

Although the primary adaptation to herbivory is the four-chambered stomach, the ruminant also has a caecum to aid in digestion. Serving as a posterior fermentation vat, the caecum allows additional breakdown of plant fibers into digestible compounds. There is no gallbladder, an organ that emulsifies fat. Since the deer diet is relatively fat-free, a gallbladder would be superfluous. The liver is large—larger than in cattle and bison.

The total length of the deer intestine is long, as with most herbivores, but not as long as in herbivores that are bulk feeders. Having adapted to eating plants that are, in the continuum of fiber foods, relatively digestible, the total length of the deer gut is only about fifteen times body length, compared with thirty times body length for bo-

FRANCIS

vines. The rectum, however, is short, indicating that deer defecate frequently.

BUILT FOR SPEED

To detect and avoid predators, deer use a combination of keen senses, including sight, smell, and hearing, and are usually aware of dangers long before the danger finds the deer. But once a predator is on to them, they must be able to flee.

The deer's skeleton and musculature are well adapted to this need. The most powerful muscles are associated with the hind legs, particularly the gluteus. These large muscles allow deer to jump great heights often exceeding 8 feet. Again, this is an evolutionary adaptation to the forest, where downed tim-

SMITH

The tapered muzzle enables deer to be selective about their forage and find the most nutritious plant parts.

Compared with bulk feeders, such as cattle or bison, deer take in smaller amounts of higher-quality food, process it more quickly, and defecate more often.

ber and underbrush are obstacles between the deer and safety.

With the hind legs providing propulsion, the front legs must steer, and they must do so accurately. The shoulder assembly of the deer, accordingly, is very different from that of humans. The human shoulder is anchored to the front of the rib cage by the collarbone, allowing a range of movements useful to a species said to have evolved in trees. But such an anchor would hinder a running animal. Without a collarbone, then, a deer has a free-floating shoulder assembly that allows not only front-to-back movement for running but also firm pivot points for turns.

A deer's lower legs, both front and rear, are nothing more than elongated feet. Deer run on two digits, comparable to the third and fourth fingers or toes of the human appendage; a vestigial toe on each side comes in contact with the ground only during jumping or in soft terrain.

The long, thin bones of the lower legs—foot bones, actually—are both boon and bane. Because of them deer can move with agility through the forest, but these bones are fragile, and deer have snapped their legs while fleeing predators.

The lower "legs" being feet and the "feet" being toes, a deer's hooves are fingernails. (The Latin word *ungulus,* fingernail or toenail, is the source of the taxonomic category *ungulate,* an animal that runs on its toenails.)

The powerful muscles of the hind quarters propel the animal in its quick escapes from danger; the muscles of the front legs provide sure steering.

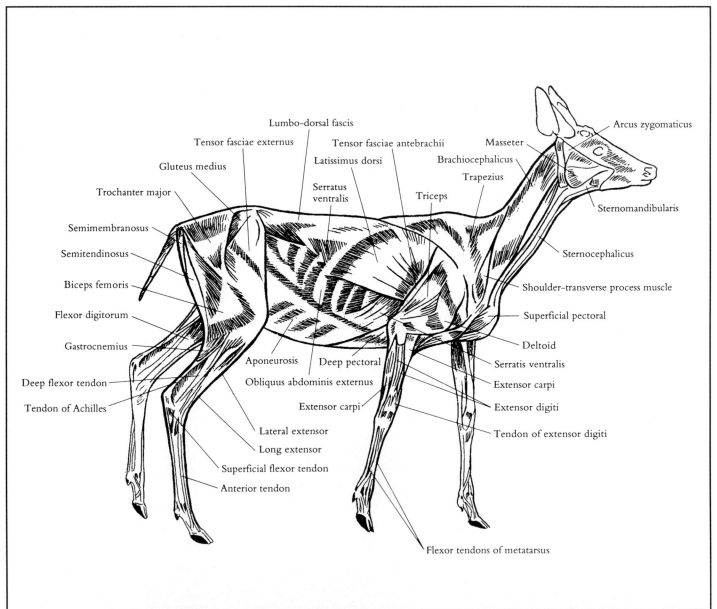

Lumbo-dorsal fascis
Tensor fasciae externus
Tensor fasciae antebrachii
Gluteus medius
Latissimus dorsi
Masseter
Arcus zygomaticus
Brachiocephalicus
Trapezius
Trochanter major
Serratus ventralis
Triceps
Sternomandibularis
Semimembranosus
Sternocephalicus
Semitendinosus
Shoulder-transverse process muscle
Biceps femoris
Superficial pectoral
Flexor digitorum
Deltoid
Gastrocnemius
Serratis ventralis
Aponeurosis
Deep pectoral
Extensor carpi
Deep flexor tendon
Obliquus abdominis externus
Extensor digiti
Tendon of Achilles
Extensor carpi
Tendon of extensor digiti
Lateral extensor
Long extensor
Superficial flexor tendon
Anterior tendon
Flexor tendons of metatarsus

BESENGER

28

DEER

The phalanx, or digit, is pointed and extends well into the hoof. The hoof itself has three parts: compact horn, sole horn, and cuneus. The compact horn is very hard and receives the bulk of impact; the sole horn and cuneus absorb much of the shock of impact. Their slender hooves allow deer to move quickly and quietly through the leaf litter on the forest floor, very unlike a human being with his broad foot.

Beneath the skin of deer is a rich array of muscles used to elevate the hair. These pili erector muscles, like the human muscles that produce goosebumps, thereby increase the amount of air space between the tips of the hair and the skin's surface and thus increase the insulative value of the fur. The same muscles also help communicate aggression and other behaviors: As a whitetail buck approaches a potential rival, for example, he appears to completely change color, from his usual gray to a very dark shade. Because deer hair, like that of many mammals, is banded in coloration, raising it exposes the darker bands and increases the amount of shadow, effectively changing the animal's color. That plus laying his ears back: There is no doubt about the buck's intentions.

The ears are important for picking out enemy footfalls in the dampened auditory world of the forest. Complex muscle groups allow deer to rotate their ears in all directions, and it is common to see an animal with one ear pricked forward and the other cocked backward: By receiving sound waves

BIGGS

Deer leap fences easily, each species in its own way. The whitetail (above) flies over in a gallop; the mule deer makes an exaggerated stott.

from opposite directions and comparing their intensity, the deer locates the source of the disturbance. Once alerted, it rotates both ears forward and stares intently at the potential threat.

CARDIOVASCULAR STRENGTH

The large heart is protected from predators by the rib cage and forelimbs. The lungs, too, are large, and can take in a great volume of air in one deep breath. Even with a bullet in its heart, a deer can run several hundred yards before exhausting its supply of oxygen.

A deer's heart rate at rest is much lower than a human's, normally ranging between forty and fifty beats per minute. But deer are nervous animals. The heart rate can zoom to more than two hundred beats per minute in a matter of milliseconds: an increase so rapid and forceful that an excited deer's beating heart can be heard by a person several feet away. It is no wonder that deer live relatively short lives.

REPRODUCTIVE ORGANS

Does are built for producing one or two

WERNER

A whitetail doe on full alert lifts her foreleg to stamp her foot in warning. Fired by adrenaline, her heart rate can jump by 500 percent in an instant.

offspring: the female reproductive tract contains a branched uterus, each horn of which can accommodate a fetus. In the unusual case of triplets or, rarely, quadruplets, two fetuses occupy one or both horns. As with other mammals, the uterus communicates with the ovary via a fallopian duct, whose tiny hairs propel the unfertilized egg to its destination in the uterus.

The uterus itself is capable of considerable enlargement, since the maximum size of young at birth is about 5 to 8 percent of body weight. A whitetail doe gives birth to some 14 to 20 pounds' worth of fawns, not including the placentas and other membranes and fluids.

A buck's reproductive system resembles

that of other mammals but is functional only for a short time each year. The testes are located outside the body, in the scrotum, but are hardly visible until they enlarge in response to rising testosterone levels during the rut. The penis is short relative to that in most deer species—particularly the fallow deer—to coincide with the female's short vaginal canal. The preputial gland in the foreskin of the penis has an as-yet-undetermined function.

—James C. Kroll

The vital organs are positioned forward in the body cavity, where the rib cage protects them from injury.

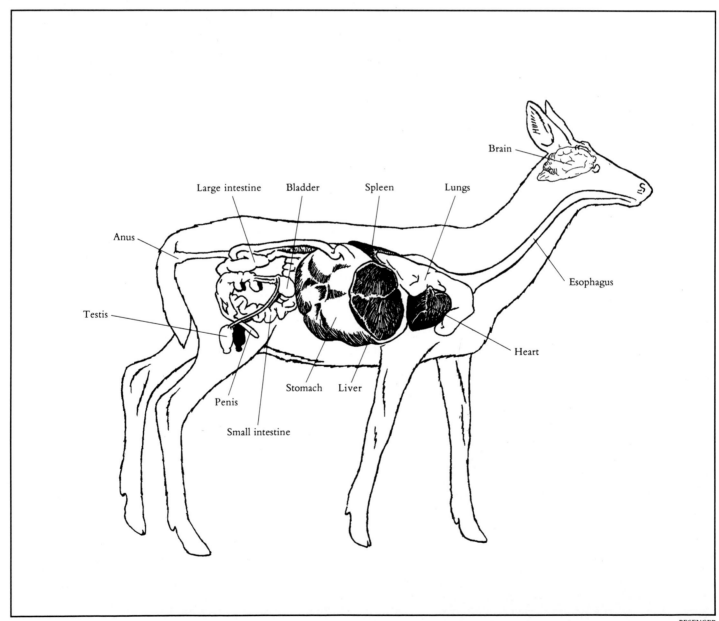

BESENGER

Antlers

---

*D*eer antlers have long fascinated humans. Ice Age man painted pictures of deer on his cave walls, and the ancient Greeks did experiments on antler growth. Buffon, a French scientist in the 1700s, thought antlers were made of wood. After all, he reasoned, they do have a "bark" that is shed as they grow. Modern research has led to a better understanding of antlers, but some mysteries and misconceptions persist.

A common error is to confuse antlers and horns. Horns are permanent structures made of dead tissue and have no blood or nerve supply. They grow from the base and are composed of keratin, a protein that also makes up hooves, fingernails, and hair. Generally, both males and females of a species carry horns.

Antlers, on the other hand, grow as living tissue and are true bone. While growing, they have both blood and a nerve supply. Antlers are deciduous—they grow, harden, and are cast each year, then replaced. Like the colorful plumage of some male birds, antlers are a secondary sexual characteristic, and except for caribou and reindeer, just the males of each cervid species have them.

Some deer, such as the Chinese water deer and the musk deer of Asia, have no antlers, but they do have tusks that can be used in battle. Other species, such as the brocket deer and pudu of South America, have very small spike antlers. Still others, like the Asian tufted deer and muntjac, have both tusks and small antlers.

ANTLER FUNCTIONS

Deer biologists and evolutionists have studied antler function for years. Most agree that antlers seem to have evolved primarily as weapons for fighting to determine male dominance for breeding rights. The question that remains is whether antlers really are needed as weapons or merely are "display organs" serving a function similar to body size or color in other animals.

Just how formidable a weapon antlers are depends on the species. Many of the smaller species, such as the muntjac, and even some of the larger ones, such as the sika deer, have straight, bayonetlike antlers perfectly suited for goring an opponent. Most deer have curved and branched antlers, however—not the best design for killing a foe. These complex antlers are used more for rubbing on trees and brush and digging in the ground or snow than for fighting. When white-tailed deer do spar or fight, they seem to take great care to lock their antlers with their opponents', thus avoiding slippage and serious injury. These battles involve a lot of pushing and twisting, much like a wrestling match. The curves and branches of whitetail and mule deer antlers are less lethal than the straight bayonets of other species. Nonetheless, fights between equal-size males can be vicious, and injuries and deaths do occur.

The regal headgear of a mature buck is among the fastest-growing tissues in the animal world. A healthy adult can grow a 3.5 to 9.0-pound (1.6 to 4.0-kilogram) rack in just three months.

DEER

Geist has found that 10 percent of all adult mule deer bucks have been injured in this way.

The display rituals of many species may obviate the need for sparring. The palmated antlers of moose and reindeer, however impressive they are to behold, are not well designed for fighting. A.B. Bubenik has shown that moose, elk, caribou, and maral deer with large antlers can intimidate rivals with smaller racks to establish dominance without actual combat.

Other theories have been offered as to why deer have antlers. Stonehouse has suggested that they are thermal radiators: growing antlers are probably the only appendages in the animal kingdom that have a temperature equal to that of the body's core. There is no question that they dissipate heat. If this were their primary function, however, we might wonder why most females don't have antlers for the same purpose, why some species (Pere David's and roe deer) grow antlers in the winter, and why there is not a direct relationship between climate and antler size.

A.B. Bubenik has theorized that antlers are used as scent markers. Velvet, the skin that covers growing antlers, does indeed have oil glands, but deer have other, more potent odor-producing glands.

In most cervid species antlers are a secondary sexual characteristic. To explain the appearance of antlers in reindeer and caribou females, biologists have suggested that the does need antlers to protect their young from predators. But don't mule deer and elk females have the same need? The final answer must be that antlers serve as many functions as there are antler shapes. Even within a species, antlers may have multiple purposes.

ANTLER GROWTH

In most species of deer, fawns are born in the spring or summer and have no antler growth that first fall. The male fawns have pedicles—skull platforms on which the antlers will develop. Some fawns may grow small antlers and become "button bucks." The buttons are cast the following spring before the first real set of antlers begins to grow. Goss has reported that the male fawns of mule deer, whitetails, moose, and roe deer all can grow such buttons. Reindeer and caribou, however, usually grow spike antlers as fawns.

Most male deer begin to grow their first real antlers in the spring, just before their first birthday. The growing antler is supplied with blood through the many blood vessels of its velvet and through its core. If the antler is damaged during its growth, it bleeds profusely, but the blood clots quickly. Injuries may cause misshapen antlers, although these can be difficult to distinguish from nontypical antlers, such as the genetically determined drop tines seen in whitetails. In fact, it is said that gamekeepers in Europe used to shoot the antlers of deer in the velvet with shotguns, in order to cause more

The elegantly curved tines of whitetail antlers allow bucks to catch an opponent's thrust, as well as lock together for spirited sparring matches.

BRYAN

Nontypical antlers, like this whitetail's palmated tines, may be caused by a variety of factors. Limited observations of such animals indicate that genetics, nutrition, and behavior could be involved.

A mule deer's antlers branch as they grow. While in velvet, the antlers are sensitive and easily damaged; a buck moves gingerly to protect them from injury. The size and shape of any particular buck's rack are determined by a combination of genetics and nutrition.

SMITH

points to grow. George and A.B. Bubenik report that serious injuries to the pedicle region will be "remembered" by the nerves, and subsequent sets of antlers will be misshapen for years to come.

There are numerous reports that injuries to other parts of the skeleton, such as the legs, have caused misshapen antlers. These reports suggest that if a deer injures or breaks a leg, the antler on the opposite, or contralateral, side will be stunted or misshapen in future years. It has been suggested that the injury caused the animal to limp, thus requiring uneven antlers to balance the gait. Others have called these reports mere coincidences, since deer have been found with misshapen antlers on the same side as leg injuries. Extensive controlled experiments would be necessary to settle the issue, but this is not the type of research many biologists would undertake.

Once the velvet antlers mature in size and shape, the velvet dies, or necroses, sometime in the fall. This apparently causes some irritation or itching to the deer, which rubs out the velvet against trees and brush. As the

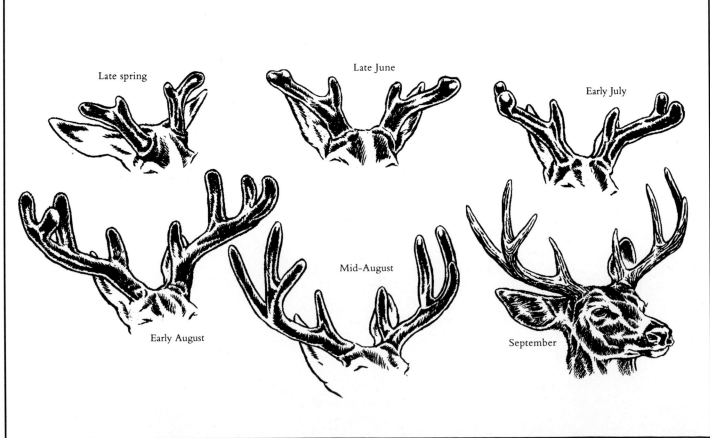

Late spring

Late June

Early July

Early August

Mid-August

September

BESENGER

DEER

velvet rubs off, minute pores are visible in the antler where the blood vessels entered. The amount of blood staining that occurs during this period determines the color or darkness of the hardened antler. The rubbing or sparring with trees may also serve other purposes. It can give the buck a better sense of the size and shape of his antlers, help sharpen the antler points, and strengthen the buck's neck muscles for the battles to come.

Rub-out occurs as the buck or stag's level of male sex hormone, testosterone, is increasing. He becomes fertile and more aggressive. Low hormone levels, perhaps caused by injuries or tumors, can cause the buck to rub out incompletely. Once the rub-out is complete, the deer is ready to compete with other bucks during the mating season.

Now large antlers are an advantage in winning the does or hinds, but they may be a mixed blessing, as dominant males often die at a younger age as a result of the stress and injuries that come from constant fighting with challengers.

As a secondary sexual characteristic and tools for fighting, antlers help bucks sort out their social hierarchy. The broken tine on this mule deer's rack can lower his status.

J. MILLER

Blood vessels supply essential nutrients to the growing bone that becomes a rack. Calcium and other minerals are supplied through the blood vessels in the velvet. By the time the velvet necroses, the antlers have stopped growing and are fully mineralized.

BRYAN

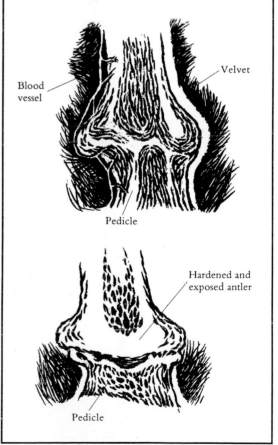

Blood vessel

Velvet

Pedicle

Hardened and exposed antler

Pedicle

BESENGER

KINNEY

Having served its purpose in nourishing the growing antler, the velvet shrivels, cracks, dies, and peels in strips.

SMITH

After the rut, a buck's testosterone level drops precipitously and his antlers are cast. The degeneration of the bone-to-bone bond between antler and pedicle is the most rapid deterioration of living tissue known. A deer can be picked up by its antlers one day, and cast them the next. There is little or no bleeding, and the two antlers usually fall off within hours of each other. When this happens, the buck's social status drops. This was demonstrated in experiments by Lincoln of Scotland, who found that a red deer's status in the herd dropped as parts of its hardened antlers were cut off, a piece at a time. In some species, such as axis deer, a new set of velvet antlers begins growing immediately. In others antler growth does not start for two or three months.

Antlers are the only regenerating living tissue in the entire animal kingdom. Hair gets replaced, but it is dead; baby teeth get replaced by permanent teeth, but just once; and broken bones and injured skin heal, but with the very different scar tissue. The only analogous replacement of an organ as complex as an antler is the growth of a lizard's tail when the original has been severed.

ENVIRONMENTAL CONTROL OF ANTLER GROWTH

The first pedicle and antler development of yearlings are largely innate and not determined by environmental cues. After that, however, antler growth is controlled by a variety of hormones that are activated by the environment. The key environmental cue seems to be light cycles, or day length. Temperature and rainfall, although seasonally variable, do not affect the antler cycle.

Antler growth usually begins when days are lengthening, between the spring equinox and the summer solstice. Rub-out occurs as days are shortening, just before the fall equinox. Goss, expanding on the work of Jaczewski of Poland, has shown that when day lengths are artificially altered, penned sika deer grow antlers six months out of phase with their normal cycle. When a twelve-month cycle is lengthened into twenty-four months, the deer grow antlers only every other year. When the cycles are shortened or condensed, the deer grow two and eventually three sets of antlers a year. That seems

DEER

to be the limit, as antlers, regardless of their size, take three to four months to grow. Goss also points out that when deer of nearly any species are transported to zoos in another hemisphere, their antler cycles quickly adapt to the new light cycle.

The farther deer are from the equator, the more defined their antler cycle. Whitetail bucks in Michigan or Pennsylvania tend to shed their antlers within a month or so of each other. Whitetails in south Texas, however, are less synchronous and shed their antlers over a longer period. Deer near the equator actually rub out and shed their antlers throughout the entire year. The specific date on which a buck rubs out or sheds is determined by its individual antler cycle. This cycle is independent of that of other bucks and believed to be centered on each animal's birth date.

Goss found that when deer were maintained under constant conditions approximating the winter solstice (eight hours of light and sixteen hours of darkness) or the summer solstice (sixteen hours of light and eight hours of darkness), the antlers cycled but at irregular intervals of about ten months. The result was the same for deer held in constant daylight, twenty-four hours a day. This suggests that an endogenous, or internal, mechanism causes the antler cycle but that changes in day length are needed to time the cycle to twelve months. Jacobson has reported a deer that was born blind and held in captivity for four antler cycles. These

WERNER

The interplay of hormones determines when a buck rubs out velvet (above) and, after the rut, casts the antlers (left). Both antlers may drop within minutes, or the second may not be cast for several days. The bloody pedicle heals quickly.

GETTLE

LEA

A mule deer's brow tines, if present at all, are smaller than a whitetail's, and each main beam usually splits into several forks on mature bucks.

cycles averaged 373 days in duration. The fact that it had antler cycles at all in the absence of day-length cues again confirms the existence of an endogenous mechanism.

HORMONAL CONTROL OF ANTLER GROWTH

Day length does not affect the first antler cycle, but hormones certainly do. More than two thousand years ago, Aristotle reported that "if stags are castrated before their first antlers, they will grow none. If they are castrated with antlers, they will not harden or be shed."

Without a doubt, the male sex hormone testosterone is the primary hormone that controls antler growth. Just how removal of

the testes affects antler growth depends on when the deer is castrated. If castrated as a fawn, the young deer grows no antlers at all. If castrated when mature, the buck grows antlers but never receives the hormonal cue to begin rub-out; he remains in velvet the rest of his life. Each year the antlers grow more points and begin to resemble a saguaro cactus. Such deer are called cactus bucks. If a buck is castrated when his antlers have hardened, he soon casts them—within a few days—and then grows velvet antlers the next season.

Such ablation experiments (in which organs were removed) were the first attempts to study the endocrinology of deer. In more recent times, scientists have removed the thyroid, parathyroid, pituitary, and pineal glands from deer. Only the removal of the pituitary, the master gland of the body, caused antler growth to stop. The pituitary produces many hormones, one of which is luteinizing hormone (LH), which controls the production of testosterone by the testes. Day length seems to control the pituitary through a pea-sized endocrine gland at the base of the brain, the pineal.

Early work on the pineal showed that its removal altered antler cycles but the mechanism was not understood. Now, however, there are ways to measure the levels of hormones in a deer's circulatory system and even ways to synthesize many of these hormones, which can then be injected in order to study their effects. The pineal produces a hormone called melatonin, which suppresses the production of LH in the pituitary and thus holds back testosterone. Studies have shown that melatonin is produced in greater quantities during hours of darkness. Some message regarding day length, probably a neural one, must be sent from the eyes via the optic nerve to the pineal gland. As nights get shorter, melatonin production decreases, releasing the pituitary to produce LH. The resulting increase in testosterone leads to velvet shedding and antler hardening. These hormonal interactions take time, so there is a lag of several months between the changing of day length and the antler cycle event.

Some questions—why testosterone levels decline rapidly after the rut, why female reindeer have antlers and cast them after their young are born – require further study. Scientists such as George Bubenik in Canada and Suttie in New Zealand have shown that the reproductive cycle and antler growth in deer can be regulated by artificially altering their light cycles or by injecting or implanting doses of melatonin. Injections of testosterone into whitetail does have been demonstrated to cause antler growth. Melatonin and testosterone, however, are only part of what must be a complex endocrine regulation of the antler cycle. Many other as-yet-undiscovered hormones are thought to be involved.

NUTRITION VERSUS GENETICS

As symbols of male dominance and sexual potency, the well-developed antlers of a mature whitetail buck inspire awe and respect. They also raise questions about whether the size of an animal's antlers is determined by its genes, or whether it is environmental factors that spur growth. Research indicates that both genetics and nutrition play important roles.

In the 1940s Austrian Franz Vogt demonstrated the effects of paternal and maternal nutrition on antler growth in red and roe deer. Starting with deer with mediocre antlers and feeding them high-energy, high-protein rations, he increased the body weights of the stags and the average size of the antlers by nearly 50 percent in just three generations. More recent experiments have been few and less spectacularly conclusive, but they have shown similar results: good nutrition means large antlers.

There is no question that antler growth puts a nutritional strain on the animal. The rack of a moose may span 1.8 meters (6 feet) and weigh 28 kilograms (60 pounds) – no less than one-sixth the weight of its entire skeleton. Imagine growing an adult human skeleton, which also weighs about 28 kilograms, in three to four months. Numerous studies have shown that restricted diets can lead to stunted antlers, as body growth seems to take priority over antler growth in all deer species when rations are short. In fact, malnutrition has been invoked to explain the rare Scottish hummel, a sort of polled red deer that never grows antlers.

WERNER

All the tines of the typical whitetail antlers grow from the forward-arcing main beams.

But the effects of poor nutrition differ, depending on the species. In white-tailed deer a restricted diet has been found to cause the bucks to cast their antlers early; in red deer it delays antler casting. Even if rations are in short supply for a time, the lack of body and antler growth will be compensated for in most deer once food becomes more plentiful.

It is difficult to separate out the effects of nutrition, but antler size is also related to the deer's body size. As one might expect, the larger the deer in body weight and shoulder height, the heavier the antlers and the longer the beam length. In fact, some evidence suggests that as the deer grows larger, its antlers become proportionally larger, thus making up a greater percentage of the animal's total body weight.

Interestingly, the overall energy requirements of all animals are equal to the body weight to a power of 0.75; in other words, as an animal gets larger, it needs proportionally less feed per pound of body weight. If these relationships hold true, then as deer get larger, they eat proportionally less but have even greater antlers. This puts greater demand on their bodies to provide minerals for the antlers during mineralization. (Antlers are made of protein as they grow in velvet, but the protein later gets replaced by solid mineral.) Cowan and others have shown that during antler mineralization, most of the calcium and phosphorus in the antlers comes from the other bones of the skeleton, not directly from the diet.

A less orthodox theory of antler size has been proposed by Bartos of Czechoslovakia. He observed red deer in pens and found that the ultimate size and number of points of the deer's antlers were determined not by body size but by the serial rank of the stag, as determined by sparring while in the velvet. He suggests that if nutrition is equal among deer, the individual deer's rank somehow affects antler size. He found that higher-ranked stags shed their velvet first and cast their antlers first, regardless of age. This must be interpreted cautiously, however, since attempts to demonstrate it in whitetailed deer have been inconclusive, and behavior of deer in pens may not match behavior in the wild.

Does all this mean genetics is not important? Of course not. There is no question that superior sires can produce superior offspring. We now believe, however, that the doe may contribute as much to the antler size of the male offspring as do the sires. This complicates the debate about yearling spike bucks, which occur in most species of deer. Some sportsmen want to protect spike bucks, believing they will grow bigger antlers later and just need a chance to mature. Others consider these animals inferior and call for them to be culled from the herd.

The evidence is conflicting. Harmel's studies in Texas showed that whitetail sires that were spikes as yearlings produced more spiked offspring than did a sire that had been a six-point yearling. Jacobson's work in Mississippi, on the other hand, showed that there was no correlation between a whitetail's first antlers and those he grew as an adult. Here's a case from my own research. A 4½-year-old whitetail sire carrying fifteen-point antlers produced eight male offspring from different does. Four of those bucks had impressive four- to eleven-point antlers as yearlings; the other four had just 1- to 2-inch spikes. Perhaps the sire failed to pass on his antler characteristics to some of his offspring, perhaps he passed on only some of the characteristics to some of the offspring, perhaps some of the characteristics were passed on by the does.

—Robert D. Brown

A coat of many functions

Standing stock-still in the gray November drizzle that darkens the naked branches and drips down tree trunks, the whitetail buck is all but invisible. His dark face and faint neck stripes blend into the brush, and it is not until he turns his head that the branches become antlers and the shadows take on the form of ears. Perfect camouflage.

No less effective was the cryptic camouflage of the fawns that same buck fathered the year before. In May, bedding down in the reddish brown oak leaves of the forest floor, the fawns in their dappled coats were invisible to predators. The summer coats these young whitetails would soon grow, like the winter coats they would acquire when the sun's warmth waned, are designed not just for camouflage, however. The deer's pelage protects the animals from both summer's scorch and winter's blasts, enabling the species to inhabit a wide range with all its temperature extremes.

Pelage even helps deer communicate with one another. The white flag alarm—a deer raises its tail, flaring the white underside, as a visual signal to the herd that danger lurks—is only the most obvious. According to one theory, a buck's black face and scrotum may cue other deer about his readiness for the rut. This coloration is known to correlate with testosterone levels in the plasma. The intensely black face of a ranking buck entering the rut has been recognized as a reliable indicator of prime age; it may also advertise his sexual strength and advise potential challengers that he is a formidable competitor for estrous does. Whether the dark face actually attracts those does has not yet been studied, however.

Despite the potentially significant role of pelage in communication, the main functions of the deer's coat are camouflage and thermoregulation.

CAMOUFLAGE

Cryptic coloration is critical to newborn fawns. Strength and coordination being marginal at this point in their lives, the young animals cannot outrun their predators; they hide to survive. The birth coat, with its white spots on a reddish brown field, provides ideal cover for blending into the fallen leaves and duff of the forest floor. The spots run in two lateral lines from ear to tail on each side of the fawn's body, and other spots appear randomly on body and flanks. When the fawn beds down, tucking both hind legs and forelegs beneath its body and turning its head back, it ceases to resemble a four-legged animal and becomes a pattern of light and dark, sunlight and shadow.

In August or September, when the fawn is weaned, it grows out of its birth pelage. The young whitetail appears scruffy and disheveled, the white spots still visible as the gray winter coat grows in. Finally the animal takes on the appearance of adults, with all the benefits of winter camouflage in the deciduous forest.

When snow covers the leaves, the whitetail's thick winter coat will blend with the gray tree trunks of the eastern deciduous mixed forest.

42   DEER

LEA

MCFALLS

The fawn's defense against predators is cryptic camouflage. When the young animal lies quiet and still, it disappears into the duff of the forest floor.

The winter coat is mainly gray with reddish brown tips, though some black-tipped hair is scattered throughout. The face is usually dark, particularly in males of prime age, with white markings around the muzzle and eyes. Pure white hair occurs on the belly, counteracting the shadow cast by the body and thus preventing a predator's eye from seeing a three-dimensional animal. Also white are the underside of the tail and a patch under the chin that sometimes extends into the upper neck. This white patch is often individualized and can be used to identify a particular animal. Faint dark stripes run down the middle of the upper neck to the shoulders, blending with the dark gray bark of deciduous shrubs and trees. The upper side of the tail is reddish brown with light beige tips.

The start of the spring molt of white-tailed deer depends on location—beginning in March in the southernmost regions of Texas, in May in the northern reaches of Wisconsin. The molt lasts for several weeks. The first hair to fall and be replaced by summer pelage is on the neck and outer forelegs;

then follow the back, the flank, and the belly. The coat change, completed in most regions of the United States by May or June, takes the deer from gray to reddish brown, again with white belly, lower jaw, and undertail as countershading. This coat is worn for four to five months, until the end of summer.

Through natural selection, deer have acquired the coat color that best blends with the prevailing tones of their environment. Slightly darker coats are seen in the humid, forested areas of the eastern regions of the United States and Canada, where it's an advantage for deer to assume the rich browns and grays of the woods. Paler deer inhabit the dry grasslands of western and southwestern North America. With those minor exceptions, however, the white-tailed deer's coloration is remarkably uniform despite the variety of habitat.

THERMOREGULATION

To survive in the northern ranges of their habitat, as well as in the higher elevations of the Rockies and Andes, deer must be able to

maintain body temperature. It is their warm, thick winter coats that insulate them from extreme cold.

Winter. The deer's winter pelage consists of coarse guard hairs and a soft, woolly underfur. Guard hairs, also known as primary hairs, are long and thick and dark; since dark colors absorb more solar energy, these hairs may play a minor role as solar collectors and help the deer reduce its energy expenditure, according to Moen.

But it is the underfur, or secondary hairs, that provides the most insulative value. Though these fine, convoluted filaments are only half the length of the guard hairs, there are many more of them—five times as many. The ratio of secondary to primary hairs in sheep's wool, by comparison, is four to one; deer, then, obtain a higher insulative value from their coats.

All these tiny, woolly filaments trap layers of air, with warmer layers closer to the skin's surface. When the fur is compressed, as when a deer lies down, the air is pushed out and the coat loses its insulative properties. It is for this reason that on arising, deer leave melted spots in the snow even as they emerge from their beds with snow still crystallized on their backs. By the same token, a deer can increase the insulative value of its fur by making its hair, in effect, stand on end. The feat is an involuntary response to cold. In mammals, a thin bundle of skin muscles, called an *arrector pili,* is attached to the hair shafts. When the muscles contract,

The fawn's first winter coat grows in to replace its natal spotted pelage. The long, waterproof guard hairs channel rain away from the insulating underfur and skin.

Summer (left) or winter (right), the deer's pelage aids in thermoregulation. Summer hairs are short and sparse, allowing air to flow and ventilate the skin. In winter, the tiny air spaces in the convoluted woolly underfur insulate the deer's skin from the bitter ambient temperatures.

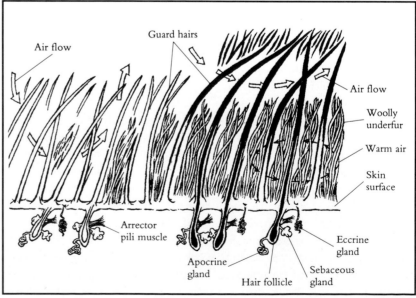

DEER

the hair stands up. In the almost hairless skin of humans, this futile attempt to prevent heat loss results in goose bumps, but in deer the erection of the hairs creates thicker layers of insulative air, thus helping the deer maintain body temperature in extreme cold.

Even deer in moderate climates would not survive if the coat lost its insulating properties when wet. Sebaceous glands in the skin manufacture water-repellent oil, or sebum, which slowly leaks onto the skin surface and coats the hair filaments. This oil keeps both hair and skin soft and elastic as well as waterproof.

Summer. In the heat of midsummer the problem is keeping cool. Deer have few sweat glands to regulate their body temperature by evaporative cooling. Panting is one solution; lightweight pelage is another.

The whitetail's summer coat has no underfur, only guard hairs, and these are shorter and thinner than the guard hairs of the winter coat. There are also fewer of them, and they are lighter in color, lacking the black hair pigment called melanin. These sparse, thin hairs enable the deer to keep cool by simple air convection: as the air next to the animal's body becomes warm, cooler air displaces it.

MOLTING

To survive—to maintain body temperature whether the ambient air is hot or cold, and to keep hidden whether the forest floor is summery brown or wintry gray—the deer needs two coats. Shedding the one and growing the other involve a complex system of external triggers and internal switches, plus a considerable outlay in energy.

A deer's first molt, at the end of the summer, is related to the time of weaning. Late-born fawns are usually weaned at an earlier age than spring fawns, but their coat changes are often incomplete, and the irregularity of the timing of their molts can persist for several years. This suggests that seasonal coat changes are determined in part by an endogenous, internal rhythm. The big trigger, however, is daylight.

Light cycles. Molting, like such other seasonal events as reproduction and antler growth, is regulated by the pineal gland, a

Diet and genetics determine the time of molt, but for does another factor is involved: not until the offspring are close to weaning can their bodies channel resources into growing new coats.

RUE III

INSIDE THE ANIMAL

45

Antler velvet

*T*hink of antler velvet as fur. Though it differs considerably from the skin and hairs that sheathe the deer's body, antler velvet is a modified skin with modified pelage. It grows each year from the skin that rims the wound on the pedicle after the dead antlers have been cast—the only example of complete regeneration of skin among mammals.

What makes this skin velvety is the profusion of short hairs, approximately twelve filaments per square millimeter, each just 5 millimeters long, that cover the antlers. These hairs do not molt, at least not in normal deer. Once the antlers are completely formed, the tissue dies because blood flow into the pedicle is interrupted, in much the same way as a heart attack occurs when blood vessels are blocked: the arterial walls harden and fatty material clogs the passageways. Dead and dry, the tissue sloughs off with vigorous rubbing.

In castrated deer, however, the antlers continue to grow, and the velvet—longer and thicker than in normal deer—molts seasonally, just like the body pelage.

The velvet lacks skin muscles but has no shortage of sebaceous glands. Shaped like elongated droplets, they reach 0.2 to 0.7

The many nerve fibers in antler velvet—which is, after all, a specialized skin with short, dense fur—are vital in controlling the normal growth of antlers. An injury to velvet antlers may reappear as a deformation for several years.

WALLNER

millimeters below the surface. Although secretion of sebum proceeds more slowly than from regular skin, oily droplets sometimes appear on whitetail antlers late in the mineralization process, apparently because the drying and contracting of the velvet pushes the sebum from the dying glands. Sebaceous glands may contain pheromones, so when the buck rubs off the dead velvet on trees, he may be leaving olfactory signals about his presence and condition. In ancestral forms of deer, A.B. Bubenik theorizes, antlers may have been permanently in velvet and served mainly as dispensers of pheromones that informed does about available bucks.

Just about everything to do with velvet is species specific: the particulars of density and length of hair, for example, differentiate whitetails from other species, as do the structure and density of the sebaceous glands. The presence of sudoriferous glands may also be species specific; such glands are known to exist in the velvet of red deer and elk stags but have not been observed in whitetail antlers.

— George A. Bubenik

pinecone-shaped organ in the center of the brain. It produces a hormone, called melatonin, and starts releasing it into the blood at dusk. When the days begin to lengthen after the winter solstice, the body receives a little less melatonin each day. The cumulative effect is a lower level of melatonin in the bloodstream. This initiates the spring molt—but not directly. The fluctuation of melatonin levels modifies the secretion of the pituitary hormone prolactin. It is the level of prolactin—rising in the spring, peaking at the summer solstice in June, and falling until the long dark night of the winter solstice—that ultimately triggers the molt.

Or does it? Another hormone from another gland may be involved as well. The thyroid produces, among other secretions, triiodothyronine (T_3 for brevity's sake), an anabolic hormone that stimulates the metabolism to provide more energy for the growth and development of skin and skin derivatives, such as hair and horns. Levels vary with day length, but on a slightly different schedule from prolactin: T_3 is at its peak in late spring and early summer (late April to early June), and then declines until the beginning of winter. The combination of peak levels of T_3 and rising levels of prolactin results in the spring molt, which throughout most of the United States, is complete by May or June. As prolactin declines in late summer, the level of T_3 is still relatively high, and the fall molt begins.

Experiments indicate that still other hormones can affect pelage, from the timing of the molt to the quality and color of hair growth. Injections of thyroxine, produced in the thyroid and eventually metabolized into T_3, greatly improve the condition of the coat in white-tailed bucks (and also increase muscle bulk). High levels of androgens, the male hormones such as testosterone, can result in darker hair and earlier molting, a finding that should not be surprising to those who have observed how prime bucks (which have particularly high levels of testosterone) have the darkest faces and are the first deer to molt in the fall. High levels of testosterone also increase the activity of the sebaceous skin glands that produce secretions to make the coat water repellent. Cortisol, the main hormone produced by the adrenal cortex, may also affect the timing of the fall molt since studies by Johnson indicate that cortisol inhibits new hair growth. Whether cortisol also affects the spring molt is not known.

Temperature. It has long been assumed that day length is the prime mover, setting in motion the complicated conversations between the body's hormones that ultimately signal shedding and regrowth of hair. But perhaps not alone. Growth of the winter coat proceeds in two stages, guard hairs first. That this first stage indeed depends on day length can be proved by penning deer in artificial light and hastening the onset of winter: as the days grow shorter, the winter guard hairs grow in. But the underfur, which would normally appear soon after, does not appear if the thermometer still reads "June." Not until the return of chilly nights in October does the woolly undercoat grow, suggesting that this aspect of molting is temperature-dependent.

Consider also two cases of temperature extremes. In the warm tropical lowlands of South America, Brokx has observed, the winter coat of whitetails, though gray, has no underfur. And in the Andes, where whitetails live at altitudes of 4,000 meters (13,120 feet) and endure near-freezing temperatures during even summer nights, deer have only winter coats; they molt gradually—or so it is believed—from gray to gray.

The cost of a new coat. Nursing does, it is well known, often keep their summer pelage longer than bucks and mothers that have weaned their fawns. One reason is chemistry. Prolactin, the hormone from the pituitary gland that, when declining and acting with other hormones, signals the body to produce the winter coat, is also the hormone that regulates lactation. The high level of prolactin associated with milk production is at odds with the low level associated with hair growth. The other reason is energy. Both processes drain the doe's energy reserves, and she cannot accomplish both at once.

For all deer, in fact—not just lactating does—molting is metabolically expensive. A buck weighing 100 kilograms (220 pounds) produces 2 kilograms (4½ pounds) of hair

The molt begins at the head and neck, progresses down the spine, then ends with the sparsely furred legs.

FRANZ

DEER

In regions with reddish soils, the difference between a whitetail's summer and winter coat is pronounced. The dark hairs of the winter pelage act like miniature solar collectors, absorbing solar energy and saving stores of body fat from oxidation.

per season, according to one estimate. To grow that much hair—good, thick hair—he must consume 2 grams (0.07 ounces) of nitrogen per day. Since nitrogen is derived from proteins, he needs a diet high in protein, which such foods as willow buds, alfalfa, and bluegrass can provide.

Protein is most important for hair growth, but a lack of essential vitamins and minerals may affect pelage by preventing certain body cells from forming or operating properly. No studies on deer have been completed, but in cattle, for example, a lack of copper in the diet causes the hair to turn gray.

The drain on energy and protein reserves deer experience during the molt explains why animals in good physical condition molt first—before weak bucks and late-born fawns as well as before lactating does. In fact, a late onset of the development of woolly fur is a better (and easier-to-read) indicator of undernourishment than the estimation of integumental fat.

Pelage may also serve as a biological measure of environmental pollution. Heavy metals, toxic to animals, can accumulate in deer hair. Although the coat of a sick deer may not appear to differ from that of a healthy animal, chemical analysis of individual segments of the hair shaft can reveal the presence of toxic pollutants and even indicate the approximate date of exposure. Studies have yet to set forth the correlations, however.

A coat of high-quality underfur is essential for winter survival, and in the colder regions of North America, it must be in place by the end of November. Deer with underdeveloped secondary hairs—or with no underfur at all—draw down their winter fat reserves fast. Whether they will ultimately succumb to exhaustion, predation, or hypothermia is only a matter of time: these deer have a poor chance of survival.

—*George A. Bubenik*

Hooves and tracks

*T*he raised head and pricked ears, the flick of the tail, then the explosive burst of speed, and finally silence: after the deer has disappeared, the human observer has only the image to recall and the tracks to study.

The two-pronged track identifies the animal as a member of the order Artiodactyla, the even-toed ungulates, along with sheep, goats, and cows. The slender shape of the deer's hooves gives minimal contact with the ground—a friction-reducing adaptation that increases the animal's speed.

When a hoof is extended—that is, when the foot supports the weight of the animal—a specialized springing ligament is stretched. As that hoof leaves the ground, the ligament

The quick retraction of the springing ligament powers each stride, enabling the deer to reach speeds of 40 miles an hour (18 meters per second).

rebounds and the hoof snaps backward, providing extra spring to the gait and increasing both the speed and the thrust of the deer's stride.

Hooves are actually modified fingernails. The outer surface, or wall, is made of highly keratinized material and is quite hard. In contrast, the sole has a softer, spongy surface that provides good contact with the ground. The two parts of a deer's hoof correspond to our third and fourth fingers (the middle and ring fingers), and the dew claws behind the hooves correspond to our second and fifth fingers.

The deer's front and hind hooves differ. The dew claws on the front feet are much closer to the hooves than those on the rear

feet. And because they bear more weight, the front hooves tend to be slightly larger, especially in adult bucks. Front hooves of an average adult buck will be about 75 millimeters (3 inches) long and 35 to 50 millimeters (1.5 to 2 inches) wide.

The growth rate of hooves appears to correspond with a normal rate of wear. This means that in areas of very soft ground, hooves can become overgrown, and in rocky, mountainous terrain, hooves tend to be shorter and more blunt. Studies at the University of Georgia indicate that deer hooves grow at an average rate of about 60 millimeters (2.5 inches) per year. Yearling bucks' hooves grow slightly faster than those of adult bucks. Hooves grow most slowly in the winter and most quickly in the late summer and early fall.

Studies have shown that there are differences in hoof sizes between male and female adult deer, and it has long been debated whether a deer's sex can be determined from its tracks.

As early as 1956, Weston argued that "No man, not even the most astute woodsman,

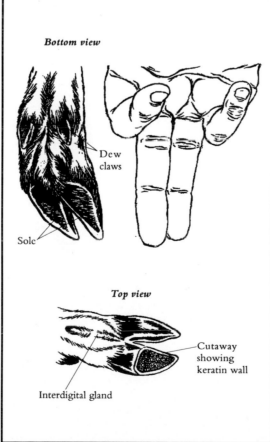

Bottom view

Dew claws

Sole

Top view

Cutaway showing keratin wall

Interdigital gland

With the relatively large, wide-spreading hooves and sturdy dew claws giving good traction even on steep, rocky terrain, the sure-footed mule deer is at home in the western badlands.

An outer wall of keratin, the same substance that constitutes fingernails, surrounds a spongy interior. Note that the artiodactyls—the even-toed ungulates—do not have a digit that corresponds to the human thumb.

INSIDE THE ANIMAL

The imprint of the dew claws appears directly behind the hoofprint; the dew claws dig in behind each hoof, adding support. Drag marks, like those visible in the light snow (below), are often presumed to be from a buck. Determining sex from hoofprints, however, is a chancy business.

can positively and consistently identify the [sex of a] white-tailed deer by its track alone." A few years later, McCullough reported on a scientific study regarding the sex characteristics of black-tailed deer hooves. His results indicated that there were significant differences in both length and width between the sexes of yearling and older deer. But he cautioned that though these differences do occur, there is some overlap, which means that in most cases one would not be able to determine sex accurately from tracks in the wild. Most adult males and the larger yearling males, however, can be identified with a high degree of certainty.

In a similar study of white-tailed deer in Georgia, Swiderek reported that, except for adult and large yearling males, the sex of a deer cannot be determined by measurements of its track.

In addition to size, there are other clues one can look for in determining a deer's sex from its tracks. A mature buck's hooves may have more rounded tips than a doe's, although hoof wear can be affected by terrain and soil conditions. It has also been suggested, but not proven, that a buck's feet tend to produce drag marks on light snow whereas a doe's feet do not.

An observer can also make an educated guess by following the tracks and interpreting the animal's behavior, and by looking at the tracks of other deer accompanying it. There is, however, only one way to be absolutely certain about the sex and size of the deer that makes a particular track, and that is to find the track while the deer is still in it.

—Karl V. Miller

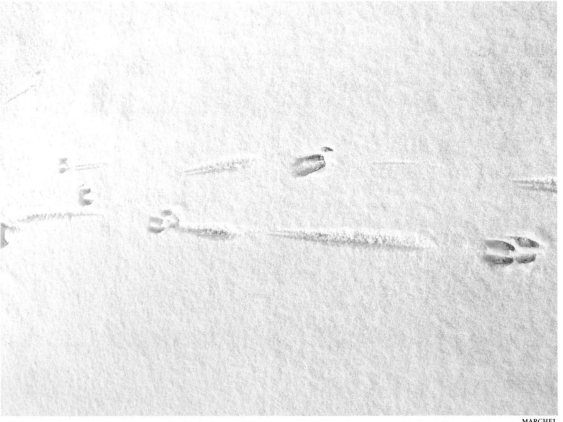

Skin glands

Deer have the same five senses that humans do but place very different importance on each of them. We rely primarily on sight to gather information about our environment and on sound to communicate with other humans. Deer, on the other hand, use their sense of smell as the primary means of both gathering information and communicating with other deer.

Chemical signals that are part of an olfactory vocabulary may be produced by a number of sources, including the reproductive tract, urine, feces, the respiratory system, and specialized skin glands. Although the other sources of scent are undoubtedly important in conveying information among deer, the skin glands are notable because of their wide distribution over the deer's body and their variability in structure and function.

All odocoileids—mule deer, black-tailed deer, and white-tailed deer—are richly endowed with scent-producing skin glands. As early as 1877, the presence of some of these glands was reported by Canton. Since these deer are closely related, they have essentially the same glands, which serve similar functions, although there are some differences among the species.

SKIN GLAND HISTOLOGY

Each of the specialized skin glands is composed of one or both of two basic types of glandular tissue: sebaceous and sudoriferous. Both types are found distributed over the skin surface, but they tend to be greatly concentrated and enlarged in the specialized skin glands.

Sebaceous gland tissues are usually associated with a hair follicle, although this is not always the case. Commonly, sebaceous glands are connected to a hair follicle by a short duct. When viewed under a microscope, a group of sebaceous glands looks like a tiny cauliflower. The secretory product of the sebaceous glands is always oily and rich in fatty materials called lipids. The sebaceous glands themselves apparently do not produce any scent important in communication, but their secretions appear to be vital for holding substances—produced elsewhere in the body—that do convey information. This lipid material then can either be trans-

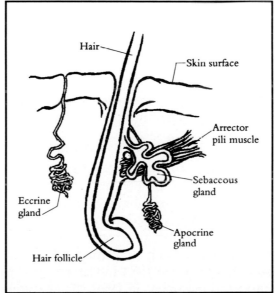

Both sebaceous and sudoriferous glands lubricate the skin and waterproof the hair. The lipids they produce, though they have no scent of their own, are a vehicle for olfactory messages.

ferred to a tree branch or some other object in the environment or be held on the deer's body to allow bacteria to change it into an odor important for communication.

There are two types of sudoriferous or tubular sweat gland tissue: eccrine and apocrine. Both consist of a secretory coil located deep in the skin and a duct leading to the skin surface. The duct of eccrine glands opens directly at the skin surface; that of apocrine glands generally leads to a hair follicle. Eccrine glands are responsible for thermoregulatory sweating in humans, but they typically are not very important in other animals. Apocrine glands, on the other hand, are confined to the pubic, perineal, and axillary regions of the human body but are widely distributed over the skin of most other mammals. Apocrine glands are much more important than eccrine glands in chemical communication; they can produce airborne odors or, more commonly, a material that is altered through microbial action into a scent.

Several of the specialized skin glands of deer are associated with areas of specialized hairs. These hairs are important in odor transmission. They can control air circulation to the skin surface, increase the area for evaporation of odors, provide a substrate for the growth of odor-producing bacteria, and serve as a brush for transferring materials to objects in the environment. In addition, each hair is connected to an arrector pili muscle, which, when contracted, can cause the hair to "stand on end."

Researchers have thus far identified eight regions of the deer's body that have specialized glandular development of potential communicative importance: the forehead, preorbital, and nasal glands on the head; the interdigital, tarsal, and metatarsal glands on the legs; the caudal and preputial regions.

THE FOREHEAD GLAND

According to Müller-Schwarze (1971, 1972), black-tailed deer rub their foreheads on dry twigs and branches, and these marked branches become centers of social attention. Similar observations of white-tailed deer marking were made by Moore and Marchinton in 1974 and later by Marchinton and coworkers in 1990. These studies found that in both species, scent marking with the forehead gland is done by both males and females, although males mark more often than females.

In black-tailed and mule deer, a microscopic anatomy (or histology) of the forehead skin reveals that the sebaceous and sudoriferous gland tissues here are only slightly, if at all, larger than those in the skin of other parts of the deer's body. In their studies conducted in the 1970s, Quay and Müller-Schwarze did not observe any differences in the activity of these glands according to the age or sex of the animal. Nonetheless, behavioral observations do indicate that this is an important scent-producing region in these deer.

A slightly different situation exists with white-tailed deer. Microscopic examination of the forehead region reveals greater numbers of tubular apocrine sudoriferous gland tissues than are found in other areas of the deer's skin. During summer, these glands exhibit little activity in either male or female deer. During breeding season, however, glandular activity increases somewhat in females and greatly in males. These glands are most active in dominant males and least active in young fawns.

THE PREORBITAL GLAND

The preorbital gland—also called the antorbital gland, preocular gland, suborbital pit, or lachrymal sinus—consists of a shallow, hairless pocket that opens to the surface through a slit. It is located in front of the corner of the eye. This pocket is essentially aglandular in black-tailed and mule deer. The edges, or lips, of the pocket in both sexes have sebaceous and sudoriferous gland tissues that are only slightly larger than those occurring elsewhere on the body surface. The histology of this gland in white-tailed deer has not been investigated, but there is little reason to suspect that it differs substantially from that of the other two species.

In all species, the preorbital gland is under muscular control; bucks commonly flare theirs open during dominance displays, does often do so while their fawns are nursing. Inside the preorbital sac there is often an accumulation of material that likely consists of dead skin cells, drainage from the eye, and

ANTUS

LEA

foreign matter. Investigations by Volkman and his coworkers demonstrated that black-tailed deer react to the scent from the preorbital gland. This reaction indicates that the scent conveys some information to other deer, but exactly what information is not yet known. The researchers suggested symbiotic bacteria inhabiting the sac as a possible source of this scent.

THE NASAL GLAND

Nasal glands were first reported in both mule and white-tailed deer by Atkeson and his coworkers in 1988, and it is very likely that black-tailed deer also have them. These glands, consisting of oval cavities located just inside the nostril, connect to the nostril by a

short duct. The glands are hairless and contain many sebaceous gland tissues but no sudoriferous ones.

The function of the nasal gland is unknown, but it does not appear to be involved in scent communication. It is similar to the nasal gland reported by Jacob and van Lehmann in 1976 in the closely related marsh deer from South America. Secretions from this gland were shown to consist primarily of lipid material that has a very low volatility. Because the molecules do not readily pass into the air, it is unlikely that these secretions emit a behaviorally important scent. It seems that their primary purpose is to lubricate the nose, although their possible role in signpost communication should not be ignored. Additional research may someday clarify the importance of the nasal gland.

THE INTERDIGITAL GLAND

Between the toes on all four feet are invaginations, or saclike folds, called interdigital glands. For all three types of deer these glands probably serve to leave a scent trail—depositing a telltale odor with each step. There are, however, differences among the species in the anatomy of this gland; therefore the source and type of scent produced likely differs also.

In white-tailed deer, the interdigital pockets are characterized primarily by greatly enlarged sebaceous gland tissues, although sudoriferous gland tissues do occur. There is

BESENGER

a tendency for the sebaceous gland tissues to enlarge as the deer ages, according to Quay. Often a yellowish, waxy material called sebum is present in the interdigital sac.

In mule and black-tailed deer, in contrast, the interdigital contains both enlarged sebaceous and sudoriferous gland tissues. In the blacktail, at least, the sebaceous and sudoriferous layers also appear to be thicker.

THE METATARSAL GLAND

The metatarsal gland is located on the outside of the deer's hind foot, or metatarsus. It is a curious structure consisting of a central, oval patch of highly cornified, hairless skin surrounded by an oval tuft of white hair. There is considerable variation in its size among the species of deer. In mule deer this gland is 100 to 150 millimeters (4 to 6 inches) long; in black-tailed deer it is considerably smaller, 60 to 100 millimeters (2.5 to 4 inches). In whitetails the gland is even smaller—just 20 to 35 millimeters (.75 to 1.5 inches)—and interestingly, it varies in size among the different whitetail subspecies. In the northern United States and Canada, the gland is fairly large. In the southern states, the gland is smaller, and in subspecies inhabiting parts of Central and South America, the gland may be completely absent.

The central, hairless ridge contains no glandular elements. Quay hypothesized that this structure has a sensory function, such as circulatory thermoregulation, although experimental evidence is lacking. The fact that

this gland is larger in colder climates does support his suggestion, however.

The skin underlying the oval ring of hair contains both enlarged sebaceous and sudoriferous gland tissues. The sudoriferous tissues are much more highly developed in black-tailed and mule deer than in the whitetail. Müller-Schwarze has demonstrated that the metatarsal of black-tailed deer produces a garliclike odor that serves as an alarm signal, but his studies, and later those of Atkeson, failed to demonstrate that the whitetail metatarsal produces an alarm scent. These findings are consistent with the differences in the histology of the organ between the two species.

THE TARSAL GLAND

The tarsal gland is probably the most important gland in all three types of deer. It is used to identify other deer and likely also contains information on dominance position, physical condition, and reproductive status.

The gland consists of a tuft of elongated hair on the inside of the hind leg at the tarsal joint, or ankle, and large numbers of enlarged sebaceous and sudoriferous gland tissues in the skin underneath this tuft. Though these skin glands likely contribute to the odor of the tarsal gland, the primary source of the tarsal odor appears to come from urine.

All deer commonly urinate onto their tarsal glands in a behavior called rub urination or scent urination. The sebaceous gland tissues under the tarsal tuft produce a lipid that coats the tarsal hairs. This lipid selectively retains certain compounds from the urine while permitting other materials to pass. In black-tailed deer, the tarsal hairs have specialized comblike structures that help hold the lipid on the hair. Müller-Schwarze called these structures osmetrichia, which is derived from the Greek *osme* ("odor") and *thrix* ("hair"). White-tailed deer do not have these specialized structures, but the tarsal hairs are still capable of holding large amounts of lipid.

The skin underneath the tarsal tuft also has well-developed arrector pili muscles, which allow the deer to flare the tarsal gland to release a burst of scent. Deer often flare

The tarsal gland, on the inside of the hind leg, grows a brush of hair that the deer can wash with urine. Certain chemicals (lactones) in the urine interact with the lipids from the gland to produce significant scents.

RUE III

LEA

FRANCIS

The role of the metatarsal, on the outside of the hind leg, is only partially known, but its size differs greatly between the species. The whitetail's gland is small, round, and white; the mule deer's may be 6 inches long.

this gland in response to physical or social trauma—a painful injury, harassment from other deer.

In black-tailed deer, the main component of the tarsal scent was identified by Brownlee and his coworkers in 1969. They found that a compound called *cis*-4-hydroxydodec-6-enoic acid lactone, which originates from the deer's urine, is present on the tarsal glands of males. Subsequent studies indicated that this compound is effective in eliciting approach, sniffing, and licking responses from other deer, although it must be accompanied by several other tarsal constituents for maximal response.

Although the compounds that provide the scent to the tarsal gland in white-tailed deer have not yet been identified, they certainly have their origin in the deer's urine and are likely similar to those of black-tailed deer.

CAUDAL GLANDS

Caudal glands have been described for black-tailed and mule deer only. These glands are located on the dorsal and lateral areas of the tail and consist of moderately enlarged sebaceous and sudoriferous gland tissues. As with the tarsal gland, the skin in the caudal area contains enlarged arrector pili muscles. Müller-Schwarze reported that blacktail fawns produce a peculiar odor from their tails when excited. This odor can also be found in adult males. The caudal area of white-tailed deer also may function as a scent gland, but it has not been examined histologically nor have any behavioral observations suggested it as a source of scent.

PREPUTIAL GLANDS

The existence of preputial glands in white-tailed deer was reported in 1991 by Oden'hal and his coworkers, but their function has not yet been determined. They consist of greatly enlarged sebaceous gland tissues and a few long hairs that protrude from the penal sheath. These long hairs become covered with a lipid material in the same manner as the tarsal hairs.

The preputial area in black-tailed and mule deer has not yet been investigated.

—*Karl V. Miller and R. Larry Marchinton*

The senses of deer

*I*magine standing 75 yards away from someone. You cannot see him—he has concealed himself in a dense fir thicket. He stands downwind of you, facing you, with his hands behind his back. Would you hear him clicking his fingernails?

You wouldn't, but a black-tailed doe actually did.

That report, from Linsdale and Tomich, is not unusual in the annals of deer sensorial feats. Deer are well known for keen senses of hearing, sight, and smell—so keen that mere humans can scarcely measure their extent.

HEARING

Like a satellite dish pointed to the heavens, collecting signals for the owner to sort out and tune in, a deer's ears point toward the source of sound and gather essential information.

When the ears, or pinnae, are stationary and at rest, the deer can tell whether the sound comes from ahead or behind. The pinnae can move independently of each other; by comparing the signals each ear receives, the deer locates the source of the sound. One measure of comparison is intensity: a louder signal in the right ear indicates that the sound comes from that direction. But deer use another measure as well. They can evaluate the difference in time it takes the sound to reach each ear, especially if the frequency, or pitch, of the sound is high.

The deer can also evaluate sounds with just one ear. Monaural hearing helps the deer locate sounds in the horizontal plane, revealing whether the source of the sound is near or far. By swiveling one pinna toward the source of a sound, the deer effectually amplifies the signal. Although monaural hearing is also essential in determining vertical location, deer usually pay little attention to what is above them: in their natural world, predators from the sky are not to be feared. Increasingly, this predator is man, hunting from a tree stand, but even this development seems to have had little effect on deer behavior. In Europe, tree stands have been used successfully by generations of roe deer hunters who have seen no need to change their strategy.

Deer are able to hear frequencies higher than those audible to human beings but not as high as those perceived by dogs—or so researchers infer from studies of the taxonomically and ecologically not-too-distant domestic goat. Goats pick up sounds from 78 Hz to 37 kHz and are most sensitive at 2 kHz. This places them between the ranges of human hearing—16 Hz to 20 kHz with greatest sensitivity at 2 to 2.3 kHz—and dogs—15 Hz to 40 kHz.

Thus equipped with sensitive ears, deer rely primarily on hearing to detect the presence of animals around them, Linsdale and Tomich concluded. Anatomy, behavior, and habitat all work together here. Red deer, Darling observed, live in "zones of silence" with little or no wind and can therefore detect the sounds of approaching creatures

LEA

TIETZ

CRANDALL

while they have time to take evasive action. North American deer that live in the midst of constant background noise—the rustling leaves of Northeast woodlands, the patter of raindrops in the Pacific Northwest, the winds and whispering grasses of the West—learn to listen for alien sounds. Habituated to the familiar sounds of their environment, they filter out all but the significant, potentially threatening auditory signals.

Deer whistles, devices mounted on vehicles to warn deer of the machine's approach, are designed to take advantage of the animal's sensitive ears, but their effectiveness has yet to be determined accurately. These whistles produce sound at a frequency between 16 and 20 kHz, but Stattleman, testing a single white-tailed deer, determined that the animal could not hear sounds in that range. Muzzi and Bisset reported that, in Ontario, railroad engines equipped with these whistles struck fewer moose than did engines without them; the engine crews also had to perform fewer moose-warning maneuvers—blowing whistles, ringing bells, dimming lights, changing engine noise—than did the crews of engines without whistles. On the other hand, Romin and Dalton reported that free-ranging mule deer in Utah reacted no differently to a test truck when it traveled with or without a deer whistle.

VISION

Astute early naturalists noted that deer see very well at night and can detect the slightest movement. And indeed, deer are often active after sunset, even in the darkest hours. Like other animals that are adapted for crepuscular and nocturnal behavior, deer have a membrane in the back of the eye that reflects light back through the receptor layer of the retina. This *tapetum lucidum,* like that of many hoofed animals, is made up of tendonlike collagen tissue. By passing light through the receptor layer a second time, the *tapetum* improves the deer's vision in dim light and also produces the eyeshine of nocturnal animals caught in automobile headlights.

Deer are active in daytime as well. Their ability to see well in bright light may be explained by a ring of pigment surrounding the cornea in the eye. This pigment, according to Duke-Elder, is most likely an antiglare device, since it is not found in mammals that are strictly crepuscular and nocturnal.

Day or night, a deer's visual acuity is excellent. Under strong light, the pupils of the eye close into a slit, focusing light onto a horizontal band across the eye's retina. In exactly this streak are clustered the nerve cells that function as signal conductors, carrying messages from the photoreceptors to the brain. The arrangement and density of the nerve cells, called ganglion cells, in the visual streak account for the deer's ability to detect danger from afar. Bruckner, in fact, suggested that the visual streak corresponds to the horizon that dominates the world view of open-country ungulates. If so, the

MARCHEL

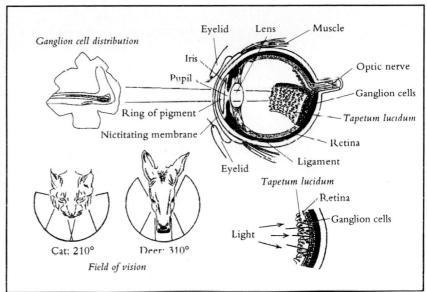

Ganglion cell distribution

Eyelid   Lens   Muscle

Iris

Pupil

Optic nerve

Ganglion cells

Ring of pigment

Tapetum lucidum

Nictitating membrane

Retina

Eyelid

Ligament

Tapetum lucidum

Retina

Ganglion cells

Light

Cat: 210°   Deer: 310°

Field of vision

BESENGER

vision of deer is particularly suited to observing intruders in flat country. The theory would also account for the observation that mountain mammals—Dall sheep, mountain goats, chamoix, and ibex among them—tilt their heads when focusing on a distant disturbance, presumably to align the visual streak with the slanted horizon of the slope on which they stand.

Other herbivores—sheep, goats, cattle, horses, red kangaroos—have a similar arrangement of ganglion cells in a horizontal visual streak. In bovines the streak is most distinct. In carnivores such as wolves and mountain lions the streak is more diffuse, with the density of receptor cells per area gradually decreasing into the surrounding areas. In human beings, there is no visual streak at all: the human eye focuses on just one spot at a time and cannot take in the whole horizon without movement of the eyes or head.

The visual acuity of deer is well demonstrated by an experiment known to researchers as the minimum separable. An animal is trained to distinguish stripe patterns so that the researchers can determine how fine a stripe can be seen at how great a distance before the pattern blurs: it's the animal equivalent of the doctor's eye chart. Red deer can distinguish 1.4 millimeter (0.056 inch) wide black-and-white stripes from gray from 0.8 meters (2.6 feet) away. This indicates a visual resolution for deer similar to that of other hoofed mammals, greater than

a nilgai antelope but less than a goat. Humans have a visual resolution about twelve times better than that of deer.

Deer see well, but do they see colors? Experiments to determine the answer to this question have to be carefully constructed: just as it is possible for us to distinguish the yellow car from the red in a black-and-white photo, so animals may use brightness (the intensity of light) to discriminate what human beings see as color (different wavelengths on the spectrum).

In an outdoor test that did not control for brightness, elk distinguished fluorescent orange from other colors and from white; the colors were painted on food buckets.

Behavioral findings indicate that red deer can discriminate colors. Each deer in the study learned to press a lever when a light came on to signal that food was available; press the right-color lever and food appears. The deer distinguished red, orange, yellow, yellow-green to green, and blue both from one another and from gray. A red deer hind spontaneously was attracted to green but, in the words of Backhaus, "disliked" blue and "threatened to become neurotic" when he tried to condition her to prefer blue over shades of gray.

In another study, red deer were found able to see colors in very dim light. Landscape painters have long observed that colors fade into gray at dusk, when, physicists tell us, light measures a mere 0.01 Lux. Paint the same scene at high noon on a sunny day—at

The tapetum lucidum, a thin layer of reflective tissue, bounces light back across the receptor cells, effectively brightening a dimly lit image; it accounts for this axis doe's eyeshine. The eye's visual streak—the concentration of ganglion receptor cells—focuses visual acuity in a linear pattern. This, along with the wide field of vision, lets the deer see across a wide area and focus on the horizon, where predators might appear—all without turning its head.

10,000 Lux—and the palette must be vivid. But what is the intensity threshold at which deer start to see color? For yellow, it is just 0.007 to 0.01 Lux. Humans require 0.1 Lux (about the brightness of a full moon) to perceive color. Reds and greens require a slightly higher level of light before they become visible to deer as spectral colors.

Two whitetails, in an experiment like that for the red deer, learned to discriminate spectral colors that were controlled for brightness. They distinguished orange (with a wavelength of 620 nanometers) from other colors with long wavelengths more readily than they distinguished green (500 nanometers) from other short-wavelength colors, such as blue.

This difficulty in picking out green is surprising, considering that deer forage among myriad shades of grassy and leafy green. Perhaps color is not important for white-tailed deer after all. Noting that the doe took only seven days to discriminate between the presence and absence of light but needed twenty-six days to learn color (the buck was slower: twenty-eight days and forty-four days, respectively), Smith and his colleagues concluded that deer may not need to distinguish colors in their natural environments, even though they can do so in the laboratory.

Deer appear to have the anatomical apparatus for color vision, though again, not all studies agree. In vertebrate eyes there are two kinds of photoreceptors: rods, which respond to single photons and enable vision in dim light, and cones, which account for color and daylight vision. The mix of rods and cones—or the absence of one form altogether—determines what kind of vision an animal has.

Cones have been found in the retinas of elk and whitetails. For whitetails, Witzel and his colleagues counted 10,000 per square millimeter, compared with 20,000 cones per square millimeter for monkeys and human beings, and 25,000 for cats.

According to a different study, however, whitetails do *not* have cones. Using scanning and transmission electron microscopy, Staknis and Simmons clearly distinguished cones and rods in the retina of the pig but found no cones in whitetail eyes. Because deer are well adapted for low-light vision and

thus have many rods in the retina, it may be that the cones were not easily detected, especially if not all sections of the eye were scanned. Unlike some mammalian eyes (including the human eye), in which the cones are concentrated in a central area called the fovea, the deer's eye could have them spread across a larger area.

In another study, Murphy and colleagues measured the electrical activity of the photoreceptors in the retinas of nine whitetails to find not only cones, but their photopigments and the specific colors to which they respond. Pigments in the cones responded to light with a wavelength of 537 nanometers (yellow-green) and 455 nanometers (blue); pigment in the rods was most responsive to light with a wavelength of 496 nanometers (blue-green). These findings suggest that deer are less sensitive to light of long wavelengths (orange and red) and actually rely upon their perception of only two colors—yellow and blue.

Deer can become blind. Cervid eyes are susceptible to cataracts, which accounted for the visual impairment in ten of seventeen apparently blind moose in a Swedish study. The lenses were deformed, reduced, and milky white or brownish gray, with granular and uneven surfaces. A microscope revealed fluid accumulation between the lens fibers, according to Kronevi et al.

CHEMICAL SENSES

What we refer to as the senses of taste and smell is the reception of molecules of chemical compounds. When the molecules of food or odor bind with receptor molecules in the animal's tongue or nose, a response is triggered. It's no longer enough, however, to talk about a deer's senses of taste and smell; there is another sense that guides numerous aspects of deer behavior, a true sixth sense unknown to early deer researchers. Vomolfaction, like taste and smell, is a chemical sense involving, in this case, the vomeronasal organ.

Taste. A deer's sense of taste is the important gatekeeper for food ingestion. Deer drop undesirable plants from their mouths, along with saliva. Bitter forage is known to be unpalatable, but a better understanding of taste sensitivity and selectivity would en-

BINEGAR

able researchers to develop repellents to protect agriculture, from backyard gardens to cornfields to vast forest plantations. Byers et al. found that various repellents kept white-tailed deer from feeding on apples and apple shoots, but only for a time. After one to six days the deer overcame their reluctance to feed on the treated forage. The effectiveness of chemical repellents may depend on how many deer are competing for how much food: if deer are few and other food is available, the treatments are likely to work longer.

Like other ruminants, deer have long, mobile tongues. The tastebuds are arranged in groups on fungiform (mushroom-shaped) or circumvallate (moated) papillae. The circumvallate papillae, which contain more tastebuds, run in two rows on either side of the midline of the tongue. Just behind the highest point of the upper surface of the tongue is a prominent cluster of fungiform papillae. Elsewhere, papillae are scanty.

The significance of the arrangement and forms of tastebuds is unexplored, but it is known that ruminants have more circumvallate papillae (sheep and ox, twenty-four; antelope, fifty-two) than carnivorous mammals (dog, four to six; cat, seven; skunk, two).

Smell. The hunter whose quarry is downwind knows all too well the deer's keen sense of smell. The animal's sense of smell aids in finding and selecting food, detecting predators, alerting other deer, identifying members of the herd, attracting mates, determining the sexual readiness of potential mating partners, bonding between doe and fawn, tracking of mates and mothers and fawns—in short, as Cowan put it, "This is the paramount sense of the deer."

Yet little is known of thresholds of olfaction. Only one species, the black-tailed deer, has been studied for olfactory performance. Findings by Müller-Schwarze et al. indicate that deer are capable of three levels of olfactory discrimination. All the experiments involved Z-4-hydroxydodec-6-enoic acid lactone, a thick, oily, unsaturated liquid that naturally occurs in deer urine and tarsal gland excretions.

In one experiment, a biological dose (an amount similar to that found in the wild) of natural lactone was applied to the hock of a fawn and the responses of its penmates—five- to twelve-month-old fawns—were recorded. The fawns sniffed and licked the spot: they had smelled it. Then the researchers applied comparable amounts of very similar synthetic lactones. Three other unsaturated lactones were sniffed and licked significantly

Foraging begins with smell. Once a deer has tested food with the nose, it takes an experimental nibble. The long, mobile tongue has taste buds that test for toxins; bitter and otherwise unpalatable plants may be spit out. The deer at the left is an endangered Columbia whitetail.

WERNER

less, and three saturated lactones prompted even less response. When the amounts were increased a hundred-fold, the fawns still ignored the saturated lactone but responded to the unsaturated ones just as they would to an actual tarsal scent comprising urine, bacteria, and tarsal secretions.

In a second experiment, blacktails discriminated between two versions of lactone, the naturally occurring Z form and the synthetic E form, whose only difference, chemically speaking, is the position of one hydrogen atom at the molecule's double bond.

Some pairs of molecules, called enantiomers, differ only in the arrangement of four groups of atoms around a carbon atom. Mirror images of one another, such molecules are said to have "handedness" by analogy to a pair of hands: Because of their orientation one cannot be superimposed on the other,

Compounds of low volatility cannot be smelled; they must be examined with the vomeronasal organ. Having licked a sample of a doe's urine, this mule deer buck uses a lip curl to pump the compounds into the VNO duct in the upper palate.

GEIST

just as a person's right hand cannot be superimposed on his left. These two versions of the same molecule have identical physical and chemical properties, except for their ability to rotate polarized light in different directions, denoted by (+) or (−). To humans and animals, however, enantiomers can appear quite different. For example, the (−) form of carvone has a distinct spearmint odor, but the (+) form has an odor of caraway. When the deer were challenged to differentiate between a pair of such molecules of a lactone that both occur in the natural tarsal scent, they could smell both versions, albeit to different degrees. The natural scent of the deer's lactone contains 11 percent (+) lactone and 89 percent (−). When the two forms were separated, deer were found capable of distinguishing between them by responding more to the (−) form than to the (+).

Besides lactone, deer respond to other social odors produced by their skin glands, urine, and feces. Response may be to each compound individually, or perhaps the compounds in a mix of deer excretions may interact in ways as yet unknown. In other mammals, chemical signals called pheromones often consist of mixtures of compounds, in which the effect of one substance depends on the admixture of another, or in which two compounds have little effect on their own but a synergistic effect when combined, or in which two compounds are basically redundant.

Vomolfaction. It's no longer enough to talk about a deer's senses of taste and smell; there is another sense that guides numerous aspects of deer behavior, a sense unknown to early deer researchers. Vomolfaction, like taste and smell, is a chemical sense involving, in this case, the vomeronasal organ.

The best example of vomolfaction occurs during the rut, when bucks appear to lick fresh urine from a doe approaching estrus. The buck's grimacing flehmen, or lip curl, mechanically transfers the odoriferous material to a pair of pores, called the incisive foramina, in the roof of the mouth. Tongue movements are important in this mechanical process, but the deer also has a vomeronasal pump. Small muscles contract to empty blood vessels around the vomeronasal or-

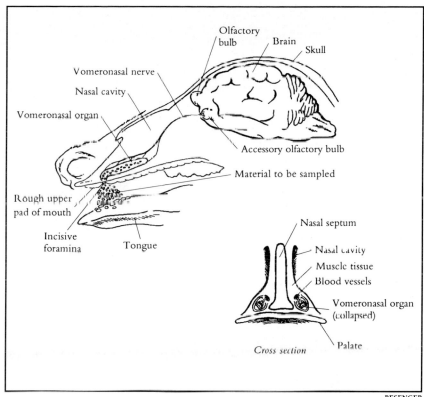

BESENGER

gan, exerting negative pressure on the organ, in effect, creating a weak vacuum. A narrow tube leading into the dead-end organ widens and sucks in material to be tested. Once the chemical analysis is done, the muscles relax, the blood vessels engorge with blood, and the resultant pressure forces the material out of the vomeronasal organ. The organ is then ready to sample the next batch.

Unlike olfactory receptors, which detect molecules in vapor, the receptors in the vomeronasal organ are sensitive to nonvolatile compounds. Not being airborne, these compounds must come into direct contact with the chemoreceptors. When the buck seeks to ascertain the readiness of the doe he is pursuing, then, he must examine her urine at close range by licking it.

—*Dietland Müller-Schwarze*

The lip curl causes the blood vessels around the vomeronasal organ to empty, creating a vacuum that the sample rushes in to fill; the compounds then are read by chemoreceptors in the olfactory bulb of the brain.

Digestion

As members of the order Ruminata, deer have a kinship with all other animals that chew their cud, such as cattle and sheep. The similarities in anatomy and morphology of the digestive systems of ruminants are much greater than their differences. For this reason, it was once thought that deer could be raised and maintained on hay and grain. This basic misconception has often led game managers, sportsmen, and landowners astray in the management of habitat and the supplemental feeding of deer, including food plots.

The Digestive System

When a ruminant eats, its food is actually digested—prepared for absorption—by four means. During mechanical digestion, plant parts are broken down into smaller particles by chewing and mixing. In chemical digestion, hydrochloric acid in the stomach dissolves plant particles. During enzymatic and microbial digestion, enzymes and microbes break the chemical bonds of larger compounds, such as starch or protein, to produce smaller nutrients, such as glucose or amino acids, which can be absorbed directly into the bloodstream. These enzymes are produced by the walls of the small intestine, the pancreas, and also by microbes in the digestive tract.

As a deer eats, it chews its food only enough to allow swallowing. While being chewed, the often dry and fibrous food mixes with saliva, which helps it pass more smoothly down the esophagus. Saliva production is impressive in ruminants, reaching levels of several gallons a day in large animals, and several quarts a day in small ones. From the esophagus the food passes through a valve and into the first of the stomach's four compartments—the rumen.

The rumen is where the main digestive process takes place. Here the food is mixed further with other rumen contents, especially microbes (bacteria and protozoa) and more saliva. Buffers in the saliva help keep the rumen from becoming too acidic. Microbes attack the food particles, breaking them down into nutrients, some of which are absorbed directly; others are digested more fully farther down the tract. The rumen is lined with papillae, small fingerlike projections that increase surface area for absorption. The fermentation process, that is, the breakdown of food in the rumen by enzymes produced by bacteria and protozoa, is the main difference between ruminants and monogastric, or simple-stomached, animals.

As food is digested, it circulates through the second compartment of the stomach—the reticulum, a heavily muscled chamber at the front of the rumen. Often called the "honeycomb" because of its many folds, the reticulum helps send boluses of food back up the esophagus for cud chewing. Depending on how fibrous the food is, it may stay in the rumen for a few hours or for a few days before being passed along to the next chamber of the stomach.

Food processing begins with the careful selection of nutritious plant parts—buds, leaves, seeds. The material is swallowed nearly whole and stored for later cudding.

KINNEY

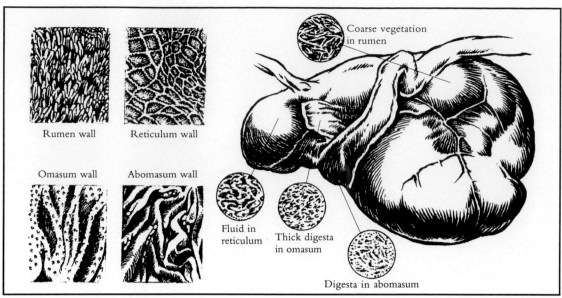

Rumen wall   Reticulum wall

Omasum wall   Abomasum wall

Coarse vegetation in rumen

Fluid in reticulum

Thick digesta in omasum

Digesta in abomasum

BESENGER

The third compartment, the omasum, serves as a pump to move the more fluid contents of the rumen farther down the tract. It is heavily muscled and has large leaves, like the pages of a book. As the rumen contents pass through the omasum, much of the water is absorbed.

The abomasum, or fourth stomach, is the deer's true stomach. This chamber is nearly identical to the stomach of monogastric animals, although the food entering the abomasum has been fermented. The hydrochloric acid produced here chemically dissolves food particles. The enzymes pepsin and rennin are released to aid in the digestion of proteins, including microbes that came along from the rumen.

Once the contents, called digesta, pass into the small intestine, enzymes from the intestinal walls or the pancreas help to digest simple sugars, peptides, and lipids. The acid from the abomasum is neutralized so that the enzymes can work. Although deer (with the exception of the musk deer) have no gall bladder in which to store bile, they nonetheless produce bile in the liver to help emulsify fats in the intestine. The small intestine's main function is to absorb into the bloodstream the many nutrients from the food that has been digested.

From the small intestine, the digesta passes into the large intestine, or colon, where more water is absorbed. Some enzymatic digestion continues to occur here, and microbial digestion may continue as well. Most animals have an outcropping of the intestinal tract called a cecum, where microbial digestion can occur, but this varies greatly among species.

BENEFITS OF RUMINATION

Ecologists have long argued the advantages of the ruminant's digestive system. Some have suggested, for instance, that even though deer may be below carnivores in the food chain, these ruminants may really have a higher niche in that they can convert foods that are not usable by "higher order" animals. The main advantage of the deer's digestive process is that it can digest cellulose and hemicellulose, the complex carbohydrates found in browse, grass, and other fibrous foods. Monogastric animals, such as humans, pigs, and dogs, lack the enzymes needed to break the bonds of these nutrients. Actually, ruminants themselves do not have the enzymes, either, but their rumen microbes do.

During the fermentation process, cellulose, along with sugars and starches, is broken down in the rumen into simple sugars, then fermented into compounds known as volatile fatty acids (VFAs). These are very small and can be absorbed right through the rumen wall. The deer uses these VFAs for energy and converts some of them back to sugars or fats for storage or for milk.

Another advantage the ruminant has is that its rumen microbes can actually produce protein. When a deer's diet lacks high-quality proteins, for example, the microbes can simply create them using whatever amino acids and other nitrogen are available. Monogastric animals do not share this ability. Of the twenty amino acids that make up proteins, about half are not manufactured in the monogastric body and have to be provided through diet; thus, protein quality depends on how many of these essential amino acids are present in the food. These animals must take in protein not only in sufficient quantity, but also of appropriate quality. Ruminants, on the other hand, need be concerned with only the quantity of protein in their diet; their rumen microbes can compensate for deficiencies of quality.

In this process, plant protein coming into the rumen is digested by the microbes first into peptides, then into amino acids, and finally into ammonia. From this the microbes build new proteins, largely in the form of new bacteria and protozoa. These apparently have about the right mix of amino acids needed by the animal because they are digested in the abomasum and absorbed in the small intestine. Thus, the deer has no need for essential amino acids—it makes its own. In addition, ruminants can use nonprotein nitrogen to make new protein. Whereas humans eliminate excess nitrogen from their bodies via urine, deer recycle urea back through the saliva into the rumen, allowing the microbes another chance to make new protein. Deer are also able to produce vitamins B and K in their digestive tracts and therefore have no need for these vitamins in their diets.

The above system is not perfect, though, as we now know. In some ruminants, such as dairy cattle, the microbes do not always produce the very best mix of amino acids. This has not been studied in deer, however.

There is one other advantage to the rumination process. Since deer are often the prey of carnivores, it is to their advantage not to expose themselves for long periods while grazing or browsing. If they had to chew their food completely as they consumed it, they would spend most of the day in this activity. As it is, deer can simply select what they want to eat, chew it just enough to get it down, then retire somewhere safe and hidden where they can regurgitate the food and chew their cuds. Hence their exposure to enemies while feeding is minimized.

Diet

There are forty-one species of deer, and we now know that there are some subtle and some not-so-subtle differences among these species in their ability to digest their food. Evolutionists disagree as to whether different diets led to these differences in the morphology of the deer species' digestive tracts or whether the deer choose different diets because their digestive tracts differ.

Hofmann of Germany has classified all ruminants into three types: grass or roughage eaters (grazers), intermediate feeders (adaptable mixed feeders), and concentrate selectors (browsers). Grazers, such as cattle, have very large rumens and a slow rate of passage of their digesta, which allows time for the microbes to act. Most deer tend to fall into the intermediate category; they are opportunistic, mixed feeders that will browse when they can but will graze when necessary. In general, they have rumens that are smaller in proportion to their body weight than do grazers, and they have larger salivary glands to help neutralize their more acidic diet. Controlled studies have shown that deer are often less efficient than cattle and sheep at digesting low-quality forages. The domestication of red, axis, and fallow deer, however, shows that they can be raised on pastures.

Some deer species, such as white-tailed and mule deer, are concentrate selectors. They have even smaller rumens and larger salivary glands. They must be highly selective, choosing browse that is easily digested. They must also feed more frequently, since digesta passes through their digestive tracts more quickly. There seems to be a relation-

SMITH

Deer are concentrate rather than bulk feeders: they select the most nutritious plant parts available instead of consuming vast amounts of less digestible food. In the Northwest the Coues whitetail may resort to evergreen forage for the winter.

The rumen's microbes—essential for digestion—adapt to the deer's diet. When a deer accustomed to twigs and other starvation food is fed corn and hay, the rumen needs several weeks to adjust; meanwhile, the deer starves with its stomach full.

MASLOWSKI

ship here between body size and feeding strategy, since large cattle graze, large deer are mixed feeders, and smaller deer are opportunistic. The anomaly is the moose, which most certainly is a concentrate selector, despite being the largest of living cervids. These differences in digestive tract anatomy and feeding strategies have implications for managing deer habitat or supplemental feeding. For example, food plants or supplemental foods for white-tailed or mule deer should be more digestible than those intended for axis deer or elk.

Harmel's studies in Texas illustrate the differences in food habits between two deer species. Six whitetails and six sika deer were put in a fenced rangeland pasture. In nine years, the sika deer population increased to sixty-four. The whitetails increased to a total population of nineteen, then they died out completely. No doubt there was an overpopulation of deer in the pasture, and when droughts hit, the adaptable sika deer were able to survive on a lower-quality, higher-fiber diet; the concentrate-selecting whitetails could not.

The digestive tract of whitetails and mule deer can change with diet, but it does so gradually. Saliva production, papilla development, and rumen size change with the seasons to adjust to fibrous winter diets or the more luscious foods of the spring greenup. Reports abound of well-meaning but ill-fated efforts to save starving deer in North America in the winter. Uninformed sportsmen and landowners often put out corn or hay for deer to get them through the winter. But it takes two to three weeks for rumen microbes to completely adjust to a new diet. Thus, deer adapted to a winter diet of highly fibrous food will die of acidosis—a buildup of lactic acid in the rumen—if they overconsume grain.

Remarkably, deer need little food in the winter, and in fact, they voluntarily reduce their food consumption and lose 20 percent or more of their body weight by using their fat stores. This is because deer have evolved to withstand the stresses of feed restriction in the winter. In fact, Hershberger and Cushwa found in Pennsylvania that deer can survive at least a month with no food at all! On occasion, supplemental hay is put out too late, and deer overeat when their rumen microbes are not present in sufficient quantities to digest the hay. Those deer can starve to death with their rumens full.

Deer also face the problem of lignin. The substance that makes woody browse woody, it is present in many deer foods, especially winter ones. Not only is it indigestible, but it can make other nutrients in the food less digestible by binding to them. And secondary plant compounds such as tannins and other phenolics can make both protein and cellulose less digestible.

The ability of deer and other ruminants to utilize natural forage and browse is an ecological advantage. Some species of deer can be domesticated, as deer farmers in Europe, New Zealand, and North America have proven. But efforts to treat deer in the wild as though they were cattle, by excessive supplemental feeding, diminishes the place of deer in our lives and culture and also may leave them vulnerable to the predation, disease, and nutritional inadequacies that they have become adapted to avoid.

—*Robert D. Brown*

Dentition of deer

The teeth of deer, like those of most mammals, vary in both structure and function to reflect feeding strategies and food preferences. Naturally enough, the shape and arrangement of teeth in herbivores that snip and grind leaves and twigs are different from the teeth of carnivores that capture, hold, and tear animal flesh, and different, too, from those of omnivores, such as bears, that feed on both plants and animals. Deer have no carnassial or true canine teeth, only incisors and molars. These teeth are specialized for foraging on plant material and aiding in digestion of cellulose.

The incisiform teeth of deer are located on the sides of the front lower jaw, or mandible, and are used to pluck plant material. The molariform teeth—premolars and molars—are the cheek teeth, located toward the rear on both sides of the upper and lower jaw. These teeth have cusps shaped like half-moons for grinding forage. Like other large herbivores with compound, ruminating stomachs, deer swallow their forage basically intact, with little chewing. After feeding, the deer beds down and regurgitates a bolus of food, also called a cud, and mechanically breaks it down with a side-to-side grinding action of the molars.

Compared with other ruminants, deer have relatively small and simple compound stomachs. This requires the selection of more easily digestible plant parts that are primarily liquid or soluble material and low in structural fiber. A narrow mouth, the small, narrow incisors, and a hard, bony pad in place of upper incisors allow the deer to select and snip off the tender tips of woody plants and the buds and leaves of herbaceous forage. With its dextrous lips and tongue, the deer selects its food, then uses its lower incisors and bony pad like a pair of scissors to sever the morsel from the plant. Deer are thus able to select not merely what plants they eat but even which specific parts of those plants.

Through evolution of dentition among artiodactyls generally, and more specifically in family Cervidae, the lower canine has been modified to serve as a lateral incisor. Typically, the canines of carnivores and omnivores are elongated and larger than incisors and serve to grasp and tear. Such a function would be unnecessary or even detrimental to deer in meeting their forage and nutritional needs.

In more primitive artiodactyls, the first premolar took on the form and function of a canine, but this tooth is missing in deer; they have, however, retained the second, third, and fourth premolars, which have low crowns and cusps, similar to the molars, to assist in grinding vegetation.

Although upper incisors and canines generally are absent in ruminants, a rare individual among white-tailed and mule deer may have small, vestigial canines on the upper jaw. Other species of deer have retained the upper canines. These include more advanced species, primarily members of the

Using her molars, this mule deer grinds a bolus of partially digested food. The more succulent and less fibrous the browse, the fewer episodes of cudding.

DEER

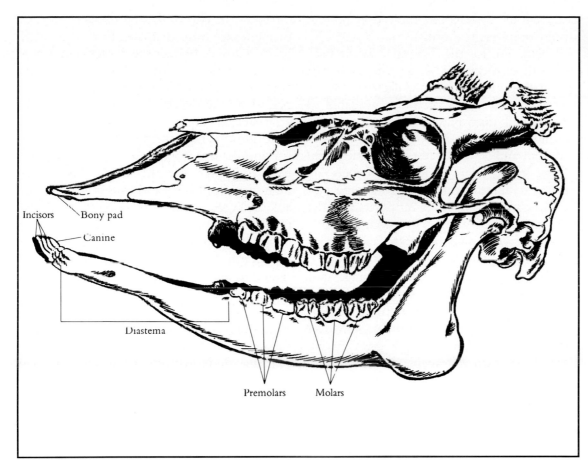

Incisors
Bony pad
Canine
Diastema
Premolars
Molars

BESENGER

SERRAO

Having a rough pad in place of incisors on the upper jaw, or maxilla, a deer cannot make the clean snips of a rabbit or hare. Plants browsed by deer show distinctive shredded tips.

genus *Cervus*, such as North American elk and European red deer *(Cervus eluphus)*. In more primitive species that lack antlers, such as musk deer *(Moschus* spp.) and Chinese water deer *(Hydropotes inermis)*, the upper canines are well developed as sharp tusks. About 7 centimeters (2.75 inches) long, these tusks serve as weapons for contesting other males and defending against predators.

Adults among both mule and white-tailed deer possess thirty-two teeth: twenty mandibular (lower jaw) and twelve maxillary (upper jaw). On each side of the mandible are three incisors, one incisiform canine, three premolars, and three molars. Each side of the maxilla typically contains only three premolars and three molars. Among zoologists the pattern is expressed as a formula, in which the first of each pair of numbers refers to teeth on each side of the upper jaw, and the second, to teeth on each side of the lower jaw:

$$\text{incisors} \quad \begin{matrix}\text{incisiform}\\\text{canines}\end{matrix} \quad \text{premolars} \quad \text{molars}$$
$$(0/3, \quad 0/1, \quad 3/3, \quad 3/3) \times 2 = 32$$

The dental formula is similar for all deer, and all have six incisors and two incisiform canines on the mandible at birth. The milk teeth (or deciduous teeth) consist of incisors, incisiform canines, and deciduous molars that are replaced by premolars.

The time required to replace milk teeth and develop the full complement of adult dentition varies among species. The extremes among family Cervidae reported by Whitehead include red deer *(Cervus elaphus)*, which need thirty months to acquire a full mouth, and roe deer *(Capreolus capreolus)*, whose dentition is complete in about thirteen months.

The entire process of tooth eruption and replacement occurs at a slower pace among mule deer than among whitetails. The medial (center) incisor (adult I_1), for example, is completely erupted at six to eight months of age in whitetails but not until eleven or twelve months in mule deer. All adult incisiform teeth are fully erupted in whitetails by thirteen months but not in mule deer until about eighteen months of age. Whitetails have the full complement of adult teeth by twenty-four months but mule deer do not until twenty-eight months.

Explanation for the difference in the pace of tooth replacement is, for the moment, speculation. Environmental factors may be involved. The types of forage available to white-tailed deer may favor a more rapid maturation of teeth compared with the rugged, dry, and generally less hospitable world of the mule deer. Indeed, whitetails are known to mature earlier, and in some particularly amiable habitats 30 percent of the does may breed at just six months. Mule deer doe fawns, by comparison, rarely breed successfully in the wild.

The quantity and quality of forage may account for variation in the timing of tooth eruption and replacement within species as well as between species. On many mule deer ranges, an abundance of lush green herbaceous vegetation is available for only a very brief time. Robinette noted that in mule deer, most incisor and premolar replacement and molar M_1 and M_2) eruption occur during late spring to early autumn, when food conditions are most favorable. Young and subadult—sexually mature but not yet physically able to compete—deer attain their maximum increment in annual body growth during this same period.

AGING DEER BY THEIR TEETH

A unique feature of the mandible of ungulates is the diastema, the space between the incisiform teeth and the premolars. This separates the part of the mouth used for capturing forage from that used to mechanically break it down. In deer the diastema increases in length with age, up to three to four years among females and perhaps over a longer period among males.

Diastemal length can be used as an index of condition and growth over time or among subpopulations because it is directly related to mandibular growth; skeletal tissue has high growth priority and thus is a more reliable indicator than body weight. Environmental conditions severe enough to delay or retard body growth should be reflected in the length of the diastema. Among deer of the same sex and age, a comparatively longer diastema indicates better habitat. In one study the interacting effects of animal density and precipitation largely explained yearly variation in mean diastemal length among yearling male whitetails, as reported by Dusek and associates.

The technique may not be so easily applied to yearling mule deer, many of whom are replacing the deciduous incisiform canines during late autumn; yearly samples during this period, which coincidentally follows a period of rapid body growth, are most readily obtained from deer killed by hunters.

Teeth provide the only reliable basis for determining or estimating a deer's age. Chronology and timing of tooth eruption and replacement provide a reliable means of determining age up to two years.

The ability to select and consume high-quality forage quickly depends on the condition of the teeth. Deer whose teeth are too worn to snip or grind efficiently must either risk predation during long foraging sessions or starve.

LEA

FRANCIS

Because deciduous incisiform teeth in deer are smaller than the adult teeth that replace them, fawns may be readily distinguished from older deer. Fawns also have only four cheek teeth per side on the upper and lower jaws (three deciduous molars and one molar).

Yearlings can be distinguished from older deer because they still have deciduous molars; these will be replaced by adult premolars by age two. The deciduous molars are smaller than the adult premolars, and they exhibit considerable wear compared with the recently erupted adult molars immediately behind. The third deciduous molar (DM$_4$) has three cusps, whereas the adult tooth that replaces it (P$_4$) has only two.

For older deer, age may be assigned by examining wear on the occlusal, or grinding, surface of the mandibular cheek teeth. This technique is highly subjective, however, because of considerable variation in wear patterns among individuals and populations. Tooth wear patterns vary widely both locally and regionally, probably reflecting differences in the amount of dust and other abrasive material adhering to vegetation. Minor differences in the timing of tooth eruption also may affect wear patterns. The rate at which teeth wear can have biological implications for individuals and populations of deer. Because tooth wear affects efficiency in feeding and chewing of plant material, and thus survival, it also affects longevity.

Age also may be determined by sectioning the root of an incisor or a molar and counting annual rings in the cementum, in much the same manner as one would age a tree. As with all mammalian teeth, the root of a deer's tooth has a layer of cementum over dentine (the crown, the portion exposed beyond the gum, has enamel over dentine). With some exceptions, annual cementum layers consist of alternating light and dark bands; the light layer is normally deposited during summer and the dark band during winter. In warmer climates characterized by less seasonality, these alternating bands may be less distinct and thus lend more subjectivity to assigning ages. Nevertheless, this technique is somewhat less subjective than evaluating wear patterns on cheek teeth.

Comparison of the two aging techniques—with deer whose ages are known either through birth records or that were first examined as fawns or yearlings—strongly suggests that cementum analysis is more accurate than analysis of wear on the cheek teeth, at least for deer two years of age and older. The successful practice of cementum analysis lies in being reasonably certain of the age at which the tooth erupted. Minor variation in timing of tooth eruption notwithstanding, the technique should allow for assignment to correct year classes.

—*Gary L. Dusek*

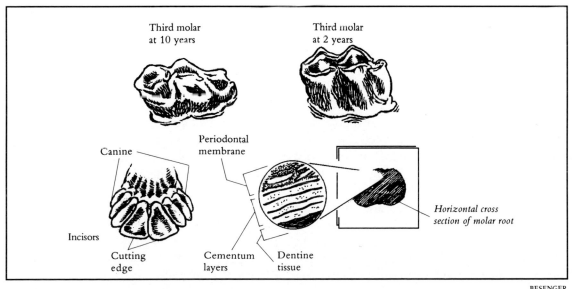

Third molar at 10 years

Third molar at 2 years

Canine

Periodontal membrane

Incisors

Cutting edge

Cementum layers

Dentine tissue

Horizontal cross section of molar root

At the same time that the teeth are growing annular layers of cementum, the incisors and molars are being worn down from tough, gritty forage. Counting the rings in a cross section of tooth reveals the deer's age.

BESENGER

Taking their world in stride

The deer of North America are well known for their fast getaways. They are as well adapted, however, for walking stealthily and trotting purposefully as they are for escaping at high speed.

THE WALK

When relaxed, deer move at a leisurely walk. This gait is, technically, the cross walk: the lifting of the right front foot is followed by lifting of the left rear. While the right front foot reaches to a new position on the ground, the right rear leg applies power, the left front supports the weight of the body (and thus is directly underneath the animal, close to its center of gravity), and the left rear is finishing its power stride, ready to be lifted and placed in the same spot where the left front had been.

In the cross walk, then, body support and power are applied diagonally. It is a symmetrical gait: the actions of left and right limbs mirror each other, and the footfalls are evenly spaced.

Normally, the rear hoof falls right on the track of the front hoof of the same side. Deviations from that pattern can tell the tracker something about the animal. If the rear hoof struck the ground well behind the front hoof, the deer was walking very slowly—almost lazily. But if the rear hoof fell ahead of the front hoof, the deer was walking fast.

Splayed rear hooves suggest a deer heavy in the rear—a pregnant doe. Hoofmarks that do not range far left or right of center are likely from a doe; bucks, having broader bodies, tend to have a wider stance. Another difference between does and bucks: Females tend to lift their hooves off the ground cleanly, leaving no drag marks, but bucks drag their hooves low over the ground when walking, particularly during the rut.

The cross walk is the same for all species and subspecies of *Odocoileus*, but there are some differences between whitetails and mule deer in the "stealth gait"—the very slow pace at which deer walk while concealing themselves. White-tailed deer may crouch low to the ground, head and neck outstretched, while stealing through low cover. (The rutting buck may approach a doe in estrus in this same crouch, as may a subordinate buck inviting a large male to a sparring match.) Mule deer, in contrast, silently pick their way through shrubbery, and though they may duck under an overhang or tree limb, there is no consistent low crouch like the whitetail's crawl. Both species may slowly sink and lie down behind a screening bush to watch a disturbance.

A deer may accelerate from a walk into a trot. As in the cross walk, the contralateral pairs of legs move more or less simultaneously, and this gait, like the cross walk, is symmetrical. A trotting deer may move forcefully enough that all four legs leave the ground. This suspended phase appears to be more common among mule deer than among whitetails. While trotting, whitetails often flag their tails.

A whitetail can accelerate from a standstill to full speed in a few bounds. In the gallop the animal keeps its body close to the ground, gaining forward motion, it directs some of its energy into expensive lift, but most goes into horizontal motion.

REZENDES

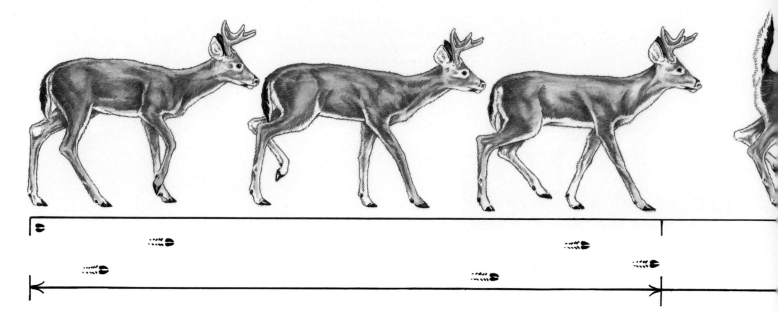

At low speeds, all North American deer use symmetrical gaits known as the cross walk and the cross trot, in which power is applied diagonally.

The cross walk (and trot) of deer differ from the pacing walk (and its accelerated version, the rack) practiced by many open-plains dwellers, such as African gazelles and camels. In the pacing walk, the lifting of the right front foot is followed by the lifting of the right rear. The center of gravity is suspended over the supporting front leg, while the hind leg on that side simultaneously applies power. Because the legs act in lateral pairs, body support and power are applied on the same side of the body, and thus the pacing or racking animal throws the body from left to right. (Little wonder that riding camels at a fast rack can be a bruising experience.) To increase speed in this gait, the animal increases its stride. The pacing walk and the rack may increase endurance–important attributes for life in the open plains.

But North American deer do not generally inhabit wide-open expanses; they prefer edges and small openings and rough terrain that offer hiding places and escape cover. To reach safety, they need quick bursts of speed and agility.

THE GALLOP

The gallop used by all species of deer is the rotary gallop, so called because during a stride the sequence of footfalls rotates left rear to right rear, then right front to left front. The next stride begins again with left rear to right rear, and so forth; the footfalls proceed in a circle around the four legs.

A transverse gallop, by comparison, would be right rear, left rear, then right front, left front, with the front legs repeating the right-left footfall pattern of the hind legs. This is the usual running gait of species adapted to open plains, such as horses, bison, and camels. The rotary gallop, however, is faster, better for life-or-death getaways, and thus preferred for rapid bursts even by species that normally favor the transverse gallop.

The rotary gallop fits logically with the adaptation of deer to their habitat. While galloping, they must be able to dodge obstacles and adjust their footfall patterns accordingly. They may therefore switch the rotation from clockwise to counterclockwise and back again, changing "leads" midstride to negotiate a sharp turn or avoid a boulder.

Though the gait is the same for both species of *Odocoileus,* it is executed somewhat differently. The white-tailed deer strives to cover as much distance as possible with each stride. As the hind legs propel the animal forward, its front legs, neck, and back follow a low trajectory into the extended suspension phase of the stride. This low trajectory lengthens the stride and conserves energy in the costly fight against gravity. The mule deer follows a steeper trajectory. Although the resulting vertical movement is useful for jumping over obstacles, it requires additional energy and can reduce the animal's speed.

After its front legs leave the ground, the galloping whitetail has a brief gathered suspension, enabling the stride to cover greater

DEER

Using the same motion that would propel it into a gallop, the white-tailed buck makes an observation leap to survey the trail ahead.

distance. And the whitetail's hind legs over-reach the front legs, generating an even longer leap. This aspect of the whitetail's gallop is easily seen in tracks: the front hooves are placed neatly one behind the other, with both rear hooves to the outside and in front. The mule deer lands on one of its hind legs behind a front leg that, for a moment, is also in contact with the ground.

As a result of all those subtle differences, the gallop of the white-tailed deer appears smoother than the rocking gallop of the mule deer. It is also faster. The whitetail reaches farther with its legs and body to cover more ground, applies power longer, has less body lift per stride, and avoids long jumps—and thus attains speeds of 6.3 to 10.9 meters per second (14.1 to 24.5 miles per hour), compared with 5.7 to 8.5 meters per second (12.8 to 19.1 miles per hour) for mule deer. Those rates were obtained in experimental conditions with animals accelerating from a standstill; in the wild, free-living deer of both species have been clocked at still greater speeds, approaching 18 meters per second, or about 40 miles per hour.

To move from a walk into a high-speed galloping escape, the whitetail quickly

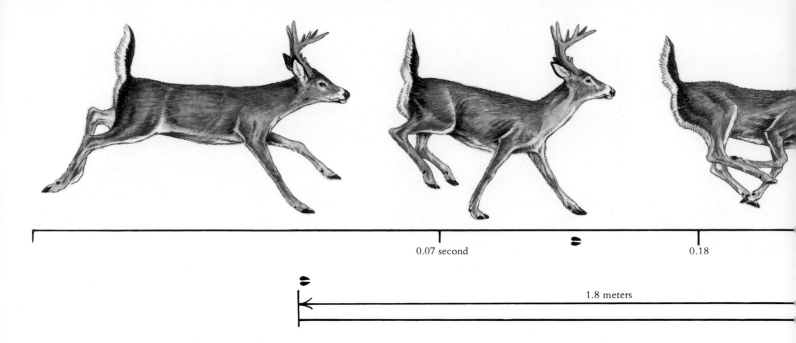

0.07 second   0.18

1.8 meters

The whitetail gallop (above) is fast and efficient. In a single stride, the deer is suspended twice. By remaining airborne in the gathered position, the animal covers more distance than if a leg were touching the ground. During the extended suspension, the whitetail stays low, not sacrificing energy, time, or distance for height. The stotting mule deer (below), on the other hand, strives for height. As the animal lands, the force of its weight is absorbed by the hind legs, then released into the suspension. Despite the height of the leap, the trajectory is more horizontal than vertical, and thus the muley's stott is almost as fast as the whitetail's gallop.

crouches. Its haunches contract, and the front hooves dig in while pulling the body forward. At the push of the hind legs, the deer's body drops even lower until caught by the quick recovery of the sharply angled front legs. The deer executes several short, synchronous thrusting steps with each pair of front legs and hind legs, thus rapidly applying energy to the ground at the expense of lift. This keeps its body low while generating forward speed. Within a few such bounds, the deer has burst into the rotary gallop and is soon gone.

THE STOTT

When sudden or severe danger appears, mule deer and blacktails don't gallop off;

they stott. This specialized jumping gait is as fast as the mule deer's gallop—9 meters per second (22 miles per hour) in experimental conditions, 8.9 to 12.3 meters per second (20 to 30 miles per hour) in the wild.

To leave the ground when stotting, the deer propels itself forward and up at a 10- to 15-degree angle. The suspended phase that follows seems impossibly long. Despite the height attained, the animal's path is much more horizontal than vertical. While airborne, the deer slowly moves both pairs of legs forward, then lands nearly simultaneously on all fours. Depending on the terrain, the front hooves may touch first, but because all the legs strike the ground virtually at the same time, the hind legs absorb

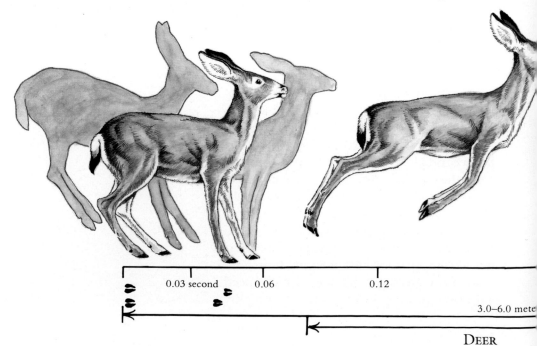

0.03 second   0.06   0.12

3.0–6.0 mete

80   DEER

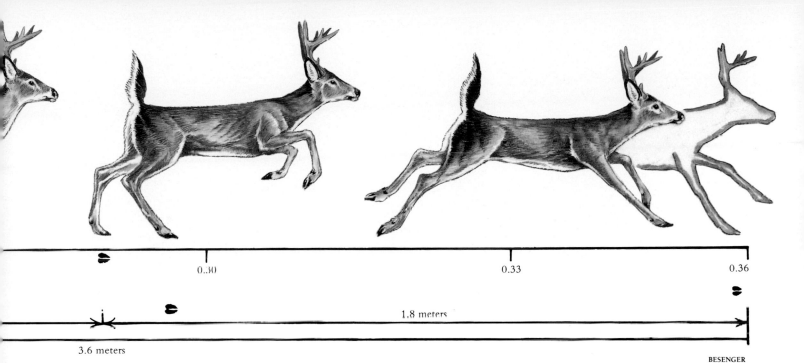

0.30   0.33   0.36

1.8 meters

3.6 meters

a substantial part of the force; in the gallop, the front legs catch the animal's weight.

Upon landing, the limbs flex as the force of the body continues forward and downward, absorbing shock and likely storing elastic energy in tendons. The body remains level while pivoting forward: it seems to float across the ground even as the legs touch down. The stability of the body's position, from descent through landing, and the animal's horizontal trajectory indicate that considerable forward momentum is conserved from one stride to the next. The mule deer is in contact with the ground for only 35 percent—about 0.16 second—of its stride.

The entire stride cycle of the stott lasts 0.4 to 0.6 second, longer than the stride cycle of the gallop (0.3 to 0.4 second), and the deer may cover 5 to 7 meters (16 to 23 feet) in a stride. But the advantage of the stott lies not with speed but with versatility. The stott allows mule deer to chase an adversary, keep obstacles in the path of a pursuer, ascend a hill straight on, and even evade a pursuer by dashing off at unpredictable angles.

Indeed, the stott appears to be the mule deer's and blacktail's adaptation to its rough, mountainous terrain peppered with windfalls and impenetrable shrubbery and punctuated by cliffs and gorges. Stotting deer may sail over the obstacles and uneven jumble at speeds hardly less than a gallop; their would-be predators are soon left behind, panting.

— Valerius Geist and Susan Lingle

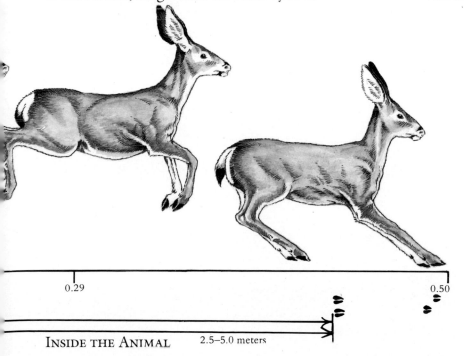

0.29   0.50

C. MILLER

White-tailed deer

Whitetail diversity

A single species can encompass enormous diversity. Consider the canine world, in which animals of a multitude of shapes and sizes can all interbreed. The genetic material that spells *whitetail* is elastic, too: if the tiny deer of the Florida Keys is the Chihuahua of the whitetail world, the imposing deer of the northeastern United States and Canada is the Great Dane.

White-tailed deer exhibit tremendous variation in color as well as size, ranging from the dark gray deer found in the mountains of North America to the orange-cinnamon deer of South America. Whitetails rank, in fact, among the top 5 percent of all mammals for genetic variation. To account for all the forms, such variable species are generally subdivided into subspecies—local populations that can be distinguished on the basis of some set of characteristics but are still able to interbreed with other populations if given a chance to do so.

The diversity in size, shape, color, and even antler form should not be surprising, given the whitetails' incredible diversity of habitats: tropical rain forests, mixed pine-oak and deciduous forests, farmlands, scrub vegetation of various types, even deserts. Some of these environments provide conditions ideal for growth and reproduction, others less so, and as a consequence, white-tailed deer in different regions grow at different rates and to different extents. Because these environments also vary in color and shade of soils and vegetation, the color of deer often varies.

The recognition of a subspecies is signified by an additional Latin name after the genus and species designations. For example, white-tailed deer on Big Pine Key in Florida are called *Odocoileus virginianus clavium,* with the name *Odocoileus* designating the genus, *virginianus* the species, and *clavium* the subspecies.

DISTINGUISHING CHARACTERISTICS

Early taxonomists used a wide variety of characteristics to describe white-tailed deer subspecies. Most important among these were such external characteristics as overall body size, antler shape and size, and coat color. Some subspecies descriptions included information about other characteristics, such as the shape of the skull and teeth. External characteristics have been considered the most important because large skeletal collections did not exist for most of the subspecies when they were first described. But some external characteristics, such as body size and antlers, are of questionable validity because such large variation already exists *within* subspecies.

The degree of distinctness of subspecies depends upon the criteria used to formally recognize them. The "eighty-twenty" rule is often used by scientists who study mammals. This rule refers to distinguishing characteristics: 80 percent distinct and 20 percent overlap, but other values have been

BRIERE

used in certain circumstances. The figures—and therefore the rule—are general guidelines. Because so few specimens from certain areas are available for study, the actual degree of overlap between distinguishing characteristics has never been quantitatively determined for the majority of the recognized whitetail subspecies. As a result, statements that deer are "generally larger," "seem to average smaller," or "have summer pelage that is redder" are given in place of more precise descriptions for most of the subspecies of whitetails.

Almost half of the subspecies were initially split off as separate species and later lumped back together as subspecies within a single, geographically widespread species. An excellent example comes from South America, where what are now eight subspecies were thought to be one distinct species, *Odocoileus cariacou*, different from North American whitetails, *Odocoileus virginianus*.

Such changes in taxonomy have occurred at the species-subspecies level as well. Without appreciation for the elasticity of the species, early taxonomists saw different

forms of deer in the species *Odocoileus virginianus* and designated each as a subspecies. At first, for example, deer in New York were recognized as being larger than those from Florida and on that basis were considered distinct. With more information, researchers recognized that larger deer tend to come from more northerly latitudes and smaller deer are found closer to the equator, with those of intermediate size occurring at midlatitudes. This latitudinal trend is also seen in other mammals and is often referred to as Bergman's Rule. It is thought that latitudinal trends in body size occur because the surface-to-volume ratio (which is directly related to heat loss) is lower for larger animals of the same basic shape: the large size retains more heat.

In addition to this latitudinal trend, island subspecies tend to be smaller than their mainland counterparts. The smallest of the subspecies include the Key deer in Florida *(O. v. clavium)* and the white-tailed deer on Coiba Island in Panama *(O. v. rothschildi),* which weigh 23 kilograms (50 pounds) or less as adult males. All of the island forms off

That the Key deer of Florida are among the smallest of all North American odocoileids is an example of two general rules for mammals: within a species, smaller individuals are found both closer to the Equator and on islands.

the coast of the southeastern United States are smaller than those on the adjacent mainland.

The largest deer, such as *O. v. borealis,* come from high montane environments and from the northern parts of the United States and Canada. In the northern parts of their range, male whitetails sometimes weigh more than 136 kilograms (300 pounds).

Geographic trends in body size complicate the interpretation of other character differences among subspecies. Large bucks, for example, tend to have large antlers, and if the effects of differences in body size are taken into account, there may not be any relative difference in the antler size between subspecies. Certainly, designating subspecies on the basis of size differences alone can be misleading, especially when nutritional conditions are not the same.

Coat color has often been used to help describe subspecies, albeit imprecisely. Deer in many parts of the range change their colors seasonally through molting, and there are often geographic trends in coat color, with deer from moist areas tending to be darker and those from tropical rain forests being redder. Coat color has traditionally been a comparative—and subjective—characteristic, but it can and should be measured quantitatively. Determining the reflectance, or specific distribution of reflected wavelengths of light, of coat colors would provide just such measurements. With these figures differences in coat color would be

exact and verifiable quantities rather than subjective guesses, making coat color a much more useful characteristic for identifying subspecies.

Internal characteristics have also been used to help identify subspecies. Measurements may be based on the shape or relative relationship between various body or skull parts.

NATURE VERSUS NURTURE

Identification of a particular group of animals within a species as a subspecies implies that there is something unique about the genetic characteristics of the group. A subspecies is designated because it is thought to exhibit a set of morphological characteristics that is different from that of others in its species. For example, several subspecies of whitetails were designated in 1940 on the basis of a variety of color, skeletal, and antler characteristics. Implied in these designations was that these characters had a genetic basis, but this assumption was never proven.

Morphological variation used to distinguish subspecies may result directly from differences in genetic characteristics, or indirectly from the responses of the same genes acting under different environmental conditions. Sorting out what is genetically different and what is an environmental response is a challenge for those who would understand this elastic species that has adapted to a wide range of habitats.

Subspecies are often considered to be

Lechuguilla is a preferred succulent food of the Sierra del Carmen whitetails of Mexico and the American Southwest. Geographic isolation from other whitetail populations can lead to genetic differences that become the basis for subspecies designation.

DVORAK

adapted particularly well to their habitat. But when subspecies are initially described, there usually are no data to prove that this type of adaptation exists, and in fact, no data of this type exist for any of the subspecies of white-tailed deer. Adaptation depends upon differences in survival and reproductive rates of animals under a variety of environmental conditions, and deer of various sizes and colors are expected to have varying degrees of success given the diversity of environmental conditions in which this species thrives. Deer whose coat color contrasted with the background colors of their habitat, for example, probably did not survive as well as deer whose coat color provided camouflage: large predators probably caught and ate more of the conspicuous deer.

Evolution of subspecies as a result of adaptation to environmental conditions occurs over long periods of time. The survival and reproductive successes of specific animals with certain characteristics in particular types of environments are important determinants for evolution in white-tailed deer and the differentiation of its subspecies.

Nine subspecies of white-tailed deer have been assessed for genetic characteristics, through laboratory studies using tissue samples. The characters depend upon the presence, absence, and variation of particular gene products. Unlike body size, these types of characters are usually not affected by short-term environmental variation. Mathematical techniques have been developed to use these discrete characters to provide standardized estimates of the differences among subspecies. In one case, use of genetic characters suggests that the Key deer subspecies may not be restricted to the islands but may also be found on the Florida mainland.

Often it is environmental conditions rather than specific genes that cause variations of physical characteristics among individuals within a species. Two animals with exactly the same set of genes for a particular characteristic may differ in this characteristic if they consume different amounts or qualities of food or live in dramatically different habitats. Nutrition and other environmental factors play a larger role than do the genes in the final expression of some characteristics, such as body or antler size, within popula-

tions. For example, studies of *Odocoileus virginianus virginianus* show that 40 to 50 percent of variation in adult antler characteristics is attributable to environmental factors. The result of two levels of food quality and availability may be two groups of deer, each of similar genetic composition but of quite different sizes.

Some morphological distinctions used to identify subspecies do not have a clear underlying genetic basis. Recent studies of several mainland whitetail subspecies in the southeastern United States found no genetic basis for those classifications. In addition, when animals of one of the island subspecies were transplanted to the mainland, their offspring responded to the new environment by growing large, becoming nearly as large as the resident mainland subspecies.

Nevertheless, the most genetically distinct whitetails in the United States are the island deer off the southeastern coast. This observation holds for other animals as well: subspecies can be especially distinct in their genetic characteristics if the group is isolated.

REASSESSING THE SUBSPECIES

Nearly half the whitetail subspecies recognized today were once classified as separate species. Taxonomists changed the classifications, splitting here and lumping there, from 1870 to 1940 as variations within the species were discovered. Now that genetic tests are among taxonomists' tools, the subspecies designations of white-tailed deer probably should be reassessed. Recognizing heretofore unappreciated differences in characteristics and measuring enough characters to properly designate subspecies should result in a more accurate classification.

Genetic methodology can provide data for a large number of characteristics to determine the cumulative differences among subspecies. Genetic characteristics have already been used to assess differences among several whitetail subspecies. The most differentiated subspecies come from islands and from Central and South America. A more thorough study of deer on islands would probably lead to the need to recognize additional subspecies. In Central and South America, the genetic differences are so great that some subspecies may turn out to be different species.

The Columbian whitetail of the Columbia River basin overlaps the range of blacktails. Its dwindling population is endangered by development in the Pacific Northwest.

BINEGAR

There are also other ways in which the subspecies designations could be reevaluated. More detailed studies of the relative dimensions of the various parts of the skull, for example, could provide a good quantitative basis for distinguishing among subspecies. Many characteristics of the skull could be used for this purpose, and the specimens needed for such morphometric and molecular examinations have already been collected.

Fascinating though the subject is, in and of itself as a scientific discipline, the correct recognition of subspecies and their ranges is important for legal, economic, and sporting purposes.

Two whitetail subspecies have been designated as endangered: the Key deer *(O. v. clavium)* and the Columbian white-tailed deer *(O. v. leucurus)*. The amount of suitable habitat for these subspecies is limited and continues to decrease with the increase in the human population. The largest Columbian whitetail population, located along the lower portion of the Columbia River, declined from an estimated 700 animals in 1939 to approximately 300 in 1975. The historical records for the Key deer are sketchy, but it is estimated that fewer than 400 of these animals remain.

Those subspecies found only on heavily developed islands, such as Hilton Head Island off South Carolina, are not yet classified as endangered but should nonetheless be of concern because their numbers are declining. If these animals are, in fact, a distinguishable and unique subspecies, their status as threatened or endangered will affect human economic interests.

It is also important to know the exact range of each subspecies. Boundaries between most of the mainland subspecies have never been quantitatively assessed and, in many cases, they have been determined arbitrarily.

As research continues, some of the recognized subspecies will probably be found not valid, and new ones will likely be described. The exact distribution of the subspecies cannot be determined until the criteria for distinguishing them have been established. Without a clear definition of what constitutes each subspecies, based on clearly defined morphological and genetic characters, there are likely to be controversy and legal actions over the subspecies and their ranges.

—Michael H. Smith and Olin E. Rhodes, Jr.

Unraveling the genes

The methods of genetic testing give scientists a new tool in the efforts to determine evolutionary relationships and speciation. In the classification of subspecies, the premise is that the morphological traits have an underlying genetic basis. With the new techniques taxonomists can examine differences in DNA sequences and in the proteins encoded by the DNA—the two most commonly used genetic approaches to taxonomic investigation.

One of the more common genetic techniques used for taxonomic analysis is electrophoresis of gene products, such as proteins. Tissues that have large concentrations of enzymes or other proteins are most useful for this procedure. These gene products are examined for differences in size, charge, and mobility. If two forms, or isozymes, of a single enzyme are detected, the researcher assumes that different genes encoded the two forms of the enzyme. Taxonomic comparisons can be made between species or subspecies based on the numbers of gene products they have in common.

Another technique, mitochondrial DNA analysis, involves counting the number of amino acid substitutions that have taken place in the maternally inherited mtDNA. Blood, muscle, or liver tissues are needed for this procedure because the cells contain mitochondria. After the mitochondrial DNA has been isolated from tissue samples, direct comparisons of differences in the mtDNA from different animals can be made. There are numerous techniques by which such comparisons can be made, ranging from amino acid sequence differences at a single gene to sequence differences (amino acid substitutions) that have randomly taken place in the mtDNA as a whole. Taxonomic comparisons can be made between species or subspecies based on the numbers of amino acid substitutions or sequence differences that are observed.

There is a drawback in making taxonomic decisions based on genetic evidence alone, however. This approach ignores the interactions between genes and specific environmental conditions. Striking variations in, say, antler size that result from differences in environmental conditions would not even be considered if genetic data alone were used to make taxonomic decisions.

—*Michael H. Smith and Olin E. Rhodes, Jr.*

The subspecies

The oldest recognized subspecies of the white-tailed deer, *O. v. virginianus,* was designated in 1780. Three subspecies of white-tailed deer were identified in the 1700s, fourteen in the 1800s, and thirteen in the early 1900s. The most recent designations came in 1940, when seven additional subspecies in the United States and Mexico and one subspecies in South America were recognized. The total comes to thirty subspecies in North and Central America, plus eight in South America.

All were defined on the basis of their external morphology and coloration: the designations were made before genetic techniques came into common use for describing differences and relationships among organisms. Many of the subspecies were based on only a small number of specimens.

Subspecies of white-tailed deer live in eighteen countries, and the number of subspecies per country ranges from one in Belize and in Panama to sixteen in the United States. Canada shares all three of its subspecies *(O. v. ochrourus, O. v. dacotensis,* and *O. v. borealis)* with the United States. In contrast, only three of Mexico's fourteen whitetail subspecies *(O. v. covesi, O. v. carminis,* and *O. v. texanus)* are also present in the United States.

White-tailed deer can be found in forty-eight of the fifty states—all but Alaska and Hawaii. White-tailed deer are present but rare in some of the western states, such as Nevada and Utah. The subspecies *O. v. borealis, O. v. dacotensis, O. v. texanus,* and *O. v. virginianus* are the most widely distributed in the United States. Most states in which white-tailed deer are found have only a single subspecies, although some, such as South Carolina and Georgia, have as many as four, including the island forms.

Eight subspecies of white-tailed deer are present exclusively on islands, five of these on islands off the southeastern coast of the United States: Bull's Island, South Carolina *(O. v. taurinsulae);* Hunting Island, South Carolina *(O. v. venatorius);* Hilton Head Island, South Carolina *(O. v. hiltonensis);* Blackbeard Island, Georgia *(O. v. nigribarbis);* and Big Pine Key, Florida *(O. v. clavium).* A single island subspecies is found in Central America, on the island of Coiba, Panama *(O. v. rothschildi).* In South America whitetail subspecies are found on the island of Curascao *(O. v. curassavicus)* and Margarita Island *(O. V. margaritae),* both off the coast of Venezuela.

Of the eight white-tailed deer subspecies represented in South American countries, only two are widespread. One subspecies, *O. v. quodotii,* lives in five countries; the other, *O. v. gymnotis,* is present in four. Three of the South American subspecies can be found in Brazil.

—*Michael H. Smith and Olin E. Rhodes, Jr.*

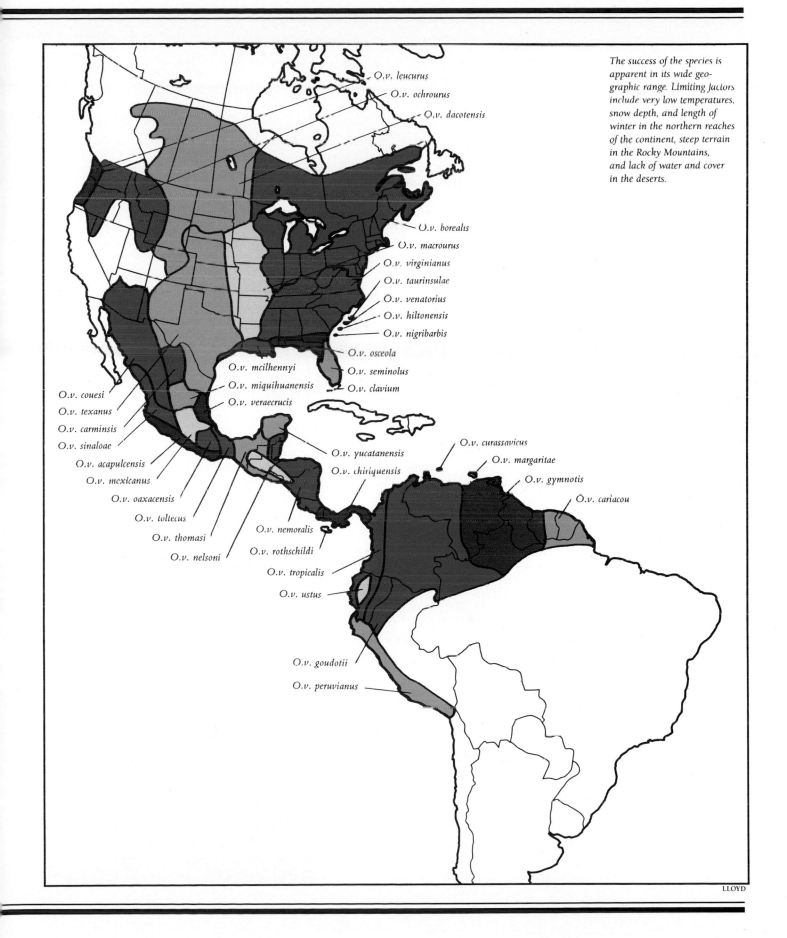

O.v. leucurus
O.v. ochrourus
O.v. dacotensis

The success of the species is apparent in its wide geographic range. Limiting factors include very low temperatures, snow depth, and length of winter in the northern reaches of the continent, steep terrain in the Rocky Mountains, and lack of water and cover in the deserts.

O.v. borealis
O.v. macrourus
O.v. virginianus
O.v. taurinsulae
O.v. venatorius
O.v. hiltonensis
O.v. nigribarbis
O.v. osceola
O.v. mcilhennyi
O.v. seminolus
O.v. miquihuanensis
O.v. clavium
O.v. veraecrucis
O.v. couesi
O.v. texanus
O.v. carminsis
O.v. sinaloae
O.v. yucatanensis
O.v. curassavicus
O.v. acapulcensis
O.v. chiriquensis
O.v. margaritae
O.v. mexicanus
O.v. gymnotis
O.v. oaxacensis
O.v. cariacou
O.v. toltecus
O.v. thomasi
O.v. nemoralis
O.v. nelsoni
O.v. rothschildi
O.v. tropicalis
O.v. ustus
O.v. goudotii
O.v. peruvianus

LLOYD

A catalog of the subspecies

Thirty subspecies of whitetails range across North and Central America. The full taxonomic name of each includes the name of the first researcher to describe the subspecies and the year in which he did so.

Acapulco white-tailed deer (*O. v. acapulcensis* Canton, 1877)

Northern woodland white-tailed deer (*O. v. borealis* Miller, 1900)

Carmen Mountains white-tailed deer (*O. v. carminsis* Goldman and Kellogg, 1940)

Chiriqui white-tailed deer (*O. v. chiriquensis* J. A. Allen, 1910)

Florida Key white-tailed deer (*O. v. clavium* Barbour and Allen, 1922)

Coues white-tailed deer (*O. v. couesi* Coues and Yarrow, 1875)

Dakota white-tailed deer (*O. v. dacotensis* Goldman and Kellogg, 1940)

Hilton Head Island white-tailed deer (*O. v. hiltonensis* Goldman and Kellogg, 1940)

Columbian white-tailed deer (*O. v. leucurus* Douglas, 1829)

Kansas white-tailed deer (*O. v. macrourus* Rafinesque, 1817)

Avery Island white-tailed deer (*O. v. mcilhennyi* F. W. Miller, 1928)

Mexican Tableland white-tailed deer (*O. v. mexicanus* Gmelin, 1788)

Miquihuana white-tailed deer (*O. v. miquihuanensis* Goldman and Kellogg, 1940)

Chiapas white-tailed deer (*O. v. nelsoni* Merrian, 1898)

Nicaragua white-tailed deer (*O. v. nemoralis* Hamilton-Smith, 1827)

Blackbeard Island white-tailed deer (*O. v. nigribarbis* Goldman and Kellogg, 1940)

Oaxaca white-tailed deer (*O. v. oaxacensis* Goldman and Kellogg, 1940)

Northwest white-tailed deer (*O. v. ochrourus* Bailey, 1932)

Florida coastal white-tailed deer (*O. v. osceola* Bangs, 1896)

Coiba Island white-tailed deer (*O. v. rothschildi* Thomas, 1902)

Florida white-tailed deer (*O. v. seminolus* Goldman and Kellogg, 1940)

Sinaloa white-tailed deer (*O. v. sinaloae* J. A. Allen, 1903)

Bulls Island white-tailed deer (*O. v. taurinsulae* Goldman and Kellogg, 1940)

Texas white-tailed deer (*O. v. texanus* Mearns, 1898)

Texas whitetails (Odocoelius virginianus texanus) can display decidedly wide, huge antlers in years when good rainfall brings superior forage.

RUE III

Mexican lowland white-tailed deer *(O. v. thomasi* Merriam, 1898)

Rain forest white-tailed deer *(O. v. toltecus* Saussure, 1860)

Hunting Island white-tailed deer *(O. v. venatorius* Goldman and Kellogg, 1940)

Northern Veracruz white-tailed deer *(O. v. veraecrucis* Goldman and Kellogg, 1940)

Virginia white-tailed deer *(O. v. virginianus* Zimmerman, 1780)

Yucatan white-tailed deer *(O. v. yucatanensis* Hays, 1874)

Common names have not been as readily applied to the eight subspecies of South American whitetails.

O. v. cariacou Boddaert, 1784

O. v. curassavicus Hummelinck, 1940

O. v. goudotii Gay and Gervais, 1846

O. v. gymnotis Wiegmann, 1833

O. v. margaritae Osgood, 1910

O. v. peruvianus Gray, 1874

O. v. tropicalis Cabrera, 1918

O. v. ustus Trouessart, 1910

—*Paul R. Krausman*

Florida whitetails (Odocoelius virginianus seminolus) are among the smallest of the whitetail subspecies in North America.

DVORAK

New York's white deer herd

While growing up in the Finger Lakes region of New York State, I was captivated by stories of ghost deer, a completely white local variety of whitetail. There weren't many of these beautiful animals—most were taken at a very young age by hunters—but in the 1950s and 1960s a small group of them received special protection on the grounds of the Seneca Army Depot. As a result of this protection, the white deer increased their numbers until they became what may well be the most famous herd of deer in the United States.

CHARACTERISTICS

Two distinctive physical characteristics set ghost deer apart from other whitetails: coat color and antler formation. Adult ghost deer are white, often the pure white of new-fallen snow, but there are a few other colors to be found among them. Some fawns are born with a tan cast to their coats, giving them a dirty appearance, but this is replaced with the adult color by the middle of their second year. Many of the tan fawns have faint spots arranged in the same pattern found on typical whitetail fawns. One-fifth to one-fourth of all mature bucks have a brown patch of hair around and between their antlers. Hair around the tarsal gland—on the inside joint of each rear leg—of both males and females is usually dark, but this is likely the result of staining caused by glandular secretions.

With their white coats and areas inside the ears and nose and around the eyes made pinkish by blood vessels showing through pale skin, ghost deer are often mistakenly thought to be albinos. But white is the natural color of ghost deer, just as it is of polar bears and Dall sheep. Albinos of any species lack color pigmentation in their skin, hair, and eyes. Without the protection of these pigments, albinos tend to be very sensitive to strong sunlight and exposure, and often die at an early age. Ghost deer, however, do not share the physical infirmities associated with albinism, and many individuals survive well into old age. Nor do ghost deer have the pink eyes typical of albinos; instead they are born with clear blue eyes that darken with age.

The antler formation of the ghost deer is also fascinating. Young bucks sporting their first set of antlers usually exhibit surprisingly uneven development, which may manifest itself in one of two patterns. In the more common form, both antlers are spikes but one is up to twice the length of the other. In the other pattern, one antler grows at an unusual angle or curve. This uneven development is usually not carried over into adulthood.

Adult ghost deer antlers generally follow the basic whitetail configuration, but here again two unique patterns emerge, each with distinctive characteristics. The most famous ghost deer racks, those that have attracted the most attention, are nontypical. These antlers often carry extra tines—usually pointing inward—and exhibit a tendency toward palmation. In a palmated rack, antler beams and tines have angular, knifelike ridges, and the spaces between tines may be webbed. The Finger Lakes region is full of stories about ghost deer with racks as palmated as those of moose, but these flat-antlered creatures inhabit only the fields of local folklore. Palmation may be especially pronounced on the brow tines of nontypical antlers. One rack in my possession has two points on the left brown tine and three points on the right, each connected by bony webbing. The fact that such brow tines often have multiple points and are unusually long suggests that genetically they may be a combined form of a typical brow tine and the first point on the main beam.

The majority of ghost bucks carry more typical racks that bear no evidence of palmation or extra points, yet they frequently lack brow tines. Some racks sweep upward, producing Y-shaped antlers. In an extreme expression of this tendency, two bucks on the depot had points growing off the rear of the main beam.

Though fascinating, such examples should not be interpreted to mean that the average adult deer at this location produces asymmetrical antlers; this is certainly not the case. The brown deer that I believe to have the largest rack on the depot is a magnificent animal in the prime of life with massive, nearly perfectly matched, twelve-point antlers having an inside spread of approximately 2 feet and extremely long tines. The largest white buck is an older, shyer animal with an equally tall but narrower nontypical rack that appears to have fourteen main points and several short auxiliary points.

GROWTH OF THE HERD

Located between Seneca and Cayuga lakes in the Finger Lakes region of central New York, the Seneca Army Depot is home to the greatest known concentration of ghost deer. Established in 1941, the depot is spread out over approximately 10,000 acres that include overgrown fields, small woodlots, and swamps—all prime deer habitat. Because human access to these habitats is restricted, wildlife has flourished in this area. Migratory birds such as ducks, geese, and swans have been photographed on the depot's ponds. Birds of prey are especially common—during our study I confirmed the successful nesting of northern harriers at one site. A bald eagle from the nearby Montezuma National Wildlife Refuge was once a

A white deer (left) has blue or dark eyes, not the pink eyes of an albino. Both have pink muzzles and ears because the blood vessels in the skin show through the pale fur.

CHAPMAN

SMITH

A white deer is a healthy animal exhibiting genetic variation, but its startling coat betrays its presence to predators, while its conventionally colored relatives are better camouflaged.

regular visitor. Although the inaccessibility of the depot has benefited many species of wildlife, it has also, for a time, been a dangerous liability for the deer, as shown in the following chronology.

1941: Construction work began on the Seneca Army Depot. A 7-foot-high chain-link fence was erected around the base perimeter, and about thirty deer were enclosed within the fence. It is assumed that a number of deer regularly entered and exited the base by leaping this fence until modifications were made.

1951: The depot herd had increased to about four hundred deer, and a white deer was sighted for the first time. Some unsubstantiated stories suggested this deer's birthdate to have been as early as 1949. One report mentioned a second white fawn in the early 1950s.

1953: Because of the base's mission, no hunting had been allowed on the depot. The deer herd had now grown to seven hundred, in excess of the area's carrying capacity.

1954–1955: A two-year live-trapping program proved ineffective for managing the deer population. Despite the removal of more than three hundred animals, the total population climbed to fifteen hundred.

1956: As the deer population reached two thousand, large-scale starvation occurred. The body of the white buck seen in 1951 was discovered, but the exact cause of death was undetermined.

1957: After the deer population reached an all-time high of twenty-five hundred, controlled hunting was introduced to reduce the size of the herd.

1958: A newborn white fawn was observed. By order of the base commander, this and future white deer were not to be harvested by hunters. From this year on, multiple births of white deer took place.

1961: Controlled hunting brought the total deer population to well below one thousand. In the fall of this year, five to seven white deer were known to live on the base. Soon a healthy herd size of up to four hundred deer in summer and three hundred in winter was reached. Except for a brief fluctuation at the end of the decade, this population size would be maintained. The number of white deer continued to increase.

1967: For the first time, a limited number of white deer were included in the fall harvest. More than one hundred white deer now lived on the depot, making up about one-fourth of the total population.

In the mid to late 1970s the proportion of white deer climbed to one in three. By the late 1980s white deer had become the dominant color group in at least some herds.

Where to See a Ghost Deer

Access to the Seneca Army Depot is tightly regulated (it was necessary to obtain special permission from the Pentagon just to take the photographs found in this chapter). Nevertheless, there are places where one can observe ghost deer. Some animals have escaped from the depot and been spotted in the woods along Sampson State Park on the eastern shore of Seneca Lake as well as along Routes 96 and 96A between the towns of Romulus and MacDugal. The best time of day to look for them is early morning or near dusk.

Ghost deer were once thought to be nothing more than "white whitetails." It is now believed that they represent a unique genetic variety of white-tailed deer, one whose range, while concentrated in central New York, may extend from Michigan to North Carolina. In the only breeding study of ghost deer done to date, researchers for the New York State Department of Environmental Conservation found the gene for a white coat to be dominant to the gene for a brown coat in both male and female ghost deer. These results were based on a very small sampling, however, so they must be interpreted with caution.

(From a study carried out by William Kent Chapman and Maj. Alan E. Bessette, with the permission of the United States Army and the Seneca Army Depot.)

— William Kent Chapman

Reproduction

In evolutionary terms, the white-tailed deer is a success. It has weathered ice ages and thaws, it has colonized mountain and swamp, and it thrives in the midst of the disturbances caused by the destructive invader of its world, man. One of the reasons for its success is its reproductive strategies: the whitetail can breed at an early age, select the best sires in a herd, produce more than one offspring per year, arrange for the young to be born at a favorable time of year, even alter the sex ratio within the herd to maintain a healthy population. In fact, the white-tailed deer is one of the most prolific mammals and the most productive deer species.

Whitetails reach puberty and breed at a very early age—but only under the right conditions. To reach puberty, a deer first has to obtain a critical body size, about 80 to 90 pounds for northern races of white-tailed deer and about 70 pounds for the smaller southern races. Up to 80 percent of the doe fawns in the midwestern farm belt reach puberty and breed at 6 to 8 months of age. In the southeastern United States, this number is generally much lower, with only 10 to 40 percent of doe fawns breeding in their first year under good range conditions.

Whether a doe reaches puberty in her first year of life depends on when she herself was born, and on the quality and quantity of food she eats in her first six months. In poorer habitat, such as the Florida pine flatwoods, deer do not reach puberty until they are 1 year of age or more. Good habitat, in and of itself, does not mean good nutrition, however: herd density can rapidly reach the point where quality forage is no longer available. The growth rate of fawns is slowed and puberty is delayed until their second year.

Biologists, then, often use fawn reproduction as an indicator of current range conditions. In well-managed deer herds, fawn reproduction is generally high, the one exception being the northern extremes of the white-tailed deer's range, where bitterly cold winters and deep snow make survival unlikely for offspring of inexperienced doe fawns. Researchers Ozoga and Verme found that even among supplementally fed deer in the upper peninsula of Michigan, fawn does did not carry fawns, whereas in the farmland of the lower peninsula more than 60 percent of the female fawns carried young.

Both protein and energy are important to the reproductive process and the onset of puberty. Protein is required for body growth; energy, in the form of carbohydrates and fats, appears particularly important to the production of female hormones. Researchers in Virginia demonstrated that female fawns on high-energy diets had higher levels of the hormone progesterone than fawns fed low-energy diets (different protein levels had no effect on progesterone values). These differences in hormonal levels relate directly to the female's ovary production and release of eggs and thus to the ability to breed.

Male fawns respond to nutrition and time of birth in the same manner as their female counterparts. In general, the same proportion of each sex reaches puberty as fawns. Sexually mature male fawns have calcified antler "buttons." And, as with female fawns, this sign of sexual maturity usually appears long after the normal rut for adult deer. Thus, it would be rare for a buck actually to participate in the rut during his first year of life unless it was to breed a female fawn.

Timing

The ability to breed does not necessarily mean that a species can reproduce: for a population to remain stable or grow, the young animals must survive to adulthood and themselves begin to reproduce. The renewal of life for white-tailed deer depends on favorable birthing times. In most regions that whitetails inhabit, only certain periods of the year allow newborns and their mothers to thrive and survive. Unlike domestic farm animals, which breed year-round, deer require a restrictive breeding period, timed so that the resulting embryo will become a completely developed fawn and be born at a time that favors survival. The mechanism by which breeding takes place at just the right time of year is an ingenious adaptation.

That the breeding of the white-tailed deer might be regulated by photoperiod was expounded in 1970 by McDowell, who observed a difference in timing between North and South: from mid-October to mid-December above the 36-degree latitude, and from the autumnal equinox (September 22) to the vernal equinox (March 21) in the South, between 28 and 36 degrees latitude.

What accounts for the different breeding seasons in North and South is the difference in the length of daylight: a deer, like other mammals in temperate zones, has in the brain a pineal gland, whose function is to measure photoreception and respond to changes in photoperiod. This small, pea-sized gland is regulated by the optic nerves from the eyes. (Indeed, the gland is itself embryologically developed from the same tissue from which eyes are.) In darkness, the pineal gland secretes a hormone called melatonin, which apparently regulates the repro-

The interplay of hormones prompts a rise in sexual energy among bucks and does. The rut is timed so that the fawns are born when weather and resources can best ensure their survival.

ductive hormones produced by the pituitary gland. That melatonin can regulate breeding has been demonstrated by New Zealand researchers Barrell and Lapwood. These researchers were able to advance the breeding of red deer by more than a month through daily administration of melatonin.

The white-tailed deer is unique among deer species in that its range covers both tropical and temperate zones. Deer near the equator have been shown to breed during all months of the year. In Venezuela, Brokx found that white-tailed does not only bred at all times of the year but, unlike their northern cousins, also can breed again shortly after giving birth and thus can fawn more than once in a single year.

Most bucks reach sexual maturity as yearlings but even then cannot compete with larger rivals for does; this fawn buck's buttons reveal his immaturity.

STRACENER

Although photoperiod appears to be the prime regulator of breeding timing, other factors may be at work. Consider the breeding records of deer at the same latitude: South Carolina deer breed starting in September, but Mississippi deer don't begin until November. That the rut is occurring at different times within the same latitudes suggests that photoperiod is not the only controller of breeding timing.

We now have evidence that genetics is likely involved with breeding timing. Deer transported from Michigan to Mississippi maintained the same October and November breeding dates that they had in the North, even as their native Mississippi penmates bred in late December and January. Crossbred offspring of Michigan and Mississippi deer bred over the whole range of both parents.

Though it is true that in the tropics whitetails can breed in every month of the year, it also is generally true that deer in any one locality are still somewhat synchronous in their breeding. Klein reported that in Honduras most whitetails breed between July and November. Deer in the Cocoa Beach area of Florida breed from the last of May through early December, with the peak around September 25. Near Labelle, Florida, just over a hundred miles south of Cocoa Beach, deer rut between mid-June and mid-September, with the peak rut near July 22. Why these tropical deer breed at such different times than northern deer is likely a result of different selection pressures. Perhaps biting insects or annual flooding has caused these populations to breed when they do. In any event, it appears likely that it is an interplay of photoperiod and genetics that regulates reproduction.

Nutrition has a small part in the timing of reproduction. From dietary studies conducted by Verme, we know that deer placed on low-quality diets breed later and have pregnancy periods four to six days longer than well-nourished does. Although nutrition is important to reproductive success and fawn survival, as a mechanism in the timing of breeding, it is very limited.

There is a myth among hunters that the timing of the rut also depends on the weather. Indeed, deer appear to be more

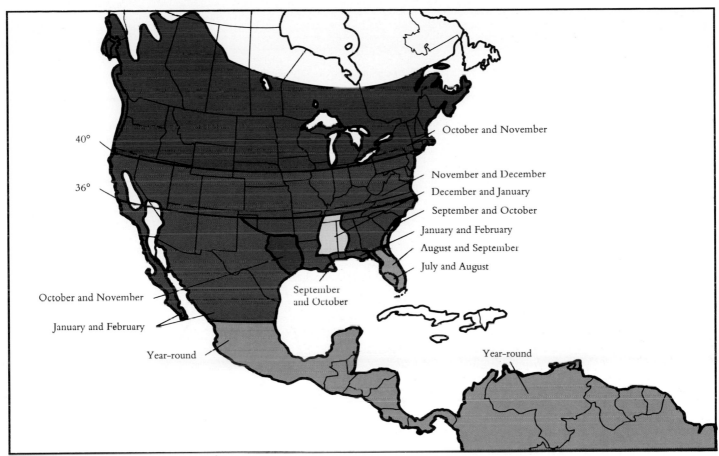

October and November

November and December
December and January
September and October
January and February
August and September
July and August

September
and October

40°

36°

October and November

January and February

Year-round

Year-round

active on cold or cool fall days than during an unseasonal heat wave. There is, however, no evidence of any correlation between breeding timing and weather conditions. Most likely, deer just feel better and are more active in cool weather. Displays of aggression, moreover, generally occur well before breeding begins. Like such physical changes as swollen necks and hard antlers, aggressive behavior helps bucks establish dominance rankings but does not necessarily coincide with the peak of breeding.

Another factor that has been suggested as a regulator of breeding timing is the phenomenon called biostimulation. In theory, the presence of individuals in breeding condition stimulates other members of a group to breed at the same time. At present there is little evidence for this, but we still have a great deal to learn about the influence of pheromones and social factors on white-tailed deer behavior.

What is known to affect the breeding season of a deer herd is the ratio of does to bucks. Herds with more does than bucks have a prolonged breeding season and a later

peak rut than herds with an approximately 1:1 sex ratio. Separate studies conducted in Mississippi by Jacobson and in South Carolina by Guynn have demonstrated that as a high doe-to-buck ratio returns to a balanced sex ratio, the breeding period shifts from later to earlier, with the peak of the rut occurring two to three weeks earlier than it was with an unbalanced sex ratio.

THE RUT

The rut is initiated by a sequence of hormonal changes in both male and female deer. This begins with melatonin stimulation of the so-called reproductive clock. The

SMITH

In North America the onset of the rut generally occurs later in the South than in the North. Actual dates are determined by local climate and have evolved so that newborn fawns are spared late-winter storms, spring floods, and hatches of biting insects.

A doe's readiness to breed — and her ability to bear more than one fawn — depends on age and good nutrition. Some fawn does are bred during their first fall, but they rarely bear twins.

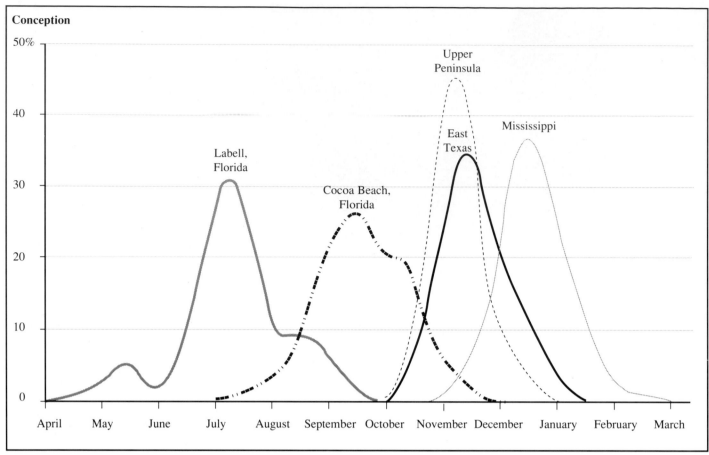

Conception

50%

40

30

20

10

0

April   May   June   July   August   September   October   November   December   January   February   March

Labell, Florida

Cocoa Beach, Florida

Upper Peninsula

East Texas

Mississippi

ZIEGENFUSS

Although the two Florida populations of deer live only about 100 miles apart, they have dramatically different peak breeding periods. Similarly, the Mississippi and East Texas deer are in the same latitude yet breed at different times. Deer in the Upper Peninsula of Michigan have the most synchronous breeding, probably because fawns born only a few weeks too early or too late will have little chance of survival.

exact mechanism is not known, but the end result is that three hormones are produced by the pituitary, a gland in the brain. These hormones are follicle-stimulating hormone (FSH), luteinizing hormone (LH), and lactogenic hormone, also called prolactin (LTH). In bucks LH initiates the production of the hormone testosterone by the testes. Testosterone and FSH together allow the manufacture of sperm. Testosterone is also responsible for many of the changes that bucks undergo in preparation for breeding, both physical and behavioral, from the hardening of the antlers and the sloughing off of velvet to aggressive challenges and antler rubs. LTH appears to act synergistically with the other hormones to increase the amount of testosterone.

The same three pituitary hormones in the female have different functions and produce different results. In does, FSH causes growth of follicles in the ovary and stimulates production of the hormone estrogen by the ovaries. Estrogen in turn causes increased development of the female sex organs and prepares the uterus for receiving

the eggs. It also contributes to secondary sex characteristics and behavioral changes, causing the doe to become restless and to seek out bucks for mating. The time when the female is receptive to mating is referred to as estrus, a period that in the white-tailed deer normally lasts about 24 hours.

Shortly after the level of FSH begins to increase, there is an increase and then a surge of LH, the luteinizing hormone. This further stimulates the follicles, which contain the developing eggs, to grow rapidly and rupture, releasing the eggs. No one knows for sure precisely when this occurs, but researchers' best guess is that the eggs are released about 10 to 20 hours after the doe first allows a buck to mount her. This means that fertilization of the eggs occurs within the oviduct, well before they reach the uterus.

Once the follicle containing an egg has ruptured, it actually becomes a gland, known as the corpus luteum. The release of LH and LTH by the pituitary causes this gland to secrete the female hormone progesterone. The most important function of pro-

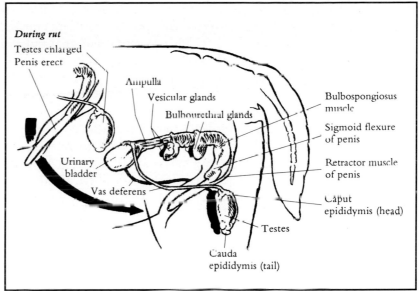

During rut

Testes enlarged
Penis erect

Ampulla

Vesicular glands

Bulbourethral glands

Bulbospongiosus muscle

Sigmoid flexure of penis

Retractor muscle of penis

Caput epididymis (head)

Urinary bladder

Vas deferens

Testes

Cauda epididymis (tail)

BESENGER

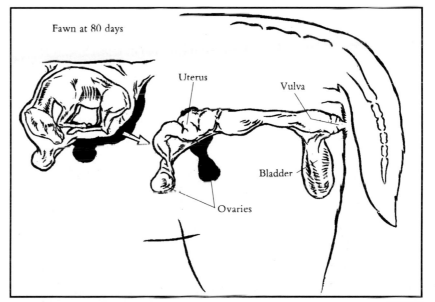

Fawn at 80 days

Uterus

Vulva

Bladder

Ovaries

BESENGER

gesterone is to prepare the uterus for implantation by the egg. If the egg is fertilized, it produces a hormone, called chorionic gonadotropin, that maintains production of progesterone by the corpus luteum and fosters the early stages of pregnancy.

Without the hormonal signal from a fertilized egg, the uterus instead secretes a hormone called prostaglandin. Prostaglandin has many functions, but at this stage of reproduction it causes the corpus luteum to regress and the uterus to return to normal so that the estrous cycle can begin all over again. The whole sequence of events takes from 22 to 28 days.

If a doe is not bred on her first estrus, then, or if for some reason the embryo does not implant in the uterus, she will again come into estrus 22 to 28 days after the first cycle. White-tailed deer that do not conceive have been documented to go through as many as six estrous cycles in a single breeding season.

For bucks, the pituitary and testes are most important to reproductive success. But there are four accessory organs involved in the male reproductive function: the epididymis, the seminal vesicles, the prostate gland, and cowper's glands. These organs show seasonal changes in the white-tailed deer and are their largest and most active during the peak of breeding.

The epididymis is where sperm mature to their fertile state. Seminal vesicles secrete a number of substances, including amino acids and sugars, that provide nutrients for the sperm. They also secrete small quantities of prostaglandin, which causes uterine contractions and helps propel the sperm toward the oviduct where fertilization occurs. The prostate secretes a milky fluid during ejaculation that helps neutralize the acid environment of the vagina and therefore increase sperm motility and survivability. Cowper's glands, also referred to as bubo urethrae glands, supply mucus to the urethra and lubrication that aids in ejaculation.

GESTATION AND BIRTH

The white-tailed deer has a gestation period of about 200 days, during which nutrition is critical to the survival of both fawn and doe. Up to a point, does deplete their own body reserves to provide nutrients for the growing fetus. Fetal death and reabsorption, however, are common among deer in overpopulated range.

In preparation for fawning, does begin to avoid contact with other members of their social group. Just before giving birth, a doe

The gravid doe needs highly nutritious food. Undernourished does may abort their fetuses, or the unborn fawns may be reabsorbed into their mothers' bodies.

BINEGAR

may shift her home range to an area outside of the normal home range or at its edge, according to Bartush and Lewis's study of whitetails in Oklahoma. Does have a marked fidelity to their birthing sites, returning to the same area to give birth from one year to the next.

Among captive deer, a period of restlessness and pacing signals the beginning of the birth process. This is particularly true of first-time mothers. A doe nearing labor generally shows enlarged and swollen mammary glands. She also adopts a peculiar walk; her tail is extended out and down, but with a fishhook-shaped crook. She seeks out a secluded area to give birth.

As with other mammals, labor begins with the bursting of the water sac. Labor often lasts a long time—twelve or more hours has been clocked in captive does—but deer are known to be able to stop the labor process if disturbed. After birth, the doe chews off the umbilical cord and eats the afterbirth. Whether she does so for nutritional purposes or to make it more difficult for predators to find the birth site is only conjecture, but both guesses are reasonable explanations for this behavior.

The doe immediately licks her fawn dry and establishes the bonding that lets her distinguish her fawn from others. She nurses it shortly after birth and remains with or near it for the first twenty-four hours. Does with twins may move the fawns to separate bedding areas within a few hours of birth. Bartush and Lewis found that the distance between the beds used by sibling fawns increased each day for the first eight days of life. This separation of twin fawns presumably increases the chance of survival for one: a predator that finds one fawn is not likely to find the other.

FAWN MORTALITY

Body weight at birth is critical to the fawns' survival. Except for the subspecies of small whitetails, like Key deer, fawns with body weights less than 5 pounds have little chance for survival. The normal birth weight for a healthy fawn is 6 to 9 pounds; fawns 12 pounds or more are not too unusual.

The mother's nutrition affects maternal behavior. Abandonment of the young is

Having eaten the afterbirth,
the doe licks her fawn dry and
waits for it to stand and begin
to nurse. Her winter coat
has not yet finished molting.

SMITH

common in undernourished deer herds, particularly by first-time mothers. In a study conducted by Langenau and Lerg in Michigan, 27 percent of the mothers on low-quality diets abandoned their fawns, versus only 2 percent abandonment rate for well-fed does.

The biggest danger for fawns in poor habitats is predation. An astounding mortality rate of 80 percent has been recorded for some areas, generally in overpopulated range and areas that lack protective escape cover. In the brush country of southern Texas and the prairies of Oklahoma, for example, coyotes are effective predators of fawns because they can observe a doe going to her young from a distance. Protective ground cover to conceal fawns is important: In overpopulated range, much of the protective cover that would otherwise shield fawns has been eaten by the deer themselves. In healthy deer populations, fawn survival is usually high in most forested regions of the country, even when predators are numerous, because such habitats have bushy understories that provide escape cover.

Some fawns succumb to disease. Although high mortality can occur among captive deer under crowded conditions because of diseases or parasites, in wild populations disease does not take a high toll on well-nourished fawns. Bacterial diseases, screwworm flies, stomach worms, lung worms, and ticks can cause problems though.

WHITE-TAILED DEER

Poor cover and inexperienced or undernourished mothers can leave fawns vulnerable to predation.

A variety of bacterial diseases can affect newborns, but the most serious are those that cause diarrhea. Salmonella outbreaks in captive deer facilities have resulted in the death of nearly all fawns. With wild deer, bacterial diseases among fawns are less significant because contagious spread is unlikely. Screwworms occur only in Latin American countries and occasionally in the border region of Texas and Mexico; they have been controlled in the United States. Screwworms can be a serious problem because the flies deposit their eggs on the newborn's umbilical cord, where the larvae can gain entry to the body. Stomach worms and lung worms take their toll on stunted and undernourished fawns and are most likely to be a problem in overpopulated range. Tick parasitism can be a significant mortality factor in some areas. One Oklahoma study attributed 37 percent of fawn losses to tick parasitism in the post-oak region. A combination of high deer density and hot, humid oak forests seems to favor the ticks, which can kill fawns by causing them to lose blood and by spreading secondary infections.

Accidents take an incidental number of young animals. Fawns may break legs and necks when they run into fences and other obstructions. Hay mowers, farm machinery, and automobiles probably account for most accidental deaths of fawns. Flooding may be a significant mortality factor for some white-tailed deer fawns in river bottoms and swampland areas.

Though the dieoffs that cause great crashes in deer population are certainly dramatic, they are the exception. The interplay of factors that can maintain a healthy population is more subtle. Reproduction and fawn mortality are the two most important factors. High reproduction and low fawn mortality generally characterize healthy deer populations, whereas just the opposite is true in overpopulated herds

FECUNDITY

The doe with her gamboling twin fawns is a common sight. Triplets are not rare, and even quadruplets are born on occasion. Whether a doe has one fawn or four depends on a complex of factors—age is one.

A fawn doe, if she conceives, generally gives birth to just one offspring. For most of the country, yearling does average 1.5 to 1.6 offspring per pregnancy, and adult does, 1.7 to 1.8.

Habitat has an effect on fertility of the white-tailed deer, too. Does from the midwestern farm country generally have the highest fertility rates, and those from the sandy forests of the South's coastal plains, the lowest. The difference is nutrition. Deer herds that are in balance with the area's forage have the highest reproductive rates, whereas few fawns are produced on overstocked ranges. Both energy and protein are important. Does given high-energy diets before the breeding season have a much higher incidence of twin and triplet births than those on low-energy diets; protein is critical to growth and survival of the fetus and also the mother's nutritional well-being.

The last factor that may bear on fertility is genetics. The subject has been well researched for domestic animals; in sheep, genetics can be very important in determining reproductive rates. Comparatively little is known about the role of genetics in reproduction in white-tailed deer, but genetics may explain regional differences in fertility rates. Tropical does rarely have twins, for example, but can have more than one fawn a year and may breed as early as a month after the last fawns were born. Poor soil fertility and lower nutritional quality of plants in the tropics would make it difficult for a doe to get sufficient protein to support twin fetuses, even under the best of conditions. Thus, it is reasonable to assume that these populations would evolve genetic controls of reproductive rates to match their environment.

SEX RATIOS OF FAWNS

Whitetails, as populations, have the ability to change the sex ratios of their offspring under different nutritional conditions. Look at the facts, all well documented by several researchers:

• Well-nourished white-tailed deer have a higher number of female offspring than male offspring.

• Poorly nourished deer and herds on overpopulated range produce more males.

• Fawn does conceive more male fetuses.

• Maiden yearling does on high-quality diets have a high proportion of female offspring.

• Maiden yearling does on low-quality diets produce more males.

• Well-nourished captive does with single births have higher numbers of female offspring.

• Well-nourished captive does with twin offspring run close to equal sex ratios.

• Well-nourished captive does with triplet offspring have a higher proportion of males.

The basis for all these differences, researchers suspect, may be female hormonal levels at conception. These hormones cause higher probability of one sex or the other because they affect the uterine environment and thus the relative motility of sperm. It is the sperm cell that determines the sex of offspring depending on X or Y chromosome presence. Perhaps these hormones cause changes in acidity within the uterus, which make the X-chromosome sperm swim faster or slower and thus reach the ova earlier or later than the Y-chromosome sperm.

Breeding timing and social factors may also be involved. Ozoga and Verme first proposed that deer bred early in their estrous cycle would conceive more females, and deer bred late in their cycle would have more male fawns. This same mechanism can help explain how social factors can affect offspring sex ratios. In herds with more does than bucks, the dominant adult does could be

A pair of healthy young fawns indicates that their mother is of prime age and has been eating a high-quality diet. The doe keeps her offspring free of any odors that might attract predators.

NAGLE

Mutual grooming helps forge a strong bond between mother and young and thus improves the fawn's chances for survival.

expected to breed earlier in their estrous cycle than subordinate and yearling does. The does that were bred later in their estrous cycle would produce more male offspring, and thus deer herds with high buck mortality and low buck-to-doe ratios could be expected to produce more male than female offspring.

These changes in sex ratios enable white-tailed deer herds to adapt to changing environmental conditions. In good times, a high percentage of female births allows the herd to increase rapidly. When the population grows too large, or range conditions are poor, more males are born, slowing the growth of the herd.

From an evolutionary perspective, a doe may have the best chance of making a genetic contribution to the herd if her first fawn is male. If she survives her first year, it may then be best to have female fawns; because females have a lower mortality rate, they have a greater probability of reproducing. Males, however, if they survive to maturity, can sire many more offspring than females. Therefore, for a doe 2 years old or older, it might be best to have an equal proportion of male and female offspring to ensure the passage of her genes to subsequent generations.

—Harry A. Jacobson

DEER

The rut

A dominance fight between mature whitetail bucks is truly awesome. With impressive speed, agility, and strength, the two animals battle each other. The clash of their antlers rings in the forest, and their racks rattle as they twist and push. Finally one buck retreats and the victor stands panting, his breath condensing in the chill air.

Such scenes occur only when males are in rut—the peak of breeding condition. Their antlers are polished and hard, and high levels of the male sex hormone testosterone course through their blood. Bucks' breeding capability may not be limited to the period during which they have hard antlers, however. On rare occasions bucks in prerut, with late velvet, and bucks in postrut that have shed antlers have been observed copulating with estrous does; it is not certain that they have sufficient sperm to father offspring.

The rut includes the normal breeding period, which, at least in temperate climates, is most intense near the middle of the hard-antler period. We think of the rut as when bucks are doing things associated with readiness to mate, such as rubbing and scraping. These occur to some extent throughout the entire period of hard antler. But the peak of the rut is determined by the time when most does come into estrus, or heat. The bucks stay ready to breed over several months, but their swollen necks and deeply stained tarsal glands bespeak the peak of rutting condition just as or just before large numbers of does start coming into heat. The chase that follows—"running," as some hunters refer to the courtship phase—is the result of does' coming into estrus.

Intensive breeding activity may last as little as two weeks or can be spread out over a much longer period. Each doe's heat lasts only twenty-four to thirty-six hours, although she will cycle again if not bred. Research at the University of Georgia by Knox, White, and others found that a doe that is not bred may cycle as many as eight times over a seven-month period. In a population with enough mature bucks, however, most does are bred during their first heat.

In temperate climates the rut usually occurs during the fall. Day length, or photoperiod, is the most important trigger initiating reproductive activity and related physical changes in both does and bucks. A portion of the brain called the pineal gland responds to photoperiod changes and acts like a chemical clock. Differential secretion of the hormone melatonin from the pineal initiates a chain of events in other glands within the deer's body, such as the hypothalamus, the pituitary, and finally the reproductive organs themselves.

Whitetails are referred to as short-day breeders because their cycle is usually activated by decreasing day length in the late summer or fall. Nevertheless, the timing of the phases of a whitetail's reproductive cycle varies in different parts of its geographic range. Near the equator, for example, where

Because not all females come into estrus at the same time, the dominant buck in an area can breed the majority of does

day length changes little, Branan and Marchinton have seen whitetail bucks in every stage of antler development throughout most of the year.

Whitetails' reproductive cycle has become adapted so that fawns are born at the time most conducive to their survival. In northern areas this results in late spring or early summer births, when ample food is available from new plant growth. These relatively early births enable the fawns to grow large before they must face the harsh winter. In parts of the southern United States and in Central and South America, the breeding season varies greatly from area to area and may even be spread out over much of the year. Breeding in areas without extremely cold weather is influenced by other, more subtle factors that affect fawns' survival, such as seasonal rains, droughts, and food sources. For convenience this chapter will generally refer to the timing of rutting activities typical of the northern and central United States, as well as some southern areas. Even within small areas, however, there can be minor differences in timing caused by the density, structure, and social organization of the population or by other environmental factors.

LEADING UP TO THE RUT

The rut consists of a number of phases extending over several months. The progression of events begins with the formation of bachelor groups.

Though female groups tend to be closely related by maternal descent, bucks usually associate with unrelated individuals. Older bucks spend a long, quiet spring and summer in bachelor groups. During this time, they recover from the loss of physical condition caused by the enormous effort expended during the previous rut and the rigors of winter, and they grow a new set of antlers. Early summer to midsummer is an especially quiet time for bucks. "Male bonding" may be too anthropomorphic a description, but they do spend this time learning about each other.

Membership in buck groups is constantly shifting. In late spring or early summer, when yearlings of both sexes are driven out of family groups, they often try to associate with the older bucks. They may be tolerated but are frequently driven away for no apparent reason. Perhaps because of this, male and female yearlings are often seen together in exclusive yearling groups during the summer. By early fall, yearling does are no longer found with buck groups, and aggression toward yearling bucks by members of older buck groups is less apparent.

McCullough and other researchers have presented evidence that bachelor groups live in different areas than the does. They also may fill different niches and occupy poorer habitats if good ones are in short supply. This behavior could be a natural selection advantage, because bucks can maximize the survival of their offspring by relinquishing the best habitats to them and their dams during this critical phase of the fawns' survival and development.

While in bachelor groups during the spring and summer, bucks' testicles are small and the production of testosterone, the most important sexual hormone, is very low. As the summer nears an end, the testes begin to enlarge and the spermatogonia lining the seminiferous tubules start the process of producing sperm. The Leydig cells increase in size and begin to manufacture testosterone. Rising levels of testosterone in the blood slow antler growth and start the hardening process. Around September 1 the antler's velvet covering is shed. In 1977 Hirth observed that loss of velvet is likely to occur first among older animals. Older bucks also experience earlier and higher peaks in testosterone levels, according to Miller and others.

As the bucks lose their velvet, they enter a time often referred to as the prerut. The entire process of removal rarely requires more than one or two days. A few bucks have been observed eating their velvet; Hamilton reported seeing one buck eat the velvet from another penned deer, but it is not known if this is common in the wild.

Even before the velvet is completely gone, bucks begin to test their new weapons on trees and bushes. The new antlers, particularly those of mature animals, are adorned with prominent pearling—many small bumps usually found near the bases but sometimes extending well up the main

BRYAN

beams. These are useful in removing tree bark but will become smoother as rubbing and sparring wear them down.

Now the bucks have these wonderful polished antlers on their heads and a rapidly rising concentration of testosterone in their bodies. A transformation in behavior occurs.

ESTABLISHING A HIERARCHY

During the rut, the social organization of bucks can best be described as a dominance hierarchy in which the highest-ranked individual is the one most likely to do the breeding. Animal A is dominant over all others, animal B is dominant over all others except A, and so forth. Since this phenomenon was

With swollen neck and stained tarsals, the buck trails does that are approaching estrus. Chemicals in their urine alert him to their readiness.

By the time bucks are in hard antler, their breeding hierarchy is well established. The smaller males will nevertheless seek to breed if the dominant buck is with one doe while another comes into heat.

KINNEY

Bucks often engage in the highly ritualized act of sparring. One animal invites another to spar by lowering his antlers. Carefully locking antlers to avoid injury, they twist necks; disengagement follows. The smaller buck then licks the dominant animal's face and forehead, possibly to memorize his scents.

described first in poultry, it has also been called a pecking order. Hierarchies occasionally can be nonlinear and become more of a web or matrix—for example, animal C may be dominant over animal D, and D over E, but E dominates C. This is not often the case among whitetail bucks, however. If there are sufficient numbers of bucks in the population with a good range of ages, they will have established hierarchies by the breeding season, and usually a clear dominant type will emerge in a particular area.

Some animals organize themselves by territories, with each territorial male controlling and breeding females that occupy or enter his area. According to Marchinton and Atkeson in 1985, whitetails basically follow a social hierarchical ranking, but there seems to be a spatial element at times. Those authors suspect that the site of an encounter between two high-ranking bucks can have a bearing on the outcome and determine which gets to breed the doe.

It is during the prerut, after velvet has been shed from antlers, that bucks begin to spar with each other. Townsend and others in 1973 pointed out that the function of sparring seems to be to establish a well-defined hierarchy among bucks. Sparring is not to be confused with fighting. True dominance fights may come later, but for now the buck is simply comparing his antlers and strength with those of others. He does this by touching his antlers to another buck's and pushing almost casually or playfully. Marchinton and Hirth observed that sparring matches often begin when one buck lowers his antlers toward another. If the second buck accepts the challenge, the two engage antlers in what can best be described as a pushing match. The smaller of the two bucks is likely to be pushed backward.

Both bucks learn something about their proper place in the dominance hierarchy from this experience. These authors also noted that "small bucks often challenge larger bucks only to be forced into a hasty retreat. On other occasions, larger bucks will tolerate the challenges of small bucks, often standing still while yearlings push at them with all their strength." Sparring matches may last for several minutes. Contests between bucks of the same size, when the outcome is in doubt, are likely to become more serious. Younger bucks spend more time sparring than do older animals and may continue even into the breeding season. Older, clearly dominant animals seem to be more secure in their hierarchial positions.

Before the actual engagement of antlers in a sparring match, it is common for the subordinate buck to groom the face and forehead of the larger buck. Forand and Marchinton in a 1989 study speculated that the subordinate may be licking the forehead gland and memorizing the smell of the adversary. This would not only aid in recognizing the larger animal in the future but also allow identification of the animal's dominance areas, which are marked by his signposts, or rubs.

What physical attributes and behavior are characteristic of dominant bucks? Certainly age is a factor. Bucks reach physical maturity around 5 years of age. Where there are few bucks older than yearlings in a population, clearly formed hierarchies may not occur. Where older bucks are present, the most mature individuals are likely to be dominant until they begin to deteriorate physically as a result of advanced age, debilitating injury, or disease. When old age becomes a negative factor varies. Some bucks may be over the hill at 6 or 7 years, but others can maintain

dominance well into their teens. The caliber of competition from younger bucks certainly plays a role.

Other important factors involved in achieving dominance are body size and strength and antler size. Antlers are pretty good indicators of overall body size and health. They serve as symbols of the buck's age and physical condition in addition to being weapons. Geist has noted that antler size itself can be intimidating to smaller bucks.

Occasionally smaller bucks or those with lesser antler development become dominants, but this is not especially common, Hirth pointed out in 1973. Studies at the University of Georgia suggest that testosterone levels play a role in the aggressiveness of bucks. Dominant bucks usually have high concentrations of this hormone in their blood. There is evidence that winning sparring matches or dominance fights may increase the production of testosterone by the winner and decrease it in the loser. It is not altogether clear, however, whether being dominant results in higher levels of testosterone or whether high levels of testosterone cause bucks to be more aggressive and achieve higher rank. There is scientific evidence to support both theories.

DOMINANCE FIGHTS

Early in the rut, dominant bucks are fairly tolerant of subordinates, but when does begin to come into heat, the hierarchy becomes more rigidly enforced. How does a dominant buck express his position behaviorally? Aggressive intentions, Thomas and others pointed out in 1965, are expressed by stereotypical postures. The lowest level of threat is a direct stare with the ears laid back along the neck. Often this is all that is neces-

sary to cause a subordinate to retreat. If the subordinate does not leave, the dominant buck erects his body hair, making himself appear larger and darker—in short, very formidable. He advances or sidles slowly toward and around the other buck with a deliberate, stiff-legged gait. A vocalization described by Atkeson, Marchinton, and Miller as the grunt-snort-wheeze is sometimes produced in these situations. This is considered to be the most threatening sound a whitetail buck makes. If the other buck does not retreat or assume a subordi-

Small, young bucks frequently spar with much larger rivals. Once into the breeding season, while the dominant animals are mating, these low-ranking bucks continue sparring among themselves.

Erect hair, darkened coat, ears laid back, hard stare: a buck approaches a challenger in a dominance display.

nate posture, the dominant animal threatens with his antlers. Unless the bucks are very closely matched, the lesser one usually yields. If neither yields, a dominance fight likely ensues.

Dominance fights generally do not last more than thirty seconds, but they sometimes go much longer before a winner is established. Injury to one of the combatants is not the inevitable outcome. Usually one of the bucks withdraws quickly without being harmed.

Nevertheless, injuries do occur — a broken antler tine, a broken antler main beam, a puncture wound. These may not be serious, but fatalities have been observed. Sometimes even the winning animal may receive head wounds that become infected, forming brain abscesses that result in death months later. A number of these cases have been reported by Nettles and Davidson at the Southeastern Cooperative Wildlife Disease Study laboratories.

On fairly rare occasions, large, evenly matched bucks' antlers become locked together so tightly that they cannot disengage and both bucks perish from starvation or predation. Instances have been recorded in which one of the locked animals remained alive even after his adversary was partially consumed by coyotes or other predators. Bucks staggering around with the head of another buck locked onto their antlers have been observed.

SIGNPOSTING

Because mature bucks and does tend to remain separate from each other except during actual courtship and breeding — a process that usually lasts only a few days — some sort of signposting or advertising *in absentia* is necessary for social communication. To accomplish this, whitetails have developed an elaborate system of licking branches, rubbing, and scraping.

Licking branches. Throughout the sexually quiescent spring-summer period, when their new antlers are growing, bucks communicate with one another using an olfactory language. This is done through communal licking of branches. How these branches are selected is not clear, but they often are the

same ones under which scrapes are made during the rut. They are most likely to be branches that are located over a trail or along the edge of a field and that are slightly above the buck's head when he is in a normal walking position. Bucks seem to prefer to reach up, and sometimes they actually stand on their hind legs to mark a branch. Rearing up on the hind legs is more likely to happen where branches of the proper form and right height are in short supply or where long-term use of a site has eliminated suitable lower branches.

Marking involves mouthing the branch and sometimes rubbing it with the forehead or preorbital glands. At the same time, bucks apparently smell and taste marks already there. Many bucks may use the same licking branch. Outside the rut, at least, no proprietary tendencies are evident, and there is communal use of the licking branch by all bucks in the area. The function of year-round licking of branches is not fully understood, but buck behavior suggests that it communicates identities and status and may facilitate social bonding.

Rubbing. Bucks begin rubbing as the velvet is being shed. Twenty-five years ago it was assumed by scientists and hunters alike that the primary purposes of rubbing were to remove velvet and build up neck muscles for fighting. But intensive studies of rubbing by Moore and Marchinton, beginning in the late 1960s, revealed that its function was far more than that. Rubbing during and shortly after velvet removal is rather violent and likely to break branches and destroy bushes. Though rubbing probably does serve to strengthen neck muscles and may help remove velvet, testing out the new weapons is likely a more important function.

As the rut progresses, rubs change to the more typical, highly visible signpost type, in which the buck uses his antlers to tear the bark of bushes, saplings, or trees, exposing the lighter-colored wood underneath. He then anoints the exposed wood with scent from his forehead gland. He may stop periodically to carefully lick his handiwork. These rubs obviously have important communicative functions: the buck is passing on information for other deer to read, through

scent, rub appearance, and the sound of his making the rubs. The scent on rubs remains detectable for several weeks, as Moore and Marchinton demonstrated with trained dogs.

These early signpost rubs, Ozoga and Verme pointed out, are usually made by the more mature bucks; yearling bucks make only about half as many rubs during the breeding season as older animals.

There is a distinct relationship between a buck's age and the size of the rub. Older bucks are likely to rub much larger trees. A typical yearling rarely rubs bush stems or saplings larger than about 5 centimeters (2 inches) in diameter, but a fully mature buck may rub pole trees 15 centimeters (6 inches) or larger. There have been observations of rubbed trees exceeding 30 centimeters (1 foot) in diameter. The larger trees used by mature bucks seem to have special scent communication functions, as bucks may repeatedly return to them. Recently Woods and others, using automatic cameras, demonstrated that not only bucks but also does come to inspect these larger rubs. Much of the activity is late at night, however, and so is usually unobserved by humans. Smaller rubs are much less frequently rerubbed, although does occasionally do inspect them. Buck and doe behavior associated with the large rubs suggests that older bucks are depositing some important information on them and that they play major roles in the sociobiological functioning of the herd.

What kind of bushes and trees do bucks select for rubbing? Proper growth form is important; limbs very low on the bole prevent easy access by the buck. Bucks seem to prefer aromatic trees, such as cedar or sassafras, when available. These may draw attention to or enhance the scents the buck leaves on the tree.

Scraping. Another very important and obviously complex signpost made primarily by bucks is the scrape. Scraping has been observed from July through March but is usually done when the bucks are in hard antler. Several researchers have found that only mature, dominant males produce significant numbers of scrapes. Scraping by dominant bucks is most intense just before the peak of breeding; subordinates, if they scrape at all, are more likely to begin later. Once does begin to come into heat in large numbers, dominant bucks no longer need to advertise their availability, as they are fully occupied handling their breeding duties. There is some evidence that scraping activity picks up again after the peak of rut.

The full scrape sequence is a combination of overhead branch marking, pawing, and urination. A scrape involves several scent sources and probably has multiple functions as a signpost communication system. Scraping behavior typically begins with a buck walking under a limb hanging just above his head. He sometimes rubs it with his forehead gland or his preorbital gland, rattles it with his antlers, or does both. He then takes

LEA

a twig into his mouth and moistens it with saliva. By doing so, he also may detect chemicals left by other deer.

After the overhead limb is marked, the buck normally paws away the leaves below it; the area cleared varies, but a 3-foot-diameter circle is common. The buck then steps forward and urinates on the bare soil. This usually involves urinating onto the tarsal glands while rubbing them together, a behavior known as rub-urination. The urine of a mature buck leaves a persistent odor and may stain the soil dark even after it has dried. It appears that the urine of bucks, especially mature or socially dominant ones, has special qualities that enhance its communicative significance.

Does sometimes approach scrapes, and the scents they perceive may play a role in priming their reproductive cycles. Also, as Moore and Marchinton reported, does apparently leave "calling cards" in the form of scent when they are approaching receptivity. Clear documentation as to how this is done is still lacking, but urination in or near the scrape is thought to be involved.

Subordinate bucks may create fewer scrapes because of behavioral or pheromonal suppression by dominants. Subordinates often approach scrapes and mark the overhanging limbs just as they lick branches during the summer. Young bucks are unlikely to perform the full scrape sequence if there are adults around, however. Furthermore, when does coming into heat are nearby, or for

other reasons known only to deer, a dominant buck sometimes does not tolerate even a subordinate's presence near a scrape. The lesser buck may be repulsed by a hard look or aggressively chased away from the scrape.

It is apparent that signposting is an extremely complex scent communication system with important functions within the deer herd; even though a great deal has been learned about signposting behavior since the 1960s, its mysteries still are not completely unraveled.

COURTSHIP AND BREEDING

Many aspects of reproductive behavior among animals are directed toward ensuring their survival as a species. As the does approach estrus and the bucks sort themselves out for breeding rights, signposts help deer become aware of each other and identify hierarchical status, conveying pheromones that prime reproductive processes in both sexes and providing information about possible sexual partners.

Who seeks out whom when the breeding season arrives? It depends. Probably the sex in the minority is courted more aggressively. Bucks do most of the seeking when the number of males is adequate, and they may move about in search of receptive does. There is evidence that some males become superdominants, or floaters, and travel over thousands of acres. Because of their physical superiority, they can intimidate bucks wherever they go. On the other hand, if mature

To scrape, the buck first marks an overhead branch with his forehead gland or preorbital gland (or both) and licks it to pick up scents from other bucks. He then clears a circle in the forest floor and urinates, rubbing his hind legs together so that chemicals from his tarsal glands are captured by the flow. The scrape holds the buck's scents for passersby. He periodically returns to determine whether any does approaching estrus have urinated near the spot.

bucks are in short supply, does may leave their normal range to seek a mate. A doe is aided in her search by the bucks' signpost advertising. These excursions in search of a mate may last only a day or two, but if she is not successful, she will likely try again in about four weeks when she cycles back into heat.

It is likely that does are selective in choosing mates when choices are available but not if the number of bucks is small. Ozoga suggests that a doe is more receptive when courted by a male of approximately the same age. There is evidence that when given a choice, an adult doe selects mature bucks over yearlings or precocial fawns. She sometimes accomplishes this by leading her younger suitors to a dominant male, who then displaces the lesser bucks in the courtship chase.

The whole process of chasing and courtship is a very visible one that exposes participants to risk from predators, both human and otherwise. This is the only time of year when white-tailed deer, particularly bucks, forsake cover and put themselves into vulnerable positions. Given the obvious selective disadvantage, why doesn't such behavior get bred out of the population? The reason is that it also provides very strong *positive* selective values. It allows the doe to be bred by the most physically superior buck in the area. She dashes around—in anthropomorphic terms, making quite a spectacle of herself—so that the local bucks become aware of her impending receptivity and join her entourage, at least until they are displaced by the largest buck. This competition among suitors usually assures that her offspring will be sired by the best buck she can find.

Dominant bucks will probably breed any doe, but they too may be selective if there is more than one doe in heat at the same place and time. Subordinate bucks are able to breed does when the dominant buck is not present, which can happen when several does cycle simultaneously. In other words, being dominant may not give a buck exclusive breeding rights, only first choice.

As the breeding season gets close, bucks begin checking does for signs of estrus. A doe nearing estrus telegraphs this by certain behaviors and by changes in her chemical cues, or pheromones. Does practice a special coquetry. They run from an approaching buck but not so far or so fast that he cannot find them. Sometimes several bucks join in, but if the doe is very close to estrus, usually the most dominant is first in the line of pursuing suitors.

A doe thus being chased often stops to urinate, apparently to provide the chasing buck with a pheromonal message about her reproductive status, to prime his reproductive processes, or both. The buck approaches the spot where she urinated and performs flehmen behavior, whereby he draws chemicals from her urine into the vomeronasal organ receptacles located on the roof of his mouth just inside the upper lip. If she is not nearing estrus, he may break off pursuit and search for another doe. Young bucks are less able to discriminate and are more likely to harass does that are not ready or even close to being ready to breed. Older, more experienced bucks waste little time with a doe that is not close to breeding.

Courtship or chasing of a doe approaching estrus may last a day or two and usually involves running circles several hundred meters in diameter. When the doe allows the buck to come near, breeding is imminent. Brown and Hirth noted that males employ a tentative low-stretch posture in virtually all

close approaches to females in or coming into estrus. The buck's head is lowered so that it is even with or below the line of his back. He usually moves his tail from side to side or flips it rapidly up and down.

The time when a doe is receptive is coordinated with ovulation so that eggs are available for fertilization by the buck's sperm. When she is physiologically ready for conception, she allows the buck to catch her. Warren and others reported that the buck licks her urogenital region or proceeds directly to chin-resting behavior, in which he presses his chin on the doe's rump. This seems to immobilize her. At this point the chase is over and she allows him to mount. Sometimes mounting proceeds without the chin rest, but it does seem to be an important behavioral cue. One way to determine whether a captive doe is in heat is for the human observer to place a firm hand on the top of her rump. If a doe responds by assuming the breeding stance, she is in heat.

In mounting, the buck slides his chin along the doe's back while straddling her with his forelegs. She may run out from under him on his first attempt, but more than likely intromission of the penis occurs. Intromission is quickly followed by the pelvic thrust, which can be violent. Both of the buck's hind legs sometimes leave the ground while he clasps the doe tightly with his forelegs. His entire weight may be placed on the doe, which drives her forward and down. She may even be knocked to the ground if the buck is very large or if she is small. The entire process from mounting to disengagement usually lasts only fifteen seconds or less.

Following copulation, the doe often exhibits a hump-backed postcopulatory stance. The tail may also be raised, giving her

what has been described by Hamilton as a "Halloween cat" appearance. The position is associated with contractions in the abdominal region. Warren and others observed repeated contractions of the vulva, and sometimes after several breedings, fluids dripped from it. This behavior may facilitate movement of the sperm to the egg or eggs.

After the first breeding, the buck tends the doe and often is observed licking his preputial area. The pair may or may not copulate again over the next several hours or even a day. While tending, the buck threatens others that approach by body postures, the grunt-snort-wheeze vocalization, and some-

To test her readiness to breed, or perhaps prepare himself for copulation, the buck licks the doe's fresh urine and, with a set of muscle contractions that produce the lip-curl grimace, transfers the material into his vomeronasal organ.

times rubbing his antlers on nearby bushes. When his right to the doe is seriously challenged, a dominance fight will occur. Such a fight is an all-out struggle that can result in injury or, on rare occasions, death of one or both adversaries.

When mature bucks are not present in the population or at least the immediate area, yearlings assume breeding duties. It is not clear whether they have as well-defined dominance hierarchies or are as defensive toward other bucks. Presumably the larger, more physically capable yearlings do most of the breeding. No documentation of this is available, however.

Just how many does a buck breeds in a season would certainly vary, depending on many factors. Severinghaus and Cheatum reported a situation in which twenty-one does were left in a pen, and a small buck with very small antlers was accidentally left with them. Nineteen of the does became pregnant. Obviously this buck did not have any competition, nor did he have to search for receptive does.

The rut is stressful to breeding bucks. They eat little during its peak and lose up to 25 percent of their body weight before it is over. This places them in a difficult situation as they enter the winter. Supplies of body fat may be exhausted just when the bucks need energy to get them through the winter. This is why the long, quiet summer is so important to bucks: it is the time when they replenish their reserves and grow their antlers. For bucks younger than 5½ years, it is also the time for physical growth. Marchinton and Miller have suggested that bucks may grow larger if they do not become breeders before their growth is complete—which can happen only if adult bucks are available for breeding duties.

Good breeding-season success depends on the food supply in summer and early fall. High-energy foods, such as berries during summer and acorns during fall, are critical. It is also important that populations be maintained at reasonably low levels and have balanced sex and age ratios. Wildlife biologists have sought to determine the harvest levels that can maintain herds in proper balance in the absence of natural predators. The concept of quality herd management, popularized by Brothers and Ray, is a good effort.

The length and intensity of the breeding season vary according to area and the characteristics of the herd. It is likely to be short and intense in the north and longer and less intense near the equator. The sex ratio and ages of bucks and does also seem to be factors. If the number of bucks, particularly older ones in the herd, is inadequate, some does may cycle late or not get bred during their first cycle. They may continue to come into heat for six months or more if they do not conceive during their first heat periods. But if enough mature bucks are present, breeding of adult does is essentially over in about three weeks. Fawn does that are large and fit enough to breed may come into heat later, thus stretching out the breeding season a little.

THE RUT ENDS

Bucks' sexual interest in the late season is affected by many things. After most does are bred, younger bucks that were not allowed to breed during the main part of the season may become more active and assertive in the search for any does that remain unbred. Miller and others noted that the testosterone levels and therefore sexual interest of young bucks go up after the larger bucks' activity begins to wane. Forand and March-

inton found that where the does come into heat over a long period and breeding effort is of lower intensity, the most dominant bucks stay active and maintain high levels of testosterone well into the winter or until all does are bred. But if breeding is very intense, they may burn out early, allowing younger bucks to breed.

Falling testosterone levels eventually precipitate antler drop. Poor nutrition or a highly intensive, stressful rut can cause early drops. In the Northern Hemisphere, bucks often lose their antlers before January, and most have lost them by mid-April. Regrowth is likely to begin in early May. Preparations for the next rut begin with the initiation of new antler growth, and the buck's annual cycle starts again.

—*R. Larry Marchinton and Karl V. Miller*

LEA

Doe behavior during breeding season

As bucks begin to rub the velvet off their antlers and engage in a long series of sparring encounters, adult does are found in family groups with their fawns of the year. By October and November, however, the adult female becomes less protective of her fawns, and the family group is frequently joined by yearlings, which Hawkins and Klimstra have shown to be her daughters. In parts of the United States and Canada where deer commonly feed in prairies or open pasture lands, larger groups with several does and their fawns may graze together, though in most whitetail range, where deer feed in or near woody cover, doe groups are small and represent a single family unit.

By fall, fawns have been weaned and direct physical contact between mother and fawns is limited to occasional grooming. The doe responds to occasional nursing attempts by the fawns with a kick or by walking away. Nevertheless, the experience, leadership, and social status of the doe are still important to fawns. Maternal experience may aid fawns in making seasonal changes in food. In northern parts of deer range, fawns follow their mothers to wintering areas, or deeryards, which may be some miles from their summer ranges.

Fawns enjoy their mother's protection and the benefits of her social status when they are with her; fawns without a mother have the lowest rank in the social system and can be harassed by any other deer, according to Townsend and Bailey. This harassment may be particularly critical in northern areas where food becomes scarce in winter and access to food and sheltered bedding sites becomes difficult. Intuitive as this may seem, in the one study that has looked specifically at the effects of orphaning in the late fall, Woodson and his associates could not demonstrate that the loss of a mother had any negative effects on the survival of fawns or yearlings. This work was done in Virginia, however, and the authors are careful to note that the loss of a mother could have a more serious impact in areas with more difficult winters.

TIMING OF BREEDING

In North America the whitetails' breeding season is triggered by changes in day length. As day length decreases in the fall, physiological changes result in readiness for breeding in both males and females. Does show no outward sign of change, but their approaching estrus is noted by bucks, perhaps

KINNEY

The doe releases small amounts of urine to communicate to bucks her reproductive status.

through scent. At least a month before breeding takes place, bucks begin to chase does on a regular basis. These early-season chases are frequent but lack intensity and usually don't cover more than 200 yards. Chases often terminate when the doe pauses to urinate. The buck responds by sniffing the urine spot on the ground and immediately seems to lose interest in the doe, departing in another direction.

Whitetails breed during November and December except in much of Florida and the Gulf Coast region, where winters are short and mild. Richter and Labisky have shown that peak breeding dates in Florida vary by as much as six months from the Everglades to the Panhandle. The breeding dates that they report for the Everglades population are more than two months earlier than breeding dates observed by Hardin in the Florida Keys—early August versus mid-October. Although these areas are less than 100 miles apart, different environmental conditions have selected for very different breeding seasons. What's important, apparently, is not when breeding occurs but when fawns are born: fawning occurs at the time of year most favorable to the young animals' growth and survival.

It is not clear what serves as the timing device for breeding among southern whitetail populations, which extend as far south as Colombia, Venezuela, and Suriname in northern South America. Breeding in these populations is still seasonal but apparently timed so that fawning does not occur during periods of adverse weather. In the coastal marshes of Suriname, for example, Branan and Marchinton found that the long breeding season was timed to avoid fawning in the fall dry season. And on the plains of eastern Colombia, Blouch reported, the breeding season was also long but timed to avoid fawning during a period of heavy rains in the summer. Because these areas are both within a few degrees of the equator, it seems unlikely that it is changes in day length that trigger breeding as in North America. Instead, these whitetails have adapted to local variations in annual weather patterns.

The duration of the breeding period varies with latitude. Near the northern limits of whitetail range, severe winter weather has a strong influence on the timing of births in the spring and therefore on the breeding season in the fall. Although fawns should not be born too early in the spring, their chances for survival are much greater if they are as old as possible at the start of winter. In northern areas of the United States and in Canada, the majority of does may be bred within a two-week period. In the South, however, MacDowell has shown that breeding may occur over a much longer period of time, one or two months in many cases.

Although decreasing day length is the primary timing device for estrus, the passage of a cold front may also be an important stimulus. A cold front in the second half of November may cause many does in a popu-

A young buck approaches a matriarchal group of does, focusing on one in particular; the other family members scatter. The selected doe keeps a watchful eye on him as he examines her urine spot.

lation to come into estrus simultaneously, with the result that rutting activity in bucks can be seen everywhere. Deer hunters frequently notice marked differences in buck activity that relate to stage of estrus. If few does in a local population are in estrus on a given day, there may be little movement of bucks, but if a cold front has just passed, bucks may seem to be recklessly traveling in all directions looking for receptive does.

OLFACTORY SIGNALS

Scent is an important medium for communication in most mammals, and it is a very significant part of the deer's world. Scent is used to communicate reproductive condition throughout the breeding season, but because humans' olfactory abilities are poor and we do not have the technology to study these scents outside a laboratory, the detail and subtleties of this form of communication are not known.

About one-third of all does will exhibit a bloody rump after copulation.

Early in the rut when bucks begin to chase does, it is apparently the scent of a doe's urine that causes bucks to give up their pursuit. This suggests that chasing at this stage of the rut occurs in response to changes in the buck's hormone levels and not to an obvious change in the doe's scent. Throughout the rut, bucks continue to test does by chasing and sniffing urine spots. The first real change in does' scent is signaled when bucks start to perform a lip-curl, or flehmen, after inspecting a urine spot. After lip-curling, a buck may continue to pursue the doe or he might give up the chase in favor of another doe. The work of Plotka and his colleagues has shown that progesterone levels in does suddenly increase ten to twenty days before estrus, and this change, or perhaps that of other hormones associated with estrus, may be reflected in the scent of their urine. When does are finally in estrus, scent is clearly important in conveying this information to bucks, although there are some behavioral changes as well.

THE ESTRUS CYCLE

In studies of deer in closely monitored pens, Warren has shown that the period of estrus in whitetails lasts about forty-eight hours. If a doe has not conceived within that time, her chances of producing a fawn the next spring are not over, because she will cycle again and come back into estrus at twenty-five- to thirty-day intervals over the next several months. In southern regions the survival of fawns that are born late may not be greatly jeopardized, but in the North fawns conceived in later estrus cycles and born in midsummer may have much less chance of surviving their first winter. Natural selection has set the timing of first estrus at the best date for birth of fawns in the spring, and those young born later in the season are less likely to make it through the winter.

During estrus, does become more restless than in the previous weeks. Ozoga and Verme have shown that the activity level of does in pens increases greatly the day or two before they become receptive to bucks. Studies of free-ranging deer with radio collars have shown several different activity patterns associated with breeding, however. Beier and McCullough in Michigan and Hölzenbein and Schwede in Virginia found that does typically remain within their normal home ranges during estrus and breeding. In fact, does even confine their activities

WERNER

to the core areas of their home ranges. This behavior makes the location of a doe more predictable to bucks that are searching and testing for does in estrus. Perhaps it is more efficient for half the deer population to remain in the same place while the other half tries to locate those members, rather than having the entire population roving simultaneously.

Scent marking by does within a small home range would make them easier for bucks to locate. Both Sawyer and Ortega have found, however, that some does may suddenly leave their normal home range for a short time (less than a day) during the breeding period and then return. It is tempting to speculate that these does left their normal areas because they weren't being discovered or visited by bucks. This might also explain why penned does without access to bucks become restless during estrus.

Older does and does in good condition come into estrus earlier than female yearlings and fawns. Working on the George Reserve in southeastern Michigan in 1979, McCul-lough showed that does generally conceived a little earlier as the deer population on the reserve was reduced and does were in better condition. In addition, yearling does conceived later than adult does; fawns, when they bred at all, were the last to come into estrus. Similar observations were made on the Welder Wildlife Refuge in south Texas by Kie and White in 1985. These authors reported that the mean dates of conception varied annually by as much as twelve days because of differences in the condition of does.

BREEDING BEHAVIOR

During the month before breeding, does are frequently chased by bucks testing their reproductive status. Otherwise there appears to be little change in the does' lives. Their home ranges remain the same, and they continue to associate with their fawns and other female family members. Chasing by bucks becomes more frequent as estrus approaches, however.

When a doe finally comes into estrus, a buck forms what is referred to as a tending

After the rutting buck has examined her urine, the doe allows him to sniff her. If she is ready to be bred, he will attempt to mount.

WERNER

FRANZ

Once a tending bond has been established, the doe is shadowed by the buck as she feeds and beds. Unless interrupted by another buck, the two will remain as a pair until they have copulated repeatedly.

seeing a buck chase a doe so hard that she lay down in apparent exhaustion. The doe Michael observed lay down three times in succession. In the case I noted, the buck nosed the doe's rear end until she got to her feet, ran slowly for a short distance, and stood for copulation.

After copulation, the buck stands next to the doe and may feed with her but with none of the tension that is so evident prior to copulation. There is no further physical contact between them. This postcopulatory stage is easy to recognize in the field because it is the only time during the breeding season a doe will allow a buck to stand side-by-side with her without trying to walk or run away.

It is not known how long two deer remain together following copulation, but I have observed pairs for more than an hour before losing sight of them, and Michael reported watching a pair for three hours. During this time, the buck continues to defend the doe from other bucks, just as he had done before copulation, and a postcopulatory buck may sometimes be driven away from the doe by a larger buck, just as happens before copulation.

There are several possible reasons for a buck to stay with a doe during this time rather than immediately starting to search for another doe in estrus. The chances for a doe to conceive may be better if she is allowed to stand or graze quietly after copulation. Or she may be willing to stand for copulation a second time, thereby increasing the odds that that buck will be the father of her offspring. Does in pens have been shown to copulate several times during a single estrus, and it may occur in the wild as well, although it has not been observed.

Bucks and does have entirely different patterns of breeding success. Does produce one or two fawns each spring from the time they are 2 years old. Bucks, on the other hand, are excluded from the breeding population until they are able to physically dominate most of their local rivals. Thereafter, bucks may breed a number of does. Clutton-Brock's work on red deer in Scotland has shown tremendous variation in the breeding success of different males, measured in terms of the total offspring sired, whereas there is

bond with the doe, and they separate from other deer. The tending buck attempts to stay with the doe until she is ready to stand for copulation.

Does appear to have little choice about which bucks tend or copulate with them. The breeding system among whitetails clearly ensures that the largest and fittest bucks in a given population will do most of the breeding. If a doe were to choose a smaller buck for some reason, he would very likely be displaced by a larger buck during the tending period.

Occasionally copulation may be forced on a doe that either is not ready or perhaps is trying to avoid a particular male. Both Michael in 1966 and I in 1977 have reported

The tending bond

In 1977 I pointed out that tending-bond status prior to copulation is easy to recognize in the field: The buck remains 5 to 10 yards behind the doe, staring at her, while she continues to graze or bed. If the doe turns to look at him, the buck looks down, thus avoiding eye contact with her, and takes a few mouthfuls of food. Every ten or fifteen minutes the buck slowly approaches the doe to test her readiness to stand for copulation. If she walks away when he advances, the buck stops and continues his vigil. During this time, the buck scarcely feeds. He beds only occasionally, when the doe he's tending has also bedded, and gets to his feet immediately if the doe gets up or if he sees another buck. The strategy of a tending buck is clearly to disturb or alarm the doe as little as possible. He will have little chance to breed her if he causes her to run from him by advancing too aggressively. And other bucks may discover her if he forces her to run.

Other bucks do in fact frequently discover tending pairs. Even if an estrous doe does not run, she cannot prevent her scent from attracting other bucks. Any buck is capable of tending and breeding a doe, but in most instances it is only the largest bucks that are able to establish tending bonds. Even a tending bond does not guarantee that that buck will be the one to breed the doe, however. In south Texas, where large deer populations afford greater opportunities for observation, it has been reported that a series of large bucks may tend the same doe before she is finally bred. Two or three tending bucks may be driven away from an estrous doe by successively larger and more dominant bucks in the course of one afternoon.

While a buck tends a doe, he also watches for other bucks that may be approaching. Smaller bucks are driven away quickly, but some small males are persistent and a tending buck may have to drive them away repeatedly. Yearling bucks may dash in on a tending pair in an effort to chase the doe away while avoiding any contact with the tending buck. If a buck that is clearly larger appears, the tending buck usually walks away from the doe with little hesitation. Apparently a fight is not worth the time, energy, or risk when the outcome is a foregone conclusion. At this point in the breeding season, aggression between bucks is serious, and a fight could result in injury or a broken antler.

Displacement of a tending buck can occur up until the last second. I observed one buck that had already mounted a doe get displaced by a larger buck before intromission could take place. The larger animal approached at a dead run, which caused the mounting buck to slide off the doe and flee. While the larger buck chased his rival, the doe ran off in the opposite direction and escaped both of them, temporarily at least. On another occasion a buck was driven away from a doe after copulation had taken place, and the new, larger buck took his position beside the doe.

The duration of tending bonds is not well established. It is difficult to keep a pair of deer under observation from the time a tending bond is formed until copulation takes place. Tending bonds certainly don't last for more than a day, and commonly a tending pair probably stays together for only a few hours. I reported one instance in which a marked buck and a doe were together for only forty-five minutes to one and a half hours before copulation took place.

—*David H. Hirth*

The doe may have led the buck in a circle, perhaps a quarter-mile or more in diameter, or forced him to negotiate obstacles before allowing him to rest his chin on her back and then mount her.

ANTUS

far less variation in the reproductive output of females.

POST-BREEDING SEASON

After estrus has passed and most does are pregnant, the excitement of the rut disappears. Does and their fawns can feed without continual harassment by bucks. Does maintain condition as best they can on poor winter forage. In northern regions, because herbaceous vegetation is covered with snow and ice, deer are limited to a diet of buds and the current year's woody shoots. South of the snow line they feed on dried forbs and grasses in addition to woody browse. In both regions winter is a time to minimize energy expenditure.

Studies by McCullough, Hirth, and Newhouse in 1989 using individually marked animals and by Beier and McCullough in 1990 using radiotelemetry have shown that bucks and does select different types of habitat, and therefore different types of food, during winter. Bucks choose areas that have greater quantities of lower-quality food. Does, on the other hand, occupy areas with smaller quantities of higher-quality food. They consume more grasses and less woody browse than do bucks, resulting in a winter diet with a higher protein content, as found by Beier in 1987 and 1988.

The selection of habitat is probably the result of the different metabolic demands placed on the two sexes. Because bucks are larger, their energy requirements are lower on a per-pound basis—they have lower metabolic rates—and they can afford to eat lower-quality food. Such food is easier to find, especially in the winter, so bucks can save energy by foraging less. Does, on the other hand, have higher metabolic requirements because of their small size and demands placed on them by pregnancy, and they must therefore select areas with higher-quality forage. It is not clear whether does actively exclude bucks from these areas with better food, or whether differences in habitat selection come about for reasons of efficiency.

—David H. Hirth

Does and their young

From the moment of birth, a whitetail fawn and its mother are partners in a clever and careful program designed to bring the newborn safely to maturity. Mother and fawn follow a cunning strategy of hiding and isolation to outwit predators. They go through the months-long activities of nursing, grooming, and playing until the fawn is prepared to join the greater deer family and the mother is ready to begin again with the next generation.

HIDING FROM PREDATORS

A whitetail fawn spends its first few weeks hidden in dense cover, visited only for brief periods each day by its mother. Mere hours after birth, the fawn stands for the first time. It also nurses for the first time, while either standing or lying down. Research by Bartusch and Lewis shows that after this initial bonding period, a doe may leave its fawn or fawns at the birth site but stay within about 90 meters (100 yards) for at least the first twenty-four hours after birth. Within the first day, twin fawns are moved to separate spots by their mother. By their second day, twins are on average about 90 meters apart. A study by Bartusch and Lewis and another by Jackson and colleagues indicate that for the next week or so, a doe visits her fawn or fawns only two to three times a day.

Separation of siblings and infrequent visits are key components of the hider strategy used by white-tailed deer. With twins widely separated, the chance discovery of one fawn by a predator does not jeopardize the other. By making only infrequent visits, the mother reduces the chances that she will give the hiding place away to predators that either see her or catch her distinctive scent. Newborn fawns themselves have little scent to attract predators.

In its first few days, a fawn begins to select a bedding spot away from its mother and to

HARRIS

The fawn's hiding locations are characterized by good cover and yet allow the young animal a view of its surroundings, even in the middle of a swamp.

Mutual grooming reaffirms the fawn-doe bond, which is essential for the fawn's survival. This fawn is old enough to be losing its spots but will continue to seek contact with its mother for up to a year.

LOCKE

DEER

move this hiding place frequently. Observation indicates that after nursing, a fawn walks some 14 to 28 meters (15 to 30 yards) from its mother to a bedding site in dense cover. The doe seems to pay no attention to the fawn's departure or to the location of the bedding place. By picking its own spot and changing it frequently, the fawn avoids having its mother's scent associated with its hiding place. Researchers discovered that when a doe is ready to see her fawn again, she simply returns to the general area where she last saw it. The doe may call the fawn with a soft bleating sound, or the fawn, already alert, may run to its mother before being called.

NURSING

Does let their newborn fawns nurse as long as they want. The first nursing bouts in an activity period have been observed to average about four minutes, with any additional bouts lasting about a minute each. But weaning takes place quickly. Gauthier and Barrette report that after two or three weeks, does terminate more than half of all nursing bouts. About this time, the fawn's stomach, especially the rumen, takes on adult proportions. By three weeks of age, fawns have begun eating vegetation after they finish nursing. By six weeks, does end almost all nursing bouts and fawns spend more and more time grazing. By ten weeks does reject most nursing attempts and terminate successful tries after only a few seconds. The fawns are now functionally weaned, obtaining almost all their food on their own by grazing or browsing.

LICKING AND GROOMING

During the first two to three weeks after giving birth, a doe typically licks the perineal region of her fawn while it is nursing, stimulating defecation by the fawn. The doe consumes the fawn's feces in the process, thereby removing another potential source of scent for predators. A doe seldom does this after a fawn is about three weeks old and less vulnerable to predators.

After a nursing bout, a doe usually spends several minutes grooming her fawn, concentrating on the head and neck. A doe will groom a fawn regularly through its first four

KINNEY

A fawn struggles to enter an atypical but excellent hiding place. It will remain there till its mother signals for its return.

months, although the frequency drops rapidly after four to six weeks. But in the fall, long after fawns are weaned, a doe will still occasionally pause to groom her fawn.

Grooming serves to reinforce and strengthen the mother-young bond that is so critical to the fawn's survival. During each grooming session, a doe is reminded of her own fawn's scent, and this enables her to distinguish her fawn from those of other does. In addition, by grooming the fawn's head and neck, the doe can remove any ticks or other ectoparasites that her young charge cannot reach on its own.

PLAYING

Play is a form of behavior that we think of as characteristic of young mammals, and whitetail fawns are no exception to this generalization. I reported in 1973 that week-old fawns begin short, infrequent bouts of playing. The basic component of play is a sudden dash away from the mother and back again, often with tail flagged. In fawns only a week or two old, these runs take the fawn 10 to 15 meters (33 to 50 feet) away from its mother. By the time the fawn is one to two months old, it may run as far as 50 to 100 meters (165 to 330 feet) from the mother. Does seem oblivious to this activity and continue to graze. As fawns become older their play runs are punctuated with bucking and zigzagging as they seem to dodge imaginary opponents or predators. My own observations and those of Michael in 1968 show

that fawns play only in the presence of their mothers and not while waiting for a mother to return. Play always occurrs after, not before, nursing.

Twin fawns most commonly play by themselves, and not together, but some interaction has been observed in which fawns playfully chase or kick at each other. In south Texas, where a number of does and their fawns may feed together in open areas, play by one fawn may stimulate play by the fawns of other does. Fawns continue to play often throughout the summer but do so less frequently by fall as they begin to assume adult behaviors.

The significance of play by fawns is probably twofold. First, it gives them practice in running and in eluding predators before they have a real need to do so. And second, the "playful" nature of this activity makes it clear to nearby deer that this is just make-believe, an important message to get across for play involving bucking, kicking, and other forms of mock aggression.

TIME TOGETHER

As a fawn gets older and makes it through the period of greatest danger from predators, mother and young can spend more and more time together. Jackson and colleagues have shown that visits by a doe to her fawns gradually increase from two or three a day during the first week after birth to as many as eight per day as the fawn enters its second month. The duration of each visit also in-

DRAKE

Successful mothers

*A*ge and experience seem to be important in the successful rearing of fawns. After observing a herd of captive whitetails in Michigan, Ozoga and his colleagues reported that fawns of experienced mothers (four years old or older) had lower mortality rates, even in the absence of predators, than fawns of younger mothers. The difference in maternal success was greater still when predators, in this case black bears, were present.

The researchers attribute these differences to the social dominance of older does. The older mothers were able to claim the best areas for their fawns in an enclosure almost a square mile in size. They used aggressive behavior to exclude other does and fawns from these sites and reared their fawns in the same areas year after year. The fawns of dominant does moved shorter distances during their first weeks of life, and siblings were more widely separated than the fawns of younger, subordinate does. These factors, along with better bedding cover, gave the fawns of the dominant does a greater chance of survival than those of less experienced does.

—David H. Hirth

MORRISON

Right: Fawns often play after nursing, while their mother is still in the immediate area. Twins don't usually play together until they are at least a month old.

If startled or aware of a potential threat, fawns freeze and experience a marked decrease in heart rate, called alarm bradycardia.

creases, going from less than thirty minutes to about an hour each time.

Twin fawns start to appear together with their mothers at about four weeks of age. No one has reported seeing siblings being reunited for the first time since birth, but it is easy to postulate that it happens when one fawn simply follows its mother as she moves off to tend her other fawn. After siblings are reunited, they seem to stay together whether or not their mother is present.

Research indicates that by the time fawns are between ten and thirteen weeks old, their daily activity patterns approximate those of their mothers. From this point on, fawns stay with their mothers all the time.

MATERNAL GROUPS

In woodland areas where groupings of deer are typically small, a fawn has contact only with its mother and sibling through the summer and early fall. By October, yearling does start to appear, and they remain part of these family groups through winter and early spring. Studies by Hawkins and Klimstra using marked deer show that these yearling does are daughters of the older doe. The yearlings may have spent much of the summer near their mother but were prevented from coming closer by the mother's aggressive behavior. Less frequently, extended family groups composed of several generations of does and their offspring also may appear.

In western portions of whitetail territory, where deer feed more often in the open and in larger units, fawns may be introduced to larger feeding groups by three or four months of age, as I reported in 1973. It is not known whether these larger doe-fawn groups are extended family units or are simply random collections of does and their fawns. In either case, the social experience of these fawns is much different from that of fawns with the limited contacts of the more typical woodland habitat.

Fawns stay with their mothers through winter and early spring. But as the May birthing season approaches, does prepare for their new offspring by isolating themselves from each other and from their previous fawns, which are now eleven months old. These new yearlings are driven away by their mothers and forced to strike out on their own. Yearling does may remain in the general vicinity of the mother, waiting for fall and their return to the fold, but male yearlings associate with other bucks and never rejoin the family group.

—David H. Hirth

WALLNER

Orphaned fawns

Occasionally a fawn tries to nurse from a doe that is not its mother, but these attempts are rarely successful. Although a fawn seems willing to nurse from any available doe, does seem very wary of being exploited by any fawn that is not their own. In a 1985 study, I observed that each time a fawn approached the wrong doe, the doe paused to touch noses, suggesting that scent is the key factor in identifying the fawn.

The subsequent reaction of the does was evenly divided between cases in which the doe simply ignored the fawn and those in which the doe repeatedly struck the fawn with her foreleg driving it away. In each of the few instances that the strange fawn did manage to nurse, the doe's own fawns were also nursing. My observations indicate that orphaned or lost fawns are seldom adopted by other does.

Other observers, however, Palmer in 1951 and McGinnes and Downing in 1970, reported adoptions by does that had lost their own fawns. In 1949 Severinghaus described four penned does that had lost fawns. Two of these does rejected substitute fawns, but the other two adopted new fawns readily. So fawn adoption does occur sometimes—but probably rarely—and only when a doe that has just lost fawns happens to encounter an orphan.

—*David H. Hirth*

Fawn behavior

A newborn fawn develops early in life the behavior it needs to survive. Even at birth the fawn is wonderfully equipped to escape detection from its enemies. Not only does its cryptic coloration (spots) help it blend into its surroundings, but the fawn can remain absolutely motionless for long periods. A warning snort or footstomp from an attentive mother is all that is needed for a newborn to crouch to the ground and not move. The fawn will use this hiding posture throughout life. Does, in fact, will use the same posture as their fawns to avoid detection, and both does and bucks will lie motionless, their heads and necks stretched flat to the ground,

Experienced mothers select good fawn-rearing habitat with secure, thick cover.

to go undetected while predators pass within a few feet of their hiding places.

The most critical period in a fawn's life is the first few weeks after birth. During this time, both its own behavioral responses and those of its mother are important to the fawn's survival. Soon after birth the mother will lead her newborn away from the bedding site. If she has twins, she will separate them by as much as 92 meters (100 yards), thus increasing the chance that one will survive should its sibling be discovered.

During the fawn's first few days, its mother rarely ventures more than 92 meters (100 yards) away. Observations of fawns in captivity show that they nurse two to eight times a day. At first, these nursing periods are the only time the fawns are active; they remain motionless when the mother is away. Each week as the fawn matures it ventures farther afield. At three days most fawns can outrun a man. At three weeks most can outrun a coyote, and at six weeks they have a good

RACHAEL

DVORAK

When the fawn is older, it chooses its own bedding sites.

CARTER

DRAKE

chance of outrunning a bobcat or lynx.

As fawns develop physically, they become more active and independent. In a 1989 study in Virginia, Schwede and coworkers reported that home ranges of fawns and their mothers increased weekly over the first three months of the fawns' lives. During this period fawns moved about half as far as their mothers, and most movement occurred when they were in their mothers' presence. At nine weeks of age the fawns' home ranges were close to the same size as their mothers' and by twelve weeks they became as active as their mothers. Similarly, a study by Jackson showed that fawns in South Texas increased their activity from 8 percent of the day during the first two weeks of life to 12 to 16 percent by the time they were a month old. Virginia researchers Schwede, Hendrichs, and Wemmer found fawn activity to increase from about 15 percent of the day at age two weeks to 60 percent of the day by twelve weeks of age. By twelve weeks there is little difference between the activity of the fawns and that of their mothers. Both studies found male fawns were more active than fe-

male fawns. Fawns are most active during the day, but as they grow older they become more active at night. Jackson found female fawns were more active than males during nighttime hours. By twelve weeks of age, both male and female fawns are travelers and much of their movement is made without the mother.

Deer rely on a complex set of communicative skills to survive. Does call to their newborn fawns with soft bleats and the fawns, wanting maternal contact and nourishment, bleat a response. If fawns are left alone for a long period, they will stand and bleat. When they are hungry, their bleating rises to a high-pitched cry. Fawns also make what is referred to as the "nursing whine," a series of low-pitched cries and moans made while nursing or attempting to nurse. This vocalization seems to strengthen the mother-infant bond and stimulates the mother to give maternal care. During and after nursing, the mother carefully grooms the fawn and licks and cleans the genital area to stimulate urination and defecation, removing scent that might help a predator find the fawn.

WALLNER

Another important vocalization is the distress call, a very loud series of bleats fawns make when they are being chased or have been caught by a predator. Adult deer respond immediately to this call, often responding to distress calls from fawns other than their own. Whole groups of does have often been observed coming to the rescue of a fawn being chased by a coyote or other predator. Even adult bucks will occasionally respond to this call, presumably coming to the aid of the distressed animal.

As fawns age, they not only become more active but also begin to interact with other deer. Play activity helps to strengthen their muscles and skills and enables them to escape danger with lightning reflexes. Play also helps fawns perfect the skills they will need to establish their place in the social order.

Fawns' play parallels adult social behavior. Male fawns engage in mock battles with overhanging branches, and mock fights with imaginary opponents, play activities that mimic scent marking, rubbing, and aggressive postures. Once fawns reach the age of five months, they begin to establish their position with other fawns in the social order. They occasionally fight with each other at favorite feeding areas. As with adults, the more dominant individuals stand on hind legs and use their front hooves to flail their adversaries. Aggression is sometimes even directed toward a tolerant mother who has ignored her hungry and impatient fawn. Fawns also engage in grooming each other and adults—a behavior that appears to be important in establishing social bonds and social rank.

Fawns often engage in play with their mother. In one common example, a fawn engages in a backward head-waggling dance, jumping straight up and landing on all fours, running fast in a wide circle around mother and back again. The doe pays no attention at first. Then, on the next pass by its mother, the fawn stops directly in front of her and she also begins the familiar head-waggle backward dance and makes a short run around the area with her fawn at her heels. As quickly as the round of play begins, it ends. The doe regains her serious maternal attitude, alert to potential dangers.

ANTUS

By following their mother, fawns learn her home range, including its boundaries, escape routes, and feeding sites.

Many of the social skills a fawn acquires are first established among siblings. Although twin fawns are first separated from one another by their mothers, as they age they begin to form close bonds and by a month and half are almost inseparable. They travel together when not in their mother's presence and exhibit many adult social behaviors, such as mutual grooming of the face and ears. The importance of these early social bonds is unknown, but undoubtedly they play a role in the deer's ability to socialize throughout life.

While a fawn is initially dependent on its mother's milk for nourishment, it soon begins to eat the same food as the mother. By two weeks of age, a fawn is nibbling on tender shoots and beginning to develop a ruminant stomach. By two months of age the four-chambered stomach is fully developed and the fawn probably could survive on its own without mother's milk. Fawns continue to nurse until they are between five and six months of age. Although bottle-reared fawns have survived in the wild on their own, early dietary behavior is significant to a fawn's survival. By following the mother and sampling the same foods she eats, fawns learn which foods are important. Deer do learn feeding behavior. Observations show that deer with no previous exposure to corn and apples will readily ignore these otherwise preferred foods.

Watering sites may be popular with other species. In this encounter, after failing to intimidate the fawn, the raccoon responded to the young deer's nip with a bite on the nose.

The last significant changes from fawn to adult behavior occur at the time of weaning.

Although most male fawns remain attached to the family group, they become more and more independent. If this independence is hastened by the loss of its mother, the fawn alters the otherwise normal behavior for yearling males: dispersing to a new home range. In 1992 researchers Holzenbein and Marchinton found that yearling males apparently are driven from their mothers' home ranges by their mothers but, if orphaned, most remain in the area of their natal home range. Some male fawns have been observed taking up with and traveling in association with adult males. Occasionally, close social bonds develop between male fawns and adult males. It is interesting to speculate whether these associations are unusual (perhaps linked to orphaning) or normal (linked to puberty).

Female fawns, like males, become more independent after weaning. However, they generally continue to maintain close social bonds with their mothers and remain in a loose matriarchal social group throughout adult life.

—Harry A. Jacobson

BUMGARNER

WHITE-TAILED DEER

Social organization

*T*he white-tailed deer is a remarkably wily, opportunistic, and adaptive creature. The species' immense behavioral and genetic plasticity has allowed it not only to survive in the wake of human progress but, in fact, to thrive. One reason for the whitetail's success as a species is its social organization, which provides for an orderly and efficient way of life. Members of a whitetail population function cooperatively and live as a society, as opposed to an animal aggregation, in which individuals interact pretty much at random. Such social harmony, which depends on individual recognition and communication, helps minimize tension and strife among individuals, increases survivability, and assures genetic fitness within the population. These behaviorisms are genetically linked and inherited.

The whitetail's social system, like that of any mammal's, is the result of complex interactions between external forces and internal drives. Deer are constantly receiving and responding to stimuli from their surroundings through sound, sight, touch, and smell, and to stimuli from internal sources, which are generally controlled by rhythmic seasonal changes in daylight, or photoperiod.

As with other ungulates, evolution of white-tailed deer social behavior can be related to such environmental factors as food quality and quantity, habitat characteristics, and predators. Regardless of the specific environmental stimuli involved, the whitetail's inherent social system is geared to provide for certain basic necessities of life, including exploitation of resources (food, cover, and water), predator avoidance, mating, and the rearing of young. These needs are best met by somewhat different behavioral strategies in different environments.

White-tailed deer are highly social beings. They live in complex social arrangements in a very competitive world, where such things as dominance rank and social alliances sometimes determine whether a particular deer lives or dies. Therefore, population density, sex and age ratios, genetic relationships, and other factors can have profound effects on behavioral patterns in any given area. Of course, these things are not static but change as deer populations flourish or fail.

SEXUAL SEGREGATION

Despite the complexities, there are basic patterns of social behavior among populations of whitetails, patterns that are similar in many respects to those of other north-temperate ungulates. As with mule deer, elk, caribou, and bighorn sheep, whitetails exhibit sexual segregation: bucks and does live apart much of the year. The basic social unit among female whitetails is a family group composed of a matriarch doe, several generations of her daughters, and their fawns. Male whitetails, upon reaching sexual maturity, join fraternal groups of compatible bucks. The group may be as small as two individuals or as large as seventeen. At certain times of the year, however, yearlings of

both sexes, mixed groups, or aggregations of both sexes and all ages may gather together.

Male and female adult whitetails live in separate social groups outside of the rut and prefer somewhat different seasonal food and cover. Both bucks and does show strong attachment to their established ranges, returning to their traditional grounds annually. The adaptive advantages of sexual segregation are hotly debated by researchers.

In a review of the various hypotheses to explain sexual segregation among north-temperate ungulates, Main and Coblentz concluded that males and females choose areas according to different criteria: Females select habitat that is best suited for rearing offspring, and males select areas that provide the best nutrition for the body and antler growth necessary for high dominance rank and improved breeding success. This explanation seems to agree well with what is known about seasonal variations in white-tailed deer social habits.

McCullough and coworkers, conducting research in the fenced-in George Reserve of southern Michigan, found that whitetail buck and doe ranges overlap most during severe winter weather and least during fawning season. My studies in the Cusino enclosure in Upper Michigan revealed overlap during the breeding season, as might be expected, and minimal overlap during the fawning season. However, I found adults segregated by sex even in winter, if food was plentiful and well distributed.

On northern ranges adult male and female whitetails intermix soon after snowmelt in spring, as they vacate their winter yards and return to their traditional summer ranges. At that time of the year, both sexes may wander extensively and intermingle peaceably as they forage on the highly nutritious, fresh new grasses and spring flora that abound in forest openings.

Segregation of the sexes commences with fawning, generally during late May or early June in the upper Midwest. An atmosphere of mutual avoidance develops between the adult sexes at this time of the year, but it is the doe's retreat to the seclusion of her traditional fawning grounds that leads to genuine social and spatial separation. Should a buck

Well before the rut, while still in velvet, a buck may flail at other members of the fraternal group. Points of contention may be feeding sites or violations of the established hierarchy.

WERNER

enter the fawning-rearing habitat of a doe with newborn fawns, the doe becomes the aggressor. She readily challenges the buck's presence with a menacing ears-laid-back stare, referred to as an "ear drop, hard look," and may even kick and chase the intruder to drive him away. Sexual segregation normally lasts about two or three months, until late summer or until fawns begin to socialize with other deer.

Favorable fawn-rearing habitat tends to be diverse, with interspersed openings and ample hiding cover for both mother and offspring. Dense ground-level vegetation— brush or lush herbaceous growth—is especially important for young fawns as hiding cover from predators. Islands of dense shrubs or trees are important for the doe as she attempts to remain concealed while maintaining a distant yet protective vigil over her vulnerable fawns. As offspring become older and better able to escape predators, habitat requirements and survival tactics for mother and fawns change.

By comparison, adult bucks appear less concerned with avoiding predators during late spring and early summer, the antler-growing period. Their first priority seems to be maximizing body condition, as they consume large amounts of nutritious but ephemeral forage. Given the sociable nature of bucks at this time of year and their tendency to frequent open, often elevated resting sites with good vantage, group alertness

Within an established hierarchy, the mere threat of a strike is usually enough: the low-ranking individual flees.

STRACENER

means that predators can be detected and eluded from a safe distance.

Soon after returning to their traditional summering grounds in spring, adult male whitetails do considerable scent marking of overhead tree limbs, possibly with secretions from their forehead glands or nasal sebaceous glands or with saliva. In some cases, they may even paw the ground and urinate beneath the scent-marked limbs, a behavior more commonly displayed during the breeding season. Although researchers do not yet understand the precise messages being conveyed, this behavior could serve to delineate a fraternal group's summer range and assist in segregating the sexes during the non-breeding season. Such behavior may intimidate other deer, including pregnant females seeking fawn-rearing solitude, and thereby reduce competition for resources and space during the critical time of antler growth and fawn rearing.

Whatever the reason, McCullough and coworkers emphasize that this niche separation of the adult sexes leads to "resource partitioning": Bucks and does do not compete equally for the same space, food, and cover resources year-round. Consequently, problems associated with food competition and malnutrition, such as impaired growth rates among young deer and reproductive failure among adult does, are invariably linked to high female density; the abundance of bucks has much less effect.

MATRIARCHAL GROUPS

The female whitetail's social organization presents a complex set of individual costs and benefits that have not been thoroughly evaluated. It is my view, however, that this system evolved both as a means of maximizing reproductive success despite the presence of predators, and as a way of making efficient use of food and cover resources, which probably changed suddenly and frequently during primeval times as wildfires, floods, and winds swept through a herd's range.

In the deer family (Cervidae), the usual pattern of range occupation is for male offspring to disperse and for female offspring to establish and defend fawn-rearing areas adjacent to their mother's range. Hence the basic female social unit is a matriarchy, whose related members share an ancestral range outside of the fawn-rearing season and in some environments periodically associate as a close-knit clan.

Related female whitetails are sociable most of the year. They recognize one another, probably by sight and smell, and strengthen their social bonds by periodic grooming, as they lick each other especially about the face, ears, and neck. The dominant animal usually initiates such behavior.

Once fawns are born, however, each mother isolates herself by driving away all other deer. In most instances, the doe must resort to a fairly violent repertoire of aggression to drive away her 1-year-old offspring, who have been dependent upon her guidance and have followed her faithfully during the previous twelve months. Such confrontations between mother and yearling probably start with the doe giving an ear drop, hard look. The doe might also kick or slap at the younger deer with her foreleg. Quite commonly, however, such interactions progress to a chase: The doe pursues her bewildered offspring, kicking and sometimes snorting at them, until they are driven out of the fawning-rearing area.

The mother of newborn fawns becomes secretive, is boldly aggressive toward neighboring deer, and adopts a form of territorial behavior that will last four to six weeks. During that period, some form of scent communication (possibly via urine or feces) by the dominant doe likely serves to deline-

BINEGAR

A yearling doe without fawns returns to her mother after the mother's new offspring is weaned. The family group will stay together until the rut.

WALLNER

A particularly productive site may have lured this buck into fawn-rearing habitat. His high rank permits him to drive a fawn away from lush forage.

ate her area, although this aspect of whitetail behavior is poorly understood by researchers. Whatever the mechanisms involved, other deer seem to get the message and willingly avoid these grounds. Whether the doe defends an area for fawn-rearing, however, or only the vicinity of the young fawn, is not entirely clear and is debated by biologists.

A young doe fawning for the first time usually selects and defends a fawning, or parturition, area next to her mother's. As related females increase in number, crowding over a period of years causes second-time mothers (usually 3-year-olds) to move a short distance away to establish new fawning grounds. This system helps the matriarch preserve her traditional fawning grounds, allows for maximum use of available habitat, and provides for an orderly expansion of the clan's range during times of bountiful food.

The young, inexperienced mother and her offspring also benefit from this intricate social arrangement. For one thing, the young doe more likely secures familiar, favorable fawn-rearing habitat with minimal competition from other more dominant, unrelated females. Also, there are certain antipredator advantages in being near older, related females more experienced in rearing fawns. Oftentimes, these experienced does will rush to the sound of any bawling fawn within the immediate vicinity, and sometimes inadvertently defend another (related) doe's young, because does don't seem to recognize the vocalizations of their own offspring. Consequently, when fawn-rearing areas are close, it is not uncommon to see two or even three related does rush to the site of a bawling fawn. Obviously, such aggressive and defensive behavior discourages predators and enhances survival prospects for the fawns. Furthermore, as the young fawns mature, these interactions help them integrate more easily into compatible social groups. Such integration is essential on northern range, where deer must learn to migrate long distances to reach good wintering habitat.

An exception to this general pattern of female range occupation was reported on intensively farmed land in Illinois, where forest cover was limited. Here first-time mothers dispersed long distances, frequently in excess of 20 miles in spring. Nixon and coworkers attributed the many female dispersals to the high annual survival rate of fawns and paucity of forest cover. In spring, preferred sites of upland shrub and successional forest cover were already occupied by older deer, and the corn was not yet high enough to provide adequate shelter, forcing young pregnant does to travel long distances.

The mother spends the first four to six hours with her newborn fawns at the birth site before moving siblings to separate beds. This initial period of nursing, grooming, and isolation seems essential in establishing, or imprinting, the mother-infant bond. Any disturbance during this critical time can lead to a breakdown in the imprinting process and ultimately lead to abandonment and death of the young.

Although the mother imprints upon her fawns within a few hours, the offspring are a bit slower. It may be several days, or possibly even a couple of weeks, before the newborn fawns become fully imprinted upon their mother. During the interim, the fawns risk being attracted to almost any large moving object—even humans. By keeping other deer away, the doe ensures that the fawns imprint on her alone.

If her fawns die, the mother resumes a sociable lifestyle within a few days. She then becomes more active and less secretive, travels a larger range, likely centers her activities in a different part of her home range, and allows her yearlings as well as other nonproductive female relatives to accompany her.

The newborn whitetail's chief defense against predation is hiding; the mother's territorial behavior, wide spacing of young siblings, separation from the infant, and relatively long-distance movements between consecutive fawn bed sites incorporate several sound antipredator strategies.

The mother visits, grooms, and nurses each fawn separately only two or three times daily, each time leading it 200 to 400 feet to a fresh, new bed site. Siblings are placed 100 to 400 feet apart. The mother calls her fawn with a soft mewing sound, but it is unknown what signals are employed to settle the fawn at a new bed site. The young fawn might move a few feet to a shaded bed on a hot, sunny day, or stand, stretch, and lie

down again at the same site. But otherwise it is highly dependent upon the doe for guidance, and generally stays put unless disturbed by a predator. The fawn thus stays within familiar habitat, unless the mother leads it elsewhere. In the process, within one or two weeks the young animal is introduced to its mother's fawning range and learns its boundaries.

Healthy fawns grow rapidly. By two weeks of age they are more likely to run from danger than to remain in hiding, and by one month they begin to initiate periods of activity independent of the mother.

Fawn siblings start bedding together when eighteen to thirty-two days old. The timing seems to hinge on the fawns' rate of physical maturation and behavioral development. It is my impression that twins and triplets raised by prime-age does develop more rapidly and therefore start bedding together somewhat sooner than those reared by young does. The chemical composition—that is, the quality—of the milk is no different, but mature does probably produce more. Much depends on the doe's nutrition. Malnourished does may produce no milk at all, and if nutrition is barely adequate, single fawns generally grow better than twins because there is no competition for what milk the doe has. But when food supplies are good, the mature doe can produce enough milk to nourish twins. The largest fawns of all are single males born to mature mothers.

Regardless of her age, a dispersing doe incurs considerable risk and competition when seeking new fawning grounds. She may settle in unsuitable fawning habitat or attempt to rear fawns within another doe's territory. As a result, the dispersing doe is less likely to rear fawns successfully.

In southerly environments the whitetail's breeding window is relatively wide, and fawns may be born over a period of several months. More than one doe, then, may ultimately raise fawns within a given area, although not at the same time. On northern ranges, however, breeding is more closely synchronized and most fawns are born during a comparatively brief period, from late May to early June. Under such circumstances, parturition behavior sharply limits the number of successful does in a forested cover, as no two does may simultaneously raise fawns in the same area (generally 10 to 20 acres). If deer density is especially high and suitable fawning sites are limited, many first-time mothers may abandon healthy offspring because of the lack of fawning solitude and resultant psychological stress.

The 2-year-old doe without fawns reverts to yearling behavior. That is, she likely associates with related nonproductive 1-year-old females and 1-year-old males during the summer months, then reunites with her mother during early autumn. Hence, maternal success largely determines the young doe's social standing and rate of behavioral maturation. The doe that fails to raise her first litter seeks her mother's leadership and resumes a subordinate role, whereas the maternally successful doe becomes a family leader.

Hirth found that does living in forested habitat of southern Michigan demonstrated fawn-rearing behavior similar to that described above. Those he studied in the savanna grasslands of Texas, however, behaved differently. In the open grasslands, fawns were commonly left in hiding while their mothers grazed in the company of doe groups or mixed groups. These sharply contrasting environmental conditions call for different maternal-care strategies, but both allow does to cope effectively with the constant threat of predators to their vulnerable newborn fawns.

Given good reproductive success, excellent nutrition, and consequent long life spans, matriarchal groups may become large and complex. A kinship group that dominates and shares a potentially large ancestral range may include not only daughters but also granddaughters, great-granddaughters, great-great-granddaughters, and so on. Logically, the larger the group, the larger the associated ancestral range. Also, because related female whitetails readily associate with one another outside the fawning season, members of a large kinship group may be able to range widely during most of the year with minimal conflict.

Since dominance among female whitetails is closely related to age, the older matriarchs and their daughters usually occupy the best fawn-rearing habitat. Female whitetails maintain a well-ordered social structure, however, and each individual knows its social standing. Behavioral dominance is seldom expressed except at parturition and seasonally at sites offering only limited choice forage.

During the fawn-rearing period a doe's hostility toward other deer diminishes after her offspring are about six weeks old. Thereafter she will more likely tolerate adult companionship and will probably expand her range to encompass more of that held by neighboring female relatives. Generally her nonproductive yearling daughters (and sometimes sons), or in some cases her 2-year-old daughters that failed to raise fawns, become her first frequent summertime adult associates. Observations suggest that it is the offspring, not the matriarch, who pressure for such association and leadership. These associations are most common when deer density is high and during those years when adult does experience unusually high mortality of newborn fawns.

Two-month-old fawn littermates are almost inseparable and spend about half of their time traveling, feeding, and bedding with their mothers. The young fawns gradually form more-complex social groups during summer. I have found that they are forced into association with other adult relatives sooner when deer density is especially high and many young does fail to raise fawns. Under such circumstances, the ten-week-old fawn may associate with an older sister almost as often as with its mother.

On northern ranges, there is a dramatic increase in the amount of social interaction among related female whitetails and their fawns in early autumn, when fawns are three or four months old. This annual regrouping is most evident in open areas, where deer gather to graze on succulent herbaceous growth stimulated by autumn rains. Such socialization, which is not so readily observed on southern ranges, presumably permits fawns to achieve close social bonds with adult females other than their mothers.

Since many northern deer migrate long distances (sometimes more than 50 miles) from summer to winter range, the doe-fawn social bond is probably necessary for fawns to learn lengthy migratory routes. Such

Grooming is an important social behavior. For twin fawns it's reciprocal and equal; for adults it may be a sign of submission, with the subordinate animal grooming the dominant.

guidance more likely ensures that fawns will find favorable protective winter habitat, and such grouping on winter range probably provides additional protection from predators. Does and fawns remain together during winter and migrate as a group back to summer range in spring.

Nelson and Mech propose that, in northern Minnesota, deer from individual winter yards represent distinct subpopulations of genetically related individuals, referred to as demes. Adult deer from each yard they studied were found to occupy summer ranges in largely exclusive areas, with minimal overlap among deer from neighboring yards.

These investigators emphasize, "This separation can last for years since adult movement patterns are traditional. Moreover, most yearling females establish home ranges on or near their birth ranges and continue the migration pattern of their mothers. This tenacity could lead to inbreeding between daughters and their fathers since dominant bucks probably maintain breeding tenure on their ranges for more than one year. Female philopatry could also lead to inbreeding with brothers and other close kin that never disperse."

Verme, who studied deer movement patterns in Upper Michigan, reached a similar conclusion. He suggested that a massive die-off of deer within a given yard would greatly reduce deer densities on the associated ancestral summer range for many years.

FRATERNAL GROUPS

From an evolutionary standpoint, all male deer compete to produce as many offspring as possible. Social organization among whitetail bucks minimizes the chance of chaotic and potentially dangerous situations in competition for mates. It is a system that allows breeding to proceed in an orderly and efficient manner.

Since breeding prospects among whitetail bucks are strictly determined by dominance rank, an individual's chances for mating are determined primarily by his age, body size, and physical strength relative to those of other males in the population. Typically, physically and behaviorally mature bucks (generally 3½ years and older) dominate younger rivals to the extent that it is a few older individuals that do most of the breeding.

The number of bucks 2½ years and older in an established fraternal group may vary greatly. Deer density and the sex and age ratios of the herd are big factors. In some areas where hunters intensively harvest antlered bucks, few if any bucks may survive to maturity and fraternal groups may be virtually nonexistent. Habitat characteristics can also influence group size, however: there is a tendency for larger male groups—five or more bucks—to form in open habitat; in forested habitat, especially where deer density is low, a buck group may consist of only two or three animals.

Based on investigations conducted on the Welder Wildlife Refuge in Texas, Brown suggested that male whitetails be categorized according to age and degree of behavioral maturity: immature deer, subdominant floaters, group core members, and dominant floaters. Although his work was conducted with a nonmigratory deer herd living in open habitat at high density (one hundred or more deer per square mile), his classification system may be applicable to other areas.

Immature deer. Considering the white-tailed deer's social system, the young male has little choice but to associate with other males. As a sexually immature individual he

LEA

is socially tied to the mother-young (matriarchal) social unit, but he must eventually break those bonds. When sexually mature, generally at 1½ years of age, he must begin to seek out and interact with older males, achieve fraternal group membership, and engage in hierarchial competition with other males over an extended period. He also must outlive his male companions if he is to someday become a dominant breeder buck.

Subdominant floaters. Most young male whitetails spend their second summer on familiar range, then disperse in autumn when about sixteen months old, but the timing of dispersal may vary from one section of the country to the next. For example, Nelson and Mech found that only about 20 percent of the males they monitored in northern Minnesota dispersed to new range when twelve months old, shortly after their mothers drove them away in spring. Rongstad found a similar springtime dispersal rate for yearling males in northern Wisconsin. In contrast, Nixon and coworkers found that half of the yearling males they studied on intensively farmed land in Illinois dispersed from April to June, when they were ten to twelve months old. Reasons for such variation are unknown but could be related to differences in maturation rates, deer density, sex and age ratios, newborn fawn survival rates, or habitat characteristics.

Although most yearling females regroup with their families in late summer or early autumn, the yearling male approaching sex-

ual maturity is harassed, dominated, and rejected by his mother and older female relatives. The aggressive behaviors are similar to those employed by the doe when she isolates herself with newborn fawns. During autumn, however, there seems to be less chasing, and the yearling male may find himself confronted with several hostile females, all related, at the same time. Although such group aggression may consist primarily of threat posturing (that is, the ear drop, hard look), a doe may strike the yearling with one or both front feet. In the latter case, she rises on her hind legs and comes down rather heavily with both feet. In other instances, the does seem to purposely avoid socializing with young related males. If grazing in an open area, for example, the does simply leave for heavier cover when they see the young male approaching.

The yearling male is automatically relegated to a low social rank within his family group and may display submissive behavior like that of female or juvenile animals in order to avoid aggressive interactions. Oftentimes, the yearling makes low-profile, slinking movements when near female relatives—quite opposite the flaunting behavior more typical of dominance displays. As a result, the yearling male that remains with related females during the rut in all likelihood becomes a psychological castrate.

This intense social pressure from female relatives forces most male whitetails to disperse when about 16 months old, shortly before breeding starts in autumn. They may travel 2 to 20 miles. High deer density tends to create excessive intrafamily strife, which contributes to a longer dispersal distance. Those males that do not disperse at yearling age (probably fewer than 10 percent) normally do so the next autumn, when 2½ years old. Such male dispersal minimizes the chances for mother-son and brother-sister inbreeding.

Maternal domination is very important in prompting dispersal among young male whitetails. Holzenbein and Marchinton compared the behavior of male whitetails orphaned as weaned fawns (seven to ten months old) with that of others that matured with their mothers. By 30 months of age, only 9 percent of the orphans had dispersed to new range, but nearly 87 percent of the others did so. Interestingly, not only did fewer of the orphans vacate their natal range, but as a group, they also exhibited better survival rates. Since this investigation dealt with a nonmigratory deer herd, however, it is not known whether young orphaned migratory bucks would respond similarly.

Why a young, sexually mature, dispersing whitetail buck eventually settles in a certain area is unknown. As noted by Brown and Hirth, the yearling buck temporarily associates with various male and female groups during autumn, hence the term *subdominant floater*. I suspect that the young floater's acceptance by members of the resident fraternal group is a major factor in determining where he settles.

Yearling bucks with velvet-free antlers seem compelled to search out and interact with other bucks during early autumn, before breeding starts. Initially the yearlings spar with other bucks in a highly ritualistic and congenial manner, unlike the more serious push fights that may erupt later on. It is the yearlings that seem to provoke antler contact with older males—very likely an essential step in the complex social development of the young buck that is striving for fraternal group membership.

Regardless of age or body size, all bucks spar. A sparring match often begins when one buck lowers his head and presents his antlers to another. The second buck usually

REZENDES

accepts the invitation and engages his antlers with those of the challenger. The two bucks' antlers are then clicked together with minimal pushing or shoving, and the match may end abruptly with no apparent winner or loser. Such early-season sparring may involve bucks evenly matched or completely mismatched in age, size, or rack.

The amount of physical exertion involved in sparring increases as the breeding season nears, and such interactions may develop into push fights, which are true tests of physical strength. Unlike sparring matches, however, push fights almost always involve bucks of similar body and antler size. Such contests allow bucks to gradually assess one another's strength, with minimal risk of injury, and help establish a firm dominance hierarchy well in advance of the primary breeding season. This social order minimizes unnecessary fighting later on, helps conserve energy, facilitates selective mating by physically superior sires, and assures genetic fitness within the herd.

The mature buck's behavior changes markedly right before the rut and his social tolerance of other males sharply declines. Yearlings may continue to spar among themselves and possibly with low-ranked older bucks, but dominant bucks seldom tolerate such behavior during the primary breeding period.

Eye contact seems to play an important role in aggressive interactions among antlered bucks (and probably all deer at various

Yearlings of both sexes—young does without fawns and young bucks not yet accepted into fraternal groups—socialize with each other. The young bucks quickly establish dominance over the does.

ANTUS

times of the year). If two mature bucks enter an open area, look directly at each other, then approach at a walk, aggressive behavior is certain to follow, with an obvious victor and loser. Oftentimes, the outcome is predictable, even if the two are still some distance apart. The dominant buck is more likely to display elaborate threat postures – the ear drop, hard look stare, bristled back hair, and deliberate stiff-legged gait – as he approaches his adversary. He may hold his head low while turning his antlers from side to side. If the second buck assumes a similar approach, however, the two animals are likely to sidle up to one another and a push fight likely results.

Thomas and coworkers were probably the first to describe the sidle action: "The buck turned his head and body approximately 30° from his antagonist, head erect and chin tucked in, and took several sidling steps toward his adversary. Arrector pili was pronounced. If the adversary was a male, he might duplicate the action. If retreat had not occurred by this time, the 'antler threat' was employed. In this threat the head was lowered so that the tines of the antlers pointed directly toward the rival." These investigators noted that retreat nearly always occurred sometime before this stage of aggression. If not, the two bucks then might suddenly crash their antlers together in a serious push fight.

If the two rival bucks have already encountered each other, and if one had emerged the

The admittance of a new member to a fraternal group prompts a reorganization of the social hierarchy. Because these bucks are still in tender velvet, the rankings are determined not by sparring but by flailing with the forelegs.

BIGGS

victor, the subordinate individual may suddenly break eye contact, gaze almost lazily into the distance, or commence sham grazing. Such a show of submission normally causes the dominant animal to relax as well, and the two bucks might then forage together peaceably.

Group core member. According to Brown, the real stability within a given fraternal group rests with two to four mature core members that achieve true social bonds. Observations suggest that core members are unrelated and that most are 2½ to 4½ years old. Even within these groups, however, certain pairs of males develop the strongest attachments.

Aggression among mature core members of a fraternal group is generally infrequent and not very intense. And although these groups break up during the breeding season, when adult bucks become solitary travelers, core members usually reassociate following the breeding season.

Dominant floater. Called hermit bucks by some hunters, dominant floaters tend to be large, mature bucks (probably 5½ years or older) that maintain a high dominance rank. In Brown's study area, these animals associated with all sorts of deer groups, including several buck groups, but did not develop prolonged associations with any particular deer. During the rut, dominant floaters tend to travel an atypically large area, likely encompassing the home ranges of several fraternal groups.

Whitetail bucks are not considered territorial in the strict sense because they permit male associates to travel the same breeding range. The dominant individual does not defend a breeding range against other males but instead tolerates them as long as they maintain subordinate postures. The hierarchy of relationships is established among bucks before the breeding season.

Dominant rutting bucks employ a complex array of scent-marking behaviors in the form of ground scrapes and antler rubs. These convey important messages regarding male identity and dominance to both sexes. Some researchers contend that buck scrapes serve as dominance areas where the scrape maker enjoys a higher dominance rank than he might hold at some other location. Supporting evidence indicates that subordinate bucks sometimes behave cautiously in the vicinity of a dominant buck's scrapes or may avoid these sites altogether.

Because yearling males can generally be found with older bucks after the rut, it seems reasonable to assume that the yearlings achieve fraternal group membership through association with other members just before or possibly during the primary breeding season. Nelson and Mech suggest, however, that a buck may require two to three years to form a home range, at least among migratory northern deer living in areas of low density. Some male dispersers continued to visit their birth ranges and reassociate with their mothers when twenty-two

153

MASLOWSKI

severe winters, congregations of deer may exceed three hundred animals per square mile in some areas of dense conifer cover, making it difficult to identify social groups, especially after bucks have cast their antlers. On the other hand, during abnormally mild winters, even northern deer may not migrate to traditional deer yards; fraternal groups could then reform on their established breeding ranges. Whether the sexes separate during winter, then, may depend on environmental factors that vary from one year to the next.

YEARLING GROUPS

Some yearlings, both male and female, that are driven away by their mothers in spring band together into exclusive groups. These yearling groups are most prevalent in forested habitat where deer live at moderate to high density, especially if doe fawns seldom breed, adult does are routinely successful in raising fawns, and overwinter mortality is minimal. Nonproductive yearlings of both sexes, however, are more likely to spend the summer with their mothers or older sisters if the older does fail to raise fawns.

According to Hirth, exclusive yearling groups seldom develop in the savanna grasslands of Texas. In such open habitat, yearlings more commonly join doe groups, mixed groups, or sometimes even buck groups during summer.

In northern Michigan, I have observed that both male and female yearlings tend to concentrate their summer activities within familiar ancestral range as they travel the vacant corridors between adjacent does' defended fawn-rearing areas. Yearling siblings of both sexes usually remain together throughout the summer, but the males may periodically take off on brief exploratory forays several miles into strange habitat. In some cases, five or more related yearlings may coalesce. Members of such groups normally maintain close association until autumn, when the females reunite with their families and the males disperse.

MIXED GROUPS

Large mixed groups of bucks, does, and fawns can occasionally be seen in open habitat. These gatherings are especially evident

to twenty-seven months old. In one case, a male used his birth range for three months when 2 years old even though he had established a new range the previous autumn.

Whether northern bucks migrate to winter yards alone or regroup before migrating is not known. It is likely that they migrate alone, at least in some years, since inclement weather sometimes triggers movement during the breeding season, when bucks are still solitary. Once in the wintering area, however, members of fraternal groups likely reunite and spend the winter together, just as they do in nonmigratory herds.

Though sexual segregation during summer is well documented among whitetails throughout the species' range, the degree to which the sexes separate in winter seems to vary regionally. In Texas, where deer are not subjected to harsh winter weather and do not migrate, the sexes readily separate and bucks regroup after the rut.

In northern areas, however, segregation of the sexes may not be so evident (or may not occur at all, according to some investigators) after deer migrate to winter habitat. During

Sensing a threat, the doe stamps a forefoot in alarm. As is customary for deer in group settings, the animals avoid eye contact; a direct stare would be perceived as a threat

SCOTT

Bucks do not usually share range with does and young fawns. Segregation of the sexes during summer ensures that the fawns will have the food and cover best suited to their survival; bucks search out areas of high-quality food with less concern for secure cover.

LEA

during early autumn before the breeding season and seem to occur throughout the species' range.

Such complex associations may consist of a number of separate matriarchal, fraternal, and yearling social groups, with each component going its separate way when the association breaks up. Deer seem to enter into such groups voluntarily and in some instances actually seem attracted to them. For deer exposed in open habitat, this tendency to congregate may be a protective adaptation against predators.

Although large mixed groups may occur chiefly in response to concentrations of nutritious forage, the autumn gatherings seem especially timely and suspiciously social in nature. These complex associations undoubtedly permit herd members to interact and communicate critical information just before the breeding season.

As Geist has noted, both male and female whitetails may exhibit grazing postures as a signal of submission or nonaggression, especially when deer are close together. Also, subordinates may crouch, depress their backs, press their tails between their haunches, hold their heads low, pin back their ears, and avoid eye contact while moving past dominant deer. Adult does, especially, may slink on their bellies, heads and necks extended over the ground, performing turning motions with their heads as they move out of the way of large bucks.

SMITH

Certainly prerut socialization represents a unique experience for young fawns. These gatherings also encourage male interactions, necessary in the establishment of fraternal group bonds and a dominance hierarchy, well in advance of the primary breeding season. Such socialization generally ceases on northern range just about the time the first does breed.

AGGREGATIONS

In contrast to the voluntary congregation of mixed groups, an aggregation is a gathering of deer forced together by limited food or cover. One of the most common examples of such behavior occurs on northern ranges, where deer that had been scattered across summer range concentrate during winter in deer yards with dense conifer cover. Such yarding behavior is presumably an energy-conserving and predator-defense adaptation for winter survival, since the evergreens afford protection from cold temperatures and deep snow.

Matriarchal and fraternal groups may maintain their distinction in some natural wintering areas, with the males grouped in peripheral cover. Adult males, being larger and having less surface area in proportion to body size compared with younger males and females, lose less body heat during cold weather. This fact might explain the buck's ability to occupy habitat with less overhead conifer cover; such habitat usually offers more browse than the typical deer yard.

Wintertime timber harvesting and supplemental deer-feeding operations sometimes attract aggregations of five hundred or more deer per square mile on northern ranges. These practices may contribute to excessive aggression and social strife among deer as the animals compete for food. Because the dominant animals have access to greater quantities of the more nutritious foods, social position may determine whether a deer lives or dies during a prolonged winter.

Deer may initially fight viciously for food at these sites of winter concentration, especially when evenly matched individuals meet for the first time. Such an encounter likely starts with direct eye contact, followed by the stereotyped ear drop, hard look. Gener-

ally, the dominant animal strikes the subordinate with a foreleg, or sometimes lunges or rushes at the adversary while emitting a snort to enhance the effectiveness of non-contact threats. Adult does, for example, commonly employ the rush or snort, or both, to dominate adult bucks. When neither individual backs away, however, the two animals may then rise on their hind legs and slash or flail at each other with their forefeet. This action normally takes place between evenly matched animals of the same gender, or between evenly matched fawns, but sometimes involves a buck and a doe. It usually lasts for only a few seconds before the subordinate drops to a normal stance and retreats a few yards, acknowledging defeat.

Seldom do dominant animals chase subordinates long distances when competing for food in winter. Instead, submissive displays, which may be as simple as avoiding eye contact and moving aside, frequently enable subordinate animals to remain with a given group of deer and feed at the periphery.

Even in situations involving several hundred deer, a relatively stable dominance hierarchy develops in which individuals recognize one another, recall previous conflicts, and learn their social standing in the herd. As the winter progresses, the frequency of conflict over limited food may increase but the intensity of combat decreases, as most late-winter encounters are settled via stereotyped aggressive postures rather than by outright physical contact. Likewise, totally debilitated deer, including those that are injured or weakened from extreme malnutrition, lose any tendency to be aggressive.

Wherever deer compete aggressively for limited food, adult bucks (2½ years and older) usually dominate all other deer, and adult does dominate fawns. Does 2½ to 12½ years old usually rank below the large males; elderly does and yearlings of both sexes rank just ahead of most male fawns. Doe fawns commonly hold the lowest rank.

Top-ranked individuals tend to show less aggression toward smaller animals that maintain submissive, low-profile postures. Low-ranked fawns also often benefit from being closely associated with high-ranked female relatives, thereby gaining better-than-expected access to limited food. Hence, although fawns normally fare poorly in competition for food and make up the bulk of the malnutrition-related deaths, many survive prolonged winters despite their submissive behavior.

Large aggregations of deer are not restricted to dense winter yards. Even after snowmelt, deer may congregate for several weeks in open areas adjacent to conifer cover. These openings are the first to become snowfree and offer new lush herbaceous growth for grazing.

—*John J. Ozoga*

Deer talk: sounds, smells, and postures

The white-tailed deer is often called elusive, secretive, silent, wary. Descriptions like these give the impression that deer lack a complex communications system. This is far from the truth. Research by behavioral scientists is just beginning to open the doors to this animal's elaborate social communications system.

In addition to vocal signals, whitetails also use chemical and visual signs to relay information, which makes their communications system difficult to decipher. In fact, vocal communication appears to play only a minor role in the day-to-day life of the whitetail. Deciphering the other forms of communication requires intensive and detailed observation of behavior, along with sophisticated analytical equipment.

Whitetails are social creatures, living in either matriarchal or bachelor groups for much of the year. Within these groups, deer use a variety of signals to communicate with one another, including a number of vocalizations, body language, and chemical signals. The signals are often very subtle, and because they are used to communicate among members of a group, they generally are effective for only a short distance.

A different strategy is required for communication among individuals that are not members of a particular group. Whitetails live in an environment that is often thickly vegetated; therefore, neither visual displays nor vocal signals would be effective for more than a short distance. Instead, they use a system of scent communication that involves placing "signposts" throughout their range. These signposts relay information on the identity of deer in an area, including their sex, dominance status, and reproductive condition. Signposts are very important in the breeding behavior of whitetails. During the rut, rubs and scrapes communicate dominance status among bucks and also advertise the buck's availability to potential mates.

VOCAL COMMUNICATION

As early as 1926, Newsom recognized that whitetails produce a variety of vocalizations. Later, in 1937, Seton also described some of their vocal expressions. It was not until the 1980s, however, that the vocal repertoire of whitetails was recorded and characterized. This was done by Richardson and coworkers in Mississippi as well as by Atkeson and associates in Georgia.

Using sensitive recording equipment along with detailed observations, these two groups recorded a variety of sounds produced by deer. The Mississippi group distinguished seven vocalizations; the Georgia team recorded twelve. This variation generally reflects differences in the interpretation of the sounds recorded.

Alarm and distress calls. The snort is probably the most widely recognized of the whitetail's calls. It is not actually a call but a sound that results from air being forcibly passed through the nasal passages. Snorts are

A rutting buck frequently tests the air, sniffing for rivals and estrous does.

MASLOWSKI

LEA

given in two distinct situations: when startled at close range, a whitetail often gives a single, very short, explosive snort at the moment it begins its escape. When a deer detects danger at a relatively safe distance, it often will produce a series of slightly longer snorts. Hirth and McCullough found that members of doe groups are much more likely to snort than members of buck groups. They suggested that these snorts serve to alert other related members of their group.

The bawl is a very intense call given only by deer in extreme distress, such as when injured or restrained. Deer of all ages may bawl, with the pitch decreasing as the deer grows older. Bawls by fawns may elicit defense by the dam. Smith in 1987 reported that fawn bawls elicited aggressive assaults in 30 to 87 percent of the instances he observed. He suggested that the differences in the tendency to defend the fawn were related to the physical condition of the mother.

Agonistic calls. Agonistic, or aggressive, calls consist of a low, guttural grunt, with other elements added as the intensity of the encounter increases. The lowest-intensity call is the low grunt alone. It is given by both bucks and does during all seasons of the year. The low grunt coupled with other visual signals such as the "head-high" or "head-low" threat is often used to displace a lower-ranking individual.

In more intense encounters, one to four short, rapid snorts are added to the low grunt. During the rut, bucks often give the grunt-snort during dominance interactions with other bucks. Females also occasionally give this call.

The grunt-snort-wheeze, produced only by males during the rut, consists of the grunt-snort coupled with a drawn-out wheezing expulsion of air through pinched nostrils. It is the most threatening call produced by bucks and often precedes a dominance fight.

Maternal and neonatal calls. The maternal grunt is a low-intensity grunt that can be heard for only a short distance. This call is given by the female while she is approaching a fawn's bedding area. The fawn responds to the maternal grunt by leaving its bed, moving toward the dam, and often nursing. When fawns become old enough to travel with their mothers, the does often use the maternal grunt to maintain cohesiveness among the family group.

Fawns often produce a high-pitched mew in response to the maternal grunt. The mew is used to solicit attention from the mother. The fawn bleat, similar to the mew, is a more demanding care-soliciting vocalization. The bleat is a more intense call—whereas the mew can be heard for only a short distance, the bleat can be heard by humans up to 100 yards away. The intensity of the bleat is directly related to the degree of need—hunger, thirst, social contact—of the fawn. Fawns also bleat when disturbed from their bedding sites, often bringing nursing does to investigate. Fawn bleats have been used successfully by both deer researchers and hunters to attract does. The successfulness of this technique decreases during late summer as fawns grow older.

During suckling or while searching for a nipple, fawns give a brief, low-intensity nursing whine. Richardson and coworkers suggested that the nursing whine may help identify the fawn, reaffirm the maternal bond, transmit pleasure, and solicit additional attention. In response, the dam may provide continued or intensified comfort and security by grooming or additional nursing.

Mating calls. Two sounds are produced by males during courtship: the tending grunt and the flehmen-sniff. Only the tending grunt can be classified as a vocalization, however. This low, guttural call is made by rutting males, most commonly while tending a doe in heat, but also frequently while traveling in search of females. Tending grunts seem to be made most often by mature, dominant males and rarely by younger bucks.

The flehmen-sniff is a sound produced infrequently by rutting males while performing flehmen, or lip curl. This behavior is associated with the buck's investigation of urine via the specialized vomeronasal organ. The flehmen-sniff appears to be merely a byproduct of this action and most likely has no communicative function.

Contact call. The contact call is occasionally made when an individual becomes separated from a group. This call is similar to the low grunt and the maternal grunt but is longer and has higher tonality and intensity, along with varying inflection. The contact call has thus far been reported only from females.

VISUAL DISPLAYS

Social groups of deer use a number of visual cues to communicate with other members of the group. Most of these signals are very subtle and often go unnoticed by the human observer. They are readily observed by other deer, however, and are used to convey a variety of information, such as dominance status, aggressive intent, and alarm. They are also used in courtship displays and in interactions between mother and neonate.

Aggressive intent. Other than overt attacks, whitetails use two types of visual displays to communicate aggressive potential in an attempt to dominate or master another individual. Threats signal an intent toward overt aggression, whereas dominance dis-

plays serve more to intimidate or challenge a potential rival.

The lowest form of threat is the ear drop, in which the ears are laid back along the neck; this is coupled with a direct stare by the aggressor. More-aggressive postures have been defined by Hirth as the "head-high" and the "head-low" threats. The head-high posture signals the aggressor's willingness to rear onto its hind legs and flail the recipient with its front legs. This threat is used most commonly by does throughout the year and by bucks while their antlers are in velvet. The head-low threat signals an intent to chase and strike the opponent with a foreleg. During the breeding season, males also use this threat to indicate a willingness to use

A doe uses a grunt to maintain the cohesiveness of her family group. Recognizing the sound of its mother, the fawn draws near.

Failure to acknowledge the dominance of a matriarch is met with an aggressive behavior: the doe lays back her ears and fixes the challenger with a hard stare. This signals that she will rise and strike at the challenger with her sharp front hooves.

Deer exhibit extremes of aggression and submission, from this buck's threatening ear-drop and stare to the ultimate posture of appeasement, the crouch.

their now hardened, polished, and tested antlers as weapons.

In contrast to threats, dominance displays draw attention and advertise status. These displays are used almost exclusively by males during the breeding season and are always accompanied by threatening postures.

A dominance display by a mature whitetail is a sight to behold. When displaying to an unfamiliar potential rival, the buck assumes a dominance posture: the ears are laid back along the neck, the eyes are held wide open, and all of the deer's hair stands on end. This piloerection helps make the buck look darker and larger to his rival. In a dominance display, the preorbital gland and the nostrils are commonly flared open. Beads of moisture appear on the buck's muzzle, and there often is noticeable drooling.

Dominance displays include not only visual signals but also vocal and chemical cues. A buck will often thrash a bush with his antlers, rub-urinate, or make a scrape. A grunt-snort or a grunt-snort-wheeze signals his willingness to carry this interaction toward further aggression.

During dominance displays, a mature buck approaches a rival at an angle with a slow, stiff-legged gait. This behavior, called sidling, allows the buck to display his body size and his antlers simultaneously without making himself unduly vulnerable to attack. Most encounters end at this point, with the smaller buck assuming a submissive posture or retreating. A vicious dominance fight may erupt if the two bucks are similarly matched, however.

Courtship displays. The communicative displays associated with courtship and breeding have been described in detail by Warren and coworkers in 1978 and by Brown and Hirth in 1979. During estrus, females are not known to display any overt visual signal to the male indicating their reproductive status and willingness to breed. Estrous advertisement appears rather to be largely an olfactory cue.

Alarm displays. When they detect danger or potential danger, whitetails use a series of visual displays in addition to the snort. The most conspicuous is the tail flag, from which the species gets its name.

WALLNER

Upon encountering an unknown object, a whitetail assumes an alert posture. The head is held erect, and ears are cupped forward in the direction of the stimulus. Depending on the degree of alarm, the tail may be held partially or fully erect to expose its white underside and the white rump patch. This display alerts other members of the group, who likewise assume an alert posture. If the danger is not identified, the deer may either retreat with a bounding, tail-flagging gait or further investigate the unknown object. Whitetails are curious animals and often will not flee until the object of concern is identified. Apparently, deer do not have very good depth perception; thus they will move toward or parallel to the object or will move their heads from side to side to get a glimpse from another angle.

Accompanying this investigation, a deer often will stamp one or alternating forefeet. This stamping might function to urge a potential predator to move and reveal itself, or to release scent from the interdigital gland as a further warning to other group members, or both.

Unless surprised at close range or greatly alarmed, whitetails expose their "flags" when fleeing. Contrary to popular opinion, bucks and does flag with approximately equal frequency when alarmed. In a study conducted on the George Reserve in Michigan by Hirth and McCullough, buck groups flagged in 91 percent of the encounters with humans, whereas doe groups flagged in 95 percent of encounters.

But why would an individual expose a conspicuous white tail patch to a predator? Wouldn't this make it easier for the predator to pursue the animal and thereby decrease the deer's chances of survival? Perhaps the most logical explanation of the causes and consequences of tail flagging was presented by Hirth and McCullough in 1977. Many species of ungulates have conspicuous rump patches. In general, social species living in relatively open habitats, such as the elk *(Cervus elaphus)*, have white patches that are not hidden by the tails. In contrast, many solitary species that live in dense vegetation, such as the musk deer *(Moschus moschiferus)*, have no conspicuous rump patch at all. Apparently, the white rump patches have evolved among gregarious species as a means of maintaining group cohesiveness. White tails fall between these two extremes—they are social animals that live in heavily vegetated habitats. Therefore, they have evolved an "on-again, off-again" rump patch. At most times the patch is concealed beneath the tail, and they can rely on their camouflage coloration to avoid predation, but when they are discovered they can use the tail flag to maintain the cohesiveness of the social group while fleeing. Whether they flag or snort in the presence of danger depends on the closeness of the threat.

Groups of bucks or does may react differently to intruders under different circumstances. If danger is detected early, either visually or by scent, and there is a chance to escape undetected, members of buck groups and doe groups respond in very different ways. Does likely will snort to warn other group members about the possible danger. Since doe groups tend to be closely related, it is to their advantage to risk detection to warn their relatives and thereby "maximize their inclusive fitness," or help ensure the

Deer signal alarm by stamping the forefoot. In addition to that visual sign, there may be a chemical one as well: the interdigital gland is thought to release a scent that can alert nearby deer to the threat.

As a social species that depends on camouflage, the whitetail needs a visual signal that can be turned on and off. The white flag enables fleeing deer to keep together; once the animals are safe in cover, the brown top side of the tail blends into the forest.

survival of related individuals. In contrast, a buck often retreats without warning other members of his group—since buck groups are composed of unrelated individuals, there is no advantage to such a warning. Rather, it is to a buck's advantage to retreat and let the others in the group become potential prey.

If a potential predator is spotted at a more intermediate range, when an escape would certainly be detected, buck and doe groups act similarly. The members of the group flee with tail-flagging and possibly snorting. Tail-flagging may work to confuse the predator, but more important, it helps maintain group cohesion. By staying in a group, each individual reduces its chance of falling prey. In addition, the combined senses of several animals make the group more difficult to approach than a solitary individual.

If an individual is surprised at close range and the danger is severe, buck and doe groups again react similarly, with an explosive scramble for escape. This retreat may or may not be preceded by a loud snort but is rarely accompanied by tail-flagging.

Scent Communication

Though deciphering the information deer relay through vocal and visual signals is not an easy task, attempting to understand how deer use chemical signals for communicating is by far the most difficult area of investigation. Although detailed studies have not been conducted, it appears safe to say that a deer's sense of smell is many magnitudes

greater than our own. Only very recently have scientists developed equipment and techniques that can detect compounds with a sensitivity similar to the deer's nose. Even with this sophisticated equipment, however, we are not able to get inside a deer's head to determine exactly what types of information are being relayed by these scents. Instead we have to rely on observations of the deer's behavior and make subjective estimates of the significance of these odors. This is an imprecise technique at best and is open for errors of interpretation. Nevertheless, our understanding of the significance of chemical cues in the behavioral ecology of deer is growing.

Chemical signals that relay information among animals are called pheromones. This term was originally coined to describe chemical sex attractants in insects but has since been expanded to include any chemical produced by one individual that transfers information to another member of the same species; some researchers reserve *pheromone* for insects and use *chemical signals* when referring to mammals. Whatever the terminology, these signals include releaser pheromones, which evoke an immediate behavioral response; priming pheromones, which result in a physiological response; and informer pheromones, which relay information but generally do not result in a behavioral or physiological response.

Sources of communicative odors in deer include specialized skin glands, the urine, vaginal secretions, and possibly saliva. Researchers have identified at least eight areas of a deer's body that have specialized development of glandular tissues likely to be involved in scent communication.

The interdigital glands are well developed in white-tailed deer. Although their significance has never been positively identified, these glands presumably are used in marking a trail while a deer walks. Other than a preliminary investigation by Atkeson in 1983, little work has been done on the function or chemistry of the interdigital. Atkeson found that the secretions of the interdigital contained a number of volatile components, including acetic, butyric, isobutyric, propionic, and isovaleric acids. These compounds have different volatilities, evaporating at different rates, and therefore the odor of a deer's track likely would change as the track ages.

Although the metatarsal of the black-tailed deer has been shown to produce an alarm scent, several investigators have been unable to demonstrate any functions of this gland in white-tailed deer. Perhaps this gland functions primarily as a sensory organ, as suggested by Quay in 1959. Other investigators suggest that this gland is an evolutionary remnant and has no function.

The tarsal gland is undoubtedly the most important source of chemical information to deer. Whitetails obtain information on individual identity, dominance position, physical condition, and reproductive status from odors arising from this gland. The tarsal of females appears to be used primarily for individual identification. Does frequently sniff the tarsals of others in their social group, and fawns use this scent to identify their mothers.

Though the sebaceous and sudoriferous glands underlying the tarsal may contribute to the odor of the gland, the primary source of information likely comes from urine. The enlarged sebaceous glands underlying the tarsal tuft secrete a fatty material that adheres to the tarsal hairs. During a behavior called rub-urination, deer urinate on their tarsal hairs. The fatty material then selectively retains fat-soluble compounds from the urine.

Deer of both sexes and all classes frequently urinate onto their tarsal glands. Sawyer found that throughout the year, does rub-urinated an average of 1.2 times every day and urinated in a normal posture eight to nine times per day. The rub-urination occurred most commonly at night, shortly after the doe rose from her nocturnal bed. After rub-urination, the doe invariably licks excess urine from the tarsal.

Bucks also frequently rub-urinate throughout the year, and during the rut, mature, dominant males may urinate exclusively in this posture. These males no longer lick the excess from their tarsals, and the resultant staining of the tarsal and lower leg is well known to most hunters.

Little work on the chemical composition of the odors arising from the tarsal has been conducted, though at least one active com-

ponent of the black-tailed deer's tarsal scent has been identified. No compound identified yet from the whitetail's tarsal has been demonstrated to be important for communication. Atkeson in 1983 and Silverstein in 1971 investigated the odors from the tarsal gland, and both identified ortho-cresol and meta-cresol, along with other compounds. Some preliminary data indicate that there are considerable individual differences in the composition of the volatile compounds in the urine of male deer. Although these compounds have not yet been identified, the presence and concentrations of several of them appear to be directly related to the age and dominance status of the male. Some of these compounds are found only in the urine of the dominant males during the breeding season. Thus there must be differences in the odor of urine among bucks, differences that reflect each animal's dominance and reproductive status. These odors are transferred to the tarsal gland during rub-urination and, along with odors from the bacterial decomposition of other urinary compounds, contribute to the particular odor of a rutting buck.

The forehead area of the whitetail contains a large number of sudoriferous glands and is used in signpost marking. These glandular areas are found in both males and females, but the glands are most active in dominant males during the rut. Scent from the forehead gland is used to mark antler rubs during the breeding season. Females have been

Bucks rub-urinate more often than females. The urine flows over the tarsal glands, taking with it chemicals that are significant to other deer.

WERNER

A buck leaves messages on twigs and hanging vines, depositing chemicals from the preorbital gland or the forehead gland. The rival buck licks the message, enhancing its scent with his saliva. Does, too, check messages.

shown to respond to these rubs and may mark them with their own foreheads.

Bucks also mark overhanging branches throughout the year. These appear to be communal marking areas, as many bucks will use the same branches. The source of the scent left on these branches is difficult to determine, although the forehead is likely one contributor and the preorbital gland and saliva possibly are others.

Many overhanging branches become scrape sites during the breeding season. While only a dominant buck undergoes the entire scrape sequence, many bucks may continue to use the overhanging branch. Therefore, the branch appears to be important to bucks for identifying other males in an area, while the full scrape is a display of dominance by a particular buck.

Communication of estrus. How does a doe let a buck know that she is in heat and willing to be bred? Probably no other question pertaining to deer behavior has been asked more often and debated more intensely. Although it is certain that some form of chemical communication is involved, we are still

unsure of the exact mechanism used. The pieces of the puzzle are starting to fall into place, however, and we have a good guess of how it is done.

To understand how reproductive information is communicated among deer, it is first necessary to look at how a deer perceives chemical signals. Like most mammals (except primates and humans), deer have two distinct means through which to receive chemical information: the main olfactory system and the vomeronasal organ. The main olfactory system receives airborne chemicals through the nose. Inspired air passes through the nose and over the olfactory epithelium, where nerve fibers pick up olfactory information and transmit it to the main olfactory bulb of the brain. In the olfactory bulb, these nerve fibers communicate with other nerve fibers, which then transmit the olfactory information to various parts of the brain. There, information is processed and decisions or behavioral responses are made.

The little-known vomeronasal organ has an opening near the center of the roof of a deer's mouth. The organ's primary purpose appears to be analysis of other deer's urine. During the reproductive season, males respond to the urine of females using a stereotypical behavior called flehmen (a German term meaning "lip curl") After taking a small amount of urine into his mouth, the buck opens his mouth slightly, curls his upper lip, and closes his nostrils; this pumps some urine into the vomeronasal organ for analysis.

The neural impulses, or information, obtained here do not go to the same parts of the brain as information obtained through the main olfactory system. Rather, information from the vomeronasal organ travels through the accessory olfactory system, in which nerves are connected via a single synapse in the accessory olfactory bulb to a part of the brain called the amygdala, which in turn has direct connections to the hypothalamus. This is important, since the hypothalamus is the part of the brain that controls the reproductive physiology through the production of hormones. Thus, information from the vomeronasal organ can affect the deer's reproductive physiology, but it does not appear to play a major role in regulating the deer's direct behavioral response.

Another difference between these two systems, the nose and the vomeronasal organ, is that the main olfactory system appears to be used to analyze smaller, more volatile, airborne molecules and the vomeronasal system to analyze larger, less volatile molecules that are in solution in some liquid, such as urine.

Why should an animal have two such systems? What part does each of these systems play in the ecology of deer?

Although no direct experimentation has been done with deer, experiments have been conducted on related animals, such as sheep and goats, to determine the roles of these two systems. Judging from behavior alone, one might conclude that the buck determines a doe's readiness to be bred by analyzing her urine via the vomeronasal organ. Yet in experiments with sheep, if sensory input from the vomeronasal organ is blocked, a ram still has no difficulty in telling ewes in heat from ewes that are not in heat. Conversely, if the main olfactory system is

LEA

Even when she is not in heat, a doe's urine speaks to other deer, advising them of her range boundaries.

blocked, the ram cannot discriminate estrous ewes. Thus it appears that the chemical signal that indicates estrus is a volatile compound that is picked up through the nose, not through the vomeronasal organ.

A series of experiments at the University of Georgia strongly suggests that reproductive information is relayed the same way in whitetails. Tests of estrous urine and estrous vaginal secretions have shown that urine is most likely not the main route that a buck uses to identify a doe in heat. Rather, it is volatile secretions from the reproductive tract of females in heat that cause bucks to pursue and court females.

If bucks use their main olfactory system to determine when a doe is ready to breed, then what is the purpose of the vomeronasal system? Findings here are much more speculative. Some researchers have suggested that flehmen of doe urine and subsequent vomeronasal analysis is used to determine whether the doe is *approaching* estrus. This is based on data showing that bucks tend to flehmen urine from does not yet in heat more often than from does already in heat.

KINNEY

We believe, however, that flehmen is used for a much more important but perhaps more subtle purpose. Since the vomeronasal system is connected to the part of the brain that controls reproductive physiology, a male's analysis of urine through this system likely serves to prime that physiology and thereby ensure that he reaches peak reproductive condition at the same time as do the females.

The primary cue that triggers the onset of the deer's breeding season is change in day length. Certain parts of the deer's brain mediate the response to this cue through a complex system that ultimately affects the hypothalamus—the reproductive control center of the brain. The result is a window of opportunity during which the deer is reproductively active. Since the vomeronasal system also leads to the hypothalamus, it likely helps fine-tune the breeding system to ensure that males and females are in reproductive synchrony. Evidence from other animals indicates that vomeronasal stimulation causes the hypothalamus to release hormones that affect the animals' reproductive capacity. Whether this occurs in deer awaits additional experimental evidence.

—Karl V. Miller and R. Larry Marchinton

Whitetail habitats and ranges

Some white-tailed deer inhabit a tiny pocket of land – just a patch of wood bordering a bit of overgrown field left by the subdivision developer. Other deer may range over an extensive area, inhabiting one site in summer and another in winter and traveling between them in spring and fall. A host of factors figure in the difference, from geographic and environmental (elevation, climate, food, habitat, and season) to the deer themselves (sex, size, age, and number) – all of which make it difficult to generalize about this protean species. But generally, the radius of a whitetail's home range is only slightly more than a mile.

In the snowbelt region, where weather is harsh, annual home ranges average larger, generally 11 square miles, than in the milder climates of the South, where deer rarely move more than 1½ to 2 square miles, for the simple reason that deer in the inhospitable North need more territory in which to meet their needs.

The density of vegetation also affects the size of a deer's home range. In open habitats, such as prairies and open forest stands, home ranges are larger than in heavily wooded areas. As the herd increases in number, home range decreases in size.

Season, age, and sex have a bearing, too. In a Georgia study, adult bucks approximately doubled their home ranges during the rut. In Minnesota, yearlings and young adults seemed to have larger ranges than older animals. In Minnesota, Texas, Missouri, and Florida, adult bucks had home ranges that were, on average, twice the size of adult does' ranges.

Home ranges are most commonly elongated. The long oval is more efficient than a circle because it allows the deer to sample a variety of habitat types – field, edge, wood, and streamside – within a small area and thus seek cover and find food and water with less effort. Elongated home ranges, however, are less common in habitats with just one or two types of vegetation: here, access to different kinds of food and cover isn't possible anyway, so home ranges assume a more circular shape.

The whitetail's fidelity to home range is well known – deer tend to use the same area year after year regardless of its condition. Deer do move in response to flooding, which is a common occurrence in the Everglades and southern river swamps, but food is not a consideration. In fact, when malnourished deer in poor range are moved to an area with plentiful food, they return to

Some Texas whitetail habitats are subject to withering drought, and the resident deer must range across larger areas to meet their needs for food and water.

LANGFORD

In the northern Rockies, whitetails colonize forested and shrubby habitats that moderate the severe winter temperatures and provide adequate food.

JONES

DEER

the place where they were captured. Nevertheless, there are circumstances in which deer move to new range, outside of moving to high ground during floods and shifting between winter and summer quarters. The impetus is social pressure.

A young animal's first home range roughly corresponds to that of its mother. During the rut, mature bucks drive away fawn bucks, prompting them to disperse in search of new territories; dispersal is most intense for yearling bucks, too, just before and during the rut. Adult does drive away their yearlings during the birthing period, and dispersal is most intense for young does during the fawning period.

RANGING BY SEASON

Some deer do not have a fixed summer or winter range; instead, they remain in an area until either the habitat disappears or constant harassment affects their ability to survive there. Some whitetails maintain two residences because good summer habitat is not necessarily a good place to be in winter.

Seasonal shifts between summer and winter ranges vary geographically, with deer in the northern and mountainous regions traveling greater distances than deer in milder regions. Deer are pushed into winter range by the arrival of cold weather; when they return to summer range, they are responding to the pull of fresh spring forage. The average seasonal range distances traveled, figured as the mean of the mileage reported in five studies, was 14.3 kilometers (8.9 miles), and the average maximum range distance was 37.3 kilometers (23.2 miles).

In the snowbelt region, whitetails during winter concentrate in yarding areas, which amount to only about 10 to 20 percent of their normal range. In low terrain, deer wintering grounds are adjacent to watercourses. Primary cover species, needed to provide shelter from the heavy snows and cold winds of the Adirondacks, include red spruce, balsam fir, white cedar, and hemlock. Because northern white cedar and hemlock are preferred foods, they are quickly browsed out of reach.

Overwintering areas vary in size, depending on the amount of adjacent wet areas—streams, marshes, swamps—and the length

With no natural predators left on Fire Island, New York, whitetails coexist with summer vacationers. Unlike deer whose hooves are worn by rock and gritty soil, these animals have long hooves that help them move in soft sand.

LITTLEJOHN

and breadth of stands of mature, uncut conifers. Those evergreens provide essential cover, but food is necessary, too: A good wintering yard provides nearby supplies of black cherry, witch hobble, red maple, striped maple, sugar maple, blueberry, viburnums, and dogwood to browse, along with northern white cedar and hemlock. Such browse plants sprout where hardwood stands undergo periodic cutting.

Not all deer wintering areas are in spruce-fir habitat. At higher elevations with steep ledges, south-facing slopes collect considerably less snow cover and are thus suitable for deer.

Deer move to their wintering yards—to the same yards every year—when day length shortens or snow reaches a depth of 46 centimeters (18 inches) or more. Then conifer stands become attractive: the evergreen boughs reduce wind speeds and snow pack, and they provide overhead thermal cover and thus higher nighttime temperatures. The best conditions for deer include a 70 percent crown closure and 100-square-feet-per-acre basal area. As a measure of tree den-

White-tailed deer habitats in the United States

Habitat	Major tree species	Climate	Deer foods
Division I			
Northeastern hardwoods 78,800 square miles 395 to 5,900 feet elevation	Beech, yellow birch, sugar maple, black cherry, white pine, hemlock, red pine	*Growing season:* 120 to 150 days *Temperature:* Mean daily low 17° to 22°F in winter *Rainfall:* 37 to 53 inches *Snowpack:* 14 to 20 inches	*Winter:* Striped maple, red maple, sugar maple, mountain maple, northern white cedar, hemlock, viburnums, dogwoods, ashes, yellow birch, blueberry, black cherry
Spruce and fir forests Near sea level to 5,900 feet	Spruce, fir, jack pine, tamarack, aspen, pin cherry, paper birch	*Growing season:* 90 to 120 days *Temperature:* Mean daily low 0° to 27°F in winter *Rainfall:* 37 to 53 inches *Snowpack:* 14 to 20 inches	*Winter:* Striped maple, red maple, sugar maple, mountain maple, viburnums, ashes, hemlock, yellow birch, black cherry, red-osier dogwood, northern white cedar, blueberry
Northern Appalachians Near sea level to 2,500 feet	Black cherry, sugar maple, hemlock, yellow birch, black ash, American elm, red maple, hawthorn	*Growing season:* 120 to 150 days *Annual average temperature:* 50°F *Rainfall:* 35 inches *Winter:* Ice storms and deep persistent snows	*Winter:* Striped maple, red maple, sugar maple, mountain maple, viburnums, ashes, hemlock, yellow birch, blueberry, blackberry
Northern forests 140,000 square miles Flat to rolling and hilly, near sea level to 100 feet	Aspen, paper birch, red maple, jack pine, black and white spruce, northern white cedar, balsam fir, maple, birch, beech, eastern hemlock	*Growing season:* 80 to 135 days *Temperature:* Average low 0° to 20°F in winter *Rainfall:* 25 to 32 inches *Snowfall:* 50 to 200 inches	*Winter:* Northern white cedar, red maple, hemlock, American mountain ash, alternate leaf dogwood, yellow birch, mountain maple, serviceberry
Northern plains Flat to undulating steep-sided formations 655 to 3,280 feet	Ponderosa pine, white spruce, trembling aspen, birch, bur oak, American elm, green ash, box elder, Douglas-fir	*Growing season:* 90 to 240 days *Temperature:* less than 26°F to 110°F *Rainfall:* 10–15 inches (NW) to 18–23 inches (SE) *Snowfall:* Of short duration in southwest	Common chokeberry, serviceberry, skunkbush, sumac, dogwood, rose, rabbit brush, greasewood, buffaloberry, common sagebrush, bearberry, snowberry, creeping mahonia
Northern Rocky Mountains Less than 985 square miles occupied by whitetails 985 feet to 6,560 feet elevation	Ponderosa pine, Douglas-fir, cedar, hemlock, spruce, fir, croplands, lodgepole pine	*Growing season:* Less than 75 days *Temperature:* 28°F mean in west in winter, 15°F in north *Rainfall:* 15 to 40 inches *Snowfall:* 12 to 40 inches	*Winter:* Douglas-fir, western red cedar, cottonwood, quaking aspen, ponderosa pine, creeping mahonia, saskatoon serviceberry, common snowberry, red-stem ceanothus, bearberry, myrtle pachistima, arboreal lichens
Southern Appalachians 138,998 square miles 1,000 to 6,000 feet elevation	Oak, hickory, yellow poplar, black locust, white pine, eastern hemlock, eastern red cedar	*Growing season:* 150 to 200 days *Average annual temperature:* 50° to 65°F *Rainfall:* 35 inches in the north to 55 inches in the south; 80 inches in western North Carolina *Snowfall:* 8 to 10 inches	*Winter:* rhododendron, mountain laurel, Japanese honeysuckle, galax, Christmas fern, mushrooms, oak mast, blueberry, wintergreen, sourwood, succulent woody stems, greenbrier
Division II			
Eastern mixed forest 42,188 square miles 600 to 5,000 feet elevation	Sugar maple, basswood, American beech, yellow poplar, chestnut, eastern hemlock, northern red oak, chestnut oak, scarlet oak, white oak, pignut hickory	*Growing season:* 150 to 180 days *Average temperature:* 35°F in January and 75°F in July *Rainfall:* 50 inches *Snowfall:* On ground 60 days in north to 5 days in south	Strawberry bush, greenbrier, trumpetcreeper grape, black locust, red cedar, sumac, rose, blackberry, viburnum, sourwood, blueberry, maple, dogwood, serviceberry, blackgum, redbud
Division III			
Coastal plain 479,530 square miles Sea level to 985 feet elevation	*Gulf prairies:* Plains longleaf, slash pine, shortleaf pine, hardwoods, loblolly pine *Bottomland:* Oak, gum, cypress, pine, hickory, South Texas pinyon, juniper	*Growing season:* 180 days in Maryland to 300 days in south *Average temperature:* 50° to 69°F *Rainfall:* 16 inches in Texas to 60 inches in Louisiana *Snowfall:* Rare	Yaupon gallberry, blueberries, greenbrier, supplejack, palmetto berries, oak mast, dahoon holly, Japanese honeysuckle, sweetbay, blackgum, sassafras, blackberry, viburnum, redbay, Virginia sweetspire, prickly pear, acacias, cacti, honey mesquite
Piedmont 63,240 square miles 295 feet in east to 1,475 feet in west	Loblolly pine, short leaf pine, oak, hickory	*Growing season:* 187 to 225 days *Temperature:* 32° to 50°F in January, 77° to 81°F in July *Rainfall:* 44 to 53 inches *Snowfall:* Rare	Japanese honeysuckle, greenbrier, blueberry, sumac, grape, honey locust, blackberry, oak mast, mushrooms
Midwest oak-hickory 158,830 square miles 25 to 2,000 feet elevation	Oak, hickory, gum, cypress, pine	*Growing season:* 170 to 220 days *Temperature:* 24° to 38°F in January, 76° to 80°F in July *Rainfall:* 35 to 50 inches *Snowfall:* Seldom exceeds 6 inches	Dogwood, redbud, serviceberry, sumac, blueberry, strawberry bush, elderberry, spice bush, farkleberry, black haw, deciduous holly, yaupon, oak mast, agricultural crops
Midwest agricultural region 340,000 square miles Low, flat to gently rolling topography	Bluestem prairie, oak, hickory, maple, beech, birch, pines, elm, ash, cottonwood	*Growing season:* 160 days on average *Temperature:* Extremes usually are of short duration *Rainfall:* 25 inches in west to 60 inches in east *Snowfall:* Rarely a problem for deer	Corn, soybeans, alfalfa, grains, woody plant foliage, forbs, grasses
Central and southern plains 277,000 square miles Low or moderate from sea level to 3,000 feet	Oak, hickory, elm, ash, cottonwood, herbaceous vegetation and shrubs, variety of grasses and forbs, mesquite, cacti, whitebrush, acacias, condalia	*Growing season:* 120 to 220 days *Temperature:* 19° to 45°F in January, 64° to 84°F in July *Rainfall:* 11 to 35 inches *Snowfall:* Rare	Snowberry, rosa, sunflower, corn, wheat, alfalfa, farm crops, grape, common persimmon, western soapberry, chickasaw plum, shin oak, eastern cottonwood, acacia, juniper, scrub oak, saltbush, broomweed nailwort, cacti
Central and West Texas 91,720 square miles Less than 500 feet to 8,500 feet elevation	Oak, honey mesquite, ash, creosote bush, tarbush, yucca, juniper, pinyon pine, ponderosa pine	*Growing season:* 150 days in west, 240 days in east *Temperature:* −10° to 115°F in west, 15° to 105°F in east *Rainfall:* 5 to 20 inches *Snowfall:* Infrequent	Blackberry, yaupon, elm, greenbrier, hackberry, oaks (acorns), honey mesquite, common persimmon, cacti forbs, grasses, prickly pear
Southern Rocky Mountains Scattered places 3,280 to 13,780 feet; whitetails most abundant at 3,940 to 7,875 feet	Ponderosa pine, pinyon, juniper, Douglas-fir, chaparral, fir, spruce	*Growing season:* 120 to 180 days depending on altitude *Temperature:* 100°F in summer to 40° to 50°F in winter *Rainfall:* 15 inches in whitetail habitat	Vetch, fleabane, corralbell, false tarragon, sagebrush, silktassel, desert ceanothus, skunkbush, sumac, filaree, fallen leaves, mountain mahogany

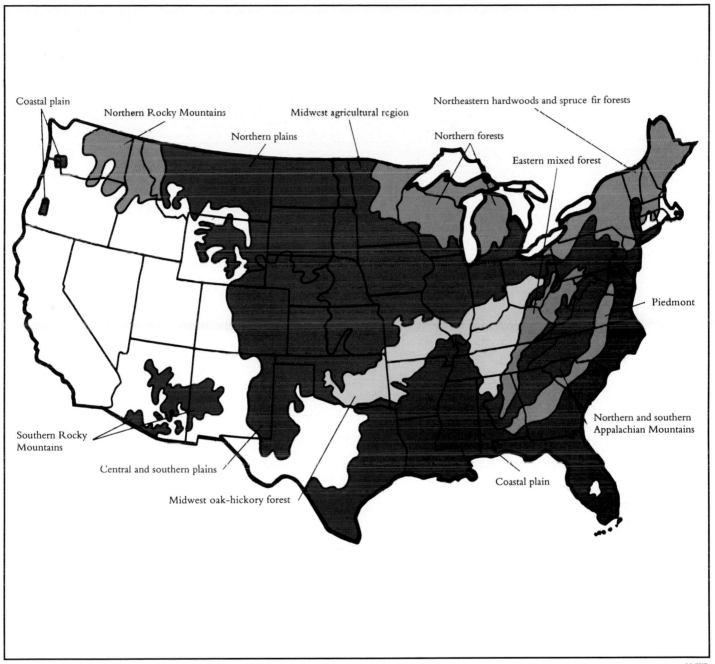

Coastal plain

Northern Rocky Mountains

Midwest agricultural region

Northeastern hardwoods and spruce fir forests

Northern plains

Northern forests

Eastern mixed forest

Piedmont

Southern Rocky Mountains

Northern and southern Appalachian Mountains

Central and southern plains

Midwest oak-hickory forest

Coastal plain

LLOYD

sity per acre, that 100 square feet—the sum of the diameters of all the trees in the given area—may include a greater number of trees if they are saplings, or fewer if they are older and larger.

Though Nelson and Mech indicate that yarding up may reduce predation, the primary reason is protection from cold: deer minimize the loss of body heat and thus conserve their energy when frigid temperatures and chill winds stress their metabolism. Shelter is so important, Verme found, that during extremely cold weather, deer stay in a yard even if the food supply is low. Deer in northern Michigan may stay in yarding areas for twelve weeks during mild winters but for twenty weeks during severe winters. Although snow depth keeps deer from moving once they are in their yarding sites, it does not appear to be the primary cause of yarding. Deer concentrate in yards before snow accumulates and remain at yarding sites even when snow conditions permit free travel.

—*Richard F. Harlow and David C. Guynn, Jr.*

A map of the U.S. vegetative regions superimposed on whitetail range reveals the extraordinary diversity of deer habitats. Although a continent apart and offering very different food and cover, the coastal areas of both the Southeast and the Pacific Northwest support whitetails. The Northwestern habitats, however, are fragmented and the deer populations are dwindling.

The home range

---

*T*he white-tailed deer is not a nomadic species. Each individual maintains a very real attachment to a particular piece of real estate. There are reasons the deer might range from this area and explore or even settle in a different area, and there are circumstances in which the boundaries may shift, but for the most part, the deer stays in its home range.

In the scientific literature there are different definitions of *home range* and various ways of delineating it. A classic definition was offered in 1943 by Burt, who explained it as the area traversed by the adult deer in its normal activities—feeding, mating, fawning—thereby excluding any migratory routes or exploratory sallies. Ungulate ethologist Fritz Walther coined the term *action area* for all the places a deer might go over its lifetime: winter range if it differs from summer habitat, for example, and the movements of bucks during the rut. Because deer live longer than radio transmitters, however, little hard information is available on their lifetime ranges.

The deer knows its home range and tends to use the same one year after year. In fact, different generations of whitetails often maintain very similar home ranges even if there are no natural or artificial "property lines," such as cliffs or fences, to keep the young deer from using feeding or bedding sites different from those of their mothers. This is particularly true of females and suggests a cultural component. In other words,

the traditional home range, and familiarity with it, can be conveyed from one generation to the next.

There exist many examples of the whitetail's attachment to its home range.

• Deer have starved to death during winter rather than leave their depleted range for an area with better food just 2 or 3 miles away. Severinghaus and Cheatum documented several such instances in New York.

• Deer in Texas sometimes remained in their home range and died from lack of food, water, or even cover, even though there were no apparent impediments to movement, as observed by Thomas et al.

• Deer tracked by radio in Alabama would not leave their annual ranges to any great extent just to reach a concentrated food supply, Byford concluded.

Ignorance of food sources not in the animals' normal range may account for such examples of home-range loyalty, but on one occasion reported by Severinghaus and Cheatum, when starving deer were actually herded into better habitat, they refused to stay.

HOW MUCH IS ENOUGH

It is advantageous, evolutionarily speaking, for an animal to become very familiar with a parcel of land. If it knows the area well enough, it can obtain the necessities of life—and escape from potential causes of death—with greater efficiency. The range must be large enough to provide sufficient

LEA

resources and cover, yet it must be small enough for the animal to know it well.

One square mile may be all the animal needs—that is what Severinghaus and Cheatum concluded in 1956 and what other researchers have since then found to be generally accurate. As far back as 1927, Ernest Thompson Seton observed that the home range of whitetails is probaby smaller than that of any other North American deer. Just how big the range is, in practice, depends on the particulars of time and space, age and sex, habitat quality and population density.

Lifetime patterns. The young fawn moves very little, in fact, not traveling with its dam at all but hiding on the forest floor until she calls it to nurse. After a few weeks it begins to run and play, moving around a bit more, and by the time it is two months old its home range begins to approximate the doe's.

Among deer with very distinct seasonal ranges, especially those in northern areas, yearlings and young adults commonly move greater distances than older animals. Tagged 1½- and 2½-year-old deer of both sexes move much longer distances than do mature

adults, according to Carlsen and Farmes. The researchers assume that deer range out during their early years and then gradually cease their wanderings. This also may be true of the more sedentary deer in the South.

Bucks have larger home ranges than does, according to most researchers, although some studies have found no difference. The greater size is more noticeable during the rut, when the buck's daily movements are less predictable. One buck studied in northern Georgia enlarged his range from 92 hectares to 244 in a six-week period—an increase of 150 percent, Kammermeyer and Marchinton reported.

In other regions, too, bucks range farther during the fall rut. Mattfeld and others observed that in New York, bucks expanded or shifted their range in the fall, while does occupied the same range they had used in spring and summer. Welch observed that Coues whitetail bucks in Arizona left their home areas in search of receptive does.

According to Brown, some large, mature bucks become highly mobile. These "dominant floaters" traverse extensive territory and

Deer graze while moving from one part of their range to another. The whitetails' well-worn trails allow them to travel efficiently from the deep forest to the edges and open fields of their range.

HERTLING

may be contenders in the social hierarchies of several populations—presumably at the top in any of the groups of mature bucks they encounter.

Does tend to remain within their home ranges, though there is also evidence that if mature bucks are not around, does in heat leave their ranges in search of them. When ready to give birth, the does sometimes move to the periphery of their ranges to drop their fawns.

Regional patterns. Northern whitetails that move seasonally from winter to summer range and back again have large annual ranges. The greater the weather changes, the more movement between ranges may be necessary.

In the southern United States, in contrast, the annual ranges are smaller and more stable. Even within these sedentary classes, however, home ranges gradually shift through time, and as a consequence, a southern deer's lifetime range is substantially larger than its home range at any one point in time. The home range of such animals looks like an amoeba: it extends a little here,

then a little there, and over time its shape and even location may change.

The survival advantages of a small home range—the deer knows it intimately and exploits its resources without expending a lot of energy or exposing itself to predators over long distances—must be weighed against its genetic disadvantages. Deer in a small area risk inbreeding.

The environment. How far the deer must travel to find food, water, and cover has an obvious effect on the size of its home range. These factors also determine the *shape* of the range.

If the necessary food, water, and cover are not located all in one place—and usually they are not—the deer must move around to meet its needs. The shortest distance between two points (or among three points) is a line, so the most efficient configuration for a home range is an elongated oval. Circular and irregular home ranges require an animal to move less efficiently and spend more energy. For this reason, the ranges of most birds and mammals, including deer, are elongated.

The extent of the elongation varies with quality of the habitat. If the habitat uniformly provides a good mix of essentials, or if the deer relies on only one type of vegetation, the oval is rather fat, and the deer ranges out in all directions from a central point to find what it needs. If the deer uses two or more types of vegetation, the oval is long and the deer's movements are more linear.

Among small mammals such as cotton rats and white-footed mice, individuals living in relatively open habitats have larger home ranges than animals inhabiting areas of dense vegetation. Studies of whitetails indicate a similar relationship between range size and vegetative density. For example, with other conditions being equal, deer in the open grasslands of the Great Plains tend to have ranges larger than those of deer in the dense forest regions of the southern and eastern United States.

Population density. Another general rule among mammals holds for deer: that average home range size decreases as population density increases. In an area of southeastern Minnesota that had fewer than two deer per square mile, Dorn reported that the deer moved extensively. In Florida surviving deer apparently expanded their home ranges when the rest of the population disappeared: Bridges and Smith, in separate studies, observed home ranges three times larger than those Marchinton had measured before and during the dieoff.

Despite such evidence, however, the inverse relationship between population density and range size does not prove cause and effect. Most deer studies, in fact, are conducted in areas with high populations, simply because there are more deer to find and observe. Comparable studies for deer in less populated regions don't always exist.

WHERE AND WHEN TO GO

Although deer are not generally considered migratory, some whitetails do have distinct summer and winter ranges. In Missouri some deer leave their small, distinct summer ranges when winter arrives, according to Progulske and Baskett. Such seasonal movement is more pronounced, however, in the mountains and northern regions of North

SCOTT

The use of established trails becomes especially important for whitetails in winter, when the animals have limited energy for forging new routes through heavy brush and deep snow.

America. And it is where the differences between seasons—both meteorologically and vegetatively—are extreme that deer move the farthest.

In Minnesota, where winter temperatures may dip far below zero, deer moved as far as 92 kilometers (57 miles) from their summer range to spend the winter, Carlsen and Farmes reported. They left behind the now sparse deciduous or mixed forests that had provided a nutritious summer diet of berries, seeds, shoots, and leaves to take shelter amid the thick, low-hanging branches of evergreens.

Like deer that do not make seasonal treks, these deer use the same summer range year after year. Although they travel to the same general area for wintering, the specific winter range may be less consistent, according to a study by Mattfield et al. Tracking both individual animals and groups of deer, Mattfield suggested that the choice of winter range varies because of differences in snow depth and traveling conditions.

Timing. When deer move from summer habitat to winter is a matter of speculation,

During the day an adult doe bedded in or near the woods, then moved into the open field to feed at night. The telemetric studies and visual observations were made by Marchinton.

as is the signal that starts them on their way. Severinghaus and Cheatum found that fall and early winter migrations appeared to be responses to weather: as the cold deepened and the snow began to fly, the deer sought areas that would shelter them from winter's worst. The spring movement back to summer range seemed connected with the need for food, as the animals, now released from the restricted winter food supply, sought succulent spring forage.

The impetus in each case involved the deer's physical comfort, but Severinghaus and Cheatum cautioned, "The immediate initiating factor that prompts migration is

Migratory whitetails do not embark on the spring movement back to summer range until weather, snow depth, and new plant growth permit.

difficult to determine, for the more obvious climatic factors and the pattern both of quality and availability of food differ widely in the whitetail range."

Similar observations and speculations have added to the literature but not settled all the questions since Severinghaus and Cheatum published that study in 1956. It still has not been determined precisely when deer move toward the yards in fall, or when they leave the winter range for summer grounds, or what actuates the movement in either direction. Among the recent observations:

• A sharp drop in temperature is important in triggering winter migration, a finding published by Verme and Ozoga and corroborated by Hoskinson and Mech, who used radiotelemetric data.

• Deer appear ready to leave the winter yard as soon as conditions—primarily the snowpack—permit them to travel freely, Verme reported.

• Does and juveniles take a fairly straight path from winter to summer range, but adult bucks are more inclined to wander, according to Rongstad and Tester.

If not confined by deep snow, whitetails leave their coniferous cover to feed on the twigs of cherry, dogwood, viburnum, witch hobble, and various species of maple.

WHITE-TAILED DEER

179

KIRKPATRICK

• Deer sometimes migrate directly from winter yard to summer range, but in other cases they make several false starts before finally leaving for good.

• The duration of the spring migration depends on when it starts: if its onset is delayed, the deer move faster, Hoskinson and Mech found. The result is that no matter when different populations begin the migration, most deer reach their summer grounds at the same time, in early May. The synchrony of their arrival may be related to the impending birth of fawns, to the availability of fresh forage, or to other, as-yet-unrecognized factors.

In the South. Southern ecosystems tend to be more biologically complex and undergo less drastic seasonal changes than those of the North. Temperature ranges do not fluctuate so widely, many broad-leaf plants are evergreen all winter, and snow never falls so deep or stays so long that it impedes travel or buries forage. There's less reason for a deer to move.

Still, shifts in centers of activity, not involving signficant changes in range, have been widely reported, most often because of shifts in sources of food.

And seasonal movements of considerable magnitude—whether they are true migrations is arguable—do occur in the South. In portions of the Everglades, deer follow the receding water south in dry times and move north ahead of rising water in wet periods. Annual movements of deer onto a refuge in northwestern Georgia have been documented by Kammermeyer and Marchinton. Some of the deer came from as far away as 8 kilometers (5 miles), and their presence nearly doubled the refuge population. Habitat conditions, herd history (the moving deer, or their dams, were familiar with the refuge, having originally been stocked on it before gradually spreading across its borders), and hunting all played roles in this movement, but hunting pressure outside the refuge was certainly an important factor. Farther south, the use of dogs to hunt deer, traditional and legal in some places, apparently makes the deer population more mobile and results in more genetic mixing.

—*R. Larry Marchinton and Karl V. Miller*

Patterns of activity

Asking where a white-tail goes in the course of a day is not unlike asking, Where does a person go? Think about that question for a minute and you will begin to see the problem. How old is the subject? Where does he live, and is it summer or winter, fair weather or foul?

The typical deer spends a typical day bedded in fairly dense cover. Chewing its cud and resting, it remains ever alert, rarely closing its eyes and actually sleeping. When sleep does come, it is for only a few minutes. Every few hours it gets to its feet, stretches a bit, relieves itself, and takes a few mouthfuls of browse. As darkness approaches, it begins moving toward a nighttime feeding area, probably just under a mile away. This area is

HANRAHAN

likely to be more open, but once darkness has fallen, it is a safe place to spend the night feeding and resting. Shortly after daylight, the deer begins moving back to the daytime bedding area of heavier cover. Browsing as it goes, the animal may not arrive until mid-morning.

ON THE MOVE

Those two areas—the forest's shrubby cover for day and the open feeding area for night—are the predictable places in which the deer can be found, but the path it takes back and forth between them is somewhat unpredictable. Because the animal is more vulnerable while it is on the move, it uses any one of several trails.

While traveling, the deer occasionally stops and browses, just a few mouthfuls at a time. Even when reaching its feeding sites, the animal is unlikely to graze extensively on any one plant—with advantages initially to the plant (stripped plants die) and ultimately to the deer itself (dead plants provide no food).

Selection of beds is a matter of individual preference. Most commonly, deer bed in the same general areas but not necessarily in the same beds. In one study Marchinton identified seventeen beds belonging to one doe, each in a different spot in her home range. Choosing a different bed every day prevents parasites from establishing themselves and also keeps predators guessing about the animal's location.

After shifting his weight onto the front knees, the bedded deer lifts his hindquarters and then straightens the front legs, one at a time, into a standing position.

Browsing overhead branches is a balancing act, not undertaken unless more easily accessible—and more nutritious—food has already been eaten.

HANRAHAN

DEER

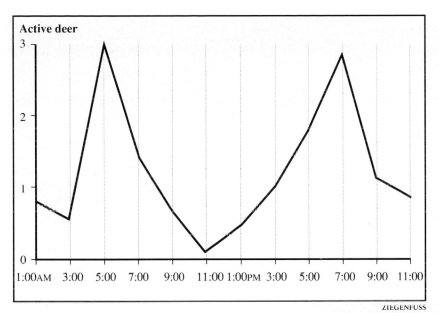

Active deer

Most active deer are observed at dawn and at dusk—a typical crepuscular pattern. At midday deer are usually bedded in safe cover.

The sweeping branches of a large hemlock deflect snow, enable the deer to bed in leaves, and protect the bedded animal from excessive heat loss on cold, clear nights.

Some beds, however, may be so desirable—so secluded and safe, so comfortable—that they are used repeatedly. One yearling buck observed by Marchinton would walk several hundred yards to his special spot whenever he wanted to rest. The bed was sheltered by overhanging vines and thick bushes, and once bedded down, the deer was both cool and practically invisible.

Aside from individual preference, many other factors affect what deer do and where deer go. Deer feeling the pressures of over-population tend to move less than deer in sparse populations, for example, and deer living in open prairies move more than deer in dense forests. Weather is another influence.

THE WEATHER CONNECTION

What effect the temperature has depends on the prevailing conditions. During generally warm or moderate weather, deer become more active if the temperature falls. In the heat of summer, deer are usually active in the coolest part of the day—that is, at night. On a very cold winter day, they are more likely to move about during the warmest time, when the sun is high. If the temperature plunges, deer may become completely inactive, and it is only when the thermometer rises again that they emerge from the thick evergreens that provide some shelter from the cold and winds. The abundance of food—or lack of it—can affect the response to cold weather: if deer can reach an abundance

HERTLING

of high-energy foods, like acorns or corn, they can afford to move around more.

Wind, humidity, and precipitation come into play as well. Light winds have little effect, but whitetails are less active if the wind is strong and gusty. Deer are likely to be most active at low relative humidities. Increased cloud cover sometimes makes them less active. Whether they move about in rain depends on how heavy the precipitation is. Whereas deer typically bed down by mid-morning, on a drizzly day they are just as likely to be active in late morning and afternoon as well. Likewise, light rain makes movement somewhat unpredictable. Heavy rainfall keeps them in their beds, as does heavy snow. In fact, deer often remain inactive for one, two, or even three days during and after a snowstorm.

Several researchers have reported that whitetails sometimes feed heavily just before bad weather, which leads to the interesting theory that they can sense the falling barometric pressure. Weather systems involve many other elements, however—temperature, relative humidity, cloud cover, wind,

Deer sleep for only a few minutes at a time. The usual posture has the head laid back along the flank and the legs tucked underneath the body.

precipitation—and sorting out which aspect the deer are actually responding to is a bit of a challenge. As Progulske and Duerre pointed out in 1964, it is probably the entire complex, rather than any single factor, that affects deer behavior.

As for astrological influences, evidence connecting activity of deer—or any other animals—with phases of the moon is far from clear. This is not for lack of attempts to find such connections, however. Solunar tables to predict fish and wildlife activity have been developed and sold for many years, but since different ones indicate different peak times, they cannot all be correct. Even rigorously

POLIN

Before bedding down, a deer paws through the snow to expose the leaves below. Once it is bedded, heat lost from the body melts a neat oval

scientific studies on the effect of moon phases are contradictory.

ENCROACHING CIVILIZATION

Where they live close to humans, deer often alter their patterns of activity. The basic change is that the deer are moving around when people are not, and vice versa. Whereas whitetails in general are crepuscular, moving around at dusk and dawn, when disturbed they can become completely nocturnal.

Hunting season is an instance of high disturbance. Older, more experienced deer quickly tend to become inactive during daylight hours; some move almost entirely at night. These animals—often mature bucks—become vulnerable to hunters only when the breeding season arrives. Then the instinct to procreate gets the better of their learned caution, and they travel in daylight to search out and court estrous does.

Not all animals can change their behavior as easily as the white-tailed deer. The wild turkey, for example, cannot see very well at night and must accomplish its daily business while the sun is up. The great horned owl, on the other hand, is active mostly at night. But the deer has a convenient anatomical adaptation: it can see relatively well day or night.

When a car headlight finds a deer, the eyes shine back at the driver because of the tapetum, a specialized membrane in the back of the eye that reflects and intensifies light. As this reflected light passes back through the eye, it is more easily detected by the rods—light-sensitive structures in the retina—thus enabling the animal to see even in very low light. Whitetails' eyes have also evolved to permit some color vision. With those adaptations for seeing in both darkness and light, deer can alter their patterns of behavior to survive in changing environments—just one of the reasons the species has been so successful.

—R. Larry Marchinton and Karl V. Miller

Dispersal of young deer

How young animals separate from their mothers and establish their own home ranges has long occupied the attention of researchers in other fields, but for white-tailed deer the subject is relatively new. In fact, dispersal was not even mentioned in landmark studies of the mid-twentieth century.

Even in the 1960s and 1970s when radio transmitters became available for tracking, some researchers missed this important behavior because they didn't study deer while the young animals were dispersing, or they were foiled by the short life and capriciousness of early radio transmitters. When researchers lost contact with a deer, they assumed it to be radio failure. In fact, the deer may have been following the common whitetail pattern: moving from his original home range and establishing a new range some distance away—*his* because the dispersing animal is most likely to be a male.

A study by Kammermeyer and Marchinton provides some context for the phenomenon of dispersal:

• Tracking nineteen tagged or radio-equipped bucks, they found that a third of them made early fall dispersal movements averaging 4.4 kilometers (2.7 miles).

• Of the ten 1½- and 2½-year-old bucks they followed, five dispersed, all during the rut.

• Of the twenty-one does tracked, only one moved any significant distance from her original range, and she did so between late August and early October—well before the rutting season.

The example of one yearling buck sketches the picture of how an animal comes to leave its birth range and settle elsewhere:

The young buck, fitted with a radio collar and monitored by Sweeney, was chased by dogs out of his home range on several occasions, as part of the 1970 study. He normally returned within a few hours, as did all the other deer studied. After outrunning the hounds on September 26, however, he bedded down 2.7 kilometers (1.7 miles) outside his original range, and instead of returning during the night, he trotted another 8.5 kilometers (5.3 miles) farther away. For the next six days he remained in an area of about 80 hectares at the new location. That proved to be a temporary site, however: for the next fifteen days after that he wandered back and forth along the route he had taken from his original range. He briefly reentered his original range twice and the temporary range once. On November 20 he began settling down in a new home area about halfway between the ranges; the population density of deer was lower here than where he had come from. Centers of activity for the new home range and his original range were 5 kilometers (3.1 miles) distant, but their borders were only 1.5 kilometers (0.9 miles) apart. A year later this buck was shot by a hunter in his new range.

Many factors, including escape from dogs, may have been involved in this animal's wandering movement pattern, followed by the establishment of a new home range. But considering his age and the time of year—just prior to the breeding season—yearling dis-

The dispersal of young males prevents them from breeding sisters and other near relatives, and their assimilation into new populations introduces fresh genetic material.

LEA

WHITE-TAILED DEER

The first few times a young buck was chased from his natal range, he returned at night. But eventually he trotted several miles away. After six days at this temporary site, he began looking for a new area and settled on a location partway back to his natal range. After a few forays back to that range and to the temporary site, he established a new, permanent home range.

persal behavior is the likeliest explanation.

Other findings by other researchers support the idea that young deer, particularly males, leave their home range:

• Marked deer observed on the Crab Orchard National Wildlife Refuge in Illinois but killed elsewhere later the same year ranged from 1 percent in 1962 to 17 percent in 1965; Hawkins et al. linked those numbers to increasing population and concluded that higher population pressure caused more deer to leave the refuge.

• During the rut, ten of nineteen young bucks (both yearlings and 2½-year-olds) temporarily moved out of their normal ranges at the Radford Arsenal enclosure in Virginia. Although a fence prevented the deer from completely leaving the area, their irregular movements suggested dispersal to researchers Downing and McGinnes. The does, meanwhile, made few unusual movements.

Most bucks leave as yearlings. A study by Hawkins revealed the following statistics on how old deer are when their ranges shift:

• 4 percent of fawns disperse.
• 7 percent of adult does disperse.
• 10 percent of adult bucks disperse.
• 13 percent of yearling does disperse.
• 80 percent and more of yearling bucks disperse.

Not always, however, is there such a big difference between the dispersal rates for yearling bucks and those for other deer. A 1991 study by Nixon et al. found that half of all yearlings of both sexes, including 20 percent of yearling does, dispersed between April and June. The study involved 286 marked and radio-collared deer on a wildlife refuge in an intensively farmed region of Illinois. Most of these deer moved 40 to 50 kilometers (25 to 31 miles) before establishing new ranges in areas left vacant because of hunting and a severe winter.

Such a high rate of dispersal for young does appears to occur primarily in very fragmented ranges like those of the agricultural Midwest. The does seem more likely to leave their natal range in spring or summer.

From such studies as these, a picture emerges: it is mostly young bucks that disperse, and they do so primarily during the rut, probably if their home range is densely populated. But how exactly do the bucks come to leave?

THE IMPETUS TO LEAVE

When a fawn is just six months old, the breeding season is about to begin. The prime big bucks that court his dam are not exactly tolerant of her offspring. Fawn bucks may even show evidence of bruises inflicted by older males during the rut. As the dominant buck chases the nearly ready female, the young animal is likely to be temporarily separated from his dam; some are never reunited. The fawns that are occasionally seen outside their home range—and thus considered to have dispersed—may be these animals.

More social antagonism awaits the fawn

HERTLING

that survives the winter in the company of its mother. When she nears parturition, she may set up a fawning territory in a selected area and drive her yearling fawn away. The young animal, especially if it is female, is likely to return once the newborn is old enough to travel with the group, but if it strikes out on its own and leaves its natal range in spring or summer, it counts as an example of dispersal.

Most dispersal, however, takes place just before and during the rut. The 1½-year-old buck is subject to antagonism from older, larger males; he cannot compete well for breeding privileges as the bucks sort themselves out in a dominance hierarchy. A more important factor, however, may be antagonism from closely related does, particularly the mother, just before breeding begins.

It is usually the mothers, then, that drive the young bucks away—a finding corroborated by an interesting study, paradoxically, of *orphaned* bucks. When Holzenbein and Marchinton radio-tracked fifteen male whitetails that had lost their dams after they were weaned, only one of these orphans was found to have left the birth range, and he had been harassed by an unrelated doe. Of nineteen bucks with mothers, eighteen had dispersed by the time they were 2½ years old.

Social pressures exist at each breeding and fawning season, and even very old males, no longer able to compete with younger bucks, may also be forced to leave. One old male

left his traditional range apparently because of competition from younger, more vigorous bucks, according to Wilkinson, who observed him on an island off the South Carolina coast. Although similar instances have been reported for old animals in other species, there are not many reports for whitetails, since most bucks die before they reach old age.

Whether administered by the mother or by her suitors, rebuffs seem to be the goad that prompts the deer to leave.

GOING THE DISTANCE

How far a dispersing animal travels depends on many factors. Distances of 3 to 10 kilometers (2 to 6 miles) are common, but dispersals of more than 150 kilometers (93 miles) have occurred. In Hawkins's study, yearling bucks were harvested an average of 8 kilometers (5 miles) from the site where they had been captured and tagged—a greater distance than for does or any other age class except adult males.

Where deer move seasonally between winter and summer ranges, the distances associated with dispersal are difficult to calculate, and indeed, dispersal may be minimal in some herds. Nevertheless, the longest seasonal movements by Minnesota whitetails were made by deer younger than 2½ years, according to Carlsen and Farmes. And in South Dakota, some long spring and summer movements by deer were termed dispersals by Sparrowe and Springer; one yearling doe had traversed 160 kilometers (100 miles).

While on the move, a deer is in danger. By roaming around unfamiliar territory, the animal encounters highways, residential subdivisions, fences, and hunters. It should be no surprise, then, that dispersing deer are less likely to survive. In their comparison of the young bucks with and without mothers, Holzenbein and Marchinton found that more orphans survived, presumably because they stayed in familiar habitat and did not expose themselves to the dangers outside.

Although movement away from a home range can be costly to an individual animal, it benefits the population as a whole. By dispersing, the young buck avoids inbreeding with closely related does, and should he sur-

BIGGS

Dispersing animals are harassed by the bucks whose home ranges they enter. The young buck must continue to search for a fraternal group that will admit him.

value of dispersal in keeping populations stable is limited at best.

Dispersal can, however, have a demonstrable effect on sex ratios among whitetails. Because the females are more sedentary, dispersal may increase the proportion of females to adult males if the departure of the males is not canceled out by an influx of males from adjacent ranges. This explains, in part, why recently established herds usually have a higher percentage of adult bucks than older, more dense populations, and why harvests of previously protected herds usually have a higher percentage of adult females.

An example comes from the Berry College refuge in Georgia. The deer population on the refuge, where hunting was prohibited, contained a lower percentage of males than did the population outside, which was less dense and subject to heavy buck harvests. The high number of does on the refuge apparently caused young bucks to disperse from it at a high rate. The extent of buck dispersal from the refuge during the fall was apparent from the decrease in the number of antlered deer that researchers Kammermeyer and Marchinton observed. At the same time, outside the refuge the ratio shifted significantly in favor of bucks.

The higher the population, the more dispersal shifts the sex ratio in favor of females—or so the data would suggest. In a population of deer studied by Urbston in South Carolina, where hunting regulations allowed the harvest of both does and bucks, the female-to-male ratio increased with population density: where the population was low, the ratio was approximately even, but where the population was very high, there were nearly three times as many does as bucks. Those sex ratios were for adults; the differences were not evident among fawns.

—R. Larry Marchinton and Karl V. Miller

vive and become a dominant buck, he introduces new genetic material to a distant herd.

The Effects of Dispersal

How the departure of young whitetails affects the herd depends on the nature of the population. If the number of deer is in balance with the limiting factors of the environment—the amount of forage, for example, and the number of sheltered places that make good cover—the dispersal of a few individuals will have no appreciable effect. Their emigration may even be offset by the immigration of animals dispersing from nearby habitat.

If the population is at or above the carrying capacity of the land, however, or if it is very low because of dieoffs, dispersal will have a more pronounced effect. The numbers of dispersing deer do seem to increase if the range is overpopulated—which brings up another factor to consider when assessing the impact of this phenomenon: the rate of dispersal. Odum, in his classic book on the fundamentals of ecology, suggested that it was the interplay of factors such as the rate of dispersal, the status of the population, and whether the numbers were increasing or declining—that would predict the effects of dispersal.

Odum, however, was speaking of animals in general. Because whitetails are polygynous, growth or decline in the deer population depends largely on the number of does. Since does, by and large, do not disperse, the

The migration of old

*T*housands of animals traversing the land, cutting fresh hoof marks in the worn trails used by generation after generation, the gravid does peeling off from the herd to birth their fawns . . .

This dramatic picture of a mass migration was handed down to the twentieth century by early settlers of the Great Lakes region. These deer—and they were whitetails, not caribou—were supposed to have traveled 125 kilometers (75 miles) from their wintering grounds in Wisconsin and Michigan near Lake Michigan to their summer range along the south shore of Lake Superior.

The spring and fall movement of whitetails had "all the characteristics of a true migration," Shiras reported in 1935. As soon as the snow depth permitted, "thousands of does worked their way north . . . traveling alone into a broad belt a little back from the south shore of Lake Superior, where just a few weeks later the fawns were born." The bucks came shortly afterward, and by early May the migration was over. So many animals following the same trails left deep cuts in the soft ground, "like the caribou trails found in Newfoundland."

Shiras believed the migrations ended when the railroad companies built wire fences along the tracks, preventing free movement of the deer and forcing them into winter yards, where they fell prey to hungry wolves and lawless hunters. The fences may not have been so significant a barrier, however; Dahlberg and Guettinger suggested that the changes in land use associated with the coming of the railroads were the greater factor.

Or did the great migrations ever take place at all? Verme expressed his doubt in 1973: "While fairly extensive deer movements do take place across the Michigan-Wisconsin border, the seasonal traffic presently goes both ways, with some deer coming north to winter. Hence, in my opinion Shiras's contention of a historic deer migration for this region quite likely is a myth."

—*R. Larry Marchinton and Karl V. Miller*

Feeding behavior

*T*he doe stands at the edge of the alder swamp in the midday sun and surveys the ridge above. After remaining motionless for almost ten minutes, she moves rapidly up the ridge. Two fawns suddenly emerge from the swamp behind her and follow their mother to the base of a large white oak. They go directly, almost as if drawn by a magnet. After again surveying her surroundings, the doe begins a methodical search. With her head near the ground, she walks around the base of the tree, moving her head from side to side in a sweeping motion. Every minute or so she stops and looks up while she chews on the acorns she has found. Her fawns follow her example.

Times are good and the mast crop is abundant. In less than fifteen minutes the deer have eaten their fill and moved farther down the ridge, where they bed in the security of a thicket of aspens. For the next three hours, the deer remain in their beds, chewing their cud.

This typical whitetail feeding behavior—locating preferred foods quickly, consuming them rapidly, and processing the food later—contributes to the success of the species. Unquestionably, the deer's senses of smell and taste aid in finding food, but those senses are likely to operate differently from those of human beings. A deer foraging for acorns, grapes, or persimmons in the forest depends on its keen sense of smell to distinguish good fruits from bad—and to avoid poisonous plants. Our tongues are sensitive to sweet and sour tastes; deer are thought to be able to detect certain oils, sugars, and amino acids. Moreover, the deer's tongue and lips have great dexterity and can pick up items as small as a kernel of corn. Since deer have no upper incisors, they do not clip their food items, but instead tear or pull herbaceous material from the stems of the plant they are feeding on. When feeding on larger stems and woody vegetation, deer chew the stems with their molars.

As ruminants, deer can ingest their feed without having to thoroughly chew it, thereby limiting the time they spend feeding and being exposed to predators. Only when bedded in a safe place do they regurgitate the cud and chew it into small particles.

Deer are opportunistic in their feeding habits. Although they have definite preferences, the choice of plants they feed on depends largely on what is available. The diet thus changes greatly through the year and around the country. While deer are feeding on acorns in Michigan, deer farther south in Alabama and Mississippi are switching from summer forbs, muscadine grapes, and legumes to leafy vines, greenbrier, and persimmon fruit. At the southern extreme of their range in southern Texas and Mexico, whitetails have subsisted on prickly pear cactus through the summer months and now add winter forbs, mesquite seeds, and browse species. In Montana, deer resort to woody browse species, such as snowberry and cottonwood, with alfalfa fields providing high-

Whitetails, like blacktails and mule deer, need easily digested forage. A deer selects the most tender, most nutritious plant parts, such as new green leaves.

LEA

Acer rubrum
red maple

Vaccinium corymbosum
high mountain blueberry

Fagus grandifolia
American beech

Pseudotsuga menziesii
Douglas-fir

Hamamelis virginiana
witch hazel

quality forage to bolster fat stores for the coming winter.

To describe the diet of the white-tailed deer, it is almost easier to say what the white-tail *won't* eat. The wide range and adaptability of the species invite all kinds of qualifications, but a few generalities are possible. Throughout their range, deer prefer fleshy fruits, such as blueberries and huckleberries, persimmons, apples, blackberries, and wild grapes.

Whitetails also relish the leaves and new growth on a variety of woody vines, shrubs, and trees, such as poison ivy, honeysuckle, greenbrier, dewberry, cinquefoil, trumpet creeper, rose, red-osier dogwood, aspen, and oak. Clover, vetch, tick trefoil, and other legumes are important sources of high-quality protein, as are many small leafy annual and perennial plants, such as aster and goldenrod. The legumes also are particularly rich in calcium. Nontoxic fungi and lichens make up a substantial part of the diet and are rich sources of energy and phosphorus.

The appeal of agricultural crops like alfalfa, peas, soybeans, sugar beets, sweet potatoes, corn, wheat, rye, and oats often leads people to consider deer a major economic pest species. Some crops, such as the winter small grains, soybeans, and beans, are eaten both as seed and in the tender growing stages.

Water, like protein, carbohydrates, fats, and minerals, is an important nutrient. Watering generally depends on the moisture content of the feed deer eat. During the spring, for example, deer rarely if ever need free water because their diet consists of succulent plants of high moisture content. In the late summer and early fall, when plants become highly fibrous and less succulent, the whitetail is likely to drink water occasionally to several times a day. In the desert, the need for water is so great that deer may even metabolize body fats to meet their water requirements.

The whitetail is a concentrate feeder. Unlike cattle and sheep, it has a small stomach relative to body size and requires, as a result,

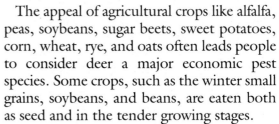

Once deer have consumed forage at ground level, they must strain to reach overhanging branches—resulting in a browse line—or go without food altogether.

AUBREY

REZENDES

a very high-quality diet. Deer prefer high-protein and energy-rich plants that are highly digestible, like browse, leafy plants, and acorns, over more fibrous grasses.

The whitetail changes its diet seasonally to meet the physiologic requirements of the rut, antler growth, pregnancy, nursing, and climatic stress in different periods of the year. Bucks have different nutritional needs at different times of the year from does, and fawns have different nutritional requirements than adults. In general, does experience their greatest nutritional demand just before weaning their fawns in the fall. Bucks are in the best nutritional condition at this time and begin voluntary food restriction until after the rut is through. It is tempting

Below: A study of deer in Mississippi from fall into early winter revealed that the animals' most intense activity was at dusk; feeding continued through the night. The deer were least active at midday Source: Jacobson.

Bottom: In Mississippi, where seasonal variations in food are less extreme than in more northerly parts of whitetail range, acorns and fruits are preferred when they are available. In winter, browse and grasses assume more importance. Source: Mitchell.

Gaultheria procumbens
wintergreen

Betula alleghaniensis
yellow birch

Diospyros virginiana
common persimmon

Gleditsia triacanthos
honey locust

Lonicera periclymenum
honeysuckle

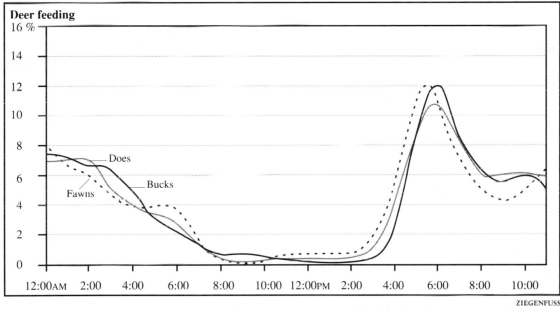

Deer feeding

Does

Fawns

Bucks

ZIEGENFUSS

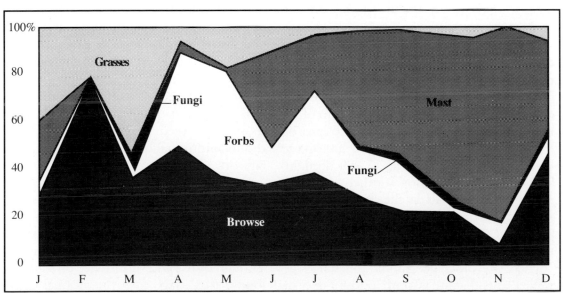

Grasses

Fungi

Forbs

Mast

Fungi

Browse

ZIEGENFUSS

AUBREY

Quercus alba
white oak

Sorbus americana
mountain ash

Prunus americana
American plum

Magnolia acuminata
cucumber tree

Juniperus communis
juniper

AUBREY

to think that this is an adaptive mechanism to ensure that does recovering from the strain of nursing will have enough food to replenish their body stores before winter arrives. Adult bucks and fawns are usually under their highest nutritional stress in late winter and early spring.

In the North, deer spend much of the early fall taking advantage of the acorn crop along with beech nuts and other high-energy fall foods. Obtaining a heavy store of lipids and fat reserves will be critical to their survival in the lean winter months ahead. Does, fawns, and bucks eat heavily during late September and early October. The bucks reach their peak condition in October and early November, just prior to the start of the rut. Once the rut starts, feeding activity takes second place to the urge to reproduce: body condition declines rapidly.

Other factors that affect what the whitetail eats are geographic location, soil types, and possibly even genetics. Geography determines what climatic stress a deer will have to endure: Stockpiling energy in the form of fat is critical for deer at the northern extremes of the whitetail's range but not so important for southern deer. Conversely, the drought and oppressive heat of a southern summer mean that whitetails in the South must be nutritionally prepared for heat dissipation and water conservation; northern herds have no such need.

There are other geographic differences as well. Plants that are favorite foods of deer in one location may be low choice or even starvation foods someplace else. Red cedar is one such plant. *Juniperus virginiana* is a preferred food in the Missouri Ozarks and in lower Michigan, but in most of the Southeast, it would be considered a low-quality starvation food. Sumac and red maple are two other browse species that are listed as highly preferred by deer in much of the Northern and Western ranges of white-tailed deer but are consumed in only low to moderate quantities in the Southeast.

The reason for such differences may be in the ground: soil types are known to affect the palatability of some forage species. But perhaps genetics offers another explanation. It is reasonable that evolutionary pressures on deer in different areas would foster different enzyme systems, allowing a race of deer in one location to digest foods with tannins or toxins that deer of another race would be unable to process. Indeed, deer have evolved different enzymes than domestic livestock: they readily consume such "toxic" plants as poison ivy, inedible mushrooms, locoweed, bracken fern, elks clover, rhododendron, mountain laurel, and tansy ragwort.

The microorganisms present in the stomach also affect what deer can and cannot eat. Deer have been known to starve to death with their stomachs full of what normally would be highly nutritious forage because, through disuse and subsistence on starvation foods, they have lost the normal rumen

196

RUE, JR.

Rubus odoratus
purple-flowering raspberry

Pinus strobus
white pine

Populus tremuloides
quaking aspen

Liriodendron tulipifera
yellow poplar

Ilex decidua
winterberry

REZENDES

*Deer kick and scratch through
the snow to reach buried
acorns and leaves. The acorns
are snipped in half by the
lower incisors and coarsely
chopped before being swallowed.*

REZENDES

AUBREY

WHITE-TAILED DEER

Sambucus nigra
elderberry

Magnolia virginiana
sweetbay

Tilia heterophylla
white basswood

Malus angustifolia
crabapple

Amelanchier
downy serviceberry

organisms necessary to digest that kind of good forage.

In general, the whitetail is said to be a crepuscular animal, actively feeding at dawn and dusk. A radio telemetry study conducted by Kammermeyer and Marchinton in Georgia documented crepuscular activity of movements by deer, but recent studies by Jacobson and Darrow using remote sensing devices at feeding stations have failed to confirm that deer are crepuscular in their feeding activity. Wild deer provided shelled corn at feeding stations during the hunting season on a wildlife management area in Mississippi were primarily nocturnal in their feeding. They fed from one-half hour before dusk until about 4 in the morning.

Personal observation over a fifteen-year period of many deer in captivity has led me to conclude that even in an undisturbed situation, deer are not particularly crepuscular in their feeding habits. I have rarely observed captive deer feeding prior to midmorning, and most daytime feeding activity does not begin until midday or later. Captive deer definitely demonstrate a feeding peak in the late afternoon and early evening hours, but also feed throughout the night.

My current study of wild deer suggests that feeding may begin in late afternoon and last throughout the night. I have conducted observations with a remote camera and timing device at feeding stations for deer accustomed to using a supplemental ration. That nocturnal feeding is an adaptation to human disturbances seems unlikely; the deer maintained this feeding schedule both during and outside of hunting season. Such feeding activity may explain the species' crepuscular movements: animals observed moving in late afternoon are going to feeding areas and those seen moving during early morning are returning from those areas.

Ultimately, perhaps, all the different research results come down to agreement: that the whitetail is a generalist feeder, that it is anything but predictable, and above all, that it is a survivor. Even in the complex man-dominated world of today, the whitetail has managed not only to exist but even to flourish.

—Harry A. Jacobson

Fleshy fruits supplement the summer and fall diets. This Columbia whitetail doe takes advantage of the plentiful cultivated apple crops of Washington.

BINEGAR

AUBREY

DEER

STRACENER

During a session of cudding, the bolus of food is chewed repeatedly and mixed with saliva before being reswallowed. The saliva contains urea, which enriches the nitrogen content of the chewed food and enhances bacterial fermentation in the rumen.

Arctostaphylos uva-ursi
bearberry

Kalmia latifolia
mountain laurel

Rhus glabra
smooth sumac

Viburnum prunifolium
blackhaw

Prunus serotina
black cherry

The Northeast, Great Lakes states, and eastern Canada

*I*n the north woods the time of plenty that coincides with acorn fall is generally short lived. Deer in the northeastern and Great Lakes states portions of whitetail range soon switch their diets to woody browse, such as blueberry, red maple, serviceberry, willow, rose, aspen, mountain laurel, and rhododendron. Agricultural crops, such as corn, sugar beets, apples, and alfalfa are used heavily where available. When the snow flies, deer are forced to retreat to winter conifer cover of white cedar and hemlock, where food will be in short supply until spring. At this time, deer eat anything available, including dead leaves, woody buds and stems, and conifers. They dig through the snow cover to get dead leaves, wintergreen, and vacciniums. American yew, ground hemlock, lichens, mountain ash, red maple, red-osier dogwood, witch hobble, and witherrod become preferred food species. However, the most important food species in the far north woods is white cedar. This is the only plant that by itself can sustain deer in the critical part of the winter. Other species must be taken in combinations with other plants to provide adequate nutrients to sustain life. White cedar also provides critical winter thermal cover for yarding deer.

By spring deer in the Northeast and Midwest begin to replenish lost body reserves with aquatic plants, goldenrod, clover, and other broadleaf herbaceous plants. Summer foods include a variety of browse species—aspen, mountain ash, cherry, maple, willow, dewberry, juneberry, and bearberry—and herbaceous species, such as clover, alfalfa, wild lettuce, and aquatic plants. Mushrooms and fruits like blackberry, blueberry, huckleberry, plum, and crabapple also are relished in the summer months.

—*Harry A. Jacobson*

AUBREY

The Northwest

*F*all foods consist of agricultural crops like wheat grain and alfalfa, plus such browse species as Oregon grape, bearberry, and common juniper. Winter foods consist of agricultural crops, buckbush, serviceberry, quaking aspen, willow, rose, ponderosa pine, Douglas-fir, myrtle, bearberry, and common juniper. Spring and summer forages include serviceberry, vetchling, American vetch, alfalfa, red clover, mushrooms, aster, spirea, dandelion, geranium, three-flowered avens, gland cinquefoil, common yarrow, and grasses.

—Harry A. Jacobson

The Southwest

*T*he white-tailed deer in the Southwest lives in habitat ranging from the semidesert brush country to prairie and intermountain regions. Winter starvation is rarely a problem, but summer drought can lead to serious food shortage. Just as white cedar and acorn mast can be critical for survival of deer in the North, the prickly pear cactus is important in the brush country. Fall food items, in addition to prickly pear, include mesquite beans, Mexican persimmon fruit, acacia seeds, grapes, acorns, kidney wood, fairy duster, mountain mahogany, desert yaupon, sumac, lime pricklyash, three-seeded mercuries, coralberry, saltbush, and other browse species, plus a variety of forbs and grasses. In some ranges in winter, a succulent plant called lechuguilla assumes the role of prickly pear in summer. Browse species such as coralberry, greenbrier, honeysuckle, bearberry, vaccinium, oak, persimmon, and juniper are prevalent in the diet. Winter forbs include spurge, birdsfoot trefoil, plainleaf pussytoes, and chickweed. Panic grasses, bromes, reed grass, and love grass are also eaten in winter, as are honey locust seeds, acorns, and—where available—agricultural plants like oats and rye. Spring and summer foods include prickly pear, lechuguilla, acacia, osage orange, grapes, sumac, oak, ash, and persimmon. Forbs like spurge, three-seeded mercuries, croton, Carolina snail-seed or moonseed, chickweed, vetch, bush clovers, false indigo, and partridge pea are also eaten in summer.

—Harry A. Jacobson

Midcentral

In the midcentral United States, seasonal changes are less dramatic than in the north woods, and deer have a wider choice of herbaceous and woody plants.

Browse species, such as poison ivy, honeysuckle, rosebuds and rose hips, buckbrush, dogwood, cinquefoil, New Jersey tea, wild grape, red cedar, dewberry, and sumac are important, along with such forbs as goldenrod, aster, wild lettuce, and English plantain. Clovers and other legumes are important fall foods. Acorns, persimmons, apples, honey locust fruit, and agricultural crops, if abundant, are heavily used. Late winter foods include mountain laurel, dewberry, red maple, greenbrier, sumac, chokeberry, rose, poison ivy, Virginia creeper, sassafras, azalea, and hawthorn. Winter wheat and corn are eaten where available. Spring foods include succulent twig growth and the new leaves of red maple, serviceberry, mountain laurel, greenbrier, rhododendron, blueberry, and deerberry. Herbaceous plants include goldenrod, violet, strawberry, galax, and aster. Summer foods include clovers, agricultural crops, legumes, aster, goldenrod, sunflower, ragweed, wild lettuce, and blackberry and plum. Succulent new leaves and twig growth of white ash, black cherry, woodbine, and other small trees and shrubs are also important.

—Harry A. Jacobson

The Southeast

Deer in the Southeast have a greater variety of foods than deer in any other region. Seldom are winters severe enough that food quantity is limiting. Only on ranges that are severely overpopulated, or during particularly severe winters, does the quantity of subsistence food become limiting. In most circumstances, the quality of food is more important.

Acorns and other fall mast crops are available for longer periods than in the North because there are more mast-producing trees and shrubs. Besides acorns, there are palmetto berries, honey locust and persimmon fruits, pawpaw fruits, and other mast—all available in the fall. Inkberry provides additional high-energy food for the winter months. Honeysuckle, dewberry, supplejack, and yellow jessamine leaves and stems are prime winter staples. Rye grass, panic grasses, winter wheat, and oats are eaten where available. Clovers, vetch, and broadleaf plants are other favorites.

Spring is a time of plenty, when deer consume succulent new growth on honeysuckle and trumpet creeper vines and herbaceous plants, such as aster, mint, ragweed, nettle, sedge, and a variety of aquatic plants. Summer foods are plentiful and include various broadleaf plants, browse species, mushrooms, and fruits like blackberry, dewberry, and wild plum. Late summer can bring seasonal stresses to deer in the Southeast, if prolonged summer drought lowers the quality of plants and causes lignification. Then deer switch to less succulent browse foods, such as greenbrier, gallberry, French mulberry, low-growing annual legumes, and less palatable herbaceous species.

—Harry A. Jacobson

The whitetail diet throughout its range

The foods of the whitetail vary from season to season and region to region, but some woody plants and their fruits are preferred browse across the United States and Canada.

CA	SE	MW	NE	NW	SW	
					•	*Acacia* spp., acacia
		•				*Acer glabrum*, Rocky Mountain maple
•		•	•			*Acer pensylvanicum*, moosewood, striped maple
•		•	•			*Acer rubrum*, red maple
•		•	•	•		*Acer spicatum*, mountain maple
•		•	•	•		*Amelanchier* spp., shadbush, serviceberry, Juneberry
•				•		*Arctostaphylos* spp., bearberry, manzanita
	•		•			*Aronia* spp., chokeberry
			•			*Artemisia* spp., falsetarragon sagebrush
			•			*Atriplex* canescens, four-wing saltbush
		•				*Berberis repens*, Oregon grape
	•					*Berchemia scandens*, rattanvine
•						*Betula alleghaniensis*, yellow birch
		•				*Betula lutea*, yellow birch
			•			*Calliandra eriophylla*, fairy duster, false mesquite
	•					*Campsis radicans*, trumpet creeper
		•				*Ceanothus americanus*, jersey tea
		•				*Ceanothus sanguineus*, redstem ceanothus
		•		•		*Ceanothus* spp., shiny ceanothus, desert ceanothus
		•				*Ceanothus velutinus*, snowbrush
			•			*Celtis reticulata*, desert hackberry
		•				*Cephalanthus occidentalis*, buttonbush
		•		•		*Cercocarpus* spp., mountain mahogany
		•				*Chamaecyparis thyoides*, Atlantic white cedar
	•					*Chamaedaphne calyculata*, leather leaf
	•					*Chionanthus virginicus*, fringe tree
			•			*Collomia linearis*, colima
•		•	•			*Comptonia peregrina*, sweet fern shrub
			•			*Condalia hookeri*, bluewood condalia
			•			*Condalia obtusifolia*, lotewood condalia
			•			*Cordia boissieri*, Mexican olive
		•				*Cornus alternifolia*, alternative-leaved dogwood
	•		•			*Cornus drummondii*, swamp dogwood
		•				*Cornus rugosa*, round-leaved dogwood
•		•	•	•		*Cornus stolonifera*, red-osier dogwood, kinnikinnick
	•					*Corylus* spp., hazelnut
	•	•	•	•	•	*Crataegus* spp., hawthorn, thorn apple (fruit)
	•					*Cyrilla racemiflora*, titi, leatherwood
◦		•	•			*Diervilla lonicera*, bush honeysuckle
	•	•			•	*Diospyros* spp., persimmon (fruit)
			•			*Dyssodia papposa*, dogweed
			•			*Erodium* spp., filaree
	•	•				*Euonymus americanus*, strawberry bush
			•			*Eysenhardtia polystachya*, kidney wood, rockbush
			•			*Fagus grandifolia*, beech (fruit)
			•			*Forestiera neomexicana*, forestiera, desert olive
			•			*Gaultheria procumbens*, wintergreen
•						*Gaylussacia* spp., huckleberry
	•					*Gelsemium sempervirens*, yellow jessamine
	•					*Gleditsia triacanthos*, honey locust (fruit)
	•	•				*Hamamelis virginiana*, witch hazel
	•					*Hydrangea arborescens*, smooth hydrangea
	•					*Ilex cassine*, dahoon holly
	•					*Ilex decidua*, deciduous holly
	•					*Ilex longipes*, Georgia holly
		•				*Ilex verticillata*, winterberry holly
	•				•	*Ilex vomitoria*, yaupon

CA	SE	MW	NE	NW	SW	
	•					*Itea virginica*, Virginia willow, sweetspire
		•		•		*Juniperus communis*, ground juniper
		•				*Juniperus virginiana*, red cedar
•						*Kalmia angustifolia*, lambkill, sheep laurel
	•	•				*Kalmia latifolia*, mountain laurel
					•	*Krameria glandulosa*, range ratany
			•			*Lindera benzoin*, spicebush
	•	•	•			*Liriodendron tulipifera*, yellow poplar, tulip tree
	•	•	•	•		*Lonicera* spp., honeysuckle
	•	•	•			*Magnolia acuminata*, cucumber tree
	•					*Magnolia virginiana*, sweet bay
				•		*Mahonia aquifolium*, mahonia, Oregon grape
	•	•				*Malus angustifolia*, crab apple (fruit)
	•					*Morus rubra*, red mulberry
			•			*Nemopanthus mucronatus*, mountain holly
	•	•	•		•	*Nyssa sylvatica*, black gum, tupelo
					•	*Opuntia lindheimeri*, prickly pear cactus
	•	•				*Parthenocissus quinquefolia*, Virginia creeper
				•		*Physocarpus malvaceus*, mallow ninebark
				•		*Pinus ponderosa*, ponderosa pine
			•			*Pinus strobus*, white pine
•		•	•			*Populus tremuloides*, quaking aspen
					•	*Prosopis* spp., mesquite (fruit)
	•	•	•		•	*Prunus* spp., plum
	•	•	•			*Prunus malus*, apple
			•			*Prunus pennsylvanica*, firecherry
	•	•			•	*Prunus serotina*, black cherry (fruit)
		•		•		*Prunus virginiana*, chokecherry
				•		*Pseudotsuga menziesii*, Douglas-fir
•		•	•			*Pyrus americana*, mountain ash
•	•	•	•		•	*Quercus*, oak (fruit)
•	•	•	•		•	*Rhus* spp., sumac
•						*Rhododendron canadense*, rhodora
•						*Ribes* spp., gooseberry
•		•	•	•		*Rosa* spp., wild rose
	•	•	•		•	*Rubus* spp., dewberry, blackberry, raspberry, currant
	•	•	•			*Salix* spp., willow
		•	•			*Sambucus* spp., elderberry
		•			•	*Smilax* spp., greenbrier
	•		•			*Sorbus americana*, mountain ash
•				•		*Spirea betulifolia*, birchleaf spirea
•						*Symphoricarpos occidentalis*, western snowberry
					•	*Symphoricarpos orbiculatus*, coralberry
		•	•			*Taxus* spp., yew
		•				*Taxus canadensis*, ground hemlock
		•				*Thuja occidentalis*, white cedar
		•	•			*Tilia* spp., basswood, linden
						Tragopogon porrifolius, salsify
•					•	*Vaccinium* spp., blueberry
	•					*Vaccinium stamineum*, deerberry
			•			*Viburnum acerifolium*, mapleleaf
•			•			*Viburnum alnifolium*, hobblebush, witch hobble
•		•	•			*Viburnum cassinoides*, withe-rod, wild raisin
				•	•	*Viburnum prunifolium*, skunk brush, blackhaw
•	•	•	•	•	•	*Vitis* spp., wild grape (fruit)
				•		*Yucca glauca*, soapweed
					•	*Zanthoxylum americanum*, lime prickly ash

CA = Canada, SE = Southeastern United States, MW = Midwestern United States, NE = Northeastern United States, NW = Northwestern United States, SW = Southwestern United States
Sources: Mathews and Glascow 1981; Goodrum and Reid 1958; Harlow and Guynn 1987; Gee, Porter, Demarais, Bryant, and Van Vreede 1991.

The nutrients for survival and growth

Late summer and early fall: that is the fat time. With plenty of forage—acorns and other mast high in proteins and oils; berries, forbs, and leaves high in energy—white-tailed deer can feed heavily. Bucks must eat enough to prepare for the rut and grow the heavy antlers that will earn them breeding rights, does must replenish their bodies now that their fawns are weaned, and animals of both sexes must lay down fat for the lean winter ahead.

GROWING A RACK

For the buck, body growth takes precedence over antler growth, so if high-quality foods are in short supply, his antlers will be small. Protein, in particular, is important at this time of the year, and the reason becomes apparent when the antlers are examined: velvet antlers are made almost entirely of a protein called collagen, and even mineralized antlers are about 45 percent protein.

A diet consisting of 13 to 16 percent protein is optimum for antler development. Should his protein intake be low, the buck, like any ruminant, can recycle urea—a nitrogen-rich by-product of protein metabolism normally excreted in urine—from the liver through the saliva back into the rumen. There rumen microbes can use the nitrogen to build new proteins.

The buck needs minerals, too. Hardened deer antlers are about 22 percent calcium and 11 percent phosphorus, but how much of those minerals the buck requires to grow those antlers has not yet been sorted out. Studies in the 1950s indicated that a diet of 0.09 percent calcium and 0.27 percent phosphorus was needed; since then researchers have published very different figures—0.64 percent calcium and 0.56 phosphorus in one study, 0.2 percent phosphorus in another, and 0.14 to 0.29 percent phosphorus in still another.

Just eating a diet high in minerals does not ensure antler growth, however. The deer's body cannot absorb calcium without vitamin D, and indeed, the levels of vitamin D circulating in the blood have been found to vary proportionally with the antler growth cycle.

Antler growth is a function of age, genetics, and nutrition. A good diet will enable this buck to grow a big rack, thus enhancing his opportunity to breed.

LEA

LEA

DEER

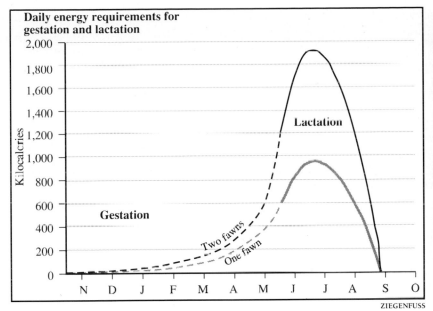

Daily energy requirements for gestation and lactation

Kilocalories

Lactation

Gestation

Two fawns

One fawn

N D J F M A M J J A S O

ZIEGENFUSS

MCFALLS

For both does and bucks, good-quality summer food is essential. The doe needs to nurse her fawns; the buck needs minerals and other nutrients to grow antlers and prepare for the rut.

Even a buck whose diet doesn't contain large amounts of minerals can still produce antlers, however. Bucks store minerals in their skeletons and transfer them to the antler if needed, which would help explain why the studies of mineral requirements don't agree. In fact, while the antlers are mineralizing, bucks undergo osteoporosis—the loss of minerals from their bones, similar to what happens to many older women. After the antlers harden, the minerals lost from the bones are replaced from the animal's diet.

In any case, for a truly impressive rack, the buck's genes will turn out to be as important as his diet.

WINTER STORES

To gain fat in preparation for winter, deer need carbohydrates. Soluble carbohydrates—starches and sugars—are a major source, and whatever a deer does not use for energy, its body converts to adipose fat. But actually, a deer eats little starch. As a ruminant, it can digest cellulose, the fiber that non-cud-chewing animals cannot digest. The tough skins of berries, the woody twigs of shrubs, the leaves of some forbs, the stems of some grasses—all the plant parts that a human being would consider inedible—furnish the deer with most of the energy it needs. In fact, fiber is useful not only for energy but for the "scratch factor" of roughage that helps keep the rumen healthy.

To make use of such high-energy foods, a deer must have healthy microbes in its ru-

men. Otherwise it may not be able to digest even high-quality foods such as alfalfa hay. The undigested roughage could build up and compact in the animal's digestive tract, possibly killing it. Similarly, if a starving deer, which would lack healthy rumen microbes, were suddenly to eat a large amount of grain, like corn, it could die of toxic acidosis—a buildup of lactic acid in the rumen.

An even better source of energy than fiber and soluble carbohydrates is lipids—fats, which are solid at room temperature, and oils, which are liquid. Lipids have two and a half times the amount of energy per gram as proteins and carbohydrates. The oils in fatty foods like acorns are thus important if the deer is to lay down its own fat for the winter.

When the breeding season begins, both bucks and does eat less, even if food is available. Their minds are on the rut, and even though the challenges and chases require more energy, especially now that the temperature has dropped, they get by with very little food. In part this is because they are drawing on the stored depot fat, which provides energy when needed, but it's also because the animal's thyroid activity and thus its metabolism decrease.

Still, the deer needs energy just to maintain body temperature when the land is locked in snow and ice. The animal also draws on its stored reserves simply to maintain body functions—breathing, walking, escaping from predators and snowmobiles, chewing and digesting what little it eats. The colder the weather, the deeper the snow, the steeper the hill—the more energy the deer needs.

Paradoxically, the bigger the deer, the less it needs, in relative terms. The large buck requires more energy on an absolute basis, but it needs less per unit of body weight than a smaller animal.

The maintenance energy—the amount needed just for basal metabolism—for a 55-kilogram (120-pound) deer in winter is about 3,192 calories (technically, kilocalories) per day, according to Ullrey and others. That's for a doe in a laboratory. Put the deer in the real world, where it must walk, run, and feed, and the actual energy requirements jump by two or three times. Since the deer isn't eating much in winter, and since what it does eat is low in nutritional quality, the animal can easily lose 15 to 20 percent of its body weight, perhaps more.

Maintenance protein requirements are fairly low, probably 8 to 12 percent of the diet. Deer can get by with very little protein for extended periods in winter. Pregnancy increases the doe's requirements—protein,

the building block of animal tissue, is essential for growth and replacement of blood, hair, and body cells—but not that much during the first two trimesters. In fact, the average fawn at birth contains just 525 grams of protein, and the doe had the six-month gestation period to produce it.

EATING FOR TWO . . . OR THREE

It is lactation that makes special demands on the doe, especially if she bears twins. The milk of white-tailed deer averages 8.2 percent protein (36.4 percent protein if the water is removed and the solids are analyzed). A shortage of dietary protein during lactation probably leads not to milk that is less rich, but simply to less milk. The doe also needs calcium and phosphorus, in approximately the same quantities needed by the buck during antler growth.

The fawn's growth is expensive. Once weaned, according to Ullrey et al., the young animal needs a diet of about 13 to 22 percent protein—more than the buck needs to grow his antlers. Besides protein for the growth of body cells, the fawn needs miner-

This doe's protruding ribs reveal her condition and underscore the importance of good nutrition during lactation, when minerals passed to her fawns are not available for her own body's needs. Her mane, though uncommon, is genetically determined, not the result of environmental factors.

DVORAK

Nutritional needs

As a white-tailed deer quickly chews an acorn or carefully nips off a bud, it takes in the nutrients necessary for proper bodily operations and good health. The nutritional requirements of deer vary, depending on factors such as the sex, age, activity, and environment of each animal. Nonetheless, certain key nutrients are essential for any deer to survive.

Fat-soluble vitamins

Stored in the body, these vitamins can become toxic if they accumulate in excessive amounts.

A	Converted from carotene, a plant compound. Deficiencies can lead to blindness.
D	Produced in the skin when exposed to sunlight. Needed for calcium absorption and metabolism.
E	Found in green plants and seeds. An antioxidant that prevents muscle disorders.
K	Produced in the rumen by microorganisms. Aids in the clotting of blood.

Carbohydrates

These are a major source of energy for deer and other herbivores.

Soluble	Starches and sugars are a part of the deer diet.
Fiber	The cellulose, converted to usable carbohydrate, provides energy and keeps the rumen healthy.

Water-soluble vitamins

Because they are not stored in the body, these are needed by most animals on a daily basis.

B complex	Produced in the rumen. Needed for many metabolic reactions.
C	Produced in the liver. Prevents scurvy; used in many metabolic reactions.

Minerals

These make up only 5 percent of deer's body, but they are vital for proper health.

Calcium and phosphorus	Present in most plants. Needed for bone and antler growth, milk production, blood clotting, muscle contraction, general metabolism.
Selenium	Drawn from the soil, this mineral can be found in most plants. Deficiencies may lead to white-muscle disease.
Sodium	Deer often use salt licks, perhaps because they need this mineral, or perhaps because they like the taste. Needed for acid-base balance and muscle contraction.

Water

This critical nutrient is available to deer in three forms; an animal may need 3 to 6 quarts per day from all sources, depending on the temperature and the deer's activity.

Free	Deer drink from ponds and streams, and lick dew on plants.
Preformed	Plants, particularly succulents like berries and forbs, contain 60 to 80 percent water.
Metabolic	This water is produced in the animal's cells as a by-product of metabolism.

Protein

Found in may plants and produced by microbes in the rumen. Deer need this component in their diets for normal maintenance (cell replacement) and for the special needs of growth, reproduction, and lactation.

---

als. A diet of 0.45 percent calcium and 0.3 percent phosphorus is best, according to Ullrey.

For the fawn, as for the doe and the buck, early fall is the time to prepare for winter, when all the animals will have to get by on reduced feed until the lush growth of spring enables them to recover.

Whitetails are well adapted for the deprivations of winter and seldom need supplemental feed. In some northern states, there may be dieoffs in overpopulated areas if the winter is long and the cold is severe, but the occasions are rare. It is the transition seasons—spring and fall—when deer need food.

—*Robert D. Brown*

Whitetail population dynamics

Years ago, when deer populations had reached critically low numbers, protection and recovery were the goal. Now the problem, at least in many areas, is controlling and even reducing deer numbers. Bringing deer herds into balance with their habitat requires an understanding of deer population characteristics and dynamics, and the first job is figuring out just how many deer there are.

Estimating Deer Numbers

Though deer numbers can be estimated and general trends recognized, actual deer numbers are not easily determined in the field. Ground-based methods for estimating a deer herd include general reconnaissance, strip census, and night spotlight counts. Strip-census counts can be made from low-flying aircraft, too. Indirect estimates of deer numbers can be made from deer sign, such as beds, tracks, trails, and pellets, and trends are apparent in harvest records, vehicle-deer collision rates, and numbers of damage complaints from farmers.

None of these methods relate accurately to actual deer numbers, however; they are most useful for showing trends. Direct counts almost always underestimate deer numbers.

Direct and indirect estimates are often converted to estimates of deer numbers with statistical procedures. Suppose, for example, ten deer are trapped and marked, and during field observations five unmarked deer are seen for every marked deer. Using the ratio of marked to unmarked deer seen, there should be sixty deer in the population: ten marked deer and fifty unmarked deer. In a study by McCullough and Hirth in 1988 on the George Reserve (Michigan) deer herd, however, "Eighty percent of the females were marked but estimates of females were inaccurate." The method is mathematically logical but appears to be much too inaccurate to apply to free-ranging deer.

If neither direct nor indirect methods for estimating deer numbers provide reliable information about actual numbers, how can deer numbers be accurately estimated at a reasonable cost? What factors affect deer population dynamics? What is the relative importance of predation compared with regulated hunting in controlling deer numbers? These and many other questions can be answered with population models that simulate real deer populations. Computer technology permits us to project deer population growth, given information about range conditions, weather, predation, hunting, numbers of does and bucks and their ages, and other aspects of deer biology.

Deer numbers have the potential to increase remarkably fast on excellent range because females in good physical condition have high reproduction rates. A population on excellent range can double in two years. Even on poor range a population grows by a factor of almost 1.7 in just four years. Rapid increases in deer numbers result in popula-

tions that are out of balance with range resources, and starvation losses increase—a scenario familiar to deer managers in many states.

The reproduction rate of a population depends in part on the age ratios of the females. A female's reproductive potential increases with age until she is past her prime—usually by age 8—and the effects of old age begin to accrue.

A better indicator of condition and reproductive capacity, however, is weight: Females that do not weigh more than 33 kilograms (70 to 75 pounds) rarely conceive. Does from 33 to 48 kilograms (75 to 100 pounds) typically conceive one fawn or perhaps none at all; does with autumn weights of 48 to 68 kilograms (100 to 150 pounds) typically conceive one or two fawns; and does weighing more should carry twins and occasionally even triplets.

And a doe's weight depends on the quality of her food. Range quality is difficult to quantify, however, and going out into the field and weighing all the does is not an option. How, then, can one easily determine

On highest-quality range, deer can double their numbers in just two years—in large part because well-nourished does can birth multiple fawns. But even on deteriorating range, a population continues to increase and can double in four years.

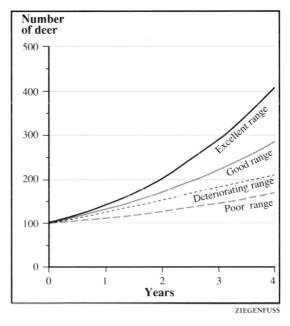

STRACENER

multiply, whereas males are simply added to and subtracted from a population. Variations in the female fraction of a deer population therefore contribute to variations in population growth, and variations in the male fraction do not.

The sex ratio at birth is not a simple ratio but a function of several biological and population characteristics, including the age ratio of does, the condition of the range, and the combined effects of age and range. Severinghaus showed in 1984 that adult does have relatively more female fawns than does bred as fawns and yearlings, which have relatively more male fawns. That's assuming good range and good nutrition. Prime-aged does on poor diets have a higher proportion of male fawns, according to a 1983 penned-deer study by Verme. As range conditions deteriorate, the age structure of the breeding population also changes, however. On poor range, females do not breed as fawns and sometimes not even as yearlings. Because prime-age and older does make up a higher proportion of the breeding population on poor range, and because their offspring otherwise tend to be females, the poor-diet trend toward more male fawns is countered by the age-structure trend toward more female fawns.

Conversely, on good range, relatively more female fawns are expected because the breeding does are in good condition. But fawns and yearlings also reproduce on good range, and younger does tend to have relatively

range quality so as to predict the does' condition and reproduction rates? As it happens, an excellent indicator of range quality is yearling antler size, for just as better range produces larger does and higher conception rates, better range results in larger bucks and bigger antlers. The average diameter of the antler beams from harvested yearling bucks can, in fact, be used to calculate the conception rate for females bred as fawns, yearlings, mature does, and older does.

Range condition:	*Poor*	*Good*	*Excellent*
Yearling beam diameters:	12mm	17mm	22mm
Fawns	0.00	0.19	0.58
Yearlings	0.18	1.22	1.98
2- to 7-year-olds	1.19	1.69	2.05
8- to 11-year-olds	0.66	1.43	1.99

Conception rates of females

SEX RATIO EFFECTS

The sex ratio is a very important characteristic of a deer population because females

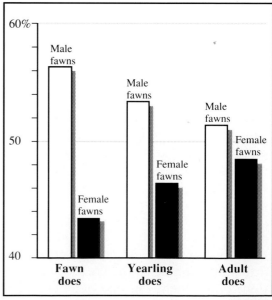

ZIEGENFUSS

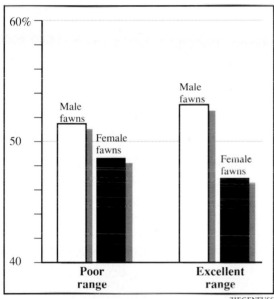

60%

50

40

Male
fawns

Female
fawns

**Poor
range**

Male
fawns

Female
fawns

**Excellent
range**

ZIEGENFUSS

*and age mortality after birth. Deer popula-
tions exposed to bucks-only hunting have
yearling and adult sex ratios that favor females. This favors population growth.
When deer numbers are high, however,
females need to be hunted if population
growth is to be controlled. Moen and
Severinghaus illustrated in 1987 that fawn
production over a twelve-year period with a
50:50 male:female ratio for both yearlings
and adults was more than twice that with a
60:40 male:female ratio. Keeping yearling
and adult sex ratios similar to those in natural populations would help the populations stay in better balance with range resources.*

*The better the range, the
greater the proportion of male
fawns.*

THE EFFECTS OF AGE

A population's age structure, or the distribution of deer numbers in each of the age
classes, depends on how many deer in each
age class die each year. As a fraction of the
yearling-plus-adult population, yearlings account for 25 to 30 percent, but more after
mild winters with little or no fawn mortality
and less after severe winters with high fawn
mortality. That assumes no hunting. In a
heavily hunted population yearlings may account for 60 percent of the yearling-plus-
adult population, or more.

Using the fraction of yearlings in a population is a good way to estimate the fractions
of other age classes. If the yearling fraction is
high, the older-deer fractions must be low,
and vice versa. Enter the variables into expo-

more male offspring than older ones. Thus
the good-diet trend toward fewer male fawns
is countered by the age-structure trend
toward more male fawns.

The net effect is that relatively more male
fawns are born in populations living on excellent range and relatively fewer are born in
populations on poor range as a result of the
interaction of the age-structure of the female
population and range quality. Note in both
cases, however, that the absolute sex ratio
favors male fawns. A 50:50 sex ratio at birth
is sometimes used as an approximation in
deer population modeling, but this leads to
errors in the results.

Yearling and adult sex ratios are a function
of the sex ratio at birth plus differential sex

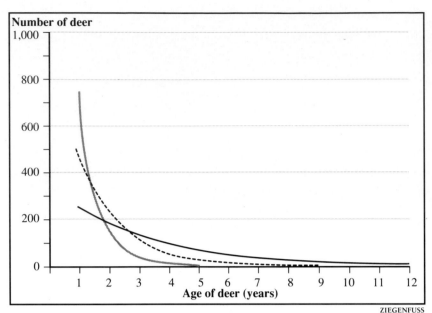

Number of deer

If there are 750 yearlings in a population of 1,000 deer, the number of older animals is very small. Conversely, a smaller proportion of 1-year-olds leaves places for more older deer.

Fawns weighing less than 1.8 kilograms (4 pounds) at birth do not usually survive.

nential equations and note that a high yearling fraction of 0.75 means there are no deer 6 years and older. At the other extreme, 195 deer out of 1,000 are 6 years or older when the age structure begins with a yearling fraction of 0.25. Obviously, a population cannot have a high proportion of both young and old deer at the same time, which explains why there are few trophy bucks in heavily hunted populations.

Such age structures are not just computer constructs; they are observed in the field. Several New York populations fit exponential equations best, and McCullough's 1979 data on the George Reserve herd in Michigan fit exponential equations for nineteen-year averages for males and females with r^2 values of 0.98 and 0.97, respectively.

After sex and age structures of a population have been determined, weighted-mean weights, metabolic rates, and forage requirements may also be determined. A higher number of smaller, younger deer, for example, results in a lower average population weight, a lower metabolic rate, and a lower total forage requirement than a population of larger, older deer. The forage required by a population, an important part of the land's carrying capacity, can be calculated when weight, metabolic rates, and forage characteristics are known.

MORTALITY RATES

Deer die from age, exposure, predators, diseases, human land-use patterns and ac-

tivities, hunting, and other causes. Some of the factors are understood well enough that the numbers can be incorporated directly into population models. Others, such as age-related mortality, can be estimated from such models.

When it comes to age, a computer model must include as many age classes as the deer has longevity. For whitetails, the oldest age class is 12 years, so thirteen age classes (0, 1, 2 . . . 12) are needed in a population model.

Fawn mortality. The first month of life is the most critical for a whitetail fawn. Summer fawn mortality is difficult to observe directly, but field studies have shown that it can vary greatly, from almost none to over 50 percent. Newborn fawns that weigh less at birth have a lower probability of survival than those that weigh more. Verme's data show that fawns weighing less than 1.8 kilograms (4 pounds) are not expected to survive (100 percent mortality) but fawns weighing almost 3.5 kilograms (7.5 pounds) are almost certain to survive.

One of the dangers for newborn fawns is predators. Newborns hide instinctively but are vulnerable if they are discovered. The hiding instinct lasts for just a week or two, depending on fawn size and development. Larger, better-developed fawns switch from hiding to running sooner than small fawns.

Yearling and adult mortality. The relative mortality rates of deer of yearling age and above increase with age. Yearlings are the least vulnerable and the oldest deer the

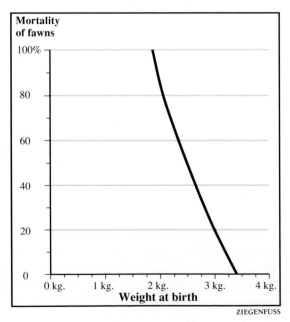

most. It is often thought that fawns are the most vulnerable because so many die in severe winters, but old deer are actually at greater risk than fawns. Few deer reach old age, however, especially in hunted populations.

Sex-related mortality. Field evidence suggests that more bucks than does succumb to winter stress. The logical explanation for this is the rut: The rapid depletion of their fat reserves in November and December makes bucks more vulnerable to the effects of poor nutrition in winter, so negative energy balances are more likely. Cold weather and deep snow compound the problem, as the bucks have little fat to draw on when they need it most. Since does draw down their fat reserves more gradually, they may still have something left late in the winter.

Weather-related mortality. Weather-related mortality includes the effects of hypothermia, starvation, and exhaustion. Hypothermia occurs when deer simply get too cold to survive. Starvation occurs when food is in short supply and the animals' fat reserve is not sufficient to maintain life. Exhaustion occurs when snow makes movement so difficult and energy-expensive that deer are confined to trails, which limits their access to food. Weather-related mortality factors are thus interrelated, not simple cause-and-effect relationships. One defense deer have is their ability to enter an energy-conserving mode in winter, with reductions in activity levels and energy metabolism, but some-

times the weather overtakes them nevertheless.

Predation. Predation may seem like a clear-cut cause of mortality, but in reality it is a complex mixture of predator, prey, and range relationships. If, for example, a deer is weak from starvation and about to die when it is killed by a predator, what is the real cause of death: predation or winter stress?

Predators need not kill live animals when dead ones are available, so deer deaths from winter stress can reduce predation on live deer. In population reconstructions for the Adirondacks in New York State, Severinghaus calculated that deer populations could not support the known harvest, heavy winter losses, and coyote predation unless coyotes became scavengers during severe winters. The tradeoff between winter kill and predation is a good demonstration of compensatory mortality.

The subject of predation generates considerable controversy among hunters, not to mention other segments of the public. Part of the controversy stems from the simple fact that if a predator kills a deer, it is neither available to a hunter nor around to contribute to population growth. This was of great importance when deer populations were low and recovering, but is of less concern today.

A widely held belief is that predators can control a deer population and keep it in balance with range resources. Calculations of predator densities, their metabolic requirements, and the caloric content of deer car-

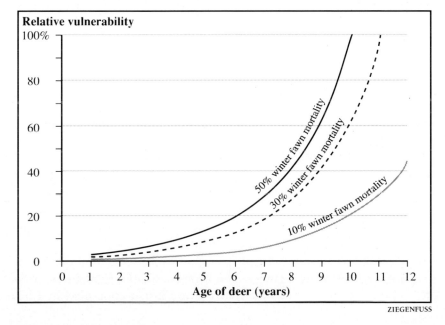

Relative vulnerability

Fawn mortality rates in winter can predict the relative vulnerability of older deer. Adults over 8 years old are more vulnerable than fawns when winter fawn mortality is 50 percent or more.

ZIEGENFUSS

MARCHEL

casses suggest that predators do not become abundant enough to control deer populations by preying on adult deer. The oldest and most vulnerable adult deer simply do not make up a significant enough portion of the population. Population control by predation is more effective if the predators learn to kill fawns.

Hunting. A deer population is usually thought of as comprising bucks and does. From the hunter's standpoint, however, the population consists of antlered and antlerless deer. Bucks with sublegal antlers and male fawns are harvested as antlerless deer, along with does and female fawns.

Mortality from hunting can be broken down into the legal harvest, illegal kill, and crippling loss. The legal harvest includes all deer harvested and reported according to hunting regulations. When antlered and antlerless deer are harvested, data should be recorded by sex for at least three age groups—fawns, yearlings, and adults—to compile an adequate picture of harvest mortality for reconstructing deer populations with a computer model.

Illegal kills are deer that are poached out of season, plus deer killed during the season but not claimed, and deer taken legally but not reported.

Crippling losses may be either legally or illegally killed deer. The subject is controversial and the data are difficult to evaluate, though computer simulations suggest that estimates by both hunters and nonhunters are probably higher than actual crippling losses.

Road kill and other accidents. Collisions of vehicles with deer seem to occur in proportion to the number of deer and to the amount and speed of traffic. Superimposed on these factors are habitat distributions and seasonal rhythms in behavior and activity. Bashore and coworkers found that road kills were significantly higher in spring and fall in Pennsylvania and were more likely to occur in edge habitat, where deer could remain close to woods but feed on herbaceous vegetation in a field.

Farm machines cause accidental deaths for fawns. The little fawn's hiding instinct works to its disadvantage if it is concealed in a hay field: the fawn hides until the last second, when it is too late for the farmer to stop the mower.

POPULATION MODELS

Modeling a deer population is a complex biological problem involving many factors. In the simplest case, a population of two deer, one male and one female, will become three deer if the female bears one young and none die.

It is often said that population growth is exponential. This generality often creates an image of numbers rising rapidly through successive reproductive cycles. Numbers can also decrease exponentially, however. Exponential calculations depend on constant natality and mortality rates, but since these rates are not constant in the real world, this is not a useful way to model and predict deer populations.

In the past, deer numbers have been estimated by multiplying some index, such as the buck harvest, by an expansion factor that represents the number of deer in the population per buck. That method is not accurate

BIGGS

enough for current deer management, let alone future needs. Legal proceedings will likely require more information on deer numbers to justify hunting; general trends in deer numbers may not be sufficient. Ecologically based population models will be needed to demonstrate deer population characteristics and dynamics, and to perform "what if" tests to simulate the effects of various actions before they are implemented.

Suppose, for example, that 100 deer are harvested from a particular herd each year. If each doe in this herd has two fawns, then 50 does are needed to replace the 100 deer killed. But not every fawn will survive, and deer die from other causes besides hunting, so more than 50 does are needed. This is a simple example of the logic underlying population reconstruction; of course, many other factors must also be considered.

The best way to estimate deer numbers and model deer populations is with a computer model based on actual deer-range relationships. Birth and death rates vary in proportion to sex and age characteristics, range conditions, and management strategies. The age-related vulnerability curve described earlier is an example of a proportional relationship. The close relationship between yearling antler-beam diameter and female reproductive rates is another example; both are proportional to range conditions. Other examples are the age distribution of harvested deer, which is proportional to summer and winter mortality rates; the fraction of yearling males, which is a function of hunting pressure; and the fraction of yearling females, which is a function of productivity. All of these important population characteristics need to be used when reconstructing deer populations.

Another challenge for computer modeling is following a class of fawns through their life span. The deer year begins with the birth of fawns. Those fawns are subject to mortality factors through the year, and at the end of the deer year, the remaining deer become yearlings; a year later, the yearlings that are left form the class of 2-year-olds; and so forth. The year-to-year continuity represents what really happens in a deer population and must be duplicated in a computer model.

One sign of an increase in a local deer herd is a rise in the number of deer-vehicle collisions. Many accidents occur, predictably enough, where roads bisect the whitetail's favored edge habitats.

The concept of biological proportions was incorporated in the Deer CAMP model I developed after attempts to design a simplified deer population model with the fewest possible variables failed. It became clear that any program to track populations sequentially from year to year had to be a proportion-based one, with as many age classes as occur in the natural life span of deer.

A population model based on sound biology can provide valuable insights into population characteristics, dynamics, and responses to different management strategies. The wealth of information on white-tailed-deer can now be used to predict deer populations and prescribe management options in just a few seconds of computer time.

POPULATION CONTROL

Some people think that deer populations regulate themselves naturally by reducing reproduction on poor range, while others maintain that regulated hunting is the only way to keep deer populations under control. In reality, deer populations are regulated by both natural and human-related factors.

To test the effectiveness of self-regulation by a deer population, suppose that a herd grows rapidly and exceeds range resources. The deer are in poor condition and their reproduction rate drops. What happens to population growth over the next several years? Computer modeling shows that the population continues to rise, though at a slower rate than if the reproduction rate had remained high. And that was assuming the lowest observed reproduction rates for poor range. The results suggest that mortality rates must increase if this population is to level off.

In pioneer days white-tailed deer became scarce because hunting was not restricted, but populations began to recover after season and bag limits were established. Recovery occurred, even with hunting, because the does were protected. With bucks-only hunting, a population grows almost as fast as when there is no hunting. Bucks-only hunting was good management when deer populations were low, but both males and females need to be harvested if populations are to be controlled.

Once reproduction rates and mortality rates (including predation, road kill, and summer and winter fawn deaths) are realistically incorporated, the computer model can suggest hunting limits that maintain population stability by limiting total mortality. A deer population on excellent range can be kept stable (zero population growth) with a legal harvest rate of 27 to 28 percent for both antlered and antlerless deer. Harvest rates of 20 to 21 percent will stabilize a deer population on good range, and harvest rates of 10 to 11 percent will stabilize a population on poor range.

Total mortality includes deaths from both natural causes and hunting. On excellent range, a legal harvest rate of 27 to 28 percent accounts for about 58 percent of the total mortality. On good range, a legal harvest rate of 20 to 21 percent accounts for about 47 percent of total mortality, and on poor range a legal harvest rate of 10 to 11 percent accounts for only 39 percent of the total mortality.

These harvest rates and mortality percentages are general guidelines only because all causes of death interact with one another to affect overall population dynamics. "What if" tests can be done with the computer model to calculate the effects, from year to year, of variations in summer and winter fawn mortality, random predation, road kill, illegal kill, and crippling losses. The interactions are so complex that a computer model is necessary to calculate their effects

Mature does are more likely to succeed in rearing their young. They select superior habitat—a range with better food—and can thus produce more milk. Good habitats also offer more secure hiding places for the bedded fawns.

KINNEY

How does' ages affect conception rates

Once the age structure of a deer population has been determined, the number of does in each age class and their conception rates may be used to calculate the weighted-mean conception rate of the herd. Note that the weighted-mean rate (1.06) is lower than the simple average for all age classes (1.44) because the population includes a larger number of young does, who are less productive than older does.

Age of doe (years)	Number of does	Fraction of total number of does	Average number of fawns per doe	Weighted-mean conception rate for the age class
1	162	0.34	0.19	0.06
2	107	0.23	1.22	0.28
3	71	0.15	1.69	0.25
4	47	0.10	1.69	0.17
5	31	0.07	1.69	0.12
6	20	0.04	1.69	0.07
7	13	0.03	1.69	0.05
8	9	0.02	1.69	0.03
9	6	0.01	1.43	0.01
10	4	0.01	1.43	0.01
11	3	0.00	1.43	0.00
12	2	0.00	1.43	0.00
Total	475	1.00	1.44	1.06

quickly enough to be of much practical use.

Total mortality in relation to the reproduction rate of the population is called the net recruitment rate. A net recruitment rate of 35 percent is possible in deer populations—high enough to cause a deer population to double in two years. Zero population growth is the goal for populations that should be kept stable, and negative net growth is the goal for populations that are too large.

The Deer CAMP computer model, developed by Aaron and Ronald Moen with the help of C. W. Severinghaus, has been tested with data from several states and was used to make management recommendations for a populated area in Massachusetts in 1984 and for a nature preserve in Kentucky in 1985. Some states use it to reconstruct deer popu-

lations in all their management units, and it has also been used to reconstruct populations for twenty-five consecutive years of harvest data in selected deer management units in New York State. The automated version of the Deer CAMP model has been tested on more than thirty years of data for the Sand Hills Wildlife Management Area in Wisconsin, and it is being applied in other areas where three or more years of harvest data are available. Management decisions should be based on a scientific understanding of population dynamics, and computer population modeling can be an excellent tool.

—Aaron N. Moen

Population change and loss of habitat

The number of white-tailed deer in North America has fluctuated over the centuries. Major changes have primarily been in response to the human beings with whom they share the continent, but the relationship has never been a simple trade-off—more people, fewer deer. The spread of human beings across the land and their changing activities have, in fact, led to more deer in many places.

White-tailed deer populations in the United States have undergone several periods of decline and reestablishment since 1500, as documented by McCabe and McCabe. From the arrival of the first white settlers until about 1800, deer populations were affected mainly by Native Americans. It is estimated there were 24 million to 40 million whitetails at the beginning of the colonial period but just 8 million to 17 million at the end. Evidence for the figures comes from early records of the fur trade. Considering how few Indians and Europeans were actually involved in this unregulated commercial enterprise, the number of hides taken annually is astounding.

Deer had long been important in the lives of the indigenous peoples. They were part of the American Indian's diet: deer remains in various middens greatly outnumber all other animal remains. Besides the meat, bone marrow was a favorite food. Deer hides were fashioned into all types of clothing, plus moccasins, headwear, and mittens. Other widely used by-products of whitetails included deerhide mats, rugs, and blankets; sinew for thread, string, bowstrings, and fishnets; and bone utensils, such as awls, digging sticks, hide fleshers, fishhooks, arrowheads, clubs, arrow straighteners, corn scrapers, cutting tools, coarse needles, daggers, and pistol-grip awls.

The decline of deer was due, in great part, to the massive harvests of deer by the Indians, who traded hides for other goods—such as knives, clothing, and cooking utensils—with the ever-increasing influx of Europeans. The hides were exported to European markets as well as used by the American colonists. To supply this trade, Natives Americans are estimated to have killed 4.6 million to 6.4 million deer each year in North America. Their methods of hunting deer included fire drive, fire surrounding, still hunting, stalking, stalking while disguised, luring, drive to snowbanks and enclosures, snaring, pens, pitfalls and other traps, drive to water, baiting, running to exhaustion, poisoning, and tracking with dogs.

Beginning about 1800 deer populations recovered modestly. The increase occurred partly because deer were spreading to new or pristine habitats and reestablishing themselves in former habitats, but also because they were no longer intensively hunted for the fur trade. The last few Native Americans of the eastern states had finally been driven from the remaining white-tailed deer range by the U.S. Army in 1837.

As a species that thrives in edge habitat, white-tailed deer were naturally restricted in number when forests covered the continent. Mammalian predators also kept populations in check.

BIGGS

The recovery did not last long, however: the growing herds of deer soon became the target for market and subsistence hunters. From 1850 to 1900 the country witnessed more hunting pressure on wildlife than at any time before or since. The intensity of the deer harvest increased as more and more hunters and settlers exploited the resource and hunted what had once been undisturbed land. White-tailed deer reached their lowest population levels and in places disappeared altogether.

With the end of market hunting and the beginning of habitat protection, deer entered a modern period of recovery. Hunting seasons and limits were established, deer were protected from illegal killing and overharvesting, refuges were established, habitat was improved, herds were restocked, predators were eliminated. As the science of game management came of age, some practices were found to be unnecessary (such as predator control) or were refined (such as habitat protection).

In fact, Downing wrote in 1987, "the pendulum of deer abundance did not swing sharply to the 'plus' side until the Great Depression of the 1930s when much of the rural human population in the South, Midwest, and East began to abandon small farms and move to the cities." When deer's worst enemy, man, moved to jobs in the city and new houses in the suburbs, the abandoned farm fields became overgrown with weeds and brush—important components of whitetail habitat. This set the stage for an unimpeded rise in the population of white-tailed deer.

REGIONAL CHANGES

Deer populations are constantly changing, even without human interference, because of natural disturbances—lightning fires, hurricanes, tornadoes, floods, blizzards, insect damage, and overbrowsing by the deer themselves. In most instances, such natural events actually benefit deer habitat. When an ice storm fells trees, or when a bolt of lightning ignites a dry forest, the canopy's opened and sunlight penetrates to the forest floor, thereby encouraging the growth of plant species preferred by deer.

The extensive farming and lumbering that cleared New England hardwood forests in the 1800s created ideal habitat for whitetails. Market hunters took advantage of this increase in the population and eliminated deer in many places.

LEMMO

The effect of human activities can be positive if, like timber cutting and agriculture, it creates good deer habitat with abundant food, but negative if, like real-estate development and highway construction, it eliminates deer habitat.

In the northern regions of New England, New York, Pennsylvania, and the Great Lake states, prolonged severe winter weather can greatly reduce overall whitetail populations. Snowpacks of 35 to 50 centimeters (14 to 20 inches) or more can form and last from December to early April. Deer may be forced to yard up, often for a hundred days or more, and can consume nearly all available food. Only the largest deer are then able to obtain any browse, and the younger animals quickly succumb to pneumonia brought on by starvation. The larger the population of deer in an area, the greater the subsequent die-off.

The usual pattern of change in these regions begins with a large increase in the deer population following logging, fire, farm abandonment, and the killing of predators. If not enough deer are killed annually by hunters, their numbers will eventually exceed the habitat's carrying capacity. If the conifers that had provided winter shelter in their usual yarding areas have been harvested, the deer will concentrate in what little good winter habitat is left, with the result that overbrowsing and ultimately starvation may occur. Such conditions cause boom-bust cycles in some white-tailed deer populations.

In parts of the snowbelt region, the bucks-only harvest tradition preferred by many hunters and sanctioned by state game commissions makes it impossible to stabilize and manage deer populations. Too many deer in an area not only results in smaller animals and large deer die-offs but also hampers habitat regeneration, preventing the growth of new forest and improved deer habitat. Also, since only bucks are harvested, few ever live long enough to reach their full potential of antler and body size.

In the northern Appalachian Mountains, severe winter weather, ice storms, and persistent deep snows along with low soil fertility limit food supplies and decrease the carrying capacity of the range. Overbrowsing and habitat depletion weaken the animals as they

C. MILLER

enter winter, making them more vulnerable to poaching, attacks by free-ranging dogs, and diseases and parasites.

Much the same conditions exist in the Great Lakes region as in northern New England and New York. Commercial clear-cutting of shade-intolerant trees on short rotations have produced areas of aspen roots, stump sprouts of oak and red maple, and seedlings of many kinds. These pulpwood operations benefit deer, particularly when such cuttings are interspersed in mixed stands of trees. But when deer populations become too high, the animals eliminate the better browse species and eventually prevent regeneration of desirable timber species.

Logging and tree-farm operations create deer habitat only temporarily. As the second-growth forests mature, the close-growing new trees take over and shade out the understory. Their own lower branches die, too, from lack of sunlight, and the tender twigs remaining on the treetops are now out of reach of deer. The habitat can no longer provide sufficient food and shelter, and its carrying capacity declines.

Overpopulated herds also lead to an increase in automobile accidents involving deer. In Michigan, 17,000 such accidents occur each year.

In Montana and the Dakotas, where white-tailed deer habitat is poor, extended winter storms can cause large die-offs. Here deer must compete with human beings for land. The intensive farming of small-grain

Since market hunting was outlawed and game limits instituted, whitetail numbers have rebounded, particularly in agricultural areas. Cropland supports high densities of deer.

The deep snows of severe winters are a limiting factor for deer populations in the northern Rockies. Fawns are the most vulnerable, but bucks stressed by the rut also succumb.

crops, deep-well irrigation systems, coal and uranium mining, and oil and gas development all have a direct impact on white-tailed deer habitat. Human population growth associated with these activities has increased poaching and harassment of deer by dogs and led to a general decline in habitat quality. Landowners' tolerance of deer, which cause considerable damage to agricultural crops, is the critical aspect of deer management in the region, according to Petersen. In fact, the number of deer harvested from an area is based mainly on how many deer a landowner will tolerate rather than on habitat carrying capacity.

White-tailed deer habitat in the northern Rocky Mountains is constantly undergoing change. Human activities, including housing developments, large water impoundments, clear-cutting, and cattle grazing, lead to loss of winter range and the elimination of important forages. Additionally, the deer are often harassed by dogs.

In the eastern mixed forest, southern Appalachian Mountains, and the ridge and valley province, prolonged cold weather and deep snows are not of paramount concern. Although occasional winters can be harsh, deer habitat in this region has improved and now supports a sufficient quantity and variety of forages to prevent starvation during winter. Most die-offs, not counting hunting, are due to disease, poaching, and collisions with vehicles.

The reason this habitat has changed to

benefit deer is that between 1940 and 1960, approximately 65 percent of what had been cropland was abandoned. Farmers left behind small clearings interspersed with fence-rows and mast-producing woodlands: perfect deer habitat.

In much of the southern Appalachians, a dense forest canopy of poorly formed timber prevails, the result of many years of selective cutting of the best trees. This practice, called high grading, never opens the canopy enough to allow full sunlight to reach the forest floor. Without sufficient light, many understory plants are unable to thrive; if the overstory is particularly dense, bare ground may predominate. This can result in a scarcity of deer foods. Other factors affecting deer populations include poaching, free-ranging dogs, diseases, and parasites. Deer damage to truck farms, grain farms, and fruit orchards is common in some parts of the region.

In the coastal plain, the piedmont, the Midwest oak-hickory forests and farm fields, the central and southern plains, and the southern Rocky Mountains, prolonged cold weather and deep, lasting snows do not occur often enough or last long enough to be a problem for white-tailed deer. However, high spring rainfall in the Louisiana and Mississippi floodplains can cause localized flooding and the drowning of deer. In Florida's Everglades, high water sometimes forces deer to high ground. There they forage on the best plants (willow, elderberry, primrose willow, groundsel tree, and royal fern), but if flooding persists and the high-quality forage is depleted, deer are forced to feed on low-quality foods, such as Florida strangler fig, pepper vine, vetch, and *Acrostichum*. As many as 30 percent of the deer herds may die of consequent malnutrition and starvation, according to Loveless. Similarly, when deer forages were depleted on Hahn and Taylor's experimental areas in Macon and Kerr counties in Texas and cold weather set in, 116 deer died from malnutrition and pneumonia.

Whitetail diets in the upland forests of the coastal plain consist of such plants as Japanese honeysuckle, yaupon, greenbrier, blackberry, yellow jessamine, blueberry, sparkleberry, viburnum, and blackgum. Depending on the type of site as well as the time of year, particularly late summer and fall, these browse plants are often deficient in protein and minerals, which may account for the small size and low densities of deer from portions of this region.

Some current land-use practices considered detrimental to deer habitat in the coastal plain include the conversion of bottomland hardwood forests to agricultural crops and the removal of hardwoods in mature pine stands. Real estate developments, both residential and commercial, have eliminated habitat abruptly and been followed by increased vehicle traffic and poaching, as well as harassment of deer by dogs.

In the piedmont plateau region in the 1800s, nearly all the land was cleared for farming and whitetail populations were at an all-time low; today approximately 60 percent of the land has returned to forest. Because of farmland abandonment, restocking, and protection, along with old-field succession, deer populations continue to increase, although some deer habitat is being lost to new agricultural efforts and real estate development. Probably the most serious disease in this region is epizootic hemorrhagic disease. Losses to this disease are usually confined to areas with high deer populations and are not a limiting factor across the region.

In the Midwest oak-hickory forests, limiting factors affecting deer populations include loss of habitat to agriculture, inundation of large tracts during reservoir construction, livestock grazing that reduces browse, and such competing land uses as highways, airports, railroads, urban developments, and mining. Other major causes of deer mortality in this region include diseases and parasites and legal and illegal hunting. Replanting oak-hickory forests to the faster-maturing pines after a timber harvest can reduce deer habitat quality by eliminating mast-producing trees.

In the agricultural Midwest, dam construction has inundated large tracts of deer habitat and made cultivation possible in formerly forested areas by reducing seasonal flooding. Other limiting factors in this region parallel those found in the Midwest oak-hickory forests.

TROUT

The same flexible diet that has ensured their survival across a wide range of habitats also gives whitetails their reputation as agricultural pests.

In the central and southern plains, large areas of native vegetation have been replaced by cultivated crops, winter wheat in particular. Good deer habitat has also been reduced or destroyed by livestock grazing. Quantity and quality of cover are the major limiting factors.

Landowners' tolerance of crop damage by white-tailed deer will probably limit out before the animals ever reach the carrying capacity of the habitat in most of this region. Since there is no substantial economic return to the landowner from managing habitat for deer, little will probably be done to improve conditions.

In the southern Rocky Mountains, whitetail numbers are too few rather than too many, and the mule deer is the larger, more numerous, and more popular game animal. Most statements regarding limiting factors in this marginal habitat are speculative and based on studies regarding mule deer, but the most critical factor for whitetails is the weather during the summer. During a prolonged drought, white-tailed deer have to compete for forage with cattle and mule deer. Because they are smaller and occupy a smaller home range than their competitors, they are at a disadvantage in the quest for food and free water.

Other limiting factors in this region include predation—primarily on fawns by coyotes—and hunting.

—*Richard F. Harlow and David C. Guynn, Jr.*

WHITE-TAILED DEER

Predators of the whitetail

White-tailed deer have long been important prey for large predators. Before Europeans colonized North America, deer roaming the forested region east of the Great Plains and areas along the Gulf of Mexico were hunted by wolves and mountain lions, and by Native Americans for food and clothing materials.

Today, wolves and mountain lions are largely gone from the white-tailed deer range of the eastern United States. Deer still face the threat of wolves in northern Minnesota, Michigan, and Wisconsin, and of mountain lions, to a limited extent, in Texas and south Florida. Relatively small populations of whitetails have expanded westward, showing up in the Great Plains and several areas west of the Continental Divide such as northwestern Montana, northern Idaho, and eastern Washington. More than half the prey killed by recolonizing wolves in northwestern Montana are white-tailed deer. Although it has not been well documented, these western whitetails undoubtedly also are preyed on by mountain lions.

Wolves and mountain lions have evolved as effective killers of deer but with very different physical characteristics and hunting behaviors. Of course, for their part, whitetails have found ways to protect themselves.

MOUNTAIN LIONS

A mountain lion is a solitary predator that stalks and ambushes its prey. The powerful cat usually creeps undetected to within about 15 meters (50 feet) of a deer, then overwhelms it with a rapid charge, either pouncing directly onto the deer's back or knocking it down and then leaping on top. The lion sinks its claws into the shoulders and flanks of the deer and bites the back of its neck. Death usually comes quickly from the onslaught of the lion, with its relatively heavy body, greater strength, and arsenal of claws and teeth.

Most of the scientific studies on mountain lion attacks have been on mule deer, not whitetails, but the patterns of preying are not believed to be markedly different for the two species. Most lion-killed mule deer were in poor health or were fawns, yearling females, or old deer. One study found, contrary to popular myth, that lions also will scavenge dead deer they find during cool weather, when spoilage is minimal. Going after weaker deer helps lions minimize their own injuries during attacks—a serious consideration for these solitary cats who must be fully functional to provide for themselves. There also are many documented cases of mountain lions killing the largest, fittest mule deer, including bucks in their prime, usually during winter following their exhaustion from the demands of mating.

Mountain lions are almost completely carnivorous, and deer make up most of their diet, 60 to 80 percent of it for lions in the western United States. Historical accounts indicate that whitetails were the main food for mountain lions before the big cats were

From its perch the mountain lion can pounce on its prey. The big cat catches deer weakened by disease, starvation, or age but will also scavenge dead animals. Having been eliminated from most of its historic range in the East, mountain lions take more mule deer than whitetails.

LEMMO

Aquila chrysaetos
golden eagle

Ursus americanus
black bear

Ursus arctos
brown (grizzly) bear

Felis concolor
mountain lion

HERTLING

virtually eliminated from the eastern states. A lion needs to kill a deer every four to sixteen days. How long an animal can go between kills depends on how soon the current deer carcass spoils, what other prey is available, and how great the energy demands are on the lion. For example, a mountain lion that is raising kittens needs more energy and therefore must kill more often.

WOLVES

Wolves chase their prey in packs, a hunting technique far different from that of the individual, stalking mountain lion. When not sleeping, a pack of wolves spends most of its time hunting or eating. A wolf pack travels extensively, often following a direct scent or, less frequently, fresh tracks before sighting a deer. The wolves then approach more closely. As soon as the deer detects them and begins to flee, they give chase. Cooperation between pack members increases the chances of running down and killing the faster deer, though most deer still get away.

Throughout much of their North American range, wolves rely upon white-tailed

Haliaetus leucocephalus
bald eagle

Felis lynx
lynx

Canis lupus
red wolf

Canis latrans
coyote

Alligator mississipiensis
alligator

deer as the staple of their diet. An adult wolf can consume twenty or more deer per year, half of them usually fawns. In addition to fawns, wolves typically prey on deer older than five years and those that are sick or wounded. It remains unclear whether the wolves are actually able to identify the older or less healthy deer or whether they merely have better luck in bringing down these weaker animals among all the deer they chase. If the wolves can actually identify the weaker animals, it makes sense for them to prey on these individuals, minimizing the pack's effort and risk of injury.

Winter can make the hunt easier for wolves. Deep or crusted snow hampers the speed of white-tailed deer more than that of wolves, so healthy deer often can be killed as easily as weaker ones. Then it is easier for a wolf pack to kill a new deer than to return to a nearly consumed carcass and gnaw on the remains. Indeed, Pimlott and workers found that wolves ate less from each deer killed when severe winters made it easier to capture deer than during mild winters. Thus, the common assertion that wolves, and preda-

HERTLING

tors in general, cull only the weaker members among a group of possible targets must be carefully considered for each case.

Research indicates that the size of a wolf pack is important in determining how successful wolves are in getting enough food: too large a pack and the food benefit of a kill to each wolf dips to a marginal level; too small a pack and the chances for making successful kills decline. In areas with only a single wolf or a pair of wolves, the prey is much more likely to be smaller animals such as beavers or rabbits. A single wolf can probably kill a deer without help—but it's unlikely the wolf would be able to chase down the deer in the first place.

OTHER PREDATORS

Hunting singly, in pairs, and occasionally in packs, coyotes are flexible predators that regularly prey on white-tailed deer, especially fawns. They generally do not seek out mature deer, but when they encounter one, coyotes will chase it with short bursts, testing its fitness. During spring, coyotes search for hidden but vulnerable fawns, focusing their efforts on areas near nervous does. Researchers have found that of fawns who fail to live to adulthood, up to 80 percent are the victims of coyotes. Studies indicate that adult whitetails usually fall prey to coyotes only if they are unhealthy or are under unusual circumstances, such as being hampered by deep or crusted snow. Adult deer are also vulnerable when on ice, where they sometimes congregate in the winter. Field work in Texas suggests that coyotes can kill bucks during the post-rut period, when the bucks are physically spent.

A variety of other predators will kill whitetail fawns and, less frequently, adults if they have the opportunity. These predators include bobcats, red foxes, feral hogs, raccoons, golden and bald eagles, ravens, brown and black bears, wolverines, and alligators, but they don't have any significant impact on deer populations.

SELF-PROTECTION

Alertness and speed are among a deer's principal defenses against predators. A mountain lion can travel great distances in

search of prey, but it can't carry out a sustained chase. It relies instead on hiding and then taking the deer by surprise at close range. White-tailed deer, then, can limit lion attacks by being alert to their presence and fleeing. In all but the shortest of chases, the deer will outdistance the lion. Wolves, on the other hand, give chase—but if the pack doesn't bring down the deer after a short run, usually less than a mile, the wolves give up and the deer, with its superior speed and stamina, escapes.

Deer have also developed other antipredator techniques. If there is a body of water nearby, they can escape from wolves by swimming. Herding limits wolf predation during the vulnerable winter months: the greater number of eyes, ears, and noses more effectively detect danger, the many moving bodies better distract attackers, the numerous hooves wear trails that improve mobility in deep snow, and the chance of being killed is decreased for each deer as it is spread among more animals. Does may protect their hidden fawns by distracting predators or by directly confronting them. Careless

FRANCIS

WHITE-TAILED DEER

229

With their wide paws, timber wolves have the advantage when a crust on the snow allows them to run on the surface while the deer, on its sharp hooves, breaks through. The wolf brings down the prey, then consumes the internal organs.

wolves and coyotes have been killed by slashing deer hooves; others have been backed down by displays of forefoot stamping and snorting. When a fawn remains completely motionless, its speckled coat and lack of odor during the first weeks of life help it to escape detection. Does with young fawns take up a brief solitary life with their newborns, presumably to make it harder for predators to find them than if they were in a group. Only when young deer are fleet enough to outrun predators is it safer to be in a group.

EFFECTS ON DEER POPULATIONS

Wolves and mountain lions once killed significant numbers of white-tailed deer, but as most researchers now believe, without limiting deer populations appreciably. Then began the historical decline of the wolf and lion in the eastern United States, where the deer are most abundant. During the twentieth century, neither predator has much influenced the overall whitetail population. The main limitations today are the extent of good habitat and death from recreational hunting, disease, severe winters, and vehicle collisions on highways.

There are still occasional instances in which predators have a major impact, though. In 1977 Mech and Karns reported that wolves had drastically reduced the number of whitetails in northeastern Minnesota. But this happened only after severe weather had resulted in the deaths of many deer and few, if any, wolves, skewing the normal predator-to-prey ratio. Wolves kill white-tailed deer during every season in northeastern Minnesota, yet they do not often contribute to a serious drop in the deer population.

—Daniel B. Fagre

DEER

Deer and dogs

The domestic dog, *Canis familiaris*, is the descendant of the wolf and related wolflike predators. Though a miniature poodle could never bring down a deer, it nevertheless retains the canid instinct to chase. Thus it is easy to believe the worst of dogs: that they run deer ragged, harass prime bucks, and kill fawns. In fact, however, numerous scientific studies have shown that domestic dogs in general are very inefficient deer predators; they frequently give chase but seldom catch or otherwise harm them.

In parts of the United States and many other countries packs of scent-trailing hounds have traditionally been used to locate deer and drive them toward waiting hunters. These deer hounds are specially bred to give tongue loudly so that the pack can follow the scent and the hunter can hear and enjoy the approaching chase. Of course, this baying also alerts the deer, making the dogs by themselves ineffective as predators. Teams of hounds and men can be effective, however, and are common hunting partners in the dense swamps of the southern United States.

Hunting dogs are not the only ones that enter white-tailed deer habitat. Free-ranging pets and stray dogs are almost everywhere today, and some strays become feral, able to survive and reproduce as wild animals without the aid of man. Even though they generally are not a desirable addition to the local fauna, these feral dogs rarely present problems for deer.

Deer are masters at throwing dogs off their scent, as demonstrated in radio-tracking studies by Sweeney and others in 1971 and Gipson and Scalander in 1977. Deer run through streams or swim across rivers and have been observed submerging themselves with just their eyes and nose above water. Does and fawns often run circuitous, zigzag patterns, frequently crossing their own or other deer's trails. They also may run down a road and then suddenly leap off one side. All of these behaviors make their scent trails difficult to follow. Bucks use these tactics,

Instinct prompts even well-fed domestic pets to give chase. Deer can quickly outdistance such threats but may also confuse scent-trailing dogs by crossing a creek.

REZENDES

By walking down a stream, a white-tailed deer prevents a predator from either scenting or seeing its tracks. This buck was doubling back behind its pursuer.

WERNER

too, but prefer to use their great speed to outdistance pursuers.

Under certain circumstances, dogs can cause significant deer mortality, especially in and around deeryards in the northern portions of the whitetail's range. This usually occurs when the snow has a light crust: the dogs can run across the surface but the heavier deer with their sharp hooves tend to break through, which slows them down.

Even if the dogs don't catch up, the deer is nonetheless stressed.

White-tailed deer also seem to be at a slight disadvantage to dogs in steep, mountainous terrain or when they have been re-stocked or dispersed into unfamiliar habitat. Holzenbein and Marchinton found this to be particularly true if there are many wire fences in the area: In their flight the deer often run into fences and become entangled or injured.

In a way, the harassment and chasing by dogs may actually have a beneficial effect on deer populations. A 1972 study by Corbett and others indicated that those deer occasionally caught are likely to be weakened by disease, and dogs may thus help prevent the spread of disease. Mountain lions and lynx, in contrast, pounce on unsuspecting deer instead of running them down in long chases, and are therefore less likely to remove weakened animals from the herd. In the absence of any other four-legged predators, dogs also help to hone the deer's senses and keep the deer fit. Concern about the dog-deer relationship, then, is not usually justified by the facts.

—R. Larry Marchinton

Intent on escape, this bounding deer nevertheless keeps one ear tuned to the rear—in effect watching its back.

RUE III

The parasites and diseases of whitetails

White-tailed deer host many parasites and disease-causing agents, yet these afflictions are rarely the cause of mortality—or at least not the sole cause. For 99 percent of the time, deer are the very picture of health. But when deer are stressed by other problems—a severe winter, for example, or inadequate food—these organisms can become pathogens, robbing deer of processed food or body fluids, depositing their wastes or toxins, or invading critical body tissues.

There are two basic types of parasites and disease-causing agents: microorganisms too small to be seen with the naked eye, such as viruses, bacteria, and parasitic protozoans; and larger parasites, such as helminths (flukes, tapeworms, and roundworms) and arthropods (ticks and lice).

VIRUSES

Viruses are minute infectious agents that replicate only within living host cells. Among deer, hemorrhagic disease is the most important, especially in the southeastern United States. Whitetails can be infected by either or both of two viruses—epizootic hemorrhagic disease virus (EHDV) and bluetongue virus (BTV), both of which cause hemorrhagic disease. In its acute form, this disease causes sudden loss of appetite, disorientation, weakness, respiratory distress, and rapid death. Major dieoffs are possible.

The first documented outbreak of hemorrhagic disease was in 1955 in New Jersey; it subsequently appeared in Michigan, Alberta, the Dakotas, the Southeast, and elsewhere. Dieoffs occur suddenly and almost exclusively in late summer and early autumn, coinciding with peak populations of the vector, a small biting gnat, or midge.

Deer that contract highly virulent strains of hemorrhagic disease may die within seventy-two hours of becoming ill. Yet many infected deer live longer and show only mild signs of disease, such as lameness or reduced activity—or no signs at all. Lesions vary; in severe cases there is edema of the head, tongue, and neck, and hemorrhages throughout the body, particularly in the stomach and intestine.

Human beings are not susceptible, and there is no treatment for deer.

BACTERIA

Bacteria are in a taxonomic category called prokaryotes. These are the smallest of cellular organisms, and genetic material within their cells is devoid of any nuclear membrane. Bacteria are usually unicellular and microscopic and vary in shape from spherical through cylindrical to helical.

Whitetails host a number of bacterial pathogens, including the causative agents of necrobacillosis (footrot), abscesses, anthrax, salmonellosis, and pneumonia. Several outbreaks of necrobacillosis have been reported in western Canada when deer feed on stacked hay or in cattle yards in late winter.

In 1975, Wobeser and others reported that the causative agent was *Fusibacterium necrophorum*. The bacterium is spread by direct contact through the feces. Deer in poor condition are most susceptible. Lesions are most common in the mouth; parts of the tongue, roof of the mouth, and around the teeth may be destroyed by the bacteria. When the feet are involved, bacteria attack the skin above and between the toes; the feet become swollen and cracked.

Anthrax is an often fatal disease of deer, bison, cattle, and other livestock. It is caused by the bacterium *Bacillus anthracis*. Animals die quickly because the bacterium multiplies and spreads rapidly throughout the body. Organs and tissues swell and there is a bloody discharge from body openings. Bacteria remain viable in soil for years, particularly in organic-rich alkaline or neutral soils that undergo periodic floods and droughts; along the southern Mississippi River is a good example. Only a few outbreaks involving deaths of deer have been reported. In 1970 Kellogg and others reported the following specific factors involved in a dieoff of about 300 deer in Arkansas: dense deer population, low food supply, bottomland soils, high summer temperatures, drought, stagnant drinking water, and large numbers of biting flies.

PARASITES

At first blush deer appear to attract an extraordinarily high number of parasitic organisms—some seventy internal protozoans and helminths, plus forty-five external arthropods—but actually, deer have not been singled out for attack. Every species of wild and domestic animal is invaded by parasites, which have a knack for finding unique places to feed and reproduce. They make a good living, too, these parasites: They move into the host's food supply and chow down. And therein lies the problem for the host. Parasites rob the animal of nourishment.

Protozoa. The smallest parasites are the protozoa—units of protoplasm called eukaryotes. Unlike bacteria (the prokaryotes), they consist of highly organized cells with genetic material within a well-defined nucleus. Like bacteria, they are unicellular. In 1981 Kingston reviewed the twelve species of protozoans reported from whitetails. One, *Toxoplasma gondii,* deserves merit not because it produces disease in whitetails—that is rare—but because several hunters from Alabama and South Carolina once became infected with this potentially pathogenic organism; in 1983 Sacks and coauthors linked the infection to the consumption of raw or partially cooked deer meat.

Helminths. Flukes, tapeworms, and roundworms are multicellular parasites collectively known as helminths. Host mortality seldom results from their activities. One of the most visible helminths is a juvenile stage of the tapeworm *Taenia hydatigena,* found on the mesenteries or in the liver. It goes by two names—cysticercus to parasitologists, bladderworm in common parlance. The young tapeworm grows into a harmless adult in the small intestine of a carnivore, usually a coyote or wolf, that has eaten the cysticercus-infected liver of a deer. The adult tapeworm sheds eggs in the canid's feces, and these eggs are accidentally eaten by deer with vegetation. The eggs end up in the mesentery or liver, where they develop into the bladderworm stage and await being eaten by a carnivore.

Taenia hydatigena is common (and usually harmless) in whitetails, mule deer, and other wild ungulates throughout North America. Prevalence in deer is highest—approximately 20 percent occurrence—in the West, where coyotes are more abundant. The parasite does not infect human beings.

The liver fluke, *Fascioloides magna,* is common in white-tailed and mule deer that live in coastal, riverbottom, and lake regions. It is a particular nuisance along the Atlantic Coast from the Carolinas to Texas, in the

---

Internal and external parasites

The number of parasite species found in whitetails differs by region. Weather may be one factor at work here; certainly another would be the population density of the host animals.

	Protozoa	Trematodes (flukes)	Cestodes (tapeworms)	Nematodes (roundworms)	Arthropods (ticks, lice)	Total
Florida	10	2	3	26	29	70
South Texas	5	1	3	13	11	33
Alberta	2	3	3	10	6	23
All whitetails	**12**	**6**	**6**	**42**	**45**	**111**

Sources: studies by Forrester, Stock, Samuel, and Foreyt and Samuel.

The locations of whitetail parasites

Whitetails are hosts to a variety of parasites, most of them harmless unless the deer are in poor condition to begin with. These parasites were found on whitetails from south Texas.

Location	Scientific name	Common name
Ears	Pulex porcinus	Javelina flea
	Amblyomma maculatum	Gulf Coast tick
Eyes, ears, velvet antlers	Amblyomma americanum	Lone Star tick
Esophagus	Gongylonema pulchrum	Gullet worm
Blood	Theileria cervi, Trypanosoma sp.	Protozoan
Liver	Fascioloides magna	Liver fluke
Abdominal cavity	Setaria yehi	Abdominal worm
Small intestine	Moniezia benedeni	Tapeworm
	Nematodirus odocoilei	Thread-necked worm
	Thysanosoma actinioides	Fringed tapeworm
Mesenteries	Taenia hydatigena	Bladderworm
Wall intestine	Eimeria mccordocki, Eimeria odocoilei	Coccidia
Caecum	Trichuris sp.	Whipworm
Base of hair shaft	Tricholipeurus parallelus	Chewing louse
Skin	Solenopotes binipilosus	Sucking louse
	Amblyomma cajennense, Amblyomma inornatum	Ticks
	Lipoptena mazamae	Louse fly
Abomasum portion of stomach	Haemonchus contortus	Barberpole worm
	Mazamastrongylus odocoilei, Ostertagia mossi, Ostertagia dikmansia	Medium stomach worms
	Trichostrongylus axei, Trichostrongylus askivali, Trichostrongylus longispicularis	Stomach hair worms
Bronchioles	Dictyocaulus viviparus	Lungworm
Carotid artery	Elaeophora schneideri	Carotid artery worm
Throat pouches	Cephenemyia jellisoni, Cephenemyia phobifera, Cephenemyia pratti	Bot flies
Muscle of tongue	Sarcocystis sp.	Protozoan

Source: studies by Foreyt and Samuel.

Pacific Northwest, around the Great Lakes, in the Rocky Mountains of Alberta and British Columbia, and in the lake regions of the far northern forests of Saskatchewan and Quebec. In some of these areas, more than 50 percent of adult deer are infected.

The aquatic snails needed to complete the life cycle of the liver fluke account for its prevalence in wet habitats. The adult worms, well over an inch long, live in cysts in the liver. When cut, the cysts exude a syrupy black fluid produced by the flukes. Deer are seldom harmed by infection, but the flukes do kill sheep and make the livers of cattle and other host animals unfit for consumption.

Many whitetails of eastern North America are infected with roundworms in their cranial cavities. The parasite is called the meningeal worm; its scientific name is *Parelaphos-*

trongylus tenuis. Meningeal worm does not harm deer, but it produces an often fatal neurologic disease, parelaphostrongylosis, in many wild and domesticated ungulates that share range with infected eastern whitetails. Moose, elk, and other hosts have died from it, and some scientists attribute the turn-of-the-century disappearance of caribou from the southern part of their range in eastern North America to an influx of white-tailed carriers. The same reason has been postulated for the widespread disappearance of mule deer from Manitoba.

Some researchers have suggested that where the worm is prevalent in whitetails, moose population densities are low; others contend that the incidence of the disease in moose is related to deer density. Either way, there is a connection between the meningeal worm in whitetails and neurologic disease in other ungulates.

Arthropods. Numerous species of arthropods—the word means jointed feet—are external parasites of deer. Parasitic flies, known as deer keds, louse flies, crabs, or cooties, are common on deer. They have been reported for whitetails in the Northeast and South, and for both whitetails and mule deer in the central and western states and in Alberta and British Columbia.

The louse flies shed their wings shortly after landing on a host deer, then feed on its

Neurologic disease

One parasite that causes little harm to whitetails can cause death among other hoofed mammals. Because the meningeal worm is fatal to mule deer and blacktails, the spread of infected whitetails into the West is a threat.

Infected animals	Apparent susceptibility to fatal disease
Llama	Very susceptible
Mule deer, black-tailed deer	Very susceptible
Woodland caribou, reindeer	Very susceptible
Domestic goat	Very susceptible, but few reports
Exotic bovidae (in zoos)	Some species very susceptible
Pronghorn	Probably very susceptible
Fallow deer	Susceptible, perhaps very
Moose	Susceptible, many fatalities
Elk	Susceptible, many fatalities
Bighorn sheep	Susceptible
Domestic sheep	Resistant, but some fatalities reported
White-tailed deer	Resistant
Cattle	Resistant

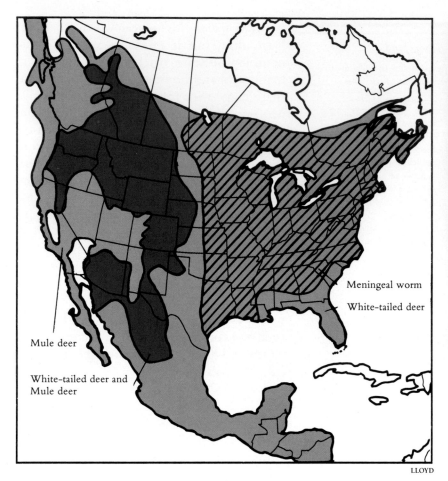

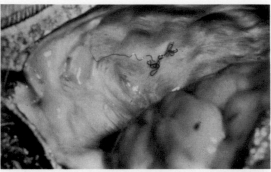

BINDERNAGEL

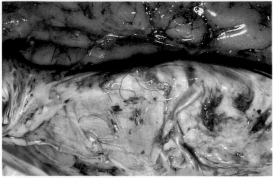

PYBUS

LLOYD

OLSEN

The adult meningeal worm infects the cranial cavity of its host. The parasite has no ill effects in the whitetail (top) but causes discoloration and bloody inflammation in the brains of other ungulates, including elk (above). The manifestations of neurologic disease caused by meningeal worms are a kinked neck, weakened or paralyzed hind quarters, and circling on the front legs. This Pennsylvania elk (left) is near death.

blood. They seldom cause problems for deer, but one animal was reported to host several thousand of these parasites.

Deer also host approximately twenty species of ticks, which are the largest of their external parasites. Although the Lone Star tick causes blindness and other problems for fawns in Oklahoma, ticks do not usually affect the health of deer.

One tick does, however, have serious consequences—for human beings. The deer tick, *Ixodes scapularis,* is involved in the Lyme disease epidemic, named for Old Lyme, Connecticut, where it was recognized in 1975. The disease has since been reported for people (and other animals) in many parts of the world. Besides the eastern seaboard from Massachusetts to New Jersey, Lyme disease is common in California, Minnesota, and Wisconsin.

The agent of Lyme disease is a spirochete bacterium that lives in the deer tick and causes flulike symptoms—fatigue, chills, fever, aches, headache—within a week to ten days after a tick bites. Far more serious complications can arise if the case goes untreated with antibiotics. Human beings are only accidental vectors in the natural cycle of transmission of the deer tick. Although many deer harbor adult ticks, it is the very small, immature nymphal stage that attaches to humans, usually between April and July, and causes infection. The usual host of the nymphal stage is the ubiquitous white-footed deer mouse, *Peromyscus leucopus.*

—*William M. Samuel*

Traumatic injuries

No one knows how many deer are injured in traumatic accidents annually, but published mortality figures indicate the numbers are high. Only rarely can mortality studies determine the actual cause of death or injury, since in most cases the animal is in an advanced state of decay when found. Still, examination of harvested deer at check stations often yields useful information concerning traumatic injuries suffered before the animal was shot.

The most common injuries are to the limbs. A deer's legs are extremely fragile, and the bones of the lower leg in particular are easily broken. Yet not only are deer capable of surviving extremely serious injuries, they seem to function quite well with significant handicaps. Deer with only three legs are observed fairly often. One such buck lived for three years after losing the lower half of his right hind leg; he could easily jump a four-foot-high fence to feed in a farmer's field. On at least three occasions the buck was seen mounting does.

Eye injuries are also common but more serious. The position of a deer's eyes give it a wide field of vision and allow it to detect potential danger. A person who loses sight in one eye experiences some loss of depth perception, but for a deer the loss of sight in one eye reduces field of vision by about 180 degrees. One-eyed deer occasionally survive by remaining close to other deer, relying on their companions to warn of dangers, but even so, they seldom live long.

Significant injuries often occur in winter. In northern climates deer break bones as a result of falls on ice. Sensing that it is almost impossible for deer to walk on ice, wolves and other predators may drive deer onto a frozen lake. The deer not only slip and fall but often dislocate their hips, making them easy prey.

In extremely cold weather, frostbite is an ever-present danger. On the northern limits of the whitetail's range, it is common to find deer with much of their ears missing from frostbite.

It is not unusual for a deer to step onto a sharp branch or back into a piercing tree limb. Harvested deer, examined at check stations, sometimes have branches protruding

LEA

Defeat in a fight may mean more than just the loss of breeding rights if the victor inflicts an eye wound: one-eyed deer seldom survive.

LEA

DEER

from wounds. One hunter-killed buck in northern Alberta had three spruce limbs imbedded in his left hind quarter, each neatly encapsulated in scar tissue. Apparently, they had been there for some time and had caused no noticeable ill effects.

INJURIES FROM OTHER DEER

Although it is commonly thought that deer lead quiet, pastoral lives, in reality these animals can be extremely violent toward each other. Observations and documentation of traumatic injuries both suggest that most injuries result from confrontations with other deer.

The social structure of deer is matriarchal. Does travel in loosely organized social groups, dominated by an alpha female. She generally rules the group strictly, meting out punishment to those who do not show the proper respect for her authority.

Fawns receive the most disciplinary attention. The doe generally is a loving but strict mother. She uses her front hooves with pinpoint accuracy, often causing damage in the process. I once observed a doe strike a young buck fawn on the forehead with such force that the animal's antler pedicle was torn from its scalp. For several years the buck was unable to produce a normal antler on the damaged side.

Does fight aggressively by standing on their hind legs and kick-boxing with their front legs. These fights, although less celebrated than the antler bouts of bucks, result in injuries to the head and especially to the eyes.

When it comes to deer-induced trauma, however, nothing compares to the rut. The combat takes place just prior to the breeding season, when the bucks' antlers are most developed. Bucks generally exhibit two antler strategies during their lives. The first set of antlers is offensive. The spikers, or yearling animals, have long, unbranched antlers, which serve to protect them from the larger, mature males. Rarely, an older animal grows spiked antlers and becomes an extremely dangerous adversary. With his powerful, fully developed body, he can use spike antlers to deadly effect.

Most mature bucks have antlers designed more for defense: they engage their oppo-

SMITH

While stretching for overhead browse, deer are vulnerable to falls and entrapment. These whitetails became caught in a fork.

nents in spirited pushing and shoving matches. The ritualized combats have evolved to minimize serious injury to the combatants, but this is not always the case. There are two times when serious injuries can occur: when two bucks' antlers become locked, and when one buck engages another with nontypical antlers.

Antlers are classified by biologists as either typical or nontypical. A typical antler has a main beam with three or more tines protruding upward. This formation allows the buck to engage and disengage his opponent cleanly. Nontypical tines complicate the situation. They prevent a clean disengagement of the antlers, often resulting in locking of the antlers.

Even typical antlers may become locked in a fatal mishap. Each year there are hundreds of reports of bucks found dead with firmly locked antlers. In one case, in Texas, one of a pair of bucks locked in such a fashion was alive, but the other had been killed and partially eaten by coyotes.

Even when disengagement proceeds normally, there can be serious injuries. As one buck spars with another, the pursuing buck attempts to stab the defeated buck repeatedly in the hindquarters. If a buck manages to knock his opponent from his feet, he immediately drives his antlers into the side and belly of the opponent, pinning him to the ground. One such battle involved two mature bucks fighting in a small field. The victor pushed the other buck over on his back and, in an impressive series of moves, repeatedly stabbed the loser along the side, back, and rump. The animal tried desperately to escape but was gored many times as he dragged himself into the forest edge. The buck later died from those wounds.

INJURIES CAUSED BY PREDATORS

Mountain lions, wolves, coyotes, and even bobcats prey on white-tailed deer. When they don't succeed in killing a deer, these large predators can inflict a variety of wounds. The canine carnivores attack deer from the rear. Coyotes and wolves pursue deer individually or in groups, and to wear the deer down and control or slow its flight, they hamstring the legs and bite at the tail. Some three-legged deer probably lost the missing limbs in canine attacks.

The catlike predators attack from ambush, trying to grip the deer by the neck or head. Even if the deer escapes, its ears may be torn and its neck and head left bleeding and scarred.

MAN-MADE INJURIES

Although man could be classified as a predator, annually harvesting millions of pounds of venison, we can examine his injuries to deer in a separate category. People—hunters and nonhunters both—are probably responsible for more injuries than any other predator.

Statistics for the crippling losses and injuries inflicted by hunters remain undocumented, but deer are more likely to recover from bow-and-arrow wounds than from the considerable trauma inflicted by a bullet. I regularly examine deer taken during the gun season whose wounds from the bow season have completely healed. Broadheads are often encased in scar tissue. Deer have survived arrow wounds for centuries: many flint arrowheads imbedded in the bones of deer

BIGGS

that died natural deaths have been recovered.

Most of the hunter-caused injuries observed in deer are similar to those inflicted by predators, with more injuries to the legs than to any other part of the body. Broken bones and missing limbs are common. One mature buck I examined had been shot through the front and back legs on his right side three weeks earlier. The bone had healed in both legs, and the only sign of injury was a small hole, which was draining, in the lower front leg.

The amount of trauma inflicted by hunters pales when compared with those caused indirectly by the actions of man. The two most common causes of injury are motor vehicles and fences. No accurate data exist for automobile-related injuries—most collisions go unreported—but the guesstimate most often cited is half a million deer-vehicle accidents annually. Many animals are killed, of course, but the ability of deer to survive impact is impressive. Injuries occur primarily to the head and neck.

In most collisions deer strike the side of the vehicle rather than the front. The head-on collisions are usually fatal, but deer frequently walk away from glancing blows, even at high speeds.

More deer die from encounters with fences than from highway collisions, particularly where deer have saturated their habitat. Poorly nourished deer weakened by winter's deprivations cannot muster enough energy

A hazard of particular danger to deer is man-made: fencing. This doe failed to clear the wire, broke her neck, and fell down dead.

to leap fences. A healthy white-tailed deer can easily jump a four- or five-foot-high fence. But the starved deer cannot get enough lift and, as it brings its hind legs forward in the normal jumping motion, catches the hind legs in the top wires; the two wires then wrap around the deer's legs.

A deer trapped in a fence may die a slow death or manage to escape—for the moment, at least—with a dislocated hip or leg. Most fence encounters are fatal.

Domestic dogs seldom kill deer directly but do cause considerable injuries. The physiological stress of the chase, especially in icy terrain, results in severe trauma and often death. Compared with its wild ancestor, the wolf, a dog is an inexperienced hunter that tends to maim rather than kill. For this reason, dogs have been banned from the woods in many areas.

Given the potential for accidents, it is no wonder that deer in the wild seldom live more than four or five years. Yet they have an enormous capacity to endure and recover from incredible injuries.

—James C. Kroll

Two accidental deaths

Last fall while I was studying feeding behavior of white-tailed deer in Georgia, I witnessed a young doe feeding in a large expanse of oaks. She was munching cautiously on acorns and pausing frequently to scan the area for potential danger. What made her nervous was the heavy wind, which rendered her exceptional hearing ineffective. Suddenly a large limb broke from a tree and fell crashing to earth behind her. The startled doe jumped, turned, and ran wildly away from the sound. She leaped into the air, striking a small tree dead center, and fell to the ground, her neck broken.

Another freak accident involved a fine mature buck. The buck was one of many deer using a trail through a cypress swamp. To cross a wide stream channel, the deer had to walk down one bank and steeply up another. The buck had no doubt made this maneuver many times, but on this trip he stumbled as he started up the opposite bank. His antler slipped beneath a cypress root, and in what appeared to be a blind panic the animal lunged forward, making the situation worse. If he had only backed up he would have been free, but it is not in the nature of deer to do so. The buck was found several days later, dead from starvation.

—James C. Kroll

Whitetails and hunters

A dramatic illustration of how much deer herds have increased in recent years is a set of figures from Tennessee. In 1952, Tennessee hunters killed 552 white-tailed deer. Ten years later the number had increased nearly fivefold, to 2,545. In 1972 it was 7,853. But those increases were small compared with the startling jumps to 40,370 in 1982 and 126,999 in 1992.

Exponential growth in the number of deer in recent years has been seen all over the country. The growth in numbers of deer harvested by hunters cannot be explained by an increase in hunters, for their number has remained stable, at 16 million. It is also doubtful that miraculous improvement in hunters' marksmanship has occurred. Even

the license to harvest does and the popularity of bowhunting and muzzleloader hunting cannot account for these huge increases in deer harvests. As the figures on deer-vehicle collisions, Lyme disease, and agricultural damage corroborate, there are simply a great many deer.

To keep herds in check and prevent massive dieoffs from starvation on overbrowsed range, wildlife managers have liberalized bag limits and expanded the seasons for deer. Though these measures subject the animals to more intense pressure from hunters, they do not appear to change the normal behavior of the whitetail.

It is legal in some places in the Southeast to chase deer with dogs while hunting. This

Deer that live near wildlife refuges have learned over the generations to take asylum in these protected areas.

SMITH

may cause deer to leave their home range, but they return within a matter of hours. Deer hunted without dogs tend to stay within their home range but seek more protective cover. Even with a heavy density of one hunter per 4 hectares (9.9 acres), deer did not leave their home range, according to Marshall and Whittington.

In a Missouri study, deer under hunting pressure remained in their home ranges, but their movements changed considerably: Bucks decreased their daily range of travel by 20 percent while does increased theirs by 25 percent. Bucks with home ranges that included unhunted refuge areas limited their activities to the refuges, leaving them only at night.

In a study of whitetails whose range bordered a refuge, Kammermeyer and Marchinton found that hunting caused some deer, mainly does, to cross into the unhunted area. Because food was abundant there, these migrants remained in the refuge until late winter, when they returned to their original home range.

Has heavy hunting pressure forced deer into the suburbs of the East and Midwest? No; the urban deer problem is rather the result of four factors. First, deer herds have increased everywhere, including areas where lots of people are living. Second, the new subdivisions, shopping malls, parking lots, schools, and golf courses built to accommodate our own growing population have displaced many deer. Third, we continue to build new subdivisions, shopping malls, parking lots, schools, and golf courses in deer habitat, bringing man and deer into close contact. And fourth, suburban areas provide deer with everything they need to thrive. Forest edge, food from mast-producing trees, edible shrubs, backyard gardens, safety from hunters: It is little wonder that deer thrive as the suburbs expand. Although research continues on the use of deer contraceptives, their widespread application is problematic. For now, for most of America, hunting will remain the primary tool for controlling deer herds.

One impact of the increased deer harvest in many eastern states is that the age distribution of many herds is skewed toward younger deer. Both bucks and does tend to

BIGGS

be younger in states with high harvests. Though it might seem that the younger bucks would enjoy unearned opportunities to mate—and thus weaken the genetics of the deer herd—no studies have shown any negative impacts. Apparently, competition among the younger bucks nevertheless ensures that only the strongest males can pass on their genes, and it is likely that some mature bucks survive and breed.

—*David E. Samuel*

In the safety of the suburbs, deer populations expand. This growth often creates a nuisance for gardeners and a hazard for drivers.

FRANCIS

Mule and
black-tailed deer

The subspecies
of mule deer

The prototypical mule deer, the Rocky Mountain subspecies, is the largest and most widespread.

"A curious kind of Deer of a Dark gray colour—more so than common, hair long and fine, the ears large and long, a Small recepticle under the eyes like the Elk, the taile about the length of the Common Deer, round (like a cow) a tuft of black hair about the end, this Species of Deer jumps around like a goat or Sheep."

So it was that Captain William R. Clark described the strange deer that members of the Lewis and Clark expedition saw along the Missouri River near the mouth of the Niobrara River on September 7, 1804. Later, Meriwether Lewis wrote: "The ear and tail of this anamal [*sic*] when compared to those of the common deer, so well comported with those of the mule when compared with the horse, that we have by way of distinction adapted the appellation of the mule deer, which I think much more appropriate." This distinction was also made by the naturalist C. S. Rafinesque, who in 1817 formally named the species *hemionus,* meaning half-ass or half-mule.

Along the lower Columbia River, Lewis and Clark found another form of deer, which Lewis described as "the black-tailed fallow deer." These were peculiar to the Pacific Coast and considered a distinct species, " . . . partaking equally of the mule deer and the common [Virginia or white-tailed] deer." This species distinction was not to hold, however: although the mule and black-tailed deer are sufficiently different to justify separate recognition and distinct

common names, they are also considered similar enough biologically to be included in one species.

Today most authorities recognize the mule deer and black-tailed deer as two groups of subspecies that broadly represent the extremes in external appearance and behavior among mule deer. Recent genetic studies generally have confirmed these groupings as well as the distinction between the mule-blacktail group and white-tailed deer. Together with morphological data, the studies indicate that the mule and blacktail races are more closely related to each other than either is to white-tailed deer. However, some authorities such as Geist also argue that the recent genetic evidence together with morphological and, especially, behavioral differences among the three forms of *Odocoileus* may be basis for reconsideration of the current classification.

Mule deer, collectively, are identifiable by their large, mulelike ears; narrow, black-tipped tails; and their typically dark gray coats with the conspicuous white to yellowish rump patches. Also characteristic are their gaits, both the stilted, stiff-legged walk and a unique four-footed bound, called stotting, in which the tail is either held down or not wagging. Adults commonly weigh 57 to 115 kilograms (125 to 250 pounds) and stand 75 to 100 centimeters (30 to 40 inches) high at the shoulder.

Deer of both the mule and the blacktail groups are readily distinguished from white-

MULE AND BLACK-TAILED DEER.

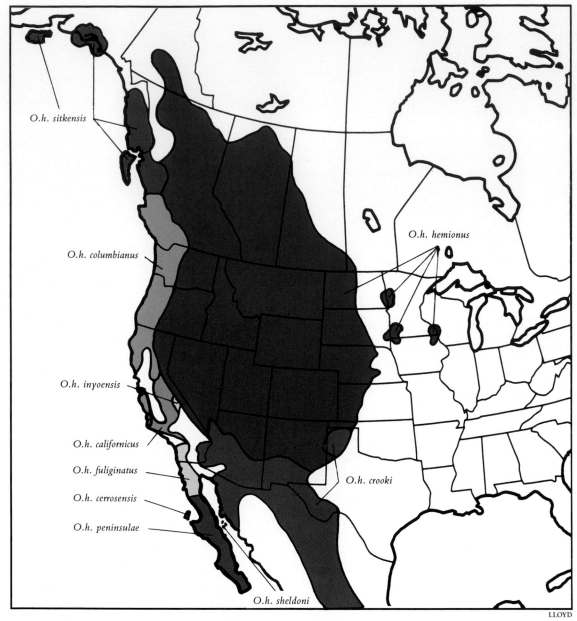

O.h. sitkensis

O.h. columbianus

O.h. inyoensis

O.h. californicus

O.h. fuliginatus

O.h. cerrosensis

O.h. peninsulae

O.h. hemionus

O.h. crooki

O.h. sheldoni

LLOYD

tailed deer by overall appearance, form and color of the tail, shape and position of the metatarsal glands on the hind legs, form of the antlers, and various behavioral characteristics, including their responses to disturbance and manner of movement when faced with danger from a predator. When threatened, the whitetail reacts immediately, bounding away along well-known trails through the densely wooded, relatively gentle to rolling terrain it inhabits, and speedily outdistances the predator. The mule deer's strategy is just the opposite. Its gait, the stott, designed for precise maneuverability in rough terrain, is relatively slow. The mule deer takes its time, using its senses to evaluate the danger and then move away very de-

liberately, stotting in any direction, uphill or down, to put obstacles between itself and its enemy. Thus it uses terrain to disappear as quickly as possible.

The geographic range of mule deer encompasses most of temperate North America between the Pacific coast and the hundredth meridian. On the east it extends into central North Dakota, east-central South Dakota and Nebraska, west-central Kansas, and northwestern Oklahoma and Texas, with scattered populations or individuals found as far east as Minnesota and Iowa. To the south, mule deer range into central Mexico along the interior highlands and throughout the Baja Peninsula. The limits in the north are the southwestern corner of Manitoba,

DEER

the southwestern half of Saskatchewan, and all but the most northerly extremes of Alberta and British Columbia. In Alaska, blacktails inhabit the coastal southeastern region, with local populations farther north on Afognak and Kodiak islands and around Prince William Sound.

Among the ten subspecies that have been recognized, such differences as body size and coloration, including the amount and distribution of black in the tail, are often relatively minor and have not been well studied or quantified. There also remains some question about the validity of some forms. Because size and other morphological characteristics on which subspecies have been distinguished can be more environmental than genetic, it is probable that future genetic studies will lead to reclassification of the races.

Great attention to date has been given to the Rocky Mountain mule deer, the largest, most massively antlered, and by far the most widely distributed of all the subspecies. Ranging across essentially all of the Rocky Mountains, Intermountain region, Great Basin, and Great Plains, this is the archetype of the species. In addition to other features, its coat is darker gray with a more conspicuous creamy white rump patch and less black in the tail than other races. At least some of these features—the large size and deep gray coat, for example—may be associated with the geographic range and the relatively cold and harsh environments this form inhabits. However, based on our current knowledge and understanding of biology, behavior, and ecology of deer, such a conclusion is speculative at best, and it remains for future comparative studies among forms across their ranges to unravel the complex environmental relationships.

Compared with Rocky Mountain mule deer, the California mule deer is slightly smaller and has a more reddish coat, a less extensive rump patch, and more black on the tail. Males have relatively large antlers, similar to the Rocky Mountain race. This subspecies is found only in southern California, in the coastal and western Sierra Nevada mountain ranges from a line drawn from San Francisco to Lake Tahoe south beyond the Tehachapi Range and into the San Bernar-

PONTON

dino Mountains west of Los Angeles. Its range overlaps widely with Columbian black-tailed deer in the coastal mountain ranges and narrowly in the western Sierra Nevada. It also overlaps the range of the Rocky Mountain mule deer along the crest of the Sierra Nevada, the range of Inyo mule deer along the crest of the Sierra Nevada and the Cascades, and the range of southern mule deer in coastal mountains around Los Angeles. Although all the subspecies are considered capable of interbreeding freely, neither the locations and widths of hybrid zones nor the role and importance of hybridization in population biology and ecology are well known.

Desert mule deer also are slightly smaller than Rocky Mountain mule deer and have much lighter, almost pallid coats with smaller, buff rump patches. These mule deer range from central Arizona and New Mexico south to the limits of the species in Mexico and west to desert mountains along the Arizona-California border. Some authorities recognize among desert-dwelling deer a separate race, the burro or bura deer, in the

Desert mule deer, like these in Arizona's Saguaro National Monument, generally have lighter coats and smaller rump patches than the archetypical Rocky Mountain mule deer.

DRAKE

The Columbia blacktail (above) is smaller than the mule deer. The Sitka blacktail (right) has a darker coat and rather more whitetaillike antlers.

LAUBER

extreme northwestern portion of the desert mule deer range.

The southern and peninsula races of mule deer are smaller still than the other forms and are generally darker throughout, with a black or blackish line down the back and tail and a relatively small rump patch. Southern mule deer inhabit only southernmost California, primarily the coastal mountain ranges south of Los Angeles and the northern third of the Baja Peninsula; peninsula mule deer are found only on the southern two thirds of the Baja.

In addition to the burro deer, three other races of mule deer have been described, though their validity may be questionable. These include the Cedros Island deer and the Tiburon Island mule deer, both found within the range of the peninsula mule deer off the west coast of the Baja Peninsula and in the Gulf of California, respectively. At least some authorities have questioned whether they should be considered distinct from the peninsula deer; others consider the Cedros Island deer an aberrant blacktail. At least one authority has doubted that the Inyo mule deer is a separate race. Said to be found along the eastern slope of the southern Sierra Nevada and Cascade mountain ranges in the Owens Valley district of California, it overlaps the ranges of both Rocky Mountain and California mule deer and could be a variant or ecotype of either.

The black-tailed deer are the smallest and darkest of the subspecies, with smaller rump patches and tails that tend to be black to brown above their black tips. Sitka blacktails tend to be slightly larger and more reddish than the Columbian blacktails and bear some resemblance to whitetails. Also, the antlers of male Sitka deer are darker with heavier brow tines and a whitetail-like appearance. Inhabiting primarily dense brush or woodlands to heavy coastal forests, blacktails also are relatively secretive compared with mule deer, and when faced with danger, they attempt to hide if possible or use the stott to place trees, fallen logs, and other obstacles between themselves and danger.

Black-tailed deer live only in a narrow strip along the Pacific coast—the Columbian race from approximately Monterey County, California, north to central British Columbia, and the Sitka race from British Columbia northward to Alaska. Except in southeastern Alaska, the blacktail's range overlaps somewhat with that of Rocky Mountain mule deer. Hybridization and intergradation of the two groups have been reported from southern British Columbia as well as from California.

—Richard J. Mackie

DEER

The subspecies

Ten subspecies of mule deer range along western North America from southeastern Alaska to central Mexico.

California mule deer *(Odocoileus hemionus californicus* Caton, 1876)

Cedros Island mule deer *(O. h. cerrosensis* Merriam, 1898)

Columbian black-tailed deer or coast deer *(O. h. columbianus* Richardson, 1829)

Desert mule deer *(O. h. crooki* Mearns, 1897)

Southern mule deer *(O. h. fuliginatus* Cowan, 1933)

Rocky Mountain mule deer *(O. h. hemionus* Rafinesque, 1817)

Inyo mule deer *(O. h. inyoensis* Cowan, 1933)

Peninsula mule deer *(O. h. peninsulae* Lydekker, 1898)

Tiburon Island mule deer *(O. h. sheldoni* Goldman, 1939)

Sitka mule deer *(O. h. sitkensis* Merriam, 1898)

—Paul R. Krausman

The bura deer?

In 1897, Mearns described the burro deer *(Odocoileus hemionus eremicus* Mearns, 1897) as a subspecies. This classification was supported by Cowan in 1936 and Hall in 1981 but has since been challenged by Anderson and Wallmo as well as Hoffmeister. "It is difficult to know," Hoffmeister wrote, "what the characters of *O. h. eremicus* really are because there is no skull for the type, and few other specimens are available from western Sonora." He concluded that all mule deer in southern Arizona are referable to desert mule deer *(O. h. crooki),* which suggests, but does not confirm, that *O. h. eremicus* is a synonym of *O. h. crooki.* In 1984, Brown argued that *O. h. eremicus* is different from the desert mule deer and the subspecies status should be retained. Brown adds that the correct vernacular for *O. h. eremicus* is "bura" deer, from the Papago and Yuma Indian name for the animal, and not the anglicized "burro" deer. They have "shorter pelage, a less distinct dorsal stripe, and a paler face and skull cap than the *O. h. crooki.* Older bucks (8+ years) also tend to be large. . . . The antlers also tend to be distinctive with wide, branching beams and relatively few tines." I have compared skulls of deer from southwestern Arizona, which Brown calls bura deer habitat, with those of sixteen desert mule deer. At least one measurement, the rostral breadth, or width of the snout at its widest point, was significantly different, and bura deer antlers were larger, as Brown suggests. Pending additional studies, the bura deer's validity as a subspecies remains questionable.

—Paul R. Krausman

Sparring, courtship, and mating

When we see bucks lower their heads and engage antlers, we think at once of aggression, of fighting. But that is not what sparring is actually about. Despite the fact that bucks engage with antlers, sparring is not combat, and the sparring partners are not enemies. Quite the contrary: they are friends. Buddies.

Sparring is a sporting engagement with hard-and-fast rules. It is the mule deer buck's means of building friendships with his peers—friendships so strong that a dominant buck may protect a smaller sparring partner against a larger buck bent on aggression. In this sense, groups of mule deer bucks are a little bit like primate societies, in which individuals do form partnerships. In mule deer this partnership is forged and expressed in sparring.

Sparring matches may be the result of strategic plans by the big bucks. That is, a large buck may select specific small bucks and diligently follow and appease them till they become his sparring partners. The purpose of this exercise appears to be to establish a ring of sparring partners in the dominant buck's mating area, which in mule deer happens to be the home range of a large doe group.

The female mule deer who are the object of a large buck's attention live in closed maternal groups that occupy well-delineated and at least seasonally exclusive home ranges. Each group excludes other mule deer. Once we observed one such group move off in unison to a distant late winter range, fight against others there, and return as a unit in early spring. Over the years one encounters the same females in the same group and in the same area.

As the time of the rut approaches, large mule deer bucks seek out these maternal groups. One large "master buck" establishes dominance over others and roams the area occupied by a group of does. His goal is to breed the mature does at the least cost to himself, and he needs his sparring partners' help in warding off other bucks of their size. As the rut progresses, he remains somewhat tolerant of the younger bucks that had been sparring partners.

The benefit of such a system to the large, master buck is that he doesn't have to guard against every unattached young buck who happens by, since his sparring partners are expected to intercept such "floaters." The benefit to the sparring partners is that when several females are in heat during the height of the rut, they may be able to participate in breeding if the master buck is busy with one particular female: master though he is, he can service only one doe at a time. So, both parties gain.

Sparring commences in various ways. It may start after a yearling buck, spotting a new, large buck that has just appeared on the females' range, goes to inspect this tantalizing stranger. The latter ignores the small buck—at least, he seems to. He allows the youngster to look him over at close range and to sniff his hocks and tail. All the while

the big buck is grazing. Then, shifting his head slightly, the large buck puts his antlers where the young buck may cautiously reach them. That's an invitation. The small buck may then gingerly step forward and cautiously engage. If the bucks are greatly mismatched in antler size, as is likely in this case, the large buck may offer the small buck only one antler. The larger is clearly cautious despite the rising enthusiasm of the smaller.

Sparring may also occur between large bucks, but it takes a longer time to start. Perhaps a large buck spots another buck—also large, but not quite his match. The big buck approaches in dominance display at a slow, plodding walk, with his body hair slightly erect and his tail somewhat elevated. He draws near at a tangent and circles the lesser buck, who moves off and glances at the displayer. The big buck may grunt-snort, and at this somewhat explosive sound the lesser trots off a dozen paces or so. The larger follows, still in display but less expressive. He may now stop to urinate on his hind legs; while the urine runs over his tarsal glands, he rubs them together. This is an act of self-marking—an olfactory dominance display known as the urine-rub.

The larger buck appears darker because he tends to erect his hair a little, while the subordinate presses his tightly against his body and looks lighter and sleeker. And while the dominant keeps his tail raised, the subordinate pinches his in. Both bucks may commence grazing, the larger following the smaller.

This may go on for a while. Eventually the larger grazes in such a fashion as to intercept the smaller. The subordinate, seeing his way blocked, turns aside and moves on. The larger follows. At some point the subordinate avoids him less and even eyes him. The larger grazes and averts his eyes. This is one of the rules of engagement: only subordinate bucks may look directly at another buck at close range. Dominants do not look at subordinates—except when the subordinate is not looking or is a long way off.

Now the larger solicits sparring. He feeds in the path of the subordinate, carefully turning his head so that his antlers are facing the smaller buck. He pauses in this stance,

Having established his dominance, the master buck has earned the right to breed this estrous doe. He follows her unchallenged, waiting for the moment.

MULE AND BLACK-TAILED DEER

253

During a highly ritualized sparring bout, bucks engage their antlers carefully without pushing or shoving. Their object is to establish a "sparring relationship."

and he waits. He may have to solicit several times if the subordinate turns and walks past him. Eventually, however, the smaller carefully walks up to him, perhaps pauses, licks his muzzle, and then slowly and carefully engages antlers. Their first sparring match is on.

Initially, both bucks are very careful. There is no pushing. They gently twist necks, antlers engaged. Suddenly the smaller bolts backward and averts his face. The larger buck responds by averting his eyes. Both stand like that for a few seconds. Then the larger animal lowers his antlers toward the lesser buck and waits: another invitation to spar.

The subordinate accepts and again engages

Sparring typically involves unequals like this yearling buck and six-month-old fawn.

GEIST

carefully. There is no pushing in this second bout of sparring; as in the first round, the bucks just twist or rotate their necks with locked antlers, though with a bit more vigor. The sparring escalates. Antlers locked, the bucks begin to move about, each apparently seeking to avoid too powerful a twist by the other. Again the smaller disengages by jumping back; again both bucks avert their eyes and stand rigid for a few seconds before the larger solicits and the smaller engages. Round three.

As the sparring match continues, the bucks become less reserved and more vigorous. Initially only the smaller engaged in sparring, but now the larger also engages and the smaller no longer runs off. They may spin around each other with antlers locked, but there is still no pushing. Then the smaller turns and begins feeding. The larger moves ahead of him and attempts to engage antlers again, but the smaller moves off. At this the larger buck averts his eyes and pauses before following him. He may repeat this solicitation several more times before abandoning the effort and merely following his sparring partner in grazing.

The two bucks graze and rest together for several days and spar vigorously every day. The larger buck is no longer cautious in his soliciting. The smaller one engages freely and even allows the larger to engage. As they walk uphill, the smaller may suddenly turn and engage, preventing the larger from going to the top. The larger accepts this without

254

any signs of impatience. In the presence of his larger sparring partner, the small buck may become rather fresh with other large bucks and even display to them—and do so with impunity. His larger sparring partner inevitably intercedes on his behalf and chases off any threatening bucks.

Sparring in North American deer is different from that in other cervids. It is always between unequals, and each participant acts out the part appropriate to his rank. The dominant buck, in between bouts of sparring, may urine-rub, even grunt-snort, and move stiffly to solicit another sparring bout. The subordinate buck never sends signals appropriate to a buck of dominant rank. He does not solicit, and it is always he who disengages and is most likely to engage. With other cervids, such as elk, when sparring does take place, it is acted out as if performed between equals: both bulls approach in dominance display, and each acts as if he were superior. These are symmetrical sparring matches, as opposed to the asymmetrical matches of mule deer, black-tails, and whitetails.

Sparring may occur when the bucks are in velvet. That's not common, and is soon terminated, apparently because the growing antlers are sensitive. This is quite apparent from the way the bucks act: they move their antlers so as not to make contact with the tender, growing tips. The fact that sparring takes place at all under such conditions is testimony to the central importance of this

JONES

sporting behavior in the life of bucks. It is, indeed, a significant bonding mechanism.

FIGHTING

Sparring matches are very common and always occur between unequals; fights are very rare, and when they do occur, they are between equals. During any one rutting season hundreds of sparring matches take place but not more than a few fights. Fights are violent and injurious. They involve distinctly different body actions and start and finish differently.

A fight might begin the following way: a large mule deer buck is patrolling the places frequented by females. He walks slowly along a trail in an aspen forest. Now and again he stops and briefly horns a shrub. He raises his head, cocks his ears, and listens, then moves on. After horning another shrub, the buck suddenly moves his head sharply and focuses his attention, fully alert, in one direction. His body hair stands erect and his tail is raised, its hairs spread. Again he horns the shrub before him, this time with a few hard, loud strokes, then snaps up

Sparring is not confined to bucks in hard antler. This small blacktail in velvet engages a more imposing buck in a match. His move is proof of his good standing with the larger animal.

GEIST

DEER

Horning is a signal of dominance, usually performed by very confident mule deer bucks. In between the frequent bouts of this deliberate thrashing, the buck rubs his face on the damaged bark and soft wood, impregnating it with his scent.

The small, very old buck on the left is insecure; he tilts his antlers at the opponent and then breaks and runs, circling past the dominant rival.

his head in the same direction as before and listens. Another buck answers by horning a shrub loudly.

The buck snorts and moves off through the forest in that direction. Again he stops to horn and listen. The other buck horns in reply. The big buck walks toward his rival. One more horning; another answer. The bucks are close now. Instead of continuing in a straight line, the first buck swings to the right, as if to just pass by the spot from which the last horning emanated. He moves with determination. A small clearing becomes visible ahead, and as he is about to enter, another large buck emerges. At once that buck begins horning tall willows. The first buck turns away from him and horns another willow bush. Then he urine-rubs.

The bucks act as if they do not see each other. Each walks as if to miss the other, but then they turn and circle. Both assume the display posture and slow display walk. Their heads are averted, ears laid back, tails raised slightly, tarsal glands widely flared. They interrupt their circling to horn shrubs. They get close. They slow down. Their hind legs are bent, their haunches lowered, their hair fully erect. As they circle and close the distance, their movements become slower still. They now crouch closer to the ground. Suddenly the stranger grunt-snorts loudly. In-

stantly, the first buck bolts away across the opening, closely followed by the stranger, who bellows a couple of times while striking the ground loudly with his front hooves. Then he stops, horns a tree trunk, and urine-rubs. He has won.

This is one possible outcome, in which one contestant loses his nerve and runs away, leaving the area uncontested. The encounter may escalate to a fight, however, which would proceed somewhat like this:

The two displaying bucks move slowly and stiffly with their hind legs bent in a crouch. They glance at each other. They crouch closer and closer to the ground. Suddenly they hurl themselves at each other and their antlers meet with a clash. They shove violently, twisting their antlers from side to side. They shove each other to a standstill. They may both dig their antlers into the ground.

Rarely, one buck suddenly backs up, pulling the other forward by the antlers. Occasionally, one is thrown high into the air and dashed to earth on his back. That ends the fight: the defeated buck scrambles to his legs

Dominance fights, unlike the sparring matches that precede the rut, involve bucks of equal size and rank. With antlers engaged, the animals strain and push until one, conceding defeat, bolts.

FRANCIS

DEER

and tries to flee as the winner gores his flanks and haunches.

Usually, however, a fight ends when one buck suddenly disengages, turns, and bolts. That is dangerous, as the winner inevitably gores the departing rival and then coughs at him, and while running pounds the ground with the front legs.

A defeated buck may run off on his own. A few hundred yards farther on he may pause, winded, and strike at a branch with his antlers. He may jump at the noise. As his confidence returns, he horns again, more vigorously. He may go into a frenzy of horning shrubs and terminate that with a loud grunt-snort, followed by a copious urine-rub. It's tempting to think he is telling himself: Only a very confident *big* buck horns and makes a racket like this.

Young bucks may skip much of the extreme display behavior described above and fight less forcefully. If a dominant notices their fight, he invariably rushes in and chases off both young combatants.

COURTSHIP

About three weeks before the beginning of estrus, mule deer bucks in the Rockies start to appear on the home ranges of the females. They are very fat, with distended bellies, and their necks have begun to swell. Bucks reappear in the same general places from year to year, though the exact home range may shift, depending on which group of does they eventually stay with.

These bucks stay in fraternal groups on or close to the females' ranges, and much sparring takes place. They feed regularly and do some cautious, half-hearted courting of females. These fraternal groups dissolve as bucks begin to roam and probe opportunities for breeding. They check out all the spots where does are most likely to be. The tempo of activity picks up only slowly as the bucks disperse and search and begin to court more and more frequently.

Then comes the time when bucks are truly active. Some run through the countryside as if pursuing an aimless task. Their tongues hang out as they zip this way and that. They may run into a patch of timber only to come running back out, then turn in another direction only to change it again. The goal of

this apparently zany dashing about remains a puzzle.

On my study area in Waterton National Park in Alberta, some bucks are distributed predictably over the female home ranges shortly before the does start coming into heat. More likely than not, a particular buck is on the range of the group of females he has chosen. The largest buck residing on such a range I call the master buck. Some bucks are floaters that are not predictable in their movements, and a very few large bucks are nonparticipants that have opted not to rut at all (more about them in a moment).

In early November the big bucks begin to show interest and stay close to certain does. That is a sure sign that these does are approaching estrus. The big bucks guard only one doe at a time; they hold no harems. Occasionally the does appear to be in a harem, but in actuality they are just crowding close to a big buck: that is where they are least harassed by small bucks. The small bucks court every doe who is not guarded by a master buck or is some distance from a large floater or another buck who might interfere. They apparently do not dare venture close to the master buck, who would then target them for attack. The master buck occasionally herds a doe he is guarding, trying to keep her on a chosen spot of land. That is, at best, only a short-term solution.

Then large bucks begin to breed does. When several come into heat, the master buck shuttles between them—and so do the

Pinching his hind legs together, a buck urinates on his tarsal brushes to deposit his scent. Only a dominant buck dare urine-rub in the presence of others.

LEA

MULE AND BLACK-TAILED DEER

small bucks on the range. Rarely, young bucks breed does that are unguarded by the master buck. More often, the small bucks disrupt a big buck's vigil over a doe in heat and occasionally chase her off and breed her before the big buck finds them.

The mule deer buck's goal in courting a doe is to obtain a sample of her urine, which tells him whether she is ready to breed. The doe rations her urine, giving him as little as possible, as there are many bucks asking for that favor. This means that the buck will have to work for it.

His first courtship strategy, by far the most common, is to play "baby" to the female. An adult male mule deer's face differs little from that of a fawn's, only a little brighter and having more contrast. The buck approaches a prospective doe with his head and neck extended and parallel to the ground, and his ears cocked. As he draws near, his head may be lowered. Glancing backward, the doe sees a baby face approaching. This superstimulus, as it is called by ethologists, is reinforced by the buck's soft bleating, a weak form of the mule deer fawn's distress call. Just before the buck reaches the doe, he stops, averts his head, and pointedly looks away from her. He holds this pose for a few seconds. Then he swings his head toward the female, bleats, and flicks his tongue. If the doe chooses to arrest his courtship, she merely glances up; he must look away.

The doe normally keeps her head low and moves forward a few steps to continue feed-

Looking back, a nearly estrous doe sees the babylike face of an approaching buck. His imitation of the entreating look and soft bleat of a fawn is a superstimulus for a receptive doe.

FRANCIS

ing. When the buck follows her, she evades him by circling him. This circle is small, usually no more than 5 to 10 meters (16 to 33 feet) across. The buck turns and courts again by addressing her and then averting his head. This goes on for a while, along with more soft bleating and tongue flicking. The doe avoids the buck each time but just barely. Then she suddenly hunches down and urinates.

Old bucks stand and allow the doe to finish urinating before moving in to test the urine. A young buck may move in and place his muzzle into the stream, an action that may disrupt the doe's urination. Having given the sample, she moves off a few paces and continues grazing. Though she holds her head low, she nevertheless keeps watch on the buck. Some does circle in such a fashion as to keep close to him; they appear to be attracted.

The buck's courtship may be drawn out, and he shows almost infinite patience. Neck outstretched and making baby noises, he follows the doe as she feeds; sometimes she circles to the buck's rear and watches him. Occasionally, however, the buck switches to a different courtship strategy. He becomes noticeably tense—a change of behavior not lost on the doe. She also tenses but continues feeding and watching the buck closely. As the buck tenses, his upper lip twitches, a motion made conspicuous by the white patches below each nostril. He may vocalize, emitting a high, continuous whine. Suddenly he bolts at the doe with a loud roar, antlers lowered. He slams the ground with his forelegs and bellows a deep, hoarse, choppy sound with each bound he takes after the fleeing doe. The chase may cover a hundred yards or more. Then the buck stops, his neck still outstretched, and the doe comes to a halt. Now she squats and urinates. This type of courtship is called the rush courtship, and its aim, like the first strategy, is apparently to make the female part with a urine sample.

Once the female has urinated and walked on, the buck moves in and nuzzles the urine on the ground. After several seconds he lifts his muzzle high while sharply curling up the upper lip. His eyes are completely or partially closed. After about ten seconds he be-

A very old drifter waits for a yearling doe to finish urinating; she is uneasy. The doe quickly lowers her head in submission as the buck steps forward to sample the urine and lip-curl.

While lip-curling to test a doe's readiness to breed, a buck appears to be in a trance.

gins to lower his head. His lips remain parted, though, and saliva may drip to the ground. Then the buck licks his muzzle and walks off.

This behavior is called the lip-curl, or flehmen. It is predicated on a small, special organ found in the middorsal line of the buck's upper palate. This is the Jacobson's organ, a small pouch of ciliated epithelium, whose nerve fibers run directly to the brain. Its function appears to be to detect from urine samples whether the female is approaching estrus. When the buck curls his upper lip, the orifice to the Jacobson's organ is exposed so that the female's urine can make contact with the organ's sensory cells.

Eventually, a few days before the middle of November in my study area, the master bucks begin to follow one particular female. They also rush at all other bucks that may come close. Large opponents are still displayed to, but small bucks are unceremoniously routed with a rush—the master buck may lower his antlers in an attempt to gore the small buck. In his aggression the dominant may thump the ground with his front

A winded buck pants after an energetic run. Chasing does and driving off challengers place great demands on bucks.

In display posture, a big buck rushes to intercept a rival caught courting the doe: his hair bristles, his ears are laid back, his tail is flared, his dark tarsal glands are open. As is typical of a dominant buck, he looks past his rival rather than directly at him.

BAUER

GEIST

hooves and vocalize, making a series of two or three rough, deep, short coughs.

During the four weeks the females are in heat, a large buck makes many charges at smaller bucks. Rarely, he connects and gores one. All his effort, however, does not deter the small males for long. They hover and may quickly take advantage of a large buck's lapse in attention to breed a doe. If one is caught at it, the big buck rushes in to gore, and the young buck may make some athletic jumps to evade the attack and escape. Though the large bucks do most of the breeding, the small males nevertheless occasionally succeed. As soon as the large buck returns to the doe he is guarding, the little buck resumes testing other does.

BREEDING

When a doe approaches estrus, her behavior begins to change subtly. She raises her tail slightly and holds it out stiffly and at an angle. She may stop feeding and stand about as though not quite well. The vulva turns pink and appears slightly swollen. She allows the buck to nuzzle her haunches. The buck becomes more lively. He may lick the vulva, a sure sign that breeding will occur within half an hour. The female allows the buck progressively longer bouts of nuzzling. Then she stands while he places his head on her croup. This escalates into the first mount. After allowing the buck to mount, the doe pauses, then bounces out from under him, turns, and circles back. Typical for mule deer is a drawn-out period of precopulatory mounts before the buck finally breeds. On this occasion he bounds suddenly upward after mounting so that his hind legs leave the ground. After disengaging, he may suddenly run after other bucks and charge them, or he may lie down.

The freshly bred female mule deer stands with a hunched back and raised tail. A few minutes after breeding, she urinates. She periodically contracts her belly sharply, a behavior not seen in whitetail does. The periodic belly contractions last for about an hour after breeding and may continue even after she lies down. Occasionally blood may be seen on the female's white rump patch.

Not all breeding activity is of this type. Sometimes a buck fails to breed a doe in full

FRANZ

heat. This may happen with his first doe of the season: it is almost as if some bucks have to relearn what to do each rut. The courtship behavior of the doe may come into play at this time. She may bounce from the buck, turn, run in tight circles around him, strike him with a front leg, and rub her head on his rump and croup. A doe occasionally may even attempt to mount the buck. All the while the male stands stiff with eyes averted. He then may nuzzle the female's vulva and copulate.

After breeding, the doe and buck stay together for about a day, and breeding is repeated. The tending buck has no easy time of it, as he is continually tested by younger bucks. Occasionally the disruption is done in a spectacular fashion, one unique to mule deer. A small buck, who has been watching the mated pair from a distance, suddenly blows the sharp alarm call and in high bounds stotts directly at them as if escaping from a predator. They bolt. At once the small buck gets behind the estrous doe and chases her. The old buck follows as best as he can. Other bucks join in. The chase may go on for several hundred yards, until the big buck catches up and chases away his rivals. Occasionally, however, the big buck runs back to where the chase began, apparently still looking for the doe that the youngster absconded with.

What's interesting here is that the young buck uses a ruse to disrupt the tending pair. He fakes escape from predators—a danger no mule deer can afford to ignore. Perhaps it's comparable to yelling "Fire!" in a packed theater. Though we recognize that the young buck is faking it, we do not know whether he does this instinctively or consciously—whether he understands the ruse. Mule deer do have relatively large brains, but we do not know if that translates into a capacity for willful, as opposed to instinctual, cleverness.

As the rut proceeds, the bucks show evidence of wear and tear. Antler tines may be broken. The fur may be streaked from antler tines that in fighting scraped across the body. Some bucks show visible wounds. The big bucks look increasingly thin and their hind legs are matted with urine. They

After copulating, the master buck guards the doe. Alert for rivals, he stands atop a snow-drift to see better. Every so often he addresses the doe in low stretch, buzzing softly and flicking his tongue. When there is no competition from other bucks, he beds beside her and rests. The pair copulates every four to six hours during her estrus.

appear less alert. Fights still break out. The young males continue to harass older bucks during tending. Then it all ends rather suddenly, as the old bucks quit rutting and withdraw into hiding.

By mid-December the does are bred, and the bucks regroup in their temporary fraternal societies. The big bucks rest in hiding and appear debilitated. The does stay on the home ranges until midwinter, at which time they move to a separate range up-valley. Here they form large herds and are joined by the bucks after they have cast antlers. At this point the bucks not only look like females, they even urinate like females. Only their striking facial markings show that they are bucks.

OPTING OUT OF THE RUT

Not all big bucks partake of the frenzy of the rut. There are a few that spend the fall feeding, resting, and ruminating while other bucks run themselves ragged. Invariably these nonparticipants are very large bucks with huge antlers and bodies. I observed several of them, and since they were very

tame, I had no difficulty following them about.

These bucks acted strangely in other respects as well. They seemed to avoid other large bucks and thus only rarely appeared in open spaces. They paused well within the screen of shrubs at the edge of the forest and scanned open spaces for other deer. On spotting a large buck, they would move into thickets and walk away, glancing back at the rival.

One of these bucks had been a normal, middle-aged rutting buck until in a fight with a old master buck he was thrown high into the air and dashed to the ground. He did not rut for several years thereafter. After a decline in the population, however, when virtually all the large bucks were lost, he rose in rank. Unchallenged, he became a master buck who enjoyed high breeding success three years running. His opting-out strategy had apparently paid off—so well, in fact, that he became the most successful buck I studied.

The opting-out strategy works when there is a die-off, as can happen in a severe winter.

When the other large bucks, exhausted by the rut, may die, he is more likely to survive, having spent the fall feeding and resting. Not only does opting out preserve the buck's fat reserves, which he may then draw on to survive lean times, but it also gives him a head start for growth the following spring and summer. This in turn increases his chances for survival and his ultimate body size and thus his ability to fight during the next rut. Moreover, following a population crash and the concomitant decline in sexual competition, a huge master buck may now breed a greater number of females. That buck thereby increases his genes disproportionately in the herd.

Thus the strategy of opting out, though chancy, appears to have big payoffs in reproduction—if and when it succeeds. Sometimes it fails. The largest buck I ever encountered was a nonparticipant. He lived at a time when the deer herd had many big bucks, and he died before it declined. I never saw him court, let alone breed, a female.

— *Valerius Geist*

Compared with whitetails

*T*here are close similarities between the sparring matches of mule deer and white-tailed bucks. I observed the latter on the Texas coast, in the Aransas Wildlife Refuge, for several weeks during the rutting season.

Whitetail bucks take a more cautious approach to sparring, and subordinate bucks make greater efforts to appease their superiors. A small buck, for example, may crawl on his belly around a displaying dominant and sniff his tarsal glands. Then he circles to the front and raises his muzzle toward the larger buck's face. The large buck lowers his head. Still crouching, the small buck begins to lick the face of the larger buck, who stands still.

Then the small buck, while licking, rises to his feet and simultaneously rolls his antlers forward, making contact with the antlers of the large buck. This starts the sparring match. Otherwise, the rules of sparring appear to be much the same as in mule deer.

The courtship of mule deer bucks is very different from that of white-tailed bucks. In fact, the differences appear to be an ethological barrier to hybridization between these two species (though interbreeding is possible and does occasionally occur in the wild). Also, the mule deer has two well-developed patterns of courting, whereas white-tailed deer (as well as other species) have only one.

Whitetails are more cautious when sparring, but when the rut begins, equal-sized bucks fight with the same intensity and vigor as mule deer.

JONES

Mule deer bucks make more precopulatory mounts than do whitetails. Some bucks seem to have to relearn the procedure each year.

The mule deer buck first plays "baby," then, if necessary, engages in rush courtship. The whitetail buck's sole form of courtship starts with behavior that is reminiscent of a fawn's suckling run: He lowers his head toward the feeding doe, then flicks his tail and comes at her on the run. The female tenses and crouches. As the buck gets close, he slaps the ground with his hooves and coughs. At this the female bolts, and the buck follows. The two may run in a wide circle, a quarter mile or more in diameter. The female whitetail is especially jumpy close to and during estrus and runs readily; the female mule deer shows no such restlessness.

In white-tailed deer there is less olfactory marking than in mule deer and the tarsal gland is often unstained. In Texas coastal whitetails, which may be a different subspecies from inland deer, the tarsal gland was darkly stained all fall in both sexes.

When the whitetail doe is close to estrus, the buck simply stands close with eyes averted. If she moves, he catches up, crouching very low to the ground, even when running. The near-estrus white-tailed does I have observed run from the courting bucks but make very small circles. They crouch submissively, look back at the buck, and wait for him to catch up. This he does,

still low to the ground, in a peculiar plodding trot. The doe curves her spine, spreads her hind legs apart, and crouches very low when the buck touches her. None of this is seen in mule deer.

There are fewer precopulatory mounts in whitetails than in mule deer. Copulation itself, however, is comparable: the buck uncoils and leaps up, his hind legs leaving the ground. After copulation female whitetails lick their legs, flanks, and tarsal glands, behaviors I have not seen in mule deer after copulation.

— Valerius Geist

Battle wounds

*Over his career, a large buck acquires many wounds—fifty per year, on average. Even this figure, based on close inspection of tanned buck skins, is probably an underestimate because small punctures go unnoticed. The largest wounds are tears that expose the underlying musculature; they may be 20 centimeters (8 inches) long. Antler points have been observed that were completely covered in blood, indicating that the wounds they inflicted were deep. Only a fraction of the wounds sustained by a buck are visible on the outside because the deer's coat hides wounds well. Moreover, the buck meticulously licks the wound, removing all blood and thus all external signs.

Large wounds in the bucks that I observed healed well enough that the animals appeared none the worse for the experience. But a deer's antlers are covered with plant debris and dirt, which are introduced into each wound struck. When large bucks rest in seclusion after the rutting season, one reason they may appear so exhausted and are occasionally emaciated may well be the cost of fighting infections. Bucks may pay a high price for being wounded; they have to recover before they can rejoin the herd for the winter and keep one step ahead of predators. These are difficult propositions for a tired, sick animal. The cost of healing the numerous wounds inflicted during the rut is not known, but it appears to be high.

— Valerius Geist

Most wounds are on the head and neck. The 2½-year-old buck (right) was wounded by a rival, but he survived. The dark rim around the wound is the result of the animal's licking it clean.

GEIST

GEIST

268

DEER

Segregation of the sexes

In polygynous species such as mule deer, the selective pressures that determine whether individuals reproduce successfully are different for males and females. Consequently, the sexes have developed different behavioral patterns. Although these differences are most dramatic during the breeding season when males engage in combat for breeding partners, there are important behavioral differences that occur during nonbreeding periods as well. In fact, it is likely that what occurs outside the rut ultimately has far more influence on successful reproduction than what happens during that short breeding period.

How females behave during nonbreeding periods determines, in large part, whether their fawns survive. Male behaviors, especially during spring and summer, influence the energy stores accumulated prior to the breeding season, which directly affect breeding success and the likelihood of avoiding starvation during winter. Because the males and females have different reproductive objectives, they often separate and form single-sex social groups during nonbreeding periods, a pattern known as sexual segregation. Among mule deer, sexual segregation is generally most pronounced during the spring and summer when forage is most abundant and of highest quality.

What are the advantages of separate social organization or different geographical distribution between males and females? In mule deer, female offspring typically establish home ranges near or overlapping those of their mother and remain in close contact with siblings and other related individuals through extended matrilineal family groups. Males, however, disperse at one or two years of age and are, therefore, the segregating sex.

POSSIBLE CAUSES OF SEGREGATION

Several hypotheses have been proposed to explain male segregation by mule deer and other ungulates. *Hypothesis One:* females claim the best habitats and males segregate to minimize competition with females, their young, and potential future offspring. Because breeding opportunities are not equally distributed among males, this hypothesis implies that nonbreeding males segregate and willingly avoid competing with unrelated offspring for available forage. Nonbreeding males would gain nothing and lose much by moving to areas with reduced forage. They would do better to remain in the best habitats to improve their physical condition and increase the likelihood of successful breeding the following year. Even successful males could avoid competing with their offspring by associating only with those females that they did not breed.

Hypothesis Two: exhausted males segregate immediately following the rut to avoid being identified by predators as easy prey. It has also been proposed that the subsequent shedding of antlers represents a form of female mimicry that enables males to rejoin

RICH

During the spring and summer, mule deer bucks move into areas that offer the best nutrition for antler growth, even at the expense of security.

female groups and minimize the risk of being selectively preyed upon by blending in. This hypothesis fails to explain why segregation occurs—and indeed is most pronounced among mule deer and many other ungulates—during the spring and summer months prior to the rut. Although the possibility exists that segregation may provide relief from predation in some situations, this has not been strongly demonstrated. In fact,

the opposite appears to be true. Male mule deer, and other male ungulates, often occupy areas where predators are abundant, and predation rates have been shown to be higher upon males than upon females in several different studies.

Hypothesis Three: males segregate to minimize rut-related aggression during periods when reproduction is not possible. This hypothesis has no scientific evidence to sup-

DEER

HANRAHAN

port it and runs contrary to the physiological mechanisms that dictate when breeding activity occurs. The increased aggressiveness observed among males during breeding periods is largely the result of an increase in systemic hormones, particularly testosterone, which is sharply seasonal among north temperate ungulates. To my knowledge, sexually motivated aggression between males during nonreproductive periods has never been reported. Even the proponents of this hypothesis fail to document any occurrences of such behavior.

Hypothesis Four: males segregate to relatively open habitats where they can maintain male-dominance hierarchies and reduce the risk of damaging growing antlers in dense vegetation. Although males are known to establish dominance hierarchies during nonbreeding periods, it seems unlikely that continual visual contact in open terrain is very important. Information from studies of mule deer in eastern Oregon and white-tailed deer in south Texas reveals the social structure of male groups to be transitory. Bucks join and disband from bachelor groups regularly, associating with many different deer throughout the summer, and older mule and white-tailed bucks are often solitary. Therefore, the individuals a buck may be with may change on a regular basis. Rather than be a detriment to assessing individual status, the males' ranging behavior and loose social structure may actually help in developing dominance relationships with

many different individuals and may later contribute to a reduction of potentially serious clashes during the rut. Also, while the risk of damage to growing antlers may influence male behavior, it seems unlikely that this can explain sexual segregation among mule deer because males remain segregated long after their antlers have hardened and become impervious to damage by brush or other objects. In addition, mule deer and many other ungulates live in open country, such as the sagebrush or desert regions of the intermountain west, where risks to growing antlers are minimal, yet these animals still segregate by sex.

Though each of these hypotheses has its proponents, none of them explain how sexual segregation improves reproductive success as well as does an explanation based on the different reproductive strategies for males and females. Above all else, behavioral patterns have evolved to maximize reproductive success. For females, this means raising fawns to the age of independence; for males, it is mating during the rut. Clearly, male and female objectives differ and, as a consequence, so do the behavioral patterns that promote them.

DEALING WITH PREDATORS

Predation, particularly by coyotes, is a major cause of fawn mortality on many western ranges and has been shown to account for more than 70 percent of fawn losses in some parts of eastern Oregon. Certainly,

In late winter and early spring, the sexes may be found feeding together in productive areas, like this aspen forest. The buck on the left will soon leave these does to join a fraternal group.

Most does move to upland slopes when their fawns are born; they are seeking succulent forage and safety from predators. This Olympic blacktail fawn is heading into its first winter. In eastern Oregon (right), utilization of slopes steeper than 10 degrees decreased as fawns became more mobile.

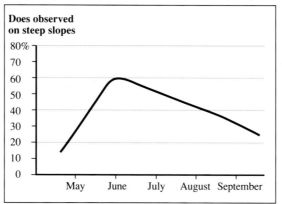

Does observed on steep slopes

those females that choose fawn-rearing sites less likely to be searched by coyotes or other predators stand a much better chance of successfully raising their offspring.

Avoidance. Observations of coyotes and mule deer in eastern Oregon show that female deer favor areas that reduce the risk of predators finding their fawns. Coyotes prefer flat terrain, and are rarely observed on slopes steeper than 10 degrees. Prior to the peak fawning period, female mule deer generally stay on level terrain but move to slopes steeper than 10 degrees around the time of fawning. As the summer progresses, and the fawns develop the motor skills needed to escape from potential predators, females and their young gradually return to more level terrain. Similar behavior has been documented for other ungulates. For example, Bergerud and colleagues reported studies in 1984 and 1985 in which caribou cows moved to mountains, coastal areas, and near-shore islands to protect calves from wolves. In a similar fashion, several studies have shown that bighorn ewe bands characteristically use steep cliffs for lambing away from coyotes and wolves.

Concealment. Concealment is another way to avoid predators. In eastern Oregon, female mule deer favor areas with greater protective cover than the areas selected by males. This is particularly true if the females are in flatter terrain. Females in these areas usually hide in dense stands of mixed browse predominated by antelope bitterbrush and mountain big sagebrush.

What about males? How do predators influence their behavior? Coyotes are a minor threat to healthy mule deer bucks during summer, and the presence of coyotes has little influence on whether or not bucks choose steep slopes or protective cover. Research by Hornocker in 1970 and others reported that mule deer males also live in areas with more cougars than those of females.

Studies show that male ungulates engage in riskier behavior and suffer higher rates of predation than females. This is typically because males tend to live in areas where predators are more abundant or can hunt more effectively. In 1977 Mech and Karns reported that male white-tailed deer were more likely to use the interior regions of wolf territories and be more vulnerable to predation than female groups that were established in the buffer zones between different wolf-pack territory boundaries. In 1989, Jakimchuk and colleagues reported that during spring migrations, caribou bulls foraged along river corridors regularly traveled by wolves and brown (grizzly) bears while caribou cows with calves remained on open tundra where these predators were less common. In 1989, Prins and Iason reported that lions killed African buffalo bulls more often than cows because bulls were usually solitary and grazed in areas that offered lions better concealment cover.

Active defense strategies. Site selection alone is often insufficient to protect offspring from predators. Females with fawns are continuously surveying the surrounding area for potential danger. When a predator detects a fawn, an aggressive defense by the dam may repel the intruder. I have often observed adult female mule deer attacking coyotes in efforts to defend fawns, a response also reported by other researchers. In general a female need only approach a coyote with her ears laid back for the coyote to retreat or give her a wide berth. Females also chase coyotes. During one observation two adult females and a 2-year-old male pursued a coyote through a meadow. The deer quickly caught up to the coyote and all three began leaping into the air and coming down with all four hooves in an attempt to strike the coyote. The attack ended when the coyote escaped and the deer made only a short follow-up chase.

Whether a coyote is a successful hunter or not depends, in part, on the number of adult deer the coyote confronts. Sometimes coyotes hunt cooperatively, and this approach appears to be particularly effective against lone deer. In one such episode two coyotes approached a single doe and fawn from different angles and forced the doe first to chase one coyote and then to whirl around and charge back to chase the second. This bait-and-switch tactic exhausted the doe and the coyotes were successful in capturing the fawn, at which point the doe ceased her defensive efforts.

Clearly, lone females are at greater risk from predators. This is especially true of

MAIN

young females that disperse from their natal ranges and then fail to establish home ranges in areas where coyotes do not like to hunt or hunt inefficiently.

Availability of food and water. The amount of locally available food and water determines home range size. Mule deer bucks have much larger home ranges than females. Unconstrained by fawns, males can travel over large areas in search of food and water. If females were to leave their fawns unattended for long periods, they would increase the risk that a predator will appear in their absence. Likewise, the greater the area that fawns travel, the greater the chances they will be detected by predators. It is not surprising then, that female groups in eastern Oregon live closer to perennial water sources than do males. On average, males were observed much farther from water, often more than 2 miles from the nearest source. Although it has been suggested that lactating females in some habitats can find all the water they require in succulent vegetation, this is unlikely in the dry, high-desert of eastern Oregon.

Steep north slopes in the high desert of eastern Oregon support snow-pocket communities of plants, such as this stand of snowbrush (Ceanothus velutinus), that provide food and cover for both does and fawns.

Bucks seek flat, open areas that are usually drier than those occupied by does.

For females to remain near their fawns while feeding, a sufficient supply of forage must be available nearby. In areas where high-quality foods are patchily distributed, such as in high-desert country, this can have a profound effect on the distribution of female groups. In eastern Oregon, female groups are concentrated in areas that support stands of palatable browse species. These preferred areas typically are dominated by snowbrush, aspen, or bitterbrush, and contain other palatable species such as mountain snowberry, wild cherry, and serviceberry. These are all good forage plants and deer often consume them. However, analysis of fecal pellets from eastern Oregon mule deer reveals that more than 80 percent of the female diet during summer (June through early September) is composed of forbs: weeds and wildflowers. That deer prefer forbs, when they are available, has also been demonstrated in other studies. This is not surprising because up until they die or become dormant, forbs are generally the most digestible and highest-quality forage available on summer range. Shrubs constitute most of the remaining diet. Grass is consumed in very small amounts, although it can be important during the early spring and sometimes also during the fall if autumn rains trigger new growth.

While females primarily consume forbs, they have browse available to supplement their diet: a security measure that appears to influence site selection and enables females to maintain smaller home ranges. However, because of the cohesive or "matrilineal" nature of female mule deer, entire groups of females and their fawns use relatively small areas, grazing heavily on favored food items, particularly forbs. Field measurements reveal that the availability of forbs is greatly reduced in areas where female groups are abundant, much more so than in areas used by males. In eastern Oregon at least, the reduced availability of forbs is not a result of poor site conditions; the female groups were primarily observed in or around snowpockets—north-and-east-facing slopes where winter snows accumulate and provide greater soil moisture and better growing conditions than windswept plateaus and south or west-facing slopes.

Male feeding sites are generally located on flat terrain in stands of mountain big sagebrush. These sites are drier, and from a casual observer's perspective, would probably look like poor-quality habitat. Mountain big sage is not a particularly good summer forage and is not eaten much by either sex. Field measurements have found that forbs are more abundant at male feeding sites, presumably because the fewer males and their mobile foraging patterns resulted in lower grazing pressure in these areas. In fact, male diets are very similar to those of females, with about 80 percent of male diet made up of forbs. But, by ranging over larger areas and avoiding places where females are abundant, males can feed in areas that are less heavily grazed and enjoy a diet rich in forbs.

Do males avoid areas used by females because of the effect that female grazing pressure has on the abundance of the favored foods? Perhaps the most compelling evidence that males respond to the availability of food and not necessarily to the presence or absence of females is the mixed-sex groups often found feeding in extremely productive areas. These groups are analogous to mixed-sex groups often observed eating agricultural crops. So it appears that if the preferred foods are available in sufficient supply, and grazing pressure by the female population is not too great, males will frequent those areas used by females. Similar conclusions were reported for Scottish red deer in 1987 by Clutton-Brock and colleagues. They found that grass, the preferred food item, was more abundant in meadows used by males, and that as female groups began using these areas, both the availability of grass and the number of males in the area declined.

REASONS FOR LEAVING

Why do males leave the areas females inhabit? Why don't males stay in these areas and live with adult females in mixed-sex groups or herds during the nonbreeding period? Do females chase them away? Do males segregate themselves to avoid competing with their offspring? Is segregation necessary to facilitate some aspect of male behavior, or some habitat requirement unrelated to females? What benefits do males get from segregation? Can the search for areas with more forage explain segregation and the riskier behavior males often demonstrate? To answer these questions it is important to recognize that everything animals do relates to and ultimately influences reproduction. The most plausible explanation for males segregating themselves is that this behavior improves their ability to find the foods necessary to condition them for the upcoming battles that determine whether they will be successful at siring offspring, even if it means they have to travel over larger areas or incur greater risks from predators to find these resources.

There is no convincing evidence that indicates adult females aggressively prevent adult males from entering particular areas. Although adult females are very aggressive toward yearling males—and this may play a role in yearling dispersal—it has not been demonstrated that aggression between adults of the two sexes maintains segregation. Mule deer males are larger than females and, during observations in eastern Oregon, were found to be dominant over females during agonistic interactions. The most common response between males and females in mixed-sex groups outside the rut is indifference—hardly what one would expect if females were actively and aggressively preventing males from using certain areas.

If females are inhabiting snowpockets and other sites with good food-growing poten-

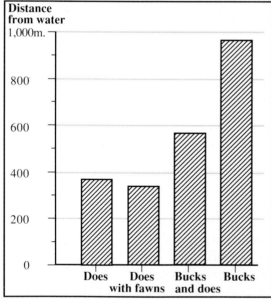

Distance from water

ZIEGENFUSS

Unless they are in a mixed group, does, with or without fawns, stay close to water. The data are for deer observed during July in eastern Oregon.

tial, and males are dominant to females, why don't males just chase females away or at least compete for the available forage in these places? Though it is impossible to determine why a behavioral pattern failed to evolve in a particular manner, it is possible to examine an animal's life history and associated behavioral patterns and explain the advantages they hold for its reproductive success. First, it is important to recognize that from birth, males compete in a race against time and each other. Most males do not survive long enough to reproduce. Of those that do, the dominant or "alpha" males breed many females while the majority of males breed few if any. Alpha males tend to be larger than average and have larger antlers and, perhaps more importantly, greater fat reserves that allow them to compete more effectively during the rut.

Since an individual male may lose 20 to 30 percent of his total body weight during the breeding period, his fat reserves at the start of the rut influence both the length of time he can compete for mates and his chances of surviving the subsequent winter. Males,

DEER

A better sex ratio

Conventional wisdom holds that a mule deer population will expand if the number of does increases. And an expanding population will naturally include more bucks.

The conventional wisdom can backfire, however. In reality, the increase in the proportion of does—which happens under bucks-only hunting—means the does use proportionately more resources, and that, in turn, may lead to fewer mature males.

As the number of does increases, they may expand into areas traditionally used by males, especially if natural pressures that historically kept does out, such as predators, are removed. The does' concentrated grazing reduces the number of bucks the area can support—or makes it unsuitable for bucks altogether. Displaced males may be pushed into poorer-quality habitat, with predictable results: more bucks fail to obtain sufficient energy reserves in summer, enter winter in very poor condition, and succumb to starvation. Male fawns are especially susceptible to winter mortality. So the mature males removed from the population through hunt-ing and winter mortality may not be replaced at a sufficient rate.

An alternative to the traditional bucks-only harvests would use what is known about sexual segregation and habitat preferences among mule deer. To maintain or create high-quality range for males, for instance, females could be intensively harvested from target areas. This would enable mature males to amass more fat during the summer, thus lowering their risk of winter starvation. The remaining does would compete less with each other, and their male offspring would be in better condition and more likely to survive their first winter. And allowing natural predators to define good and bad fawn-rearing habitat would, in effect, maintain areas for use by males.

The results of increased female harvests and predator protection—both of which fly in the face of traditional management—would be high-quality habitat for both sexes and more natural sex ratios, with greater numbers of mature males.

—*Martin B. Main*

---

therefore, need to accumulate as much fat as possible to increase their potential reproductive success.

Realistically, the bucks cannot afford to waste energy defending food resources by chasing animals—male or female—from areas, nor can they afford to forage in areas that have been heavily grazed. This is not to imply that males don't have disputes over food; they do, but these generally consist of low-level encounters in which a dominant male displaces another individual from a food source with a look or a nudge.

Aggressive interactions culminating in chases by males are extremely rare in eastern Oregon. Females, on the other hand, frequently chase other females and yearlings from areas in which they are feeding. Geist suggested in 1981 that similar behaviors by female black-tailed deer may represent a form of territoriality, and that since females are relatively confined in their movements by their fawns' limitations, this type of behavior pays off.

Because the areas grazed by females are heavily utilized, they become unattractive or unsuitable for males who cannot afford to waste energy searching for high-quality foods. Consequently, it appears that males do better searching for forage in areas where females are not plentiful and where grazing pressure is lower, even if the forage is more widely scattered.

—*Martin B. Main*

Social behavior

Deer are social animals that live, for the most part, in herds and small groups. To get along–to live efficiently and without injury to one another–they have evolved patterns of social behavior. These patterns determine who may benefit from the security and forage of joint property and who may not, help the young grow into competent members of deer society, minimize costly exertion during the rut, and sort out who mates with whom.

Deer send and receive messages using visual, olfactory, auditory, and tactile means of communication. The visual means are the easiest ones for researchers to decode. We suspect that the olfactory means are prominent and important, but we have difficulty deciphering them. Auditory signals are less important. Tactile signals are, again, a bit tough to discern, but research on tame deer has provided some information. Deciphering deer language is essentially playing a detective game.

Because deer have very sharp senses, their messages can be subtle. Better to spend time feeding and resting, with short periods of walking and body maintenance, than to use a lot of energy making grand gestures. Deviations from the common, normal daily activity are powerful signals in their own right: let one deer merely become alert, thereby disrupting the calm, and other deer close by become alert.

Deer in groups stay close together and pay attention to the positions of others; that is how they keep together and protect one another from predators. Deer also keep strife to a minimum by being exceptionally courteous to one another. A deer alone readily raises its head from feeding and glances around in all directions, but a deer in a group keeps its head down, especially when passing another deer, and avoids looking directly at anyone else. Staring is most discourteous; it is done only from a distance, or when the other party is looking away or not paying attention. A direct look is inevitably a prelude to a request. A courting buck may address a doe when he seeks to know her readiness for mating, or a small buck may graciously be allowed to admire a big buck and get a little taste of his tarsal gland, or a dominant may fix a subordinate before an aggressive rush and chase. Staring, then, is an address tied to something that is not always good. Avoiding a stare thus keeps the peace.

White-tailed deer, when passing one another within a group, not only keep the head down and eyes averted but also crouch slightly. This is a "courtesy crouch," a sign of appeasement and nonhostility. Even a dominant buck crouches to acknowledge the presence of a deer, whatever his rank. Such courtesies are an expression of respect by one individual of another, regardless of their respective stature or rank in deer society. The fact that a big whitetail buck appeases a little buck may seem puzzling, but it happens commonly.

Mule deer practice the courtesy crouch little compared with the sensitive, nervous white-tailed deer. When passing one another, mule deer do little more than lower the head. At times, however, they may not just crouch but actually crawl past one another on their bellies. Two examples show that crawling on the belly is an extreme sign of appeasement:

First, I once observed a large group of female mule deer with yearlings and fawns that had fled several coyotes. The deer stopped as a unit, densely packed, and looked back along their escape route. They stood rigid for several seconds. Then they stole tiny glances at one another and all quickly looked back whence they had come—the only line of sight that did not fix another deer with a stare. Suddenly all the deer crouched deeply and, necks outstretched, rapidly crawled away from one another in all directions. Safely apart, all rose virtually simultaneously from the crouch and commenced feeding in the somewhat dispersed group typical of foraging mule deer.

Second, a mule deer buck appearing for the first time on the home range of a doe group two weeks before the mating season may be intensely stared at by females—when the buck is not looking their way. One or several does may approach him to sniff at the tarsal glands on his hind legs. Each female crouches and crawls on her belly to get a good sniff of the stranger.

A very old matriarch leads her small band. Her crouching posture is a friendly signal. This successful doe had held the group together for many years with her courtesy, never through aggression. When others did not follow her lead, she waited patiently until they came around. After she died, the clan dispersed.

The blacktail doe makes nose-to-nose contact with a buck. Crouching in submission, she sidles alongside him. She remains crouched, and her ears are forward: a sign of friendliness. The buck acknowledges her by turning his head in a nonaggressive gesture, thereby confirming that she belongs in the clan.

GEIST

In both cases, the crawling and the avoidance of direct eye contact are conciliatory gestures.

ENERGY CONSERVATION

Why is there a need for such courtesy? And why is there so little social activity between members of a herd except during the short period of the rut?

The answers lie in the inescapable facts of all animal life: nutrients and energy are very hard to get, are digested with great losses, are inefficiently stored as fat, and are inefficiently converted into work.

Say, for example, that there are 100 joules (a joule is a unit of energy, not unlike a calorie) in an amount of good-quality hay. When it is eaten by a deer, about 44 joules is lost right away because the tough fibers are indigestible—they are passed in the feces—and another 11 joules is lost in the urine or as methane gas. Just to process the remaining 45 joules of energy costs about 5 joules, leaving the deer about 40 joules to do "work" (walking, breathing, chewing, growing) or be stored in fat as a reserve. Even if the 40 joules is used directly in work, only 10 joules of work may be accomplished because the peak efficiency of muscular work is about 25 percent. Thus 100 joules of forage results in, at best, 10 joules of work.

Even that is optimistic, however, because a solid workout has an "aftercost": it costs something to restore the muscles so that they are ready to respond to the next demand. The recovery cost, spread over several days, amounts to about 5 joules. That drops the efficiency of work from 25 percent to about 20 percent.

Matters get worse if the digested energy of 40 joules is stored as fat before it is used. At best, digested energy is converted to fat with an efficiency of 50 percent. That is, 40 joules of digested energy converts into 20 joules of fat. Reconverted to metabolizable energy, 20 joules of body fat gives less than 4 joules of work.

It is calculations like these that probably explain why animals in the tropics, where food is generally available year-round, grow very little body fat—why the carcasses of African antelope are so lean, containing less than 4 percent body fat, compared with 20 to 25 percent in well-nourished deer. Fat storage is an adaptive advantage only when a seasonal food surplus exists and can be converted to fat for use in the following lean season.

ENERGY COSTS

That accounts for energy income. What about energy expenditure? It is very high, under the best of times. When all is well, the cost of life for a deer who is not growing, lactating, or in the last trimester of pregnancy is about 500 kiloJoules (kJ) per metabolic kilogram of body mass (500 kJ [wt.kg]$^{0.75}$ per 24 h). Lactation and simultaneous restoration of the body in summer (growing a new hair coat, rebuilding depleted muscle tissue, and restoring bones that became porous because the fetus was drawing on bone salts during pregnancy) raise the cost to 590 to 790 kJ(wt.kg)$^{0.75}$. The daily intake of metabolizable energy under good forage conditions in summer is only about 670 kJ(wt.kg)$^{0.75}$, barely enough to meet the demands of lactation alone. That's one reason lactating does look like skeletons draped in moth-eaten fur and are the last to molt. They cannot afford to grow a new coat until the fawns begin to eat plant food and the demand for milk lessens. The doe, thin and haggard compared with her spunky fawn, is testimony to the difficulty of getting energy and nutrients, even when food is abundant. Animals under such constraints do not frivolously waste energy.

Maintaining the integrity—the health—of the body is of crucial importance not just because disability invites predation, but also because it takes more energy to heal and restore injury to the body than it does to grow the original tissue. The tearing down and building up of the body's tissues (as happens, for instance, during reproduction) are so costly as to invite early death. Thus a deer needs to avoid injury and unproductive activity as much as possible. Deer may be forced to make long movements to avoid predators or bad weather. Such movements are costly. Getting excited unnecessarily is also expensive. If deer seem lazy much of the time, it's for good reason. Deer bouncing about in play on a summer evening are a rare sight, and it means that the food supply is good. Not only is it pretty to watch, but it also indicates that the deer are healthy, for starvelings do not play.

A deer can quickly deplete the energy it gets from a day of good feeding. The expenditures below are given in kiloJoules per kilogram of body weight. It takes a small deer less energy to run or do other work than a large deer. In winter, a deer's income is only 290 to 420 kJ (wt.kg)$^{0.75}$ per twenty-four hours. Clearly, deer are in a serious energy-crunch even in the best of times.

	kJ (wt.kg)$^{.075}$ per 24 h.	kJ per hour for a small doe (50 kg)	kJ per hour for a large buck (90 kg)
Resting and ruminating	380	298	463
Calmly standing	420	329	511
Walking	850	666	1,035
Swimming	2,000	1,567	2,435
Slow running	2,400	1,880	2,922
Hard running	4,400	3,447	5,357

With those kinds of costs, the average deer must be an absolute miser with ingested metabolic resources and keep all energy expenditures to a minimum if it is to reproduce. Every calorie that can be saved must be saved so as not to waste nutrients vital to the deer's reproduction. In short, what energy stores there are need to be carefully husbanded.

Courtesy helps deer husband their resources. It prevents costly random aggression and enables deer to enjoy the safety of numbers, to feed undisturbed alongside

A blacktail doe charges and chases off a yearling male. He is being expelled from the maternal group and must seek membership in a group of mixed yearlings or adult bucks.

GEIST

other members of the herd, and to live a reasonably stress-free existence. This is essential if the bucks' bodies are to be restored in preparation for the mating season, and if the does are to produce abundant milk for their fawns. When deer do become aggressive—the doe chasing away her yearling fawn, the buck contesting his rivals in sparring matches—the hostility is purposeful.

THE SOCIAL CALENDAR

Deer's tolerance of one another varies through the year. When the fawns are in hiding, the presence of yearlings appears unwelcome to the doe. This may be because the fawns might join a passing yearling and be lost. The gravid does have separated from their own yearlings earlier in order to channel their milk production toward the fawns. Their precious milk supply cannot be shared with the young from the preceding year. The does interact with their fawns by licking them during suckling. The fawns reply in kind, and mutual grooming by the doe and her fawns is common in nursery groups. Reciprocal grooming also occurs between adult females in nursery groups.

Females that have fawns hidden close by may be intolerant, rushing yearlings that wander too close and chasing them off. The does withdraw, however, when large bucks show up. Yearling bucks and does roam about mostly on their own where deer are at low density, but they occasionally join one another or a buck. About six weeks after the fawns have been born, the mature does become more tolerant, and the yearlings rejoin them.

Since the objectives for successful reproduction are different for bucks than they are for does, it is not surprising that the two sexes differ in their ecology. Bucks, to grow large and lay down fat before the rut and have any hope of breeding, must take chances on predation. They tend to go to forage sites that offer the very best food, even if they put themselves somewhat at risk. Successful reproduction for a female, on the other hand, means ensuring the safety of her fawns; food is a secondary consideration. This separates bucks and does ecologically. Bucks are more likely to frequent open areas than are does. The females have a period of rather lonely existence while the fawns are in hiding, but they do come out as the fawns mature, reaccept yearlings into their company, and eventually join into nursery groups with other females late in summer.

The bucks, though they may be alone for long periods of time, tend to join with other bucks into loose associations on the summer range. They do not interact much, however. The bucks are in their red summer coat, not their nuptial "battle dress," which they grow in early fall. They feed and rest and occasionally perform dominance displays to a stranger till he leaves. The bucks in a group seem to know one another and reappear in the same area in successive years. Yearling bucks may attach themselves temporarily to one buck or another. The big bucks visit mineral licks occasionally. They roam about but are not too predictable in their whereabouts. They spend their days feeding, ruminating, and resting while their antlers grow larger day by day and the red coat is slowly displaced by the gray of winter. The time for shedding velvet is then near.

Little social behavior is observed in summer, though once in a while a young buck—that is, a 2- to 4-year-old—may join with yearlings on a cool evening in running games in a field. During the period of intense body growth, play may be a way to supply some necessary exercise. An example from another species: Adult bull moose form small "old-boys' clubs" in spring, shortly before the deciduous shrubs leaf out in May when the

Doe and fawn often groom each other, but this behavior occurs between other female members of the group as well.

FRANZ

GEIST

A deer typically strikes out with its front leg to discipline another deer.

GEIST

A female blacktail sniffs the tarsal gland of a buck. Such testing is common among blacktails but less common among mule deer and white-tails.

bulls have begun their antler growth, and may play in the morning and evening hours. I have seen nothing comparable in mule deer or white-tailed bucks of the same age at the same season, but bucks do form fraternal groups quite readily in spring and summer.

At a mineral lick, old bucks aggressively displace younger ones by striking at them with front legs, even rushing at them. They threaten subordinates in the head-up threat posture that signals the impending use of the front legs as weapons.

The does are very loyal to the home ranges where the fawns have been born, even in fall, when the young are already large and long past the hiding stage. In response to harassment, does prefer to hide and may even become nocturnal. The bucks, by contrast, are not particularly loyal to their summer ranges and readily desert them when repeatedly disturbed. They may then move off many miles and settle down somewhere else. The big bucks in summer are individually not very predictable in their whereabouts, and they range over a large area—several square miles in the Alberta Rockies.

In general, there are few interactions among mule deer during the summer. Bucks occasionally perform dominance displays and there may be a bit of overt aggression. Does and fawns spend most of their time with one another, and deer do play on a few occasions. Otherwise the mule deer show little interest in one another. This is not surprising, since during this period the renewal of their bodies and the production of milk are all-important.

BLACKTAILS

The black-tailed deer of the Pacific Northwest, the parent form of mule deer, use social signals amost identical to those of mule deer, but they differ in some respects. They form small herds organized socially into group territories. Each territory is held by deer of both sexes, who assist one another in repulsing other deer, such as strays trying to find a place to live or members of a neighboring group attempting to expand their territory. Thus members of a group territory must know and accept one another. Consequently, blacktails exhibit some behaviors different from those of mule deer. Blacktails test one another's tarsal glands rather more frequently. Subordinates crouch more expressively—there is more appeasement, and at times a subordinate deer, as if insisting upon being recognized and accepted, pursues a dominant.

—Valerius Geist

The media of deer communication

Mule deer, white-tailed deer, and black-tails all use urine as a meaningful olfactory marking fluid. Bucks request a female's urine during courtship and test it to determine the proximity of estrus, in a manner so distinct it is called the lip-curl, or flehmen. Like the male, the female also urinates on her tarsal glands, which are somewhat smaller than the buck's, and rubs them together. She normally licks off the urine shortly after performing the urine-rub, however, and consequently has considerably less of an odor than the large bucks. Fawns, too, may urine-rub to attract the attention of their mothers.

Small mule deer bucks may urine-rub during the rutting season, but like females, they lick the urine off. In the presence of large bucks, the small, subordinate bucks urinate in a crouch, just like does. Even then the closest dominant buck may approach them with lowered head, which terminates their urinating.

The urination posture itself is expressive in mule deer. Though dominant bucks urine-rub throughout the rut, they switch to urinating in the female type of crouch as soon as they are exhausted by the rut and are no longer participating. They may also switch

GEIST

GEIST

to urinating in female fashion after a defeat and always do so in the presence of a buck that dominates them. A buck's deeply crouched urination posture signals his submission to a dominant.

A large mule deer buck speaks loudly through his scent. From the hock down, the hair on his hind legs is matted with urine. The large buck urine-rubs in response to spotting a rival, after vigorously horning shrubs or small trees, after winning a fight, and when escorting a rival out of the range occupied by his group of females.

The tarsal glands of a mule deer buck are large and stained. The buck opens these tarsal brushes when excited, particularly during a dominance display. It is here that his olfactory personality appears to reside. The females, which crawl out to him on their bellies, attempt to sniff and nuzzle the buck's tarsal brushes, and subordinate bucks circle in an attempt to get a whiff of his scent.

What is the attraction here? The tarsal gland has specialized, scaly hairs with pockets of wax on their surface. This surface selectively absorbs from the urine certain volatile organic molecules, known as lactones. The many lactones form a rich mixture. Male and female deer secrete virtually the same mixture of lactones in similar quantities, but they differ dramatically in the quantity of

The deep urination crouch (far left) is typical of females in all species of North American deer. Once he has shed his antlers, a mule deer buck (left) adopts the female crouch. Blending in with the females may be an adaptive advantage, since predators know that bucks are weak after the rut. Whitetail bucks, however, continue to use a male urination posture.

one particular lactone. Yearling bucks have the same pattern of lactone secretion as females. There is a difference in lactone production between young and old deer, which suggests that lactones can reveal a fair amount about a deer's status.

Mule deer and blacktails tested experimentally each preferred the tarsal scent of their own species. Black-tailed deer frequently sniff the tarsal glands of others, and during hours of darkness the amount of tarsal sniffing rises dramatically. White-tailed deer, whose hind legs are much less stained, urine-rub over scrapes. The scrape behavior is an elaborate ritual not found in mule deer.

Other glands are involved in mule deer communication as well. The metatarsal gland, located low on the outside of the lower hind leg, appears to function as a warning: In experiments, deer shied away from metatarsal scent. Old World deer, very different in evolutionary origin from New World deer, also have metatarsal glands. The gland is particularly large in mule deer and small or even nonexistent in white-tailed deer. On whitetails the hairs of this gland are white; in mule deer, blacktails, and hybrids it is yellow-fawn. Its size is proportional to the atmospheric conditions: it is large in cold, dry climates and small in regions with warm, muggy days, probably because high humidity allows a more ready release of scent molecules. The exact function of this gland is still a mystery.

Deer also have large glands and long, secretion-soaked gland hairs between their hooves. The interdigital gland may have a role in enabling bucks to track does. Then there is the preorbital gland in front of the eye, a gland that may be opened. Bucks in great excitement open this gland wide.

We can say little beyond this. For human beings, whose olfactory powers are limited, the world of deer odors is, at present, largely beyond our ability to comprehend.

—Valerius Geist

Mule deer habitat

---

*B*eing broadly adapted, mule deer are found in practically all the major climatic and vegetational zones of western North America. The only places they cannot be found are the arctic, the tropics, and the most extreme desert. Locally, environments vary enormously in topography, physiography, climate and weather, vegetation, land use, and the kinds and abundance of other animals. Even the same place may vary from year to year, depending on weather conditions and the presence and activities of other animals. Consequently, defining typical mule deer habitat is difficult.

Having said that their habitats are many and diverse, we can generalize to say that mule deer are most often found in semiarid, open forest, brush, and shrublands associated with steep, broken, or otherwise rough terrain. Their strongholds are the mountain-foothill habitats that extend from northern New Mexico and Arizona north into British Columbia and Alberta along the Rocky Mountains and other mountain ranges. Extensive populations are also found in prairie habitats, however, especially in the Great Plains along the eastern and northeastern limits of their distribution, and in semidesert to desert shrub habitats of the Southwest.

Mule deer are well adapted—morphologically, physiologically, and behaviorally—for the relatively dry, rugged, and open terrain they inhabit. It is in such harsh landscapes that they can best survive in the presence of other large mammals and predators. Rugged topography also affects other important habitat components such as climate, microclimate, vegetation, land use, and the presence and activities of other animals. These factors, in turn, determine the availability of the habitat's resources—food, cover, space, water—and exactly how and how effectively mule deer can use them. Ultimately, the habitat determines whether any individual deer—or an entire herd—will thrive.

HABITAT TYPES

The mountain-foothill habitats occupied by mule deer span a broad range of latitudes and elevations. Topography and climates—and consequently vegetation—are diverse and variable. Moreover, most mountain deer use very different habitats in winter than in summer and are, as a consequence, migratory. Montane forest communities interspersed by meadows or parks and riparian drainageways generally characterize summer ranges, although a variety of other communities, from open steppe at low elevations to subalpine-alpine types at high elevations, may also be used, especially by bucks and does without fawns. Open, shrubby slopes and ridges of southern and southwestern aspect characterize the primary wintering areas, though deer may seek out other sites as well.

In the plains, level and rolling prairie grasslands are little used by mule deer. Instead,

Mule deer are well adapted to life in rough, broken terrain, like the slopes of the National Bison Range. Although white-tails are spreading into Montana, mule deer still have the advantage in this region.

JONES

MULE AND BLACK-TAILED DEER

DEER

FRANCIS

CAIN

deer live mostly in rough, timbered, or open breaks along river drainages, heavily dissected badlands, and brushy streamcourses and draws. Mule deer are generally not found in high densities over broad areas, though they may be very abundant locally in rough breaks or badlands and riparian areas. Evergreen trees and shrubs, such as pine and juniper, provide cover in timbered breaks and badlands; deciduous trees and shrubs may be important along streamcourses and in draws.

In the Southwest, mule deer are found in two types of semidesert-desert range, both of which are arid, sparsely vegetated, and shrubby. One such range—in southern Arizona and New Mexico, western Texas, and parts of Mexico—is characterized by creosote bush, mesquite, greasewood, and several species of cactus. In some areas, various species of oak and chaparral grow. The other type of range, called the northern or Great Basin, can be found in parts of Nevada, western Utah, and southeastern Oregon. Common plants there are sagebrush, saltbush, cliffrose, and winterfat, with juniper-

PONTON

MULE AND BLACK-TAILED DEER

YUSKAVITCH

pinyon woodlands and pine forests at higher elevations.

Deer of the black-tailed subspecies inhabit coastal, coniferous forests from northern California to southeastern Alaska, as well as woodland-chaparral habitats of the central coast ranges. Coastal rainforest habitats offer dense conifer stands and a maritime climate with cool temperatures, many cloudy days, and high precipitation. In California and southern Oregon, redwoods and Douglas-fir typify these habitats. To the north, Sitka spruce, western red cedar, western hemlock, and Douglas-fir predominate. Forest succession is very rapid, and the kinds and amounts of understory plants vary widely.

Different successional stages may be important to black-tailed deer in different areas. In western Washington, for example, deer preferred forests ten to thirty years after logging, when brush fields produced a lot of high-quality forage. But studies on Vancouver Island, British Columbia, and in coastal forests of southeastern Alaska have shown that deer prefer mature forests—over 150 years old—even more than logged habi-

tats. The explanation may be in the pattern of snow accumulation along the Pacific Coast: Snowpack is deeper in logged areas of the Northwest than in an old-growth forest whose canopy acts like an umbrella; on coastal blacktail ranges farther south, the snow is never deep enough to hinder the deer, who can then select a habitat for its forage.

California woodland-chaparral habitats consist of two major vegetation types, oak woodlands and chaparral. The woodlands, characterized by oak and pine, include a variety of shrubs and contain grassy openings. The chaparral type is dominated by numerous shrubs, and in the absence of fire or other disturbance, it becomes extremely dense—too dense even for deer.

THE VALUE OF DIVERSITY

Within any broad area, mule deer usually occupy or utilize a variety of habitats and vegetation. Their use of these different types may vary by season, with the sex and age of the individual, with the population density, and according to other variables as well, including the weather. Thus, they will also live in higher densities and reproduce more successfully in some habitats than in others.

Exactly how and how well mule deer use any habitat is determined both by the needs of the animals for food, cover, water, and space, and by the distribution of the resources that meet those needs. Some aspects of a habitat are fixed or relatively stable, for example, geographic location, topography, climate, soil, and vegetation. Fixed habitat components determine how well an area meets the inherent morphological, physiological, and behavioral constraints or requirements of mule deer, and how and where deer distribute themselves, move, and otherwise use the habitat and, ultimately, potential deer numbers in the area.

The variable aspects, called stochastic components, include weather, the presence of predators and other animals, the relative abundance of the deer themselves, and the presence and activities of humans. These factors influence the seasonal and annual suitability of and resources available in any particular habitat; their effects are expressed in reproduction rates (or fawn recruitment)

and adult mortality rates—that is, in population dynamics.

Having access to a variety of habitat types is crucial for mule deer, for several reasons. Mule deer consume a diversity of plant species. At any one time and during the course of the year, several vegetation types are needed to provide this diversity in the generally dry and variable environments the animals inhabit. Likewise, cover needs are different from summer to fall and winter, so deer need a variety of vegetation and physiographic sites for bed sites, escape, and thermal regulation. Because of this, the juxtaposition of various habitat types may be just as or even more important than any specific vegetation or terrain feature.

MOVEMENTS AND HOME RANGE

Mule deer are not distributed evenly across their habitats nor do they move randomly across them. Rather, the use of habitat is well organized at various levels, from individuals to family groups to subpopulations and even populations.

Mule deer populations are relatively discrete, complete ecological units that occupy specific areas that meet all their yearlong needs. The size and configuration of population units reflect both environmental features and patterns of deer behavior. Social bonding among maternally related individuals, for example, results in traditional movement and habitat use patterns that maintain the integrity of groups of deer and

the population as a whole. These traditional movements and patterns in turn maintain the boundaries of each population unit from generation to generation.

Within population-habitat units, individual adults of both sexes establish home ranges in suitable habitat. Adult males and females, or deer of different ages, usually select different areas—in effect, partitioning the habitat. For example, males older than yearlings often gather in clumps of two to five, occasionally more, in closely overlapping if not common home ranges. In some areas at least, these buck habitats are peripheral to areas used by does; in others, they are interspersed locally among the female areas.

In the mountains and foothills, adult male ranges tend to be in drier, more rugged habitat at higher elevations; on drier, open, and rough ridges and slopes at intermediate elevations; or in more open foothill and steppe habitats. In other areas, buck habitats—and patterns of their use—resemble those of adult females, which in summer tend to be more widely and uniformily spaced across high-quality reproductive habitat.

Segregation of the sexes may reflect differences in resource needs and behavior between males and females. It may also help assure that in the variable environments occupied by mule deer, mature females have access to the resources they need to reproduce and their fawns need to survive. Other suggested benefits of segregation to the species include predator avoidance, reduced

Males and females select different habitats. Groups of males—two to five, sometimes more—have closely overlapping home ranges in dry, rugged ridges and slopes and open foothills. Females raise their fawns in the lowlands.

ESCHER

DEER

competition and aggression, reduced risk of damage to growing antlers, and optimal foraging by males.

Within their seasonal home ranges, mule deer typically move only short distances in the course of daily activities. Longer distances are normally traversed only during migration or by males during the rut, but may also be prompted by disturbance during hunting season, very deep snow or extreme drought, and the wanderings or dispersal of yearlings or other young adults.

Occasionally, local or unusual environmental conditions may require mule deer to use a second seasonal, or accessory, home range. When forage becomes desiccated in August on the primary summer home range, for example, deer may move several kilometers to better forage on a second home range for several days to several weeks. Use of accessory areas has been reported for all seasons of the year and may enable more deer to live in an area than would otherwise be possible.

The size of home ranges and the distance deer travel daily, seasonally, annually, and over their lifetime vary widely among individuals, sexes, and populations but especially with the habitat. Deer that live in highly diverse habitats capable of meeting their seasonal needs move very little, and their annual home ranges are very small—less than 1 square kilometer (0.4 square mile). In contrast, relatively simple habitats and widely spaced seasonal habitats result in large annual home ranges. Wood reported that mule deer in an eastern Montana prairie commonly ranged 12 to 25 square kilometers (5 to 10 square miles), with some ranges as large as 66 square kilometers (25 square miles).

In semidesert habitats, large year-long home ranges of 10.6 square kilometers (4 square miles) have been reported for females, and 12.4 square kilometers (4.7 square miles) for males. In timbered, northern prairie breaks, annual ranges for does averaged 6.6 square kilometers (2.5 square miles) and varied from 1.5 to 30.2 square kilometers (0.5 to 11.6 square miles); for mature bucks, they averaged 27.1 square kilometers (10.5 square miles) and ranged from 16.6 to 33.4 square kilometers (6.4 to 12.8 square miles).

Based on studies to date, it is apparent that males generally have larger home ranges than females. Also young and very old adults may use larger home ranges than prime-age individuals, which dominate the best range and cause younger and older animals to move more widely to find food and cover.

The distances deer move and the home ranges they occupy reflect the way each deer meets its needs within the habitat and responds to the presence and activities of other deer and perhaps other animals. There is also a cultural component to movement and habitat use, especially among females: young deer follow and learn the traditional patterns from their mothers, and thus seasonal movements, home range areas, foraging strategies, and cover preferences are often passed on, to be used in turn by the young does' own offspring. This passing on of successful strategies is central in maintaining the integrity of populations or population-habitat units.

SEASONAL MOVEMENTS

Most mule deer follow one of three general patterns of movement and home range during the year. Some deer inhabit areas that meet all their resource requirements, all year long. Such deer may cluster their use of habitat seasonally in one part of their home range but may be found in any part of the area at any time, making it impossible to distinguish seasonal range boundaries.

A second group of deer—characteristic of many areas—typically move between separate, but nearby, seasonal ranges that are usually within about 2.5 kilometers (1 mile) of each other. Deer occupying adjacent seasonal ranges may occasionally move back and forth between the two at any time, and in mild winters may spend much of the time on their summer range.

The third category is the true or "classical" migratory deer: those who have distinct, widely separated seasonal ranges and do not travel between them except during migration. As the distance between seasonal ranges increases, the timing and pattern of movements of migratory deer often become highly specialized and may include use of accessory or holding areas along migration corridors.

Migratory movements between distinct seasonal ranges are most characteristic of mule deer in the mountains and foothills but may be found among deer in other habitats as well. Distances covered in migration may vary from a few kilometers to more than 160 kilometers (100 miles). Typical migrations involve moving to higher elevation in spring or summer and returning to low elevation in winter; however, the reverse also occurs, with animals migrating to lower elevation in summer and higher, drier range in winter.

Winter home ranges reported in the literature for migratory deer in mountain-foothill habitats vary from 0.3 square kilometer (0.1 square mile) to more than 12 square kilometers (4.6 square miles) but usually range from 1 to 3 square kilometers (0.4 to 1.1 square miles). Average winter home range size varies inversely with winter severity, indicating that severe weather restricts deer movement. Summer home ranges similarly vary from less than 0.3 square kilometers (0.1 square mile) to 4.5 square kilometers (1.7 square miles) but usually range from 0.5 to 2.5 square kilometers (0.2 to 1 square mile). Year-long home ranges of resident females on foothills habitat vary from 2.9 to 17.3 square kilometers (1.1 to 6.6 square miles).

Fall migrations are usually triggered by a certain depth of snow on summer and intermediate ranges; the timing of spring migration has typically been associated with snowmelt and the lure of succulent forage on summer areas. But neither is always the case.

Deer that follow different migration and other movement patterns are employing behaviors that have proven successful through time. For example, deer that must cross mountain passes often begin migrating early in the fall, regardless of snow accumulation. If these deer waited until snow covered their summer ranges, snow in the passes would block their access to winter range. On the other hand, deer that simply descend a mountain slope to winter range often wait until forced to move by deep snow; some may not even leave their summer range in years of little snow.

Such differences account for the very

ESCHER

*Deer that must cross mountain
passes to get to winter range
begin their migration early,
before the snow flies.*

BAUER

MULE AND BLACK-TAILED DEER

295

The conifers in a mule deer herd's winter range provide food when snow depth prevents foraging on dry herbs and leaves.

different schedules of adjacent herds, groups within a herd, and even individual animals within a group. Some deer in the northern Rockies regularly migrate to winter range during late October or early November; others summering only a few kilometers away may not move until later in November, December, or even January. The time of migration, like the choice of seasonal range, varies widely among individuals, maternally related groups, populations, and habitats.

Mule deer are not considered migratory in most prairie habitats but may migrate locally or use some parts of their annual range more intensively in winter than in summer. Also, deer may leave their home ranges during unusually severe storms, droughts, or other environmental conditions.

In an eastern Montana prairie, mule deer females follow three patterns of movement, depending on characteristics of their local habitat. Nonmigratory, resident deer live in prairie badlands with streams, riparian areas, and other habitats; the diversity of their habitat meets all of their food and cover needs in winter as well as in summer, so they stay there all year long. A second group, the autumn migrants, spend winter and most of the spring and summer in less diverse badland habitat. These areas meet most of their yearlong needs but apparently become dry in late summer when, to find forage, the deer travel to agricultural fields and other habitats where they stay through late autumn, at which time they return to their normal range. The third group winters in badlands that are not sufficiently diverse and too dry to support pregnant and lactating does. These deer migrate varying distances in spring to more productive summer habitats and return at the onset of winter. Such patterns of movement clearly relate to local environmental characteristics and conditions, and similar patterns have been observed for mule deer on breaks and desert ranges.

Yearlings and occasionally other young adult mule deer may move far or leave a population entirely in the process of establishing permanent home ranges. This dispersal leads to a continuous genetic interchange between populations and segments of populations. The young of both sexes disperse, but the movement appears to be more prevalent in males: 50 to 70 percent of yearling males characteristically leave their natal ranges.

—Richard J. Mackie

Reacting to weather

Living in a variety of habitats across much of western North America, mule deer are subject to vast weather extremes. Temperatures in mule deer country can range from below −60 to above 50 degrees C (−76 to 122 degrees F). While one animal struggles to stay warm in the cold, windy Rocky Mountains of northern British Columbia, his cousin must keep cool in the hot, arid deserts of Baja California. Using a number of physical, physiological, and behavioral mechanisms, mule deer are able to cope with extreme and regular temperature changes.

INTERNAL REGULATORS

Homoiothermal (warm-blooded) mammals, mule deer have an average body core temperature between 37.1 and 40.6 degrees C (98.8 to 105.1 degrees F). Lacking an extensive system of sweat glands, mule deer cannot cool down through the evaporation of perspiration, but they do possess several other very effective involuntary responses that help them maintain their body temperature.

Metabolic rate. Most deer species have the ability to alter their basal metabolic rate during times of thermal stress. Studies have indicated that deer in general increase their metabolic rate when the air temperature drops below about 7 degrees C (45 degrees F). Rocky Mountain mule deer, though, as indicated by Mautz and colleagues, do not significantly increase their metabolic rate

until the temperature drops to −23 degrees C (−10 degrees F). Both Columbian black-tailed deer and white-tailed deer increase their metabolic rate at higher temperatures. Apparently mule deer, which normally experience cold temperatures in open mountain foothill and plains environments, are better adapted to low temperatures than are other deer.

Shivering. The involuntary muscle contractions involved in shivering produce heat to help maintain body temperature when the ambient air is cooler than the animal's body. As the air temperature decreases, the animal, if uninsulated, must produce more heat, so shivering increases. Because a deer in its winter coat is generally insulated like a

Mule deer weather the desert by adapting their schedule. Not until the shadows lengthen and the hottest part of the day is past do the deer move to their foraging sites.

FRANCIS

RICH

The snow accumulating on the deer's back proves the insulative value of a winter coat. When the temperature drops below −9 degrees C (15 degrees F), the animal may seek a warmer, more sheltered spot.

person dressed in a full goosedown garment, shivering probably is less important than posture, activity, and coat characteristics as a thermoregulatory mechanism.

Panting. Panting increases the rate of respiratory exchange and heat loss through evaporation from respiratory surfaces. Mule deer in dry environments generally pant when ambient temperatures are very high or following bouts of activity, such as running.

Piloerection. When the hairs in a deer's coat "stand on end," they trap additional insulating air, increasing the depth and insulative value of the coat. This short-term solution is similar to the longer-lasting effect brought about by the animal's molt from summer coat to winter coat. The dark reddish summer coat of adult mule deer is relatively thin and made up of short guard hairs with little insulating underfur. In early fall, both adults and fawns replace their summer coats with dark gray winter coats; this pelage has long guard hairs and thick, short underfur with high insulating qualities.

Blood flow through ears. The large ears of a mule deer can function much like the

vanes of a heat sink. Blood flowing through the abundant vessels near the surface of the thinly furred inside ear loses heat to the cooler ambient air. This heat loss can be directly controlled by adjusting the blood flow through the ears—a process known as vasoconstriction.

BEHAVIORAL ADAPTATIONS

In addition to involuntary responses, mule deer also have developed deliberate movements and habits that help them cope with extremes and changes in temperature. These include habitat selection to take advantage of their physical and biotic environment.

Cover. During periods of cold, mule deer select bedding sites that afford protection from radiant heat loss and wind. Spots beneath thick conifers, heavy brush such as juniper, or overhanging rock ledges all work well as "pockets" in which the animals can conserve energy. During periods of hot weather, these same deer seek shade beneath coniferous trees and shrubs; use breezy, sheltered, mesic sites on north and easterly slopes; and seek the shelter and cool air of

DVORAK

cuts along drainageways in the rough terrain they seem to favor.

Movements. During winter, mule deer appear to be most comfortable in ambient air temperatures between −9 and 7 degrees C (15 to 45 degrees F). When the temperature in an animal's preferred range falls below this comfort zone, it may move up or down the hill or mountain, between north- and south-facing slopes, or to and from cover to take advantage of the temperature inversions at different elevations or different temperature regimes.

Posture. When faced with cold weather, a mule deer can conserve body heat by lying on its brisket and belly with legs folded under, head curled back, and nose tucked into its flank. This position reduces the amount of body, especially poorly insulated extremities, that is exposed to the chilling air and wind. Indeed, Mautz and colleagues found that mule deer spend 25 to 40 percent less time standing when temperatures fall below − 12 degrees C (7 degrees F). To dissipate heat in summer, the deer may lie with both front legs, head, and ears extended in an alert resting posture.

Activity patterns. Ever adaptable, a mule deer will adjust its schedules to those of the environment. During winter, fat reserves accumulated over late summer and autumn help meet energy needs, so the animal can feed only as necessary, usually on warm slopes or sites during the warmer periods of the day. Conversely, during summer, the animal can limit its activity and feeding times to the cooler hours—early morning, late evening, after dark—especially when the weather is warm and dry and sheltered sites are few. By limiting activity and seeking cool, moist sites in hot weather, the mule deer is able to conserve moisture and reduce its need for free water—important concerns in its typically semiarid environment.

OTHER WEATHER FACTORS

Individually, most other weather elements seem to have little effect on mule deer, eliciting reactions from the animals only in conjunction with ambient temperatures. Wind, for example, has little apparent influence except during periods of extreme cold when

Deer cannot sweat. Panting is the primary cooling mechanism, but some excess heat escapes as blood flows through the veins of the ears.

In summer, a mule deer can find refuge from the direct rays of the sun by bedding in the shadow of a rock. In winter, the same rock may help the animal prevent radiant heat loss.

SMITH

FRANZ

To conserve heat while bedded, deer curl up, with legs tucked underneath the body. This position protects from the cold both the limbs, which are thinly furred, and the internal organs.

When the snow reaches chest height, deer conserve energy by using well-traveled paths to move among the foraging sites of their winter range.

high winds force deer to seek shelter and reduce their activities. Humidity may affect the comfort of deer and thus their activities, but again it probably does not act independently of other weather factors. Some observers have suggested that deer appear slightly more nervous during periods of low atmospheric pressure. This may be related to temperature gradients, however, and to some extent to precipitation and wind. Precipitation alone, either rain or snow, has little direct effect on mule deer except when severe storms force animals to seek shelter. Whether this movement to shelter is a comfort-seeking response (escaping the force of the storm) or a security measure (finding a less vulnerable location while the storm impairs the use of senses such as sight, hearing, and smell) or both remains a matter of conjecture.

Snow depth. Perhaps more than any other single weather element, snow depth affects the behavior and well-being of mule deer. As snow accumulates, it covers and gradually decreases the kind and amount of forage available. This may force the animals to rely upon fewer or less-nutritious but more-accessible shrubs and other plants or plant parts that remain above the snow. For example, in the northern plains mule deer eat a variety of forbs, grasses, evergreens, and shrubs during winter. Increasing snow depths may reduce their diet to just a few species of shrubs such as sagebrush and juniper, or the needles of conifer trees such as

pine and fir. Greater depths also present an obstacle to movement, requiring even the largest animals to expend more energy in pursuit of poorer-quality forage.

If the snow becomes deep enough, deer will leave an area. In autumn, depths of 15 to 30 centimeters (6 to 12 inches) may be sufficient to initiate major migrations or shifts in habitat use. Depths of 25 to 30 centimeters (10 to 12 inches) may impede movement, especially among young animals; more than 50 centimeters (20 inches) essentially precludes use of an area.

In mountain habitats, normal winter snow depths can restrict mule deer to less than 20 percent of their total year-round range; under severe snow conditions only 20 to 50 percent of that already reduced range may be usable. The actual amount of usable winter range in any given area depends upon geographic location, local topography, weather, vegetation, and land use.

In the mountains, mule deer generally respond to increasing snow depths by moving down from higher elevations or climbing up from lower ones onto steep south- or west-facing slopes. They also may move to windswept ridges or into timber cover, where snow accumulates less and clears more rapidly. However, in some areas such as windswept foothills where snow shadows occur along the lee slopes of mountain ranges, even migratory deer may winter rather widespread on large winter ranges.

—Richard J. Mackie

BAUER

The desert diet

The North American desert is a harsh and unforgiving world of searing wind, sun-scorched rock, and seemingly unending hot glare. Its aridity sucks the moisture from those who would study its life forms, for human researchers have none of the ingenious adaptations of their subjects.

A desert tortoise carries its own canteen, a water bladder tucked into its upper carapace. The sidewinder, a small rattlesnake, consumes its rodent prey whole not just for food but for water as well, effectively obtaining this precious commodity secondhand. One of its targets never even takes a drink. The kangaroo rat's refreshment is a helping of dry seeds, whose 4 percent moisture content is used with utmost efficiency. The rat's urine is not liquid—flushing waste products in a dilute solution would be extravagant—but more like a concentrated paste. This animal cools off not by sweating but by panting, and lest its humid breath go to waste, its nasal passages condense and recycle the moisture with every exhalation.

It is in this world of specialized creatures that the mule deer—anatomically the same deer that inhabits the lush mountain valleys of the Cascades—lives and even thrives. Unlike the animals that have evolved physiological adaptations for desert life, the deer has changed its behavior. Without, say, the

During summer much of the water of the desert is locked in cacti and other plants; for free water, deer may have to travel extensively.

BIGGS

During prolonged droughts, desert mule deer consume more succulent forage, presumably for its water content.

desert tortoise's canteen, the deer must obtain and conserve water through different behavioral strategies.

WATER

Rainfall is scant in the Sonoran cactus desert of the American Southwest, but it comes in two seasons: winter and late summer. After a rain, when streams come alive and the gravel of dry washes sparkles under the rivulets, deer have an abundance of water to drink. Tanks and natural rock basins, called tinajas, are full. Such free water remains even into dry spells if it is shaded and deep. But as the water dries up, deer must adapt. To prevent dehydration, the animal seeks out shade during the heat of the day and be-

comes active only when the sun is below the horizon—an alteration of its usual pattern of activity recently documented by Hayes and Krausman. And to meet its need for free water, the deer travels.

In Hervert and Krausman's study of does, deer went to water an average of once a day and drank 5 liters (1.3 gallons) per visit. When the accustomed watering sites were no longer available, the deer left their home ranges and went as far as 2 kilometers (1.2 miles) in search of other sources of water. These deer returned home within an hour.

Some deer, however, shift their home ranges because of water. During the summer dry season, Rautenstrauch and Krausman found, desert mule deer in the King Valley

DEER

of southwestern Arizona migrated to ranges that offered free water. And in central Arizona, deer are known to be found closer to water during the hot dry season.

It may be that in cooler times and places, deer can "drink" enough water just by eating vegetation, but in the desert in summer, they clearly need free water. The desert summers are cruel. By July ambient temperatures may have exceeded 38 degrees C (100 degrees F) for more than 100 days, and ground temperatures can reach 49 degrees C (120 degrees F). Rain is unpredictable and may not fall for days, even weeks, at a time. This time happens to be critical for the deer: it is the end of the gestation period, and good nutrition is vital.

FOOD

Though the North American desert supports more plants than the sweeping sand dunes of the Sahara, vegetation is nevertheless sparse, and deer must maintain larger home ranges to meet their nutritional needs. Like the animals that inhabit the desert, the plants that grow here have their own adaptations.

Cacti have given up on broad leaves and some species have even abandoned needles as too wasteful, with too much surface from which water can escape. Instead, they are just stems and trunks, thick and bulky to maximize interior volume without exposing a lot of exterior surface; these green trunks and stems have taken over the leaves' food-producing role. Cacti reach out for water with their shallow, widespread root systems and store it in their spongy interiors. The barrel cactus, with its water-saving design, can live for four years without water. When the rains come, the pleated columns of saguaro and corrugated ranks of organ pipe expand. When the sun scorches the earth, the thick waxy skin of these plants holds the moisture in. When the drought is prolonged, the pulp contracts but can yet provide moisture even for flowering.

These reservoirs would stand little chance against the desert's thirsty inhabitants were it not for their defenses. Shaggy gray spines emerge in tufts from the senita cactus, the "old man" cactus. Spines long and sharp enough to make a porcupine envious defend

the hedgehog cactus. Such a thick growth of pale gold spines protrudes from the stubby arms of *Optunia bigelovii* that the common name for this species of prickly pear is the teddy bear cholla.

Cactus defenses do not discourage the deer, however. *Optuntia,* in fact, is an important forage species for mule deer in late spring and summer, constituting as much as a fifth of the diet. The deer can eat these prickly plants whole, spines and all. Using nearly prehensile lips to reach and nip the cactus, and agile tongue to position the flexible spines just so, deer chew and swallow the cactus without suffering any apparent damage.

But are cacti a preferred food? The proportion of succulents in the desert deer's diet seems to vary with the amount of rainfall: consumption of succulents decreased during rainy seasons, according to separate studies by Leopold and Krausman in Texas and by Short in Arizona. Because desert mule deer use succulents as a source of water—supplementing free water from springs and pools—this component of their diet is greater in dry periods than for northern races of deer.

Thorns and spines do not deter the deer from eating other kinds of plants, either. The acacia, a shrub that belongs to the pea family, is armed yet palatable to deer during summer, when more desirable forage is scarce. This plant does not try to store water, as the cacti do; instead, its desert strategy is to outlast the drought with small, tough,

Bright red fruits top the pads of the prickly pear cactus; their flesh is sweet and seedy.

BIGGS

CAIN

The spines of the prickly pear cactus appear formidable but do not deter browsing deer.

Foods preferred by desert mule deer

Of the plants that constitute more than 5 percent of the deer diet in the deserts of Texas and Arizona, some—jojoba and Texas ranger, for example—are eaten year-round. Other species, though, are available only during certain seasons.

Plant	Spring	Summer	Late summer or fall	Winter
Browse				
Acacia (*Acacia* spp.)	–	8–14%	8%	–
Calliandra (*Calliandra eriophylla*)	24%	13	20–71	–
Ceanothus (*Ceanothus* spp.)	–	6	8	–
Desert deervetch (*Lotus rigidus*)	–	–	–	8%
Eriogonum (*Eriogonum* spp.)	–	–	5–14	13
Gaura (*Gaura* spp.)	–	6	6	6–9
Guayacan (*Porlieria angustifolia*)	–	–	9	5
Holly-leaf buckthorn (*Rhamnus crocea*)	–	–	5	–
Ironwood (*Olneya tesota*)	–	6	9	–
Jojoba (*Simmondsia chinensis*)	12	5–21	9–35	23–27
Mariola (*Parthenium incanum*)	6	6	7–22	9
Mesquite (*Prosopis* spp.)	–	29	5	–
Milkwort (*Polygala macrodencia*)	–	–	5	–
Oak (*Quercus* spp.)	–	14–26	–	–
Ratany (*Krameria* spp.)	9	12–51	8–15	8
Sagebrush (*Artemisia* spp.)	5	–	–	–
Sumac (*Rhus* spp.)	6	12	12	9
Texas ranger (*Leucophyllum* spp.)	50–66	12–60	12	40–52
Forbs				
Artemisia (*Artemisia ludoviciana*)	–	–	12	–
Bladderpod (*Lesquerella* spp.)	–	8	–	27
Boraginaceae	5	–	–	6
Dalea (*Dalea neomexicana*)	5–19	9–36	6–41	23–55
Deervetch (*Lotus* spp.)	–	–	–	6
Filaree (*Erodium cicutarium*)	–	–	–	10
Flat-top buckwheat (*Eriogonum fasciculatum*)	38	10	6	17
Grass-nuts (*Dichelostemma pulchellum*)	–	–	–	13
Janusia (*Janusia gracilis*)	–	–	5–25	–
Lupine (*Lupinus* spp.)	18	8	–	12
Mallow (*Abutiton* spp.)	9	7	5–24	6–13
Menodora (*Menodora scoparia*)	–	–	–	10
Rockcress (*Arabis perennans*)	–	–	–	5
Scruf-pea (*Psoralea* spp.)	6	–	–	–
Spurge (*Euphorbia* spp.)	17	5–21	15–26	12–38
Tidestromia (*Tidestromia* spp.)	–	–	12	–
Twist flower (*Nerisyrenia camporum*)	6	–	10	17
Succulents				
Beargrass (*Nolina* spp.)	6	–	–	–
Lecheguilla (*Agave lecheguilla*)	48	–	5–17	9–42
Prickly-pear (*Opuntia* spp.)	9–23	19	9	13

Sources: McCulloch (1973), Krausman (1978), Leopold and Krausman (1987), Krausman et al. (1989).

waxy leaves. The ocotillo, a shrub with large, wandlike branches, casts its leaves when dry and grows new ones after a rain. These new leaves are well protected by spines, but deer still manage to eat some whenever the plant is green.

Deer browse on jojoba, a shrub 1 to 2 meters (3 to 6 feet) tall with dark, thick leaves and an acornlike fruit. About half of each fruit is lipid, a liquid wax similar to sperm whale oil. Just as that giant sea mammal's oil is unique among animal fats and oils, so too is the high-energy lipid of the jojoba: no other plant in the world is known to produce it.

Other important forage species include locoweed, a plant poisonous to livestock but eaten with impunity by deer; Texas ranger, a large shrub with thick, succulent, silver-blue leaves, whose new growth and flowers are deer favorites; and dalea, a species that ranges from small trees to large shrubs, which also loses new growth to foraging deer.

The agave or century plant consists of a cluster of thick, succulent, evergreen leaves spreading out at ground level from a short, underground stem. After several years (ten to twenty, not one hundred as the name implies), the plant rapidly grows a stalk 2 to 3 meters (10 to 15 feet) tall and then dies. Deer eat this stalk. In fact, I have seen deer consume a stalk 2 meters (6 feet) tall and as thick as a man's wrist in fifteen minutes before moving on to other forage.

As with deer in more hospitable habitat, browse provides the bulk of their diet, but forbs are also important. Like browse, forbs contain relatively high amounts of moisture and are consumed whenever available. At higher elevations deer eat the acorns of mast oaks, scrubby, low-growing relatives of the oaks that provide abundant mast in eastern forests.

Just as deer are opportunists, so there are opportunistic plants in the desert: the annuals. These plants have little tolerance for desert conditions, and indeed, they are not normally seen. But let the rain come and suddenly the annuals burst forth, hastening to grow, flower, reproduce, and set seed before the withering sun dries them to dust— or before the deer eat them. Among the

CAIN

ephemeral plants that must thus hurry through their life processes are filaree, lupine, and menodora.

These annual plants are not dependable foods for deer, because conditions may permit their growth only every three or four years. But when ephemerals do appear, they are likely an important component of the diet.

In fact, annuals aside, the desert mule deer's diet is extremely varied. The number and diversity of plants consumed changes with locale, season, and year-to-year fluctuations in climate. In the lower Sonoran Desert, in southernmost Arizona, there are few species of vegetation, and in Krausman's study, deer selected 28. But on the more diverse Three Bar Wildlife Area in central Arizona, at the northern edge of desert mule deer habitat, McCulloch and Urness counted 106 forage species. Overall, the diversity of plant life in the desert provides ample choices for desert mule deer, and their reputation as opportunistic feeders carries even into this harsh environment.

—Paul R. Krausman

The scrub oak and sagebrush of mesic sites in the Southwest provide good forage for deer.

The cost of living

Survival is a matter of balance. For mule deer and black-tailed deer, survival depends largely on a seasonal energy balance: the difference between income (the energy obtained from food and body reserves) and expenditure (the energy costs of living). The deer's daily expenditures include what is needed for body maintenance, plus the costs of moving around, keeping warm, and reproducing. Those costs change over the course of the year, as do the food resources. When income exceeds expenditure, usually during summer, the deer replenishes its reserves and puts on fat. When income drops as expenditures rise, however, as is typically the case during winter, the deer draws down its reserves. And thus weight gain and fat storage are followed by weight loss and fat depletion: an annual cycle that enables the deer to survive even in the face of harsh weather and limited food.

SOURCES OF INCOME

On one side of the balance is food. Forage is often plentiful in summer and early fall, scarce in winter and early spring. Seasonal changes aside, the choice of food is sometimes determined by the weather. When grasses and forbs lie buried under drifted snow, mule deer in the Rocky Mountain region turn to shrubs, such as bitterbrush (*Purshia tridentata*), snowberry (*Symphoricarpos* sp.), and serviceberry (*Amelanchier* sp.). When gusts of wind tear lichens from the treetops, blacktails have access to one of their favorite foods. When the rhizomes of a fern, *Dryopteris dilatata*, which is commonly eaten by Sitka blacktails throughout the winter, are locked in frozen ground, the deer eat evergreen forbs such as bunchberry dogwood (*Cornus canadensis*), trailing bramble (*Rubus pedatus*), and foamflower (*Tiarella trifoliata*), or the woody stems of huckleberry (*Vaccinium ovalifolium* and *Vaccinium alaskensis*). To a large extent, then, weather determines what deer can eat, and how much.

Although the gross energy component of forage remains relatively stable throughout the year, deer cannot always get adequate nutrition. During winter, deer turn to matured plants and woody twigs for food. Such a high-fiber diet is less digestible, so nutri-

Browse is not favored as long as other food is available; bitterbrush is one of the mule deer's starvation foods.

J. MILLER

Mule deer are very selective, nipping off buds and small, pliable twigs.

MULE AND BLACK-TAILED DEER

Prunus virginiana
common chokecherry

Balsamorhiza sagittata
arrowleaf balsam root

Salix lasiandra
Pacific willow

Phlox caespitosa
tufted phlox

Cornus canadensis
bunchberry

ents—and, therefore, energy—are not as readily available to the animals. The amount of protein deer consume also varies seasonally with the protein content of plants: the tender green shoots of spring are low in fiber, high in protein, and highly digestible, just the opposite of the tough woody stems available in winter.

Because of changes in plant quality and quantity, early winter ranges for deer are usually sufficient to meet protein needs—relatively low at this time—but are often lacking in energy provision as the animals encounter cold and snow. By late winter, when the food supplies are rapidly being depleted, ranges may not be able to meet protein or energy needs of deer.

Deer spend more time ruminating during winter to process poorer-quality, highly fibrous stems, only to extract less benefit from them. That explains why it's not just the amount of vegetation that determines whether a deer is well fed. In fact, a deer can eat only so much regardless of season. One biological limit to intake is the biting rate, which is constrained by how fast the animal can chew and swallow, and that in turn depends on the size and density of plant leaves or stems.

Blacktails, for example, can eat prodigious amounts of skunk cabbage *(Lysichitum americanum)*, with leaves that may grow 1 meter tall in southeastern Alaska. Their intake rates are much lower when eating plants

The protein content of plants rises in spring, then declines as the tissues grow and mature. It is during that short period in spring that deer must replenish protein stores that were broken down during the winter as the animals' fat stores were depleted. The data come from Hanley and McKendrick's study of blacktail foods in Alaska.

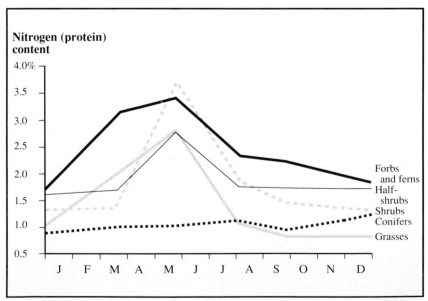

Nitrogen (protein) content

Forbs and ferns
Half-shrubs
Shrubs
Conifers
Grasses

Quercus gambelii
Gambel oak

Penstemon rupicola
cliff penstemon

Lupinus polyphyllus
blue-pod lupine

Rhus trilobata
squawbush

Juniperus osteosperma
Utah juniper

with much smaller leaves, such as trailing bramble or bunchberry dogwood.

Intake is also affected by the animal's capacity to process the food after it is swallowed. Studies of the breakdown of plants in the rumen have determined how long it takes for forage to pass through the digestive tract. Spalinger and others found that fiber slows digestion in mule deer: browse stems take two to four times longer than small forbs to pass through the animal's system. For example, 50 percent of ingested pea *(Pisum sativum)* and balsam root *(Balsamorhiza sagittata)* leaves break down in the rumen in less than an hour and a half, but blueberry *(Vaccinium* sp.) stems need much more time—almost six hours.

Besides fiber, certain chemicals in plants can reduce the animal's ability to digest forage and can even produce toxic effects. These secondary compounds, as they are known, may have evolved as a plant defense. By binding with plant protein, for example, tannins decrease the digestibility of a plant and the amount of protein that is available to the animal.

Mule deer, however, evolved along with many of the tannin-containing browse species and now have a counterattack. Animal proteins in the saliva of deer actually bind to the tannins to minimize absorption and their effects on digestibility. Consequently, deer are better able to consume and digest the twigs and buds of such plants as

FRANCIS

Windstorms break loose branches of Douglas-fir, at times littering the forest floor with small, green twigs. The foliage of treetops is less toxic than that of lower branches and mule deer eagerly feed on the windfall.

AUBREY

Amelanchier alnifolia
western serviceberry

Pseudotsuga menziesii
Douglas-fir

Artemisia tridentata
big sagebrush

Trifolium pratense
red clover

Cowania mexicana
cliff rose

AUBREY

red alder *(Alnus rubra)* and red-osier dogwood *(Cornus stolonifera)*.

Terpenoids are another group of plant secondary compounds that can have toxic effects. These are the fragrant volatile oils of such plants as sagebrush, juniper, and conifers. Terpenoids apparently destroy the rumen's natural digestive bacteria, which are responsible, through fermentation, for supplying 50 to 70 percent of the animal's energy requirements. When sagebrush exceeds 30 percent of the diet, mule deer lose their appetite and experience rapid weight loss. Given a choice, the animals prefer species that contain the lowest levels of terpenoids.

Yet deer do not entirely avoid plants that contain terpenoids and tannins, and the scientific literature abounds with examples of deer eating the very foods that inhibit their digestive abilities. One theory, advanced by McArthur and others, is that for mule deer and blacktails, the most important nutrient consideration is energy. Deer prefer forage that has high digestible energy and low concentrations of toxic secondary compounds. If deer cannot find plants with these characteristics, they select the forage highest in energy content as long as the energy obtained from it is greater than the energy spent detoxifying secondary compounds. Consequently, redstem ceanothus *(Ceanothus sanguines)* and sitka willow *(Salix sitchensis)*, even though they contain high levels of tannins, are preferred forage plants for mule deer and blacktails. If the costs of metabolizing and excreting the secondary compounds are very high, deer will choose a plant with lower energy and lower tannin content. Because deer simultaneously attempt to maximize energy intake and minimize secondary compound intake, their food preferences will vary from location to location.

ENERGY BILLS

On the other side of the balance are the expenditures. An understanding of energy costs for a deer begins with maintenance: what it spends in energy just to support such basic functions as breathing, blood circulation, tissue and organ function, muscle tone, and maintenance of body temperature. Basal metabolism rates are determined while an animal is resting, fasted, and neither heat- nor cold-stressed; in such a state it incurs no costs for being active, processing its food, or regulating its temperature under extreme conditions. The smaller black-tailed deer has maintenance metabolic rates 18 percent higher than those of mule deer, according to Mautz et al. This finding is consistent with the general rule that smaller animals have relatively higher metabolic rates. Basal energy metabolism also appears to decline during winter—by 6 percent compared with summer rates in black-tailed deer, and by 11.5 percent for mule deer. This decline coincides with wintertime reductions in food resources.

Cercocarpus ledifolius
curl-leaf mountain mahogany

Salix sitchensis
Sitka willow

Taraxacum officinale
dandelion

Opuntia spp.
prickly pear

Carex hystricina
porcupine sedge

Now factor in the realities of life in the wild and the energy costs increase dramatically.

Food intake. The digestion and processing of food may raise energy requirements by 11 percent in mule deer, according to Kautz.

Posture. Just standing takes more energy than lying down. Energy costs increase 25 percent in most wild ungulates when the animal is standing.

Locomotion. Faster travel and steep, uphill routes naturally increase energy costs for all deer, although per unit of body weight, larger animals have lower demands. For example, it costs relatively more energy for a fawn to travel across a field than it costs the fawn's mother.

Winter movement. Snow deeper than the deer's front "knees" (carpus height)—approximately 32 centimeters (12.6 inches) for an average 67-kilogram (148-pound) mule deer—makes travel expensive. If the animal periodically breaks through crusted snow, energy costs go up again. If the deer sinks into drifts up to its belly—if the snow is deeper than 58 centimeters (23 inches)—the animal resorts to exaggerated bounds at extremely high expense.

Dense, wet snow is more taxing than light powder because it drags on the legs and forces the deer to lift its legs higher to clear the snow. Energy costs for travel through heavy, belly-deep snow are eight times the cost of traveling on bare ground.

A deer uses eight times more energy to travel through very deep snow than to traverse the same distance over bare ground.

FRANCIS

AUBREY

MULE AND BLACK-TAILED DEER

311

Potentilla arguta
tall cinquefoil

Vaccinium parvifolium
red huckleberry

Melilotus officinalis
yellow sweet clover

Symphoricarpos oreophilus
mountain snowberry

Lysichiton americanum
yellow skunk cabbage

Thermoregulation in cold environments.
Deer suffer more from cold when it is windy than on a calm day, as one would expect. The effects of solar radiation are equally important. At −30 degrees C (−22 degrees F), in early winter morning, a mule deer shivers violently. As the day dawns and sunbeams strike the animal's pelage, shivering ceases. In fact, Parker and Robbins found, in full sun at −30 C (−22 degrees F), the mule deer's skin temperature may reach the same level that it does at *plus* 30 degrees C (86 degrees F) in summer. (To include the effects of sun and wind, researchers use Bakken's standard operative temperature index; similar to a windchill factor, the index also accounts for solar radiation, and thus it

By decreasing energy expenditures during winter, the mule deer makes best use of limited resources. A fawn's winter metabolic rate—the basic cost of maintenance—drops 70 percent.

represents the temperature that the animal actually feels.)

Mule deer in good condition during winter are not stressed by cold until the standard operative temperature drops to about 20 degrees C below zero (−4 degrees F). The animals erect the hair to thicken the coat and shiver to generate heat by muscle contractions. Energy metabolism then increases in an effort to maintain an adequate body temperature. Mule deer in poor condition with limited food supplies are much less tolerant of the cold and must take those compensatory measures before the temperature reaches −20 degrees C (−4 degrees F). And mule deer that have just molted their winter coats, only to experience a late-spring blizzard, will suffer if the temperature falls below 5 degrees C *above* zero (41 degrees F). In both cases, energy costs go up.

Ability to withstand cold varies among the species of North American deer. Mule deer are more tolerant than whitetails, black-tailed deer are less so—which is what one might expect from the temperature ranges of their respective habitats.

Thermoregulation in warm environments.
Maintaining an acceptable body temperature is necessary for survival; it is not just cold, however, that can cause a problem. Mule deer with heavy, well-insulated coats suffer heat stress in winter if the temperature rises above 5 degrees C (41 degrees F). In their summer coats, they are stressed by heat at temperatures greater than 25 degrees C (77

AUBREY

FRANCIS

degrees F), which often occur in the open habitats of their range. Blacktails are heat stressed in summer when temperatures rise above 27 degrees C (81 degrees F). In all of these cases, the animals must increase their energy expenditures, primarily through panting, to rid their bodies of excess heat.

Rain. In winter, rain does not appear to increase energy costs for adult blacktails. Certainly they are better adapted to rain than mule deer. The white powder that appears on the dry pelage of blacktails, visible especially between the shoulder blades, is a specialized fat covering on the hairs. In the rain it becomes a waxlike coating that sheds water. Compared with mule deer, blacktails have approximately two and a half times more of this coating in winter.

Despite this adaptation for their wet coastal habitat, black-tailed deer expend more energy in summer rains if the temperature is less than 10 degrees C (50 degrees F) than they do when the weather is dry but colder than 5 degrees C (41 degrees F) or hotter than 30 degrees C (86 degrees F). For blacktail fawns, with relatively higher energy demands, cold spring rains can be fatal.

Reproduction. If the adult doe has not had adequate nutrition during her pregnancy, she loses weight and has a lower level of body fat than a better-fed deer, and her fawn is often smaller with less chance for survival. Fetal growth varies significantly with winter conditions. Under extremely poor nutritional conditions, ovulation and conception are entirely inhibited.

The pregnant doe also needs protein, which is essential for building body tissues. In his sixteen-year study of Colorado mule deer, Robinette found that does receiving higher amounts of protein had higher pregnancy rates and fawned earlier in the spring than did less-well-fed does. Moreover, the fawns weighed more by the end of summer, and some even bred during their first fall.

For bucks—mule deer or blacktail—protein is important for antler growth in the period leading up to the rut. The rut itself is costly and requires a reserve of energy. Anderson et al. observed less fat in male mule deer than in females in winter, which they attributed to the bucks' higher activity level in autumn. Nordan's study showed significant weight

FRANCIS

loss in blacktail bucks during the breeding period.

Lactation. It is during lactation that energy costs are greater than during any other reproductive process. According to Wallmo and others, they may reach 2.3 times basal metabolic rates at the peak of lactation. The doe must produce milk of sufficient quality—concentrated energy and high protein—to enable her fawn to grow rapidly and thus become capable of escaping predators and surviving the coming winter.

Deer milk is richer than the milk of domestic animals. Among North American deer species, milk protein content averages between 7 and 8 percent, compared with 3 to 3.5 percent in cattle. The black-tailed

Lactation exacts a high cost in energy and protein, but because it coincides with the high-quality, nutritious forage of late spring and early summer, the doe can nourish her fawns. Still, she may lose weight and delay her molt.

Bucks experience extremes of fat storage and depletion, in sync with the annual cycle of forage quality. Females, on the other hand, maintain a more stable reserve but, because of the demands of lactation, cannot replenish it until late in the year. The hypothetical data for mule deer in Colorado come from Wallmo et al.

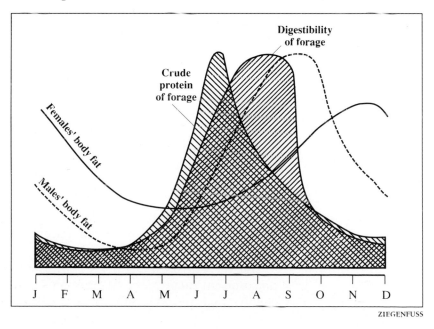

ZIEGENFUSS

To grow large enough to survive its first winter, a fawn needs high-quality nutrition. Young animals require more energy per unit of body weight than do larger adults.

deer's milk is more than 50 percent higher in energy content than the mule deer's milk. Data from Sadleir and Carl and Robbins indicate that, during the first five weeks of lactation, milk averages 1.75 kilocalories per gram in blacktails and 1.11 kilocalories per gram in mule deer (cattle have about .73 kilocalories of energy per gram of milk). The smaller blacktail fawns also grow almost 50 percent more rapidly than mule deer fawns.

To produce such a concentrated milk, the blacktail doe depends partly on high-quality forage that provides high amounts of both energy and protein. She must also break down her own body tissue reserves to meet the energy demands of her fawns. During the first five weeks after parturition, she may lose 8.5 percent of her body weight. Even though the mule deer doe's milk is less rich, the energy demands are similar, since she must produce a larger volume of milk to feed her slightly larger newborn fawns; she loses 6.5 percent of her body weight during the same time period.

Growth. The fawn's early growth depends on sufficient quantities of its mother's high-energy, high-protein milk. Then, when it turns to forage, it must find enough food of good quality to continue its maturation and grow its winter coat.

Young, rapidly growing animals generally have higher energy requirements per unit of weight than older, mature adults. Its initial growth spurt passed, the fawn's metabolism declines during the first winter, but the rates of decrease are very different between mule deer and blacktail fawns. For blacktail fawns, the metabolic rate declines about 20 percent between 5 and 8 months of age; for mule deer fawns, the drop is drastic—70 percent, according to studies by Parker and Robbins. The big decrease for mule deer fawns is an adaptive advantage in their typical winter habitat, with its extreme cold and lack of food. With lower expenditures, the young animal conserves its resources for the absolutely essential task of surviving till spring.

Even for an adult, the mule deer's winter metabolism is 11.5 percent lower than in summer. It, too, is cutting costs, trying to maintain the balance between energy income and expenditure that will enable it to survive.

—Katherine L. Parker

Profile of a mule deer population

Consider a mountain lake. A stream feeds water in; at the other end, water flows out. Rain falls, snow melts—the water level rises. Hot, dry winds blow across its surface—the level drops.

So it is with a population of animals: the interplay between births and deaths (inflow and outflow) and immigration and emigration (precipitation and evaporation) determines whether the herd grows or shrinks. The lake analogy, offered by Farner, is actually much simpler than the real-life complications of the animal world. Understanding animals is anything but simple, and no two populations exhibit exactly the same behavior. But that is just what makes the study of populations fascinating.

A population is a group of organisms of the same species that occupy a given area over a given time. It is an abstraction. Individual animals and small groups—a doe and her young, for example, or a summer bachelor group—may attract more interest, Dasmann notes, because they are real: they can be seen and observed and studied. But an understanding of populations is important because it yields information that cannot be learned from the study of individuals. When describing populations, biologists measure characteristics that individuals, by definition, lack: density, sex and age structure, mortality rates, natality rates, social structure, and movement patterns.

To obtain this information, biologists begin with natural history. Basically descriptive, it emphasizes the visually apparent aspects of a given species' population biology, from births and deaths to immigration and emigration. The lake, in other words.

BIRTHS

Although fawn mule deer can give birth, wild females normally do not give birth until their second year. Other things being equal, fawns and yearlings produce fewer young than do older mule deer females. Younger animals usually produce single deer but the most common litter size is two. When triplets are born it is to females older than four years, according to Anderson. Quadruplets are very rare but have been documented.

The number and condition of the newborn deer depends, as well, on the condition of the mother. Clutton-Brock's study on red deer (*Cervus elaphus*) found that the body condition of females was directly related to the success and number of calves born. In a study in Michigan, Verme concluded that the malnutrition of whitetail females reduced fetal weights and birth weights.

Such findings are probably applicable to mule deer as well. At birth mule deer weigh from 2.3 to 5 kilograms (5 to 11 pounds), with singles usually heavier than twins and males heavier than females.

Much of our knowledge about the reproduction cycle of mule deer has been obtained from captive animals. A buck's sperm productivity and quality generally decrease

Although there is no typical sex or age structure that characterizes all mule deer populations, adult females generally outnumber adult males by more than two to one, even in unhunted areas.

from age seven on. Does, on the other hand, usually remain productive throughout life.

Some deer never become part of the population. Up to 10 percent mortality occurs in mule deer from losses of ova (before fetal development can even begin) and postnatal mortality may run 22 to 53 percent for males and 17 to 25 percent for females, according to Connolly.

How many pregnant does carry their fetuses to term and how many newborn fawns survive determine the productivity of the herd. And those factors, in turn, depend on climate, nutrition, predation, disease, the degree of competition with other herbivores—in short, all the things that constitute mortality.

MORTALITY

Death can come to mule deer directly—from a hunter's bullet, a predator's strangling bite, or the weakening wrought by an infestation of parasites; or indirectly—from habitat loss and consequent starvation. Mortality factors do not always act independently, however, and often a compensatory

mortality process is at work, as Bartmann and coworkers have demonstrated. That is, an increase in one form of death results in decreased mortality from other causes, with the net result of zero on the overall mortality rate.

Hunting. More than half a million deer are shot annually. Recreational hunting is predicated on the notion of a harvestable surplus—a certain number of deer that can be killed each year without detriment to the breeding stock. This number varies widely from population to population. Hunting, moreover, may affect several aspects of mule deer populations: production and survival of fawns, mortality from other causes, population turnover and age composition, and the relative proportions of bucks, does, and fawns. Although hunting can alter mule deer populations, it does not operate in isolation, nor is it the only influence that can produce these effects. Connolly offers several generalizations:

• Mule deer herds can produce an annual harvestable crop of deer, the size of which varies with the age and sex class hunted.

• Controlled recreational hunting is unlikely to limit deer numbers because regulations tend to be conservative.

• Hunting only males tends to produce increasing deer herds; hunting females reduces densities.

• Hunting stimulates higher rates of fawn production and survival because in a thinner deer herd there is less competition for forage and hence improved nutrition, according to some studies.

• The average age of deer in hunted herds declines as the harvest increases.

• Hunting any specific age and sex classes—antlered deer only, for example, or antlerless—changes the age and sex composition of the herd.

Predation. Mule deer share their range with several predators—mountain lions *(Felis concolor)*, bobcats *(Felis rufus)*, coyotes *(Canis latrans)*, golden eagles *(Aquila chrysaetos)*, domestic and feral dogs *(Canis familiaris)*, and black bears *(Ursus americanus)*. The role of predation in ungulate populations has been a controversial topic because there is no universal agreement on population regulation.

In addition, human hunters often assume that a deer killed by predators is one less animal available for their own bag. Is that indeed the case? Just how do predators affect mule deer populations?

Connolly offers three possible answers, based on a review of some sixty predator-prey studies in North America. First, predators do control some ungulate populations. Bobcats and coyotes were responsible for most documented fawn mortality in Oregon, according to a 1975 study by Trainer. Controlling predators on winter deer range brought an increase in the winter survival of fawns. Similar results emerged from studies of mule deer and coyotes in Arizona, California, Utah, and Washington, and of deer and mountain lions in California: fawn survival increased where predators were controlled. If the range is deteriorating, predators can hasten the decline of a population of ungulates. Rarely, however, were predators the only direct cause of widespread declines. And in some cases predators appear to keep ungulates adjusted to the carrying capacity of the range.

Fawn survival rates affect the structure of a population. Irrigation ditches and canals pose a real hazard to young mule deer trying to cross or drink.

RICH

The second conclusion is just the opposite of the first: predators do *not* control ungulate populations. Instead, populations were found to be regulated more by habitat conditions, with predation of minor consequence. Ten studies of mule deer and predators (coyotes, black bears, mountain lions, and bobcats) in Arizona, California, Nevada, and Utah supported this conclusion. The predators did kill many mule deer, especially fawns, but predation was not the limiting factor.

To confuse the issue even more is Connolly's third conclusion: that predation may force the redistribution of mule deer on limited winter range. A study by Hornocker suggests that in response to predation, deer would spread out more and make less intense use of limited forage.

The conflicting results from biologists who have all studied similar predator-prey relationships point out a problem: comparisons are difficult when studies proceed by different methods and are conducted without controls. Nevertheless, it is safe to say that predation is a certain source of mortality for mule deer. Recent studies by Gasaway and his colleagues and by Ballard have demonstrated that ungulates in general cannot withstand the combination of high rates of hunter harvest and predation by unchecked numbers of carnivores. The same conclusion is probably applicable to mule deer in particular.

Diseases and parasites. Like predation, disease and parasites can act alone or in combination with such other factors as competition, predation, and bad weather, with a consequent loss to the wildlife population. Even when disease is not a primary mortality factor, it can still be the consequence of other predisposing factors. Hibler uses gastrointestinal parasitism by nematodes as an example: "Severe burdens of gastrointestinal parasites generally are an indication of crowding and competition, within and among deer populations, resulting in inadequate nutrition. Although gastrointestinal parasitism must be blamed as the cause of death, these parasites were only the final insult."

Determining the impact of disease is not an easy task because the biologist must usually study sick animals in the laboratory; in the wild they are quickly eliminated. In his review of diseases of mule deer, Hibler discusses viral, bacterial, and parasitic diseases.

Viral diseases include tumors, bluetongue, epizootic hemorrhagic disease, foot-and-mouth disease, malignant catarrhal fever, and the bovine virus diarrhea—mucosal disease complex.

Bacterial diseases associated with mule deer include pasteurellosis *(Pasteurella multocida)*, brucellosis *(Brucella* spp.), necrobacillosis *(Fusibacterium necrophorus)*, actinomycosis *(Actinomyces bovis)*, blackleg and malignant edema *(Clostridium chauvei* and *specticum,* respectively), caseous lymphadenitis *(Corynebacterium ovis* and *C. pyogenes)*, and anthrax *(Bacillus anthracis)*.

The parasitic diseases that Hibler documented for mule deer are the intraarterial nematode elaeophorosis *(Elaeophora schneideri)*, the abdominal worm, setaria *(Setaria yehi)*, the meningeal worm parelaphostrongylosis *(Parelaphostrongylus tenuis)*, gastrointestinal parasitism by nematodes *(Haemonchus* spp., *Ostertagia* spp., *Trichostrongylus* spp., *Nematodirus* spp., *Nematodierella* spp., *Trichuris* spp., Capillaria spp., and perhaps *Marshallagia* spp.), lungworms *(Dictyocaulus viviparus, D. filaria, D. hadweni, Protostrongylus macrotis,* and *Parelaphostrongylus odocoilei)*, foot worm or leg worm *(Onchocerca cervipedis)*, eye worm *(Thelazia californiensis)*, tapeworms (larvae stages of *Taenia hydatigena* and *T. krabbei* and adult *Moneizia* spp. and *Thysanosoma actinioides)*, trematodes or the common liver fluke *(Fasciola hepatica)* and the large American liver fluke *(Fascioloides magna)*, sarocystis *(Sarocystis* spp.), toxoplasmosis *(Toxoplasma gondii)*, bloodsucking diptera *(Hybomitra* spp. and *Tabanus* spp.), blackflies *(Simulium* spp.), deerflies *(Chrysops* spp.), mosquitoes *(Aldes* spp.), black bodega gnats *(Leptoconops* spp.), botflies *(Cephenemyia jellisoni,* and *C. apicata)*, louse flies *(Lipoptena depressa* and *Neolipoptena ferrisi)*, lice *(Haematopinus* spp., *Linognathus* spp., *Tricholipeuris* spp., and *Cervophthirus* spp.), mites, ticks *(Otobius megnini, Dermacentor albipictus, D. andersoni, Ixodes scapularis, I. pacificus,* and *Ornithochoros coriaceus)*, fleas *(Pulex irritans)*, and anaplasmosis *(Anaplasma marginale)*.

ROBBINS

Congenital anomalies also contribute to mortality in mule deer, but reports of anomalies are rare in free-ranging wild populations because malformed individuals die at a very young age.

Accidents. When it comes to accidental causes of death, most studies are not extensive or systematic, and their methods of collecting and analyzing data are highly variable. But accidents—including illegal kills, crippling losses, road kills, falls, drowning, and entanglements in fencing—are certainly responsible for losses to mule deer populations.

Crippling deaths occur when wounded deer elude the hunter and subsequently die from their wounds. Several researchers have examined these losses and documented that they constitute from 8 to a whopping 92 percent of the legal harvest.

Accidents involving mule deer and vehicles have been a serious problem in the West since the 1960s. Although accurate records have been difficult to maintain, thousands of mule deer are killed in collisions each year. In some areas this mortality can be signi-

ficant: More than 20,000 deer are killed each year on California highways—a figure that is approximately 60 percent of the average harvest each year in the state from 1970 to 1975.

Falls, drownings, and entanglements may have only local importance. Desert mule deer inhabiting extremely steep and rugged habitat in the Picacho Mountains in Arizona often fall to their death from cliffs and large boulders. Of nine collared females in a population studied by Krausman, three died from falls. Deer also fall into canals and water troughs and drown—and more than 12,000 kilometers (7,500 miles) of concrete-lined canals carry water from rivers and reservoirs to industrial, residential, and agricultural users throughout the western United States. Thousands of mule deer and other wild ungulates drowned in twenty-some canals in ten western states and Canadian provinces while attempting to cross or drink. Deer entanglement in fences is perhaps a broader form of mortality because fences thread their way all across mule deer range. Again the actual number that die after catching a hoof

Mortality rates may be high if deer already weakened by winter cannot find forage on overgrazed land.

The arrival of a coyote pack at first disrupted a mule deer herd's normal activities. After several fawns were attacked and killed, the deer left their winter range and swam across a large lake, not to return for several weeks.

or antler in wire has not been documented.

Other types of accidents include entanglement in loose wire, antlers locked with antlers of other deer, and numerous less common causes of death that have little effect on populations.

Weather. Rain or drought, early winter storm or mild spring: weather usually determines plant growth and water availability and thus affects deer populations. In the northern parts of mule deer range, however, deep and prolonged snow cover can lead directly to starvation and malnutrition. As with other forms of mortality, weather is difficult to isolate. An animal weakened by a struggle through chest-deep snow or a lack of water may be a more tempting target for a predator than if it were healthy. Ultimately, all the forms of mortality act in concert.

IMMIGRATION AND POPULATION

Deer sometimes move away from their herd in the behavior known as dispersal. Bunnell and Harestad offer a formal definition: individual movements out of an area larger than a home range that exhibit no predictable return.

How far a deer must move to be considered in dispersal varies. Bunnell and Harestad reported that movements of Columbian black-tailed deer greater than 5 kilometers (3.1 miles) were dispersive and averaged 15.2 kilometers (9.4 miles) for males and 12.2 kilometers (7.6 miles) for females. Robinette reported that Rocky Mountain mule deer dispersed up to 1.6 kilometers (1 mile) beyond established home ranges and that the dispersers established new home ranges. Robinette also reported that fawns dispersed up to 217 kilometers (135 miles).

Mortality rates of dispersing animals appear to be higher than for deer that stay with their natal herd. Scarbrough and Krausman's study of desert mule deer in the Picacho Mountains of Arizona revealed that yearling males dispersed up to 45 kilometers (28 miles) from their home ranges but died soon after dispersing.

Many biologists assume that the number of deer leaving a herd equals the number moving in, and hence immigration and emigration cancel each other out. Until more is learned about these movements the assumption will continue to be made.

The basic components of any mule deer population—natality, mortality, emigration, and immigration—are the aspects of natural history necessary to understand the population "lake." They are influenced by factors both biotic (other animals and habitats, for example) and abiotic (topography, water, climate). If researchers' descriptions of mule deer herds appear imprecise and couched in qualifiers, just recall all the possible factors and their combinations and interrelationships, from environmental mechanisms like condition of plants, grazing intensity, water availability, and climate, to population mechanisms like diseases, parasites, hunting pressure, predation, accidents, dispersal, winter mortality, and reproductive rates. Then it is not surprising that so much variation exists between mule deer populations.

—*Paul R. Krausman*

Populations and habitat

Mule deer inhabit a variety of ecosystems, but not uniformly. The exact nature and ability of each habitat to meet all the animals' needs determines, in large part, the number of deer that can comfortably live in an area.

All deer, but especially reproducing females, spend six to eight months (from spring to fall) on home ranges in habitat suitable for them to recover from the rigors of the past winter, bear and rear fawns, regain sufficient body condition to breed and conceive successfully again, and accumulate the fat and energy reserves necessary to survive the following winter. At the same time these habitats must provide adequate cover for both young and adults to avoid or defend themselves against predators.

In those places where all of these needs can be met in small areas—where food and cover are abundant and closely interspersed—individual ranges are small and many deer are able to live in the area. On the other hand, in those places where resources are limited or widely scattered, home ranges are larger and fewer deer can live in the area. Because of this relationship between resource distribution and deer numbers, deer abundance can be viewed as the product of both the productivity of the habitat (the number of deer that can be supported per unit area) and the total amount of habitat available. Overall, the largest deer populations are found where high quality habitat exists continuously over a large area; small, less dense populations are found in habitats where the resources are limited, widely spaced, or distributed in scattered patches.

MOUNTAIN FOOTHILLS

Given the species' basic requirements, it's not surprising that, of all the different ecosystems in the West, mule deer reach their greatest numbers in the mountain-foothills. In such habitat there may be as many as 4 to 8 deer or more per square kilometer (10 to 20 per square mile). One range in Utah was reported to support 16 deer per square kilometer (40 per square mile) *after* each annual hunting season from 1947 to 1956, a period of extreme mule deer abundance. In the Bridger Mountains of southwestern Montana, late winter populations numbered about 4 mule deer per square kilometer (10 per square mile) of total year-round habitat during the late 1980s. Mountain-foothill habitats are generally very complex with a great diversity of topographic features, microclimates, vegetation types, and flora. Small changes in elevation, slope, and exposure can also bring about changes in microclimate and flora. Such complexity and diversity enable mule deer to consistently meet all their seasonal needs for food, water, shelter, and escape cover within a very small home range.

Of course, such diversity also means that some isolated areas, although of the same general habitat type, might support deer populations of very different size and den-

In the Lava Beds National Monument of northern California, the large overwintering deer population may strip the understory as early as November. This doe stretches for a bite of mountain mahogany.

J. MILLER

MULE AND BLACK-TAILED DEER

323

ESCHER

DEER

Left: Males and females in one Montana study preferred different summer habitat. Males concentrated in higher, more open areas; females selected denser, sheltered areas. The sexes came together only on winter range.

sity. For example, in the Bridger Mountains mule deer are distributed in several discrete population-habitat units—complete ecological units that include all individuals in a population and the habitat required to sustain them year-round. One unit, with a total year-round range of 315 square kilometers (122 square miles), supports an average population of 2,100 mule deer. An adjacent unit, covering almost twice as much area, supports less than half as many deer. Both units are, in general, mountain-foothill habitat. Areas of high-quality habitat exist continuously over most of the high-density unit, so deer are distributed more or less uniformly across the entire area from spring through fall. In the low-density unit prime habitat is limited and found primarily around the periphery of the area, so deer live only in those areas.

BREAKS AND BADLANDS

The hilly breaks of river drainages and the steep ridges and gullies of badlands also offer excellent mule deer habitat. With an appealing diversity of topography and vegetation,

such areas as the Missouri River breaks of northeastern Montana and the badlands of eastern Montana and western North Dakota support deer populations of 1.4 to 6.2 animals per square kilometer (3.5 to 15.5 per square mile). Where localized habitat conditions are particularly favorable, even greater concentrations may be found, occasionally reaching densities of 30 per square kilometer (75 per square mile).

CHAPARRAL

At first glance chaparral, semidesert and desert shrub lands of the Southwest, would appear to be rather inhospitable habitat for deer. On desert ranges especially, the heat can be intense, cover limited, and food and water often scarce. Yet, much of this area is home to the well-adapted desert mule deer subspecies. One study in Arizona indicated that chaparral supported about 4 mule deer per square kilometer (10 per square mile) just prior to hunting season. California chaparral habitats seem to support even greater numbers of deer. There, studies have reported summer populations of black-tailed

Without abundant tree and shrub cover, the deer of the badlands often turn to topographic features—overhanging rocks, steep ridges, deep gullies—for shelter. The availabilty of these features determines, in part, population densities.

Although they make less use of agricultural crops than do whitetails, mule deer often feed in fields adjacent to their range. Wheat fields like this one in Montana can help support large populations.

deer ranging from 30 per square kilometer (75 per square mile), believed to be normal for the area, to about 55 per square kilometer (137 per square mile) on a newly burned area. Winter populations of blacktails were about 10 deer per square kilometer (25 per square mile) on unmanaged chaparral and 23 per square kilometer (57 per square mile) on managed (burned and seeded) chaparral.

PRAIRIES AND PLAINS

The rolling, open grasslands of prairies and plains generally are not conducive to an abundance of mule deer. Offering only slight, if any, topographic relief and little variety of vegetation, animals in these habitats must either travel across home ranges large enough to encompass areas that meet all their seasonal needs—food, water, cover— or concentrate in the few prime spots that can satisfy their needs more locally. Such habitats therefore usually support fewer than 2 deer per square kilometer (5 per square mile) and frequently fewer than 0.5 per square kilometer (1 per square mile). However, population densities exceeding 30 deer

per square kilometer (75 per square mile) have been recorded for some especially favorable habitat complexes, for example, where agricultural croplands are interspersed with otherwise suitable habitat for mule deer.

SEASONAL AND LOCAL CONCENTRATIONS

Although mule deer generally are not found in dense populations across their year-round range, they may concentrate in greater numbers. During winter, for example, concentrations of 30 to 50 deer per square kilometer (75 to 125 per square mile) or more are not uncommon, especially in mountain-foothill habitats. Such concentrations are usually the result of deep snows forcing deer from high-elevation mountain ranges to move to winter ranges that make up only 20 percent or less of their total year-round range. Isolated, high-density populations also may be found during any season in areas where good natural habitat is interspersed with productive cropland. Fields of alfalfa will always be attractive in late summer when natural forage plants mature, lose their succulence, and drop in nutritional quality. In winter, waste grain in barley and other grain stubble fields can provide high-quality forage sought by large numbers of deer.

POPULATION FLUCTUATIONS

In addition to the basic differences of size and density, most mule deer populations in every type of habitat are almost constantly fluctuating. At least four different patterns of change—seasonal, annual, periodic, and long term—can be identified.

Seasonal changes. These variations are the result of the dynamics of populations through the year. With the birth of new fawns, population is highest in late spring or early summer. As animals die throughout summer, fall, winter, and spring, the population is reduced to its lowest level just before fawning the following year.

The magnitude of seasonal changes depends upon the number of fawns born and patterns and rates of seasonal mortality. Fawn mortality is often very high at or immediately after parturition. Generally lower mortality prevails among both fawns and adults through summer and early fall. Notable exceptions can be found on some southern, semidesert mule deer ranges and blacktail ranges in California woodland chaparral, where drought conditions during fall may claim the lives of many fawns as well as some adults. In mule and black-tailed deer populations that are hunted—as most are—hunter harvest is likely to be the primary mortality factor during the fall.

In northern environments, winter is often a critical time for mule deer, and some mortality, especially among fawns and old adults, is typical. Occasionally, winters may claim as many as one-third or one-half of the animals present in early winter. In some areas early spring may also bring a substantial number of deaths, especially when cold and snow linger and before deer are able to regain their vigor from harsh winter conditions.

Annual changes. Year-to-year fluctuations in population size are the result of differences in the number of fawns born and the number of deer that die throughout each season. Because of this, population density during a particular season may be

KINNEY

higher or lower than that of the same population during the previous or succeeding year. For example, in the northern plains, combinations of overwinter mortality and reduced natality following a severe winter can result in a loss of one-third to one-half or more of a mule deer population by the next year. On the other hand, with good conditions attended by high reproduction and survival, a population may double its numbers by the following year.

Periodic changes. Population fluctuations spanning several years generally reflect the accrued effects of short-term developments. That is, several years of relatively high recruitment and below-average adult mortality usually result in general population increases, while low recruitment and above-average mortality result in a general population decline.

The general trend, from 1960 to 1987, in a mule deer population in the Missouri River breaks of Montana illustrates both year-to-year and periodic fluctuations. Long-term studies by Hamlin and Mackie show that the number of deer present during a particular

Winters may occasionally claim as many as half the animals on a hard hit range; bucks are especially vulnerable after enduring the demands of the rut.

season was seldom stable from year to year. There were three periods of major population fluctuation during the study, involving 2- to 4.4-fold increases or decreases. The deer population did not change in the same way each year of these fluctuations, but it *did* change, indicating a general trend: rapid growth from 1967 to 1970, 1978 to 1983, and 1986 to 1987; rapid decline from 1961 to 1962, 1971 to 1972, and 1984 to 1985.

Any factor or combination of factors that affects fawn production and survival, or adult mortality rates, will also affect the population trend. However, the role or importance of any single factor—weather, predation, hunting—may be not be simple or straightforward.

For example, the Missouri River breaks experienced exceptionally severe winters during 1968 to 1969, 1977 to 1978, and 1978 to 1979, but the mule deer population grew throughout those periods. Conversely, the region had relatively average winter conditions during 1983 to 1984 and 1984 to 1985, but the population decreased. The former winters were preceeded by excellent summer range conditions, however; the latter were relative drought years that reduced the quantity and quality of food available to deer to develop fat reserves before winter.

Long-term changes. Some changes in number and distribution of mule deer can be seen only over a long period of time. Thus, a population may fluctuate annually or periodically within either an expanding or a shrinking trend. Such trends reflect long-term, often very slow-to-develop and subtle changes in the quality and quantity of habitat available. They may be influenced by changes in vegetation, grazing, logging, farming, or other activities and developments or by long-term changes in the distribution and abundance of other competing wild animals or predators, or even by climate and weather patterns. They may also be very difficult to detect, especially in populations that fluctuate widely over shorter periods of time.

—Richard J. Mackie

Longevity

*I*n captivity, mule deer does have been known to live 22 years and bucks, 16 years. Maximum life expectancy of wild does and bucks in natural populations may be only about half that of captive deer. Studies of individually tagged mule deer in the wild indicate that females seldom live beyond 10 to 12 years of age, and males rarely beyond 8 years, although does in some populations may live to be 12 to 15 years of age.

Reasons for the greater longevity of females have not been well studied, though it appears that males in all age classes have a higher natural mortality rate than females. This may be because of physiological stress during the rut, as well as habitat preferences that may predispose males to relatively greater mortality. For example, mature males usually live apart in more open, higher, drier, or rougher habitats that are superior hunting terrain for major predators, like mountain lions. The more extensive movements and larger home ranges of males in these habitats may also expose them to more mortality factors as well. Hunting, which is often selective for males, especially older bucks, may further increase male mortality and reduce life span, but it does not explain all of the differential that occurs even in unhunted populations, where adult females usually continue to outnumber adult males by two or three to one.

Tooth wear, which affects feeding efficiency, apparently is a critical factor in determining the maximum potential life span of deer. This may be partly responsible for differences in longevity between captive and wild mule deer, between deer on different ranges, and between males and females in the same area when males use distinctly different, often drier, habitats than females. Differences in food types, soil texture, or weather conditions that leave vegetation coated with grit can affect the rate of tooth wear. Deterioration of teeth through wear that reduces the animal's ability to eat could make a 5- to 6-year-old mule deer in a dry, dusty range the equivalent of an 8- to 10-year-old in a more mesic, lusher habitat.

In wild populations, there is extensive annual mortality among both sexes, and most individuals die before reaching old age. Any habitat or other environmental factor—weather, disease, parasites, predation, competition with other wild and domestic ungulates, nutrition, and hunting—that influences mortality will influence average longevity and the age structure of the deer population. Because different factors may operate or have different effects on females than on males or on young than on old deer, and on deer generally in different habitats, longevity and ultimately population age structures and sex ratios may vary greatly among populations.

—Richard J. Mackie

Tooth wear, with its obvious impact on nutrition, is a major factor in the survival of deer. A fawn in its first winter is well equipped to forage, but a very old buck with worn teeth may not make it till spring.

GEIST

FRANZ

Predators and scavengers of mule deer

Mountain lions, gray wolves, and coyotes are responsible for the deaths of thousands of mule deer each year in western North America. In many regions, these animals are seemingly dependent on the deer and have the potential to influence their numbers. For example, Hornocker estimated in 1970 that in the absence of other prey, a single lion would require as many as twenty deer per year for survival. For an adult population of fifteen lions, this translates to a potential annual kill of about three hundred deer in an area of 200 square miles. Other studies reveal that the impact of wolves and coyotes may be just as great, especially where mule deer populations are high or where mule deer gather on their winter ranges.

Mountain lions inhabit forests and shrublands throughout much of western North America. According to Dixon in 1982, mule deer are by far the most important food for mountain lions, sometimes constituting nearly 80 percent of their diet. Lions are solitary hunters that locate their prey by sight and stalk it before attacking. They tend to select greater proportions of fawns and older male deer than might be expected if their killing habits were random. Recent protection of mountain lions in some areas has led to increased attacks on humans and domestic animals as the lions seek mule deer living near settlements.

Gray wolves have been exterminated from most of their former habitats south of Canada. In northern latitudes, though, mule deer remain an important part of their diet, along with caribou, moose, and other hoofed prey. Given a choice, wolves seem to prefer the smaller deer and frequently select the more vulnerable fawns. Wolves typically hunt in packs that at times may exceed a dozen individuals, mostly family members. They usually locate their prey by scent but also find success through tracking and chance encounters.

Coyotes are widely distributed and regionally abundant throughout the mule deer's prairie, plateau, mountain, and coastal habitats. Although coyotes eat a variety of ani-

The line between predator and scavenger is not always clear. Neither the mountain lion nor the wolverine may have brought down this mule deer, but both look to benefit from it.

FRANCIS

FRANZ

mals, mule deer are often an important food. Single or small groups of coyotes are efficient predators of fawn mule deer. They are also able to kill adult deer weakened by disease or injury, or limited by snow in their ability to escape. Proficiency in locating and scavenging deer that have died from other causes contributes to the success of coyotes as a species.

The black bear, bobcat, golden eagle, raven, and various other species either prey on mule deer or scavenge their carcasses. As a group these species are opportunists, and situations where any one depends on mule deer are rare. It is not unusual for several scavengers to make use of a mule deer killed by a coyote or by severe weather. When this happens, each species has its place in a feeding hierarchy based largely on size. Small birds like the magpie may be persistent but are nearly always last to secure a meal.

The magnitude of mule deer mortality from predators prompts important ecological questions about the ability of these predators to control mule deer populations, and experiments and observations have been

conducted in a variety of habitats. In 1981 Connolly reviewed nineteen studies of mule deer predation and concluded that lions and coyotes often do kill substantial numbers of deer. He went on to say, however, that they have yet to be proven the direct cause of a population decline. There are a few cases where gray wolves seem to control deer numbers, but they are on large coastal islands and questions remain regarding long-term relationships in these isolated settings. The entire issue of population effects has been further complicated by human pressures on predators over most of the twentieth century.

Predators have traditionally been viewed in terms of their negative effects on mule deer populations. This attitude was based largely on the fact that the public valued deer as a nutritional and recreational resource. But the killing habits of predators were also poorly understood and frequently judged in human terms of cruelty. Field research during recent decades has helped to modify these attitudes by adding an ecological dimension to traditional thinking. Predators

Although adult wolves are efficient predators, they generally have little effect on mule deer populations unless other factors – starvation, weather, disease – have already weakened the herd.

Felis concolor
mountain lion

Canis latrans
coyote

Canis lupus
gray wolf

Ursus americanus
black bear

HERTLING

and scavengers are now understood to be integral elements of ecosystems that have evolved over millennia. Though their specific roles remain somewhat of a mystery, their general presence is now recognized as important.

In the past, humans were exceptionally effective predators that not only killed all manner of wildlife but also destroyed the habitat on which many species depended. During the twentieth century, the value of mule deer and other game animals was recognized, and conservation programs were established to restore their diminished numbers. As the century ends, predators are also receiving both the legal protection of conservation laws and the intellectual support required for their continued existence. Robust populations of mule deer, their predators, and scavengers reflect not only the effectiveness of conservation programs, but also the retention of nearly all important western habitats. However, permanent loss of key sites is now accelerating as people discover and develop desirable areas such as foothill winter ranges. Land planning that includes consideration of wildlife values has emerged as a principal form of mitigation for this trend.

Wilderness plays an especially unique role in western wildlife conservation. It was in the remote Sierra Madre of northern Mexico that Aldo Leopold first saw and described a prosperous relationship among predators, prey, and habitat. In a contemporary exam-

Aquila chrysaetos
golden eagle

Felis rufus
bobcat

Gulo gulo
wolverine

ple, Glacier National Park illustrates the value of wild areas in an era of expanding human populations. During the 1980s, gray wolves returned and established a breeding population after many decades of absence. The area in and near the park is now the only place in the conterminous United States where wolves, lions, and coyotes are free to prey on mule deer as well as white-tailed deer, elk, and moose. Under these relatively natural conditions, the return of wolves has had little impact on any of the prey species, and mule deer are only a minor part of the wolves' diet. However, there are still questions about how lions and coyotes will respond to competition from wolves.

Mule deer are ecological generalists and thus found throughout western habitats under a variety of environmental conditions. Their very successful reproductive abilities and strategies help to compensate for the sometimes high losses incurred by severe weather, sport hunters, and natural predators. With these attributes, mule deer are better equipped than most wilderness species for adapting to the encroachments of civilization.

—C. J. Martinka

HERTLING

MULE AND BLACK-TAILED DEER

The parasites and diseases of mule deer

*T*he disease-causing organisms that afflict mule deer—many of which are shared with whitetails—usually become important only when the host is predisposed by some other stress in its life, such as severe weather, crowding, or competition for food. There are exceptions that prove the rule, however, and in a review of mule deer diseases, Hibler suggested that hemorrhagic disease is one affliction that can break out even among strong, well-nourished animals.

VIRUSES

There are two similar hemorrhagic diseases, each caused by its own virus: bluetongue virus and epizootic hemorrhagic disease virus. The viruses are spread from carrier hosts to susceptible hosts by biting midges of genus *Culicoides*. Humans are not affected.

Both viruses are present in most of the contiguous forty-eight states. In 1991 Sohn and Yuill reported that both diseases were pathogenic for whitetails, and that several outbreaks of bluetongue virus in mule deer and blacktails—with mortalities—had occurred. Far fewer mule deer die than whitetails or pronghorn antelope that share their range with muleys. A 1988 study by Thorne and others confirmed this observation: 2 to 5 percent of pronghorns in several areas of northeastern Wyoming died during a 1984 outbreak of bluetongue virus, but deer mortality was estimated at less than 1 percent.

Chronic wasting disease is a newly recognized disease of mule deer that will be making headlines in upcoming years. This degenerative neurologic disease is similar or perhaps identical to bovine spongiform encephalopathy—more colorfully known as mad cow disease—now epidemic in cattle in England and Europe (and possibly spreading elsewhere), and to scrapie in domestic sheep. No infectious viral agent has been isolated and the mode of transmission is unknown. It is not known whether humans can become infected, but there are several similar human diseases.

In 1980, Williams and Young described the condition in fifty-three captive mule deer from Colorado and Wyoming. The incubation period is very long, about eighteen months, and the disease progressive (three

A deer in the final throes of chronic wasting disease is weak and depressed, with excessive salivation. The agent of this illness remains unidentified.

WILLIAMS

weeks to eight months). The outcome is death. Clinical signs include emaciation, excessive salivation (probably because of difficulty in swallowing), repetitive behavior (such as walking the same path), and staring into space. So far, only animals that have been in captivity for several years are involved, but if deer in the wild carry the as-yet-unknown agent, some as-yet-unknown condition in the deer's environment could trigger an epidemic.

An apparently new disease killed large numbers of mule and black-tailed deer in California in late 1993. Signs included respiratory distress, diarrhea (often bloody), depression, and sudden death. Deer of all ages died. A virus is thought responsible.

BACTERIA

In 1976, when deer researchers and managers were dealing with declining muley populations, Prestwood and others suggested that only one bacterial disease, necrobacillosis, or footrot, was a serious threat to mule deer populations. Outbreaks occurred when deer and elk were stressed by sparse browse, crowded at winter food sites, or concentrated near muddy water holes during drought. The disease, caused by a bacterium that is spread by direct contact through the feces, results in lesions and swellings.

PARASITES

Mule deer are believed to host 79 species of internal and external parasites, compared with 112 for whitetails. As with viruses and bacteria, many of the parasites afflict both species. In 1978, Stock conducted one of the few studies of parasites of mule deer and whitetails from the same region, in this case Alberta. Mule deer hosted more parasites: 16 species of helminths (flukes, tapeworms, and roundworms), compared with 11 in whitetails, all of which were also found in the mule deer.

Two roundworms are noteworthy The carotid artery worm, *Elaeophora schneideri*, causes no clinical disease in mule deer, the

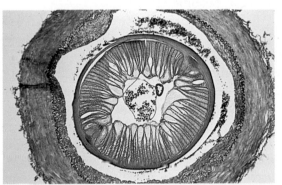

DAVIES

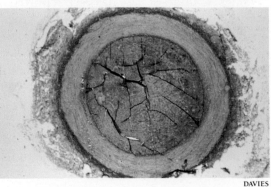

DAVIES

Cross sections show that the carotid artery worm does little damage to the arteries of the mule deer (top) but blocks the flow of blood in an elk (bottom).

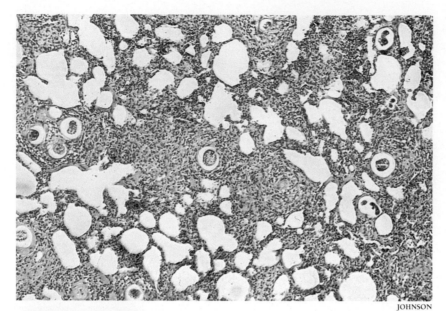

JOHNSON

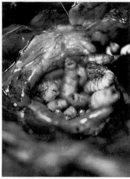

W. SAMUEL

Top: Inflamed, granular tissue surrounds the eggs and larvae of the muscle worm, here parasitizing the lungs of a mule deer. Extensive hemorrhage can result. Above: The bot fly's larvae mature in the back of the pharynx, then leave via the animal's nose.

normal host, but produces muzzle and ear necrosis, malformed antlers, blindness, and mortality in other hosts, such as elk, moose, and domestic sheep. In whitetails, *Elaeophora* infection is associated with oral food impaction. Horseflies are the vectors that spread this worm from host to host.

Adult worms live in the carotid arteries, which in mule deer remain relatively free of pathology. In the abnormal hosts, however, the worms spend many days developing in small arteries that supply blood to the head. If there are a lot of worms, some blood vessels can become occluded.

The muscleworm, *Parelaphostrongylus odocoilei*, is a close relative of the whitetail meningeal worm that lives in connective tissue and blood vessels of the musculature, particularly in the loin and thigh regions. The normal hosts are mule and black-tailed deer of the Pacific Northwest and far western Canada, but woodland caribou and mountain goat are also hosts. Deer become infected by accidentally eating infected snails or slugs. Clinical disease has been reported in mountain goats and blacktails and in experimentally infected mule deer and moose. Both muscles and lungs can be damaged extensively. A similar muscleworm occurs in white-tailed deer and caribou.

Mule deer are also host to bot fly larvae. Adult flies of the genus *Cephenemyia* harass and attack the head of a deer, squirting minute larvae into the oral or nasal openings. The larvae migrate to the posterior region of the throat, where they grow into larger larval stages, often overwintering. In spring they migrate to the nose, drop from the host, and develop into adult flies.

The effect of infection by bot fly larvae—often called throat bots or maggots—on deer has long been argued. Weight loss, trauma to the upper respiratory tract, cerebral abscesses, and death have been attributed to bot fly infection. In 1987 Cogley reported severe pathology in the throat region and discomfort for deer, but he discounted these parasites as pathogens because once the larvae left the deer, the retropharyngeal recesses healed rapidly.

The parasitic and infectious disease agents of mule deer are similar to those in whitetails but not as well known, primarily because they have been studied less. Of the 728 articles published between 1985 and 1990 in the *Journal of Wildlife Diseases,* the major periodical devoted to the subject in North America, 61 dealt with whitetails but only 14 addressed mule deer.

—*William M. Samuel*

The human hunter

Let the numbers tell the story. In the frontier that was nineteenth-century Colorado, mule deer were shot without restriction by mountain men, homesteaders, ranchers, soldiers, miners, railroad crews, and market hunters. The hunting went on every year, all year long, for a century. By 1900 there were only 6,000 mule deer left. Then, in the early twentieth century, the regulations of sport hunting were established and enforced. Throughout the century changes in the landscape favored mule deer: forests were logged and wildfires blazed, creating shrublands, for example, and existing mule deer habitat was set aside, protected, and improved. By 1990 Colorado's deer herd was estimated to be 600,000.

That is an example of the good effect that wildlife management, including regulated sport-hunting seasons, can have for deer. Other numbers tell a different story, of how mismanagement can devastate a healthy herd.

Take the North Kaibab mule deer herd in Arizona, described by Russo. Because many area hunters opposed the harvesting of does, from 1946 through 1949 the practice was eliminated. With the reproducing segment of the herd thus protected—each female adds herself and any offspring to the population, each male adds only himself—in just those few short years the population increased an estimated 30 percent, compounded annually. Realizing that the herd was out-stripping the land, the state's Game and Fish Department resumed doe hunting in 1950, albeit on a very small scale, and increased the harvest rate each year through 1954. Still the population continued to grow. In 1954, 12,000 "any deer" permits were issued, but too late: an estimated 18,000 deer starved to death that winter.

Every habitat has a limit to its capacity to provide food, water, and cover for deer. If the deer population substantially exceeds that capacity, foraging deer snip the lower branches of trees as high as they can reach, and they eat shrubs beyond the ability of the plants to reproduce, remain productive, or even survive. Very quickly the forage is out-stripped. The inevitable result is death: if the deer do not die from starvation itself, they are too weak to survive winter's cold or pred-ators' wiles. It may take many years for the habitat to recover to the point at which it can again support a viable deer population.

Scientifically based control of mule deer populations has become necessary in the United States to maintain healthy popula-tions of deer in an environment that has been altered by human beings. The primary tool of wildlife professionals to manage deer is hunting, a recreational activity for many people. Wildlife managers do not receive general tax revenues; they rely instead on hunters to generate the funds needed to per-petuate healthy herds: hunting licenses, ex-cise taxes on the sale of firearms and ammu-nition, and fines from wildlife law violations provide virtually the sole source of revenue for wildlife law enforcement, population monitoring, research, and the purchase and improvement of mule deer habitat.

The premise of hunting as a method of maintaining healthy deer herds is that each year's crop of fawns adds more deer than can survive the following winter. In a population that is at the carrying capacity of the land, that surplus of animals will succumb to starvation during the winter if they are not harvested by hunters during the fall. Without hunting, the theory goes, the deer population will self-regulate and ultimately collapse by natural causes of death—starvation, disease, predation—but perhaps only after deer have become so numerous that the habitat is severely damaged. The general pattern in an unmanaged mule deer population is one of surges and crashes, separated by long periods of habitat recovery. The objective of hunting is to keep the population relatively constant—and within the capacity of the habitat to support it.

Hunting, then, is usually considered compensatory, in that it acts as a replacement for natural mortality, and not considered additive, or in addition to natural mortality. In a test of this hypothesis in mule deer, Bartmann, White, and Carpenter stocked a large pasture in western Colorado with 133 radio-collared deer per square kilometer—a rate that simulated an unhunted herd. Two more pastures were stocked with 89 and 44 deer per square kilometer, representing hunting removals of 33 percent and 67 percent, respectively. Starvation was the leading cause of fawn mortality in all pastures, indicating a nutritional limitation at all densities, but fawns in the least-populated pasture had the best chance of survival, and fawns in the overpopulated pasture, the worst. The researchers concluded that the higher natural mortality of fawns in pastures with higher numbers of deer demonstrated that a strong compensatory mortality process was at work in that population.

Where do natural predators fit into the scheme? Another study by these same researchers looked at coyote predation. For four winters before a coyote population was reduced, more fawns fell prey to coyotes than died of starvation; in the three winters after the coyotes were killed, more fawns succumbed to starvation. That was probably predictable. But what's most interesting is that no change in fawn survival was detected: the fawns either fed the coyotes or starved to death. The researchers concluded that these results supported those from their pasture study, even though the cause of mortality differed.

Hunting mortality in mule deer is more likely to be compensatory when population densities are high, when the population is at or near the habitat's carrying capacity, and when there is a harvestable surplus. If densities are low and below the habitat's carrying

ESCHER

MULE AND BLACK-TAILED DEER

339

In the relative absence of natural predators, mule deer numbers can surpass the carrying capacity of the range; starving deer are the result. Well-managed hunting seasons and limits can keep the population in better balance with the habitat.

capacity, or if more deer are removed through hunting than would normally die of natural causes, then hunting mortality may be additive. Hunting such a population could reduce it to below a healthy level. Proper hunting management should prevent that from happening.

HIDING FROM HUNTERS

The mule deer's fidelity to its home range is well known. When a hunter enters its turf, the deer's natural inclination is to remain in the area, whose routes and rocks it knows so well. What it seeks is cover.

How any particular deer responds to hunting activity may depend on the adequacy of cover in its home range. In eastern Montana, Swenson reported that mule deer on mixed-grass prairie—an open landscape—appeared more vulnerable to hunting than those in forested habitats that offered hiding places.

Prairie deer move to upland timber during hunting season, and they learn fast, finding better cover as the season progresses.

Kufeld, Bowden, and Schrupp monitored seventeen radio-collared mule deer in the Rocky Mountain foothills west of Fort Collins one day before the first of Colorado's two deer seasons in 1983; they followed the deer again during day 2 of that season and during day 3 of the second deer season. The habitat was a mixture of shrubland and coniferous forest with patches of grassland. Part of the area where these deer lived was open to hunting and part was closed. No matter where their home ranges were, the distances the deer moved did not change after hunting began, but their destinations did: deer in the section open to hunters generally moved to brush and undergrowth that offered increasingly better cover for hiding.

—Roland C. Kufeld

340

Fearless mule deer

A mule deer buck standing broadside to a bowhunter can jump so quickly that it can evade an arrow shot from a modern compound bow at just twenty paces. Then, without breaking eye contact, it calmly watches the hunter. This precisely controlled behavior in the face of danger allows mule deer to appraise situations quickly and decide whether they are harmful.

Mule deer soon discover that native predators avoid areas of human habitation, such as the small towns in national parks, and often take up residence there, having correctly recognized that these particular humans are harmless. Such town deer feed and rest on lawns, seek shelter under verandas, and chase cats and dogs through the streets. Gardening aspirations aside, they are compatible with life in small towns provided they are not fed by hand. The dole may make some deer become aggressive when free food is not readily forthcoming from visitors' hands, but they are otherwise not dangerous.

Blacktails appear to tame almost as readily as mule deer. Within the security of national parks, blacktails become active by day and mingle with visitors. This suggests that their usual nocturnal behavior is a response to predators. Whitetails, however, are much more difficult to tame.

— *Valerius Geist*

Antler point restrictions

*I*n an attempt to increase the proportion of prime-age bucks in mule deer populations, game managers in several states—California, Colorado, Oregon, Utah, Wyoming—implemented antler point restrictions (APR) during the latter half of the 1980s. With APR in effect, no buck with fewer than three points on one antler could be legally harvested. In theory, this practice should protect yearlings and younger males until they reach maturity. In fact, however, it was subsequently concluded that APR not only failed to increase the proportion of prime-age bucks but also could harm the herd in general.

Researchers cited three primary reasons for this. First, although APR restrictions allowed most bucks to make it to their second year, relatively few survived beyond age 3 because all hunting pressure was concentrated on the older animals. Second, because antler points on mule deer are difficult to count accurately in hunting situations, many yearlings were shot accidentally and left in the field. Third, because all hunting pressure was focused on older and possibly higher-quality bucks, many of the younger animals were able to breed, which could have genetically adverse effects on the population. By 1992, several of the states had discontinued APR.

— *Roland C. Kufeld*

PONTON

The future

Where the species come together

*T*hink deer habitat as a continuum, ranging from areas occupied exclusively by mule deer to areas inhabited just by white-tailed deer. At one end of this continuum is the drier, rugged, open habitat of the mule deer; at the other are the relatively moist, less rugged woodlands and fields of the whitetail. In between these two extremes, the two species often coexist.

Mule deer and white-tailed deer ranges overlap throughout much of western North America—in the northern Rocky Mountains, across the Great Plains, and in the mountain foothills and intermountain valleys of the southern Rocky Mountains. Food and habitat preferences of the two species are quite similar, and the potential for competition exists. Indeed, concern is often voiced that one species, especially white-tailed deer, has replaced or may be replacing the other.

In general, however, the two species segregate themselves spatially even where their ranges overlap. For example, in southeastern Arizona, whitetails are usually found at higher elevations and mule deer at lower elevations, according to Anthony and Smith. Elevational segregation also occurs in the northern mountains and plains, except there it is the mule deer that occupy the higher ranges while whitetails are found in the foothills and along mesic draws and streamcourses.

Even in areas where the two species share the same habitat, they tend to occupy different niches. For example, on one studied prairie habitat where both species were common, their ranges overlapped on only 1 to 7 percent of all 25-hectare (62-acre) habitat units over a twelve-year period, according to Wood. Winter was the time of greatest overlap, and summer the least.

Mule deer and whitetails rarely associate in mixed groups. Kramer has suggested that it is a lack of familial ties rather than intrinsic avoidance that keeps the species apart. In both species, small groups of deer typically are maternally related individuals that repeatedly associate with one another. Larger aggregations consisting of several family groups may result when heavy winter snows or drought restricts the animals' range, or when the lure of agricultural crops or early spring plant growth pulls them together. Where groups of both species are present, individuals of the two species may occasionally intermingle or range near each other.

Areas occupied by both species, called areas of sympatry, are usually found where environmental elements are acceptable to both species or where one species' preferred habitat is interspersed with that of the other. In the prairies of eastern Montana, for example, white-tailed deer are most commonly found in riparian areas (hardwood draws) interspersed within agricultural croplands, while mule deer select areas of rough terrain that also include riparian areas. Therefore, habitats that contain all these components may be occupied by both species.

FRANCIS

The distribution of habitats—their abundance and proximity to one another—influences not only species overlap but also seasonal distribution, migration patterns, and population size.

Just what separates mule deer and whitetails where their ranges overlap is difficult to identify because the two species eat much the same foods and occupy similar kinds of habitat. Nevertheless, it may be less a matter of particular food items and cover types, and more a matter of the whole complex of factors that constitute habitat. Differences in the species' preferences become much clearer when viewed across the entire range of deer, however. Whitetails extend farther eastward into the parklands and forests of northern and eastern North America. They also extend farther southward into the tropical shrublands of South America. Mule deer generally have exclusive domain over much of the semidesert shrublands of the Great Basin and California.

The general pattern of distribution can be seen as one moves east from the northern Rockies into the Great Plains. In the rugged mountains, the mule deer has nearly exclusive domain. Whitetails predominate only in foothill and intermountain valley habitats where terrain is less precipitous and often associated with riparian vegetation or agricultural fields or both. The sedimentary plains of the West are relatively dry, with gentle, undulating terrain dissected by drainages. The plains support both species, and either one may predominate, its relative abundance determined by local complexes of topography, vegetation, land use, and climate.

Continue east into the riverbottom habitats of rather broad, level floodplains, cot-

Mule deer and whitetails rarely come close enough to fit in the photographer's frame, and even when they do, hybrid offspring are unlikely to result: the mule deer buck either ignores white-tailed does or is confused by their courtship behaviors.

RICH

Cropland, rather too lush and level to suit a species accustomed to harsher terrain, is not the usual habitat of mule deer, but these bucks in velvet have found a source of nutritious food. Whitetails are usually the more frequent visitors to cultivated fields.

FRANCIS

tonwood forests, and abundant agricultural croplands. Riverbottoms support white-tailed deer throughout the year and may also be used locally by mule deer, especially during autumn. Adjacent sedimentary plains may support both species year-round. Move farther east: As precipitation increases and the land becomes more productive, mule deer become less common, until eventually the landscape is occupied exclusively by whitetails.

SEPARATE NICHES

Niche or habitat segregation often occurs even in areas of substantial overlap, with each species taking that portion of the local landscape to which it is better adapted. The Long Pines of southeastern Montana offer a good example. These timbered ridges and mesas rise 350 meters (1,150 feet) above the surrounding sedimentary plains. The highest elevations contain closed-canopy forests of ponderosa pine, which gradually give way to more open savannas at middle to lower elevations. Rugged badlands and breaks of steeper terrain appear between the pine up-

lands and the lowland prairies. Both species live throughout the area during spring, summer, and autumn, according to Dusek, although whitetails make more extensive use of agricultural croplands. During winter, mule deer occupy steeper, more rugged habitats. They are seeking slopes, southwest aspects, and open timber canopies, where the snow won't accumulate beyond navigable depths and where the winter sun will raise daytime temperatures a bit. Whitetails, in contrast, concentrate in the dense pine uplands in gently rolling hills. There the forest canopy intercepts snow, reducing its depth and also providing thermal cover that minimizes temperature fluctuations. Thus, although both species are found throughout the Long Pines, they occupy separate niches because of their very different strategies for surviving the harsh winters.

Factors contributing to segregation of mule and white-tailed deer can be clearly defined at the ends, or extremes, of the habitat spectrum. Even in areas of sympatry, however, various factors promote niche segregation.

JONES

Competition between the two species is believed to be a primary factor in segregation. The concept is familiar to students of natural history: If similar species depend for their survival on the same resources (food, cover, space, and so on), only one species will eventually survive. The outcome depends on initial densities and any adaptive advantage one species may have over the other. To prove that interspecific competition influences a species' ecology and maintains spatial segregation, however, it is necessary to show that joint use of a limited resource restricts distribution or population size. Although the potential for competition has been shown, actual competition leading to improved survival of either mule deer or whitetails has not been documented. One possible reason for this is that subtle differences in morphology, physiology, and intrinsic behavior may lead to subtle differences in habitat and food preferences that have not been detected in general habitat relationship studies.

Heating and cooling. Mule deer and whitetails may seek different microclimates within the same habitat because they differ physiologically in their response to air temperature. Rocky Mountain mule deer, for example, can tolerate lower winter temperatures than white-tailed deer, and both can tolerate lower temperatures than Columbian black-tailed deer. These differences stem from each species' long-term adaptation to climate. Both mule and white-tailed deer experience colder temperatures in their northern ranges than do Columbian black-tailed deer. And though mule and white-tailed deer are exposed to similarly cold temperatures, a major difference exists in the types of habitats they occupy. Whitetails typically winter in conifer stands with dense overstories that act like a blanket to reduce heat loss, particularly at night. Mule deer occupy more open environments that experience greater extremes in temperature and sharper wind chill.

Other physiological differences may further encourage segregation between whitetails and mule deer. Cooling during summer can be as important as heat conservation during winter. Studies by Parker et al. comparing physiological processes have shown that the primary means of cooling among elk is sweating. Mule deer, however, do not sweat but rely primarily on panting to dissipate heat, thereby conserving water more efficiently than elk. As expected, elk are closely associated with wet areas, particularly during the hottest summer days. Although similar studies have not been made on white-tailed deer, this hypothesis might logically be extended to white-tailed deer, which like elk are associated with more moist habitats.

Different diets. Digestive physiology of mule and white-tailed deer may also contribute to different habitat preferences. All deer are ruminants, but each species possesses traits that predispose it to select specific types of food. According to Putman, rumino-reticular volume and the length of the intestine, both relative to body size, separate the concentrate feeders—animals that eat small volumes of easily digestible forage— from the bulk feeders, which eat larger volumes of forage that contains high concentrations of lignin and cellulose and is therefore more difficult to digest. The typical bulk

THE FUTURE

347

feeder is a larger animal with greater rumen capacity and a larger gut. Though mule deer and whitetails are both considered concentrate feeders, mule deer seem slightly better at handling larger amounts of coarse forage, and whitetails may need smaller amounts of high-quality forage. In other words, whitetails seem slightly more adapted to receive much of their nutrition from cell contents or other plant parts that are highly nutritious and easily digested, as suggested by both Hoffman and Klein. This is particularly evident in the whitetail's preference for agricultural crops.

Behavioral patterns. Behavioral factors, such as direct social dominance of one species over the other, might also lead to segregation. There is no evidence, however, that either species consistently demonstrates direct social dominance over the other. Interactions between species typically follow the same dominance hierarchy commonly observed within species, bucks being dominant over all other deer and does over fawns, as observed by Kramer. Within any one class, such as bucks, larger animals are dominant over smaller ones. In fact, direct evidence indicating that behavioral interactions do *not* promote segregation was provided by studies in Arizona by Anthony and Smith. There, mule deer are nearly two times larger and clearly dominate whitetails. Nevertheless, the researchers concluded that social dominance was not very important in separating the species because interactions were

infrequent and usually nonaggressive. Therefore, which species currently occupies an intermediate habitat acceptable to both is probably not a result of direct aggression but may simply be an indirect result of which species was first established in the area, followed by subsequent avoidance of non-family members.

Predation. Avoiding predators, which involves both morphological and inherent behavioral mechanisms, could be an important factor influencing segregation along the habitat spectrum. Lingle has found substantial differences between the species in their responses to predators. Whitetails attempt to flee, using their great speed to outdistance predators, and may also hide to avoid detection. Their gallop is faster than the stotting gait of mule deer, so they run along established trails and dart around obstacles. They also may take to water to throw predators off their scent. Mule deer, in contrast, often stand their ground when approached. They attempt to keep track of the predator's location and may actually approach a predator and assume a threat posture. When confronted at close proximity, they rely on their bounding gait and maneuverability to negotiate rough terrain, and they may use obstacles to avoid and confuse predators. In stotting, moreover, the legs remain close to its body, allowing the mule deer to kick a predator while fleeing. The gallop of a whitetail, with legs outstretched, does not allow such effective defense during flight.

Between the mule deer's stronghold in the high slopes of the Rockies and the whitetails' Midwestern plains habitat are many places where the species' ranges overlap. Even in areas of sympatry the species naturally segregate, with mule deer taking rougher terrain.

Rocky Mountains   Foothills   Valley bottoms   Sedimentary plains   River breaks and badlands

Overall, then, mule deer seem adapted to living with predators in rough terrain, while whitetails are adapted to predators in more gentle, brushy, and moist habitats. That these characteristic responses to predation are inherent and inherited is also demonstrated by Lingle's studies of flight responses of captive mule and white-tailed deer. Hybrid offspring exhibited behavioral responses intermediate to those of the parent species. They showed agitation and ambivalence in their response to a threat, they would repeatedly approach and retreat, and their flight was slower than that of whitetails and less maneuverable than that of mule deer. Thus, hybrid responses seem less adaptive than either parent species and are equally maladaptive in both mule and white-tailed deer habitats. This behavior, which potentially increases susceptibility to predation, was maintained through at least three generations of backcrosses. Such vulnerability would minimize the impact of hybridization in the wild and help maintain species segregation.

There are probably many other factors that help define species niches and maintain segregation. Each species certainly possesses many distinctive morphological, physiological, and behavioral characteristics that, over time, have resulted in niche separation. Mule deer have specialized at the more arid, open end of the spectrum, and whitetails have specialized at the more wooded and productive end.

Niche separation leads to very localized segregation and allows the two species to share broad areas that are generally suitable to both species. Joint use of an area by two or more species, with each concentrating in preferred habitats to which it is best adapted, results in the most efficient use of available resources. In such situations, each species uses available resources with maximum efficiency because it is occupying habitats where it is most competitive. This in turn increases productivity of the entire community. Also, with each population responding to different habitat characteristics, environmental variation or long-term changes in habitat conditions would have less effect on the overall animal community. Thus, joint range use results in greater community stability.

WHEN THE HABITAT CHANGES

Where their ranges overlap, each species survives and reproduces in its own niche. Changes in habitat will thus affect the two species differently and, in some cases, favor one over the other. Habitat alterations have been a major reason why the relative abundance of mule deer and white-tailed deer has shifted in many areas.

In southeastern Arizona, for example, changes in vegetation put the two species in direct competition, Anthony and Smith found. There, white-tailed deer occupied desert grassland, oak woodland, chaparral, and coniferous forest typical of higher ele-

ESCHER

Mule deer   White-tailed deer

River bottomlands   Sedimentary plains   Glaciated plains

LEA

JONES

vations, while mule deer occupied desert shrub, desert grassland, and lower chaparral plant communities. Because of hotter and drier conditions, livestock overgrazing, and fire suppression, shrubs spread into former desert grasslands, thereby expanding mule deer habitats and populations at the expense of white-tailed deer.

Most habitat changes, however, apparently have favored whitetails. Their abundance is related to the amount of overhead cover, which reduces temperature extremes not only in winter but also throughout the year. In west Texas, an invasion of shrub species in semidesert grasslands initially favored mule deer, because many of the shrubs were preferred food items. As shrub density continued to increase, however, whitetails were favored over mule deer. High-density mule deer areas had an average of 43 percent shrub coverage, whereas high-density whitetail areas averaged 63 percent shrub coverage.

Agriculture also has favored white-tailed deer in the North. Higher whitetail:muley ratios resulted from land clearing for alfalfa production in Manitoba and from increased production of irrigated corn in Kansas, according to Kramer. Additionally, agricultural developments along river systems of the northern Great Plains resulted in a variety of changes favoring white-tailed deer, as reported by Dusek and associates. Irrigation systems create shallower, more stable subsurface water flows that increase tree, shrub, and herbaceous cover. Irrigated crops also

provide a highly nutritious, easily digestible food for whitetails.

Intensive crop production brings changes in both the amount and the timing of livestock grazing—changes that promote high-quality cover. Better management of riparian habitat across western rangelands has also served to increase woody cover and thereby enhance whitetail habitat. All these factors combine to provide pockets of complex, diverse, and stable vegetation within a region that is biologically simple and of highly variable quality, as suggested by Dusek and associates. Mule deer can and do occupy these riverine and riparian systems, but whitetails seem better adapted to these conditions, as evidenced by their nearly exclusive use of such habitats. In many cases these habitats were used exclusively or almost exclusively by mule deer just thirty to fifty years previously.

Sweeping changes in land usage in the West—which include human encroachment upon what was once the domain of deer and other wildlife—have perhaps had a negative effect on mule deer. Whitetails, on the other hand, have adapted to these changes more successfully.

—Alan K. Wood, Richard J. Mackie, and Gary L. Dusek

DEER

Deer and other ungulates

At the time of European settlement, nine species of hoofed mammals shared North America with mule deer and white-tailed deer: elk, moose, caribou, pronghorn, bighorn sheep, Dall sheep, mountain goats, bison, and peccaries, each with several subspecies. Each species' different morphological, physiological, and intrinsic behavioral attributes were adapted to specific environments within the broad spectrum of habitats found across the continent. Many of these species coexisted, each occupying its own niche, and each niche defined, in part, by the presence and activities of the other species and by the ungulates' major predators—mountain lions, lynx, bobcats, wolves, coyotes, grizzly bears, black bears, and golden eagles.

Pronghorn occupied a rather broad niche across shrubby and grassy plains; to that habitat bison added woodlands of the north and east. Elk, too, occupied a relatively broad niche that included prairie border habitat across much of temperate North America. In contrast, bighorn sheep subspecies generally occupied very narrow and specialized niches, the Rocky Mountain form occupying mountain grasslands in and around steep rugged terrain and the now extinct Audubon bighorn inhabiting the most rugged portions of the plains.

White-tailed deer occupied a relatively broad niche in temperate woodlands of the eastern and midwestern United States but on western rangelands were more restricted.

Early explorers found them only along major river bottomlands that contained a diversity of riparian vegetation, along smaller plains streamcourses where riparian vegetation was interspersed in rolling grasslands, in mesic foothills of mountains, and in forested mountains and valleys of the Northwest.

The mule deer's niche was also more specific and restricted than in recent times. Early explorers and trappers found mule deer abundant primarily in the moderately rough, dry terrain of the semidesert, badlands, and mountain-foothill habitats. Such places were best suited for mule deer to survive among the other ungulates and the predators.

Once Europeans began settling the West, niche dimensions were greatly changed. Bighorn sheep were greatly reduced in number and range; the Audubon subspecies in the northern plains was exterminated. Bison were essentially eliminated, the niche of antelope was narrowed, and elk were limited to just a small portion of their former range.

Unregulated market and subsistence hunting eliminated both whitetails and mule deer from habitats that did not provide secure cover. Other deer habitats were encroached upon by humans for a variety of uses, and deer abundance was substantially reduced. Yet mule deer remained widely distributed—albeit in low numbers—across the rugged terrain that had characterized most of the species' range. Whitetails were nearly eliminated from riparian habitats in the plains and

DEER

survived largely in the inaccessible, unsettled riverine habitats and thick forests of mountain valleys.

At the same time that other ungulates, which through competition may have confined deer to narrower niches, were eliminated, large predators were also eliminated or greatly reduced, and hunting restrictions were instituted. The result: the greatly expanded deer populations of the early to mid-twentieth century.

From scattered core populations, mule deer expanded rapidly in distribution and abundance throughout the West. They came to occupy what could be viewed as relatively marginal habitats—including lowland plains, badlands, and agricultural lands—sometimes in great abundance. Some of these areas probably had not been inhabited by deer before, given the presence of both predators and other ungulates better adapted to those habitats, and the absence of agriculture. By the late 1930s and 1940s, whitetails similarly were expanding, not only reclaiming much of their historic niche but also expanding into new habitat created by agriculture and related human activities.

Today predators, too, are reclaiming portions of their historic range. Mountain lions and coyotes have been favored by less control, bears have been favored by special management, and wolves are now being considered for recovery or reintroduction efforts in certain parts of their former range. At the same time, other ungulate species have also reclaimed portions of their former ranges.

All of those changes are contributing to restoration of many of the original niche relationships that existed among deer and other major wildlife species. Some populations, however, can never be greatly expanded and may even shrink. Antelope, for example, only rarely jump fences and are thus less adaptable than deer to agriculture and other human development; it is likely, then, that they will never even approach their historical distribution and abundance. Similarly, bison, wolves, grizzly bears, and other species that conflict with existing land uses can never be reestablished except in designated areas that represent but small portions of their historic range.

The niche of whitetails, at least in agricul-tural and riparian environments, should continue to expand not just because these deer are adaptable, but also because of modern efforts to protect riparian habitats and other species. Mule deer, on the other hand, seem destined to become confined to more widely scattered habitats as land uses change and other ungulates and major predators expand, thereby restricting this species to only its most favorable environments—those they occupied before European settlement. Mule deer populations, moreover, may be smaller.

The increase in white-tailed deer has been primarily onto private lands. Here deer come into conflict with private land uses, primarily agriculture, so future increases in abundance of the species will depend largely on human tolerance of crop damage.

DEER AND MOOSE

Moose are primarily a boreal forest species, living within the range of deer across southern Canada and portions of the northern United States. In the northern Rocky Mountains both white-tailed deer and mule deer share major habitats with moose, at least seasonally.

Large differences in body size and other morphological and physiological features define different niches for these species, especially in winter, when the potential for overlap in forage preference is greatest. Moose, because of their larger size and longer legs, can tolerate much greater snow depths; their range thus extends much farther north. Moreover, in winter they remain more dispersed than whitetails. In the mountains deer concentrate on winter ranges where snow depth is reduced by elevation and dense conifer cover, and in the snowbelt whitetails yard up in conifer stands. Moose, on the other hand, are able to move about in deeper snow and usually select young forest stands with abundant deciduous browse. Deer congregate in groups in sheltered areas; moose are more dispersed and select winter habitat more for food and shelter than for ease of movement.

Browse is a major item in the diets of both moose and deer, especially in winter. Although there may be some overlap in consumption of individual plants, there is probably little direct competition except under

FRANCIS

Even though they often select the same browse, moose and deer do not usually compete for habitat: the long-legged moose can feed in marshes and deep snow.

declines. The worm has not yet been found in western North America, but its introduction to the northern plains and Rocky Mountain regions would be possible if deer or other infected ungulates were relocated from east to west.

DEER AND ELK

Elk share much of mule deer range across western North America. They overlap with whitetails through the northern Rocky Mountains, in a number of Great Plains habitats from Alberta and Manitoba south to Texas, in parts of Arizona and New Mexico, and where elk were reintroduced in Michigan and other eastern states. Wherever studies have been conducted, patterns of habitat use by elk appear generally similar to those of both deer species. Like moose, however, elk occupy a broadly different niche, and direct competition is probably minimal in most areas.

Elk, being larger, more mobile, and gregarious, move more widely and are less fussy about their habitat than either deer species. Their core habitat is the rolling grasslands of prairie borders and tree-grassland savannas of foothills, plus breaks between the rough, dry shrublands favored by mule deer. They are also commonly found in moist riparian bottomlands and deciduous woodlands used by whitetails. Because of their adaptability, however, elk may readily use many, if not all, the habitats and resources used by both deer species.

The food habits of elk also overlap broadly with those of deer, but elk are more general and flexible in their choice of forage throughout the year. For example, elk feed on the same high-quality, succulent herbs and leaves of shrubs that are preferred by deer in summer. If these are limited or not available, however, elk readily eat the leaves and stems of mature grasses, which are avoided by deer. And though they prefer grasses in fall and winter, they will eat the same browse selected by deer when the grasses are locked under snow cover. On forested mountain and valley ranges in the northern Rocky Mountains, all three ungulates may browse extensively on the same species throughout the year.

Because elk can adapt successfully to a

the most severe winter conditions. Jenkins and Wright reported that in winter, whitetailed deer in the northern Rocky Mountains favored low-growing evergreen shrubs, while moose foraged primarily on tall deciduous shrubs.

Competition strong enough to reduce the population of either species is not well documented. There is, however, one area of concern: where ranges of whitetails and moose overlap from western Manitoba across eastern North America. Here the deer is a carrier of the meningeal worm *(Paraelaphostrongylus tenuis)*. Though this parasite seldom harms infected deer, it is highly pathogenic to moose, and some moose populations in overlapping range have experienced severe wide range of environments, including those favored by both deer species, and because they are more flexible than deer in using resources, they would seem to have an advantage over deer in most competitive situations. It has therefore been suggested that competition from elk for browse on winter range could increase deer mortality or make deer resort to less nutritious, less palatable foods or less favorable habitats.

At least one study has reported that white-tailed deer may avoid elk and that competition could force whitetails into marginal habitat where fawns would be more vulnerable to predation. Avoidance of elk by mule deer, however, has not been established, though mule deer are not abundant near several major elk winter ranges. The few deer found in these areas are usually in peripheral or interspersed local habitats that elk visit only occasionally.

Nevertheless, there is little documentation that competition with elk limits populations of either mule deer or whitetails. It may be that such competition does occur but varies in effect with the type of habitat, time, weather, the presence and activities of major predators, including man, and other environmental conditions.

DEER AND BIGHORN SHEEP

The range of bighorn sheep in western North America overlaps the ranges of mule and white-tailed deer. Because the sheep prefer rugged terrain whose steep promontories and rocky crags are a safe haven from predators, there is greater range overlap with mule deer. Bighorn sheep are more selective in their habitat choices and thus are more restricted in distribution than most other native ungulates. Indeed, they can survive only where secure havens can be found near open stands of grass and shrubs for foraging.

Bighorn sheep are more gregarious than either deer species. This, together with bighorns' specialized habitat needs, helps maintain segregation between bighorns and other ungulates and serves to favor bighorns when other species attempt to use preferred sheep habitat.

The food preferences of deer and bighorns are broadly similar, particularly during winter, when browse is important, and in

spring, when all species concentrate on new growth of grasses. Despite this general similarity in seasonal diets, there does not seem to be competition for forage, even with mule deer in the same terrain. In the only study comparing ranges of bighorns, whitetails, and mule deer, Hudson and associates concluded that bighorn distribution and use of habitat was independent of both deer species; sheep were much more localized in distribution because of their need for steep, rocky terrain.

DEER AND PRONGHORNS

The pronghorn antelope's world overlaps mule deer and white-tailed deer ranges throughout the prairie, basin, and mountain valley grasslands and shrublands of western North America. The overlap is greater with mule deer because whitetails are absent from most of the Great Basin—an extensive and important habitat for both mule deer and antelope.

Though a range map would show considerable overlap, the niches of the species are very different. Pronghorn are highly adapted to open habitats with large areas of relatively flat terrain on which vegetation rarely exceeds 38 centimeters (24 inches) in height. Such habitats allow antelope to use their superb eyesight and swift speed to avoid and outrun predators. Their use of this habitat, along with their gregarious behavior and general mobility, segregates the pronghorn from both deer species. Mule deer avoid open areas of gentle terrain; whitetails prefer more overhead vegetation.

Although few comparative studies have been conducted, deer and antelope diets are generally similar and many of the same habitats may be used by all three species in some seasons. Wood found that pronghorn and mule deer on an eastern Montana prairie foraged in similar areas, especially during autumn, when the antelope moved into mule deer habitats. But the deer did not move into or make substantial use of antelope habitat. Despite some overlap in seasonal foraging areas, there is no real opportunity for significant competition between pronghorn and either deer species because each selects habitats with very different topography and vegetation.

DEER AND OTHER WILD UNGULATES

The historic interaction between bison and deer remains unknown, but present-day competition is negligible, given the decreased size and range of the bison herds.

Other wild hoofed mammals that may appear on deer ranges include the mountain goat, bison, collared peccary, Barbary sheep, and wild boar. Mountain goats live within the range of mule deer in many areas of the northern Rocky Mountain region. Other populations have been introduced in the Black Hills of South Dakota and northeastern Wyoming, where they also come in contact with white-tailed deer. Local distributional patterns, habitat preferences, and food habits of mountain goats vary from area to area. Goats occupy a broadly different niche than do deer, and though data suggest seasonal overlaps, especially with mule deer in many areas, interspecific competition between the two animals has not been considered an important factor in the ecology of either.

Bison also share some habitats with deer, chiefly in parks in the United States and Canada, but little attention or concern has been given to interspecific relations.

In the Southwest, the collared peccary and a number of other exotic ungulates introduced from other continents share mule deer range. Competition is keen between collared peccaries and desert mule deer for herbs where plants are scarce or when drought limits the supply of forage, according to Knipe. Barbary sheep that have become established in wild populations also eat many of the same plants as deer, but like bighorn sheep, they apparently frequent and concentrate their feeding on steep canyon walls and other sites little used by deer, as reported by Ogren. Most other exotics are restricted to fenced pastures on private lands, and little information is available regarding their possible interactions and competition with mule deer.

DEER AND DOMESTIC LIVESTOCK

Cattle, sheep, and horses are common on rangelands and pastures occupied by deer in North America, but mules, burros, goats, and hogs are also raised. Feral, or wild, populations of domestic species, especially horses and burros, can be found on some deer ranges in the West.

Each livestock species can have a major effect on the biotic community and greatly alter food and cover resources for deer and other wildlife. Besides sharing food and cover with wild ungulates, domestic animals and deer often have common predators, host the same or similar parasites, and can carry or be afflicted by the same or similar diseases. Thus the potential for interspecific competition or conflict is great. Indeed, in western North America, where most land is grazed by one or more domestic herbivores, livestock grazing may be the single most important factor that limits deer and other wildlife.

The danger to a whitetail buck, should axis deer escape from wildlife parks, is obvious. Whitetails evolved without morphological or behavioral defenses against such exotic species.

BIGGS

Though the opportunity for conflict exists, association between deer and livestock does not automatically mean that one or both will be adversely affected. Like deer and other wild ungulates, domestic species differ in size and form, physiology, and behavior. All are specialized to some degree in their use of rangeland, their nutritional requirements, and the kinds of plants and plant tissues they select. In fact, in some situations interactions between deer and livestock may benefit one or both species.

There also are instances in which interactions are competitive in one respect and cooperative in another, or in which they are cooperative under one set of circumstances, neutral at another, and competitive at still another. In some cases, interactions may go from competitive to cooperative at certain thresholds of distribution and abundance of one species.

Neither mule deer nor whitetails are known to directly affect the distribution, numbers, or general well-being of any domestic species on rangeland. Competition for forage has caused concern among ranchers in many parts of the West, but in studies by McKean and Bartmann, moderate grazing of Colorado cattle pastures by mule deer in winter did not reduce weight gains of calves. Disease transmission from deer to livestock may also be a possibility in some areas. Other concerns about deer on rangeland have more to do with the operations of livestock grazing—deer damage to crops, haystacks, and fences, for example, rather than to the livestock itself.

Evaluating the effects of livestock and livestock grazing on deer is extremely complex, and generalization is difficult for even single-species interactions across one type of range. Studies have shown many negative or potentially negative effects from cattle, sheep, goats, horses, mules, burros, and even hogs in deer habitat. Domestic livestock may directly affect deer habitat in the short term by consuming or trampling deer forage and cover plants. Their very presence may cause deer to avoid an area or alter their patterns of behavior and movement.

And there can be indirect effects that are often subtle and show up only in long-term changes or trends in the supply of resources or in the distribution, behavior, or dynamics of deer on a range. Such indirect impacts

Domestic livestock seem to suffer little loss of nutrition when sharing pastureland with deer, but ungulates can transmit diseases to each other.

FRANCIS

may include gradual, long-term reductions in the vigor of plants and the amount and quality of forage, or long-term changes in the kinds, amounts, and quality of vegetation available for deer food and cover.

When it comes to deer and domestic livestock, much depends on the nature of the grazing and the husbandry practices: the intensity with which the land is stocked, the species and breed of the stock, the seasonal grazing patterns, the kind of fencing, the amount of water diverted for stock, the methods of brush and predator control, and the use of fertilizers and pesticides.

Some negative impact may be unavoidable whenever livestock are raised on rangeland occupied by deer. Occasionally, however, deer and their habitat may actually benefit from their domestic relatives. The palatable shrubs and forbs that replaced grazed perennial grasses on many western ranges helped mule deer populations grow in many areas during the early to mid-1900s. Similarly, use of some plants and range sites by livestock or by both livestock and deer may improve habitat diversity, increase the amount of forage or the availability of certain seasonal plants, and provide an overall plant complex more favorable to deer. Indeed, the general increase in distribution and abundance of deer during the past century despite widespread and often abusive livestock grazing in the West is often cited as evidence that deer and livestock, especially cattle, are relatively compatible.

The same upland pastures that are suitable for grazing sheep may also attract mule deer.

ROBBINS

Livestock management practices have changed substantially over the last 150 years. Continuing changes in ranching, land use, predator abundance, and public attitudes toward resource management are reshaping the niches of our native deer. As the niches of white-tailed deer continue to expand, primarily onto private lands, opportunities for conflict will increase, and what happens in the future will depend on the level of human tolerance. Mule deer will doubtless decrease in number and distribution as other species expand and land use patterns change; this species appears destined to retreat to its traditional habitat strongholds.

—Richard J. Mackie, Alan K. Wood, and Gary L. Dusek

CAIN

Restoring the balance

Whitetails as a species seem to have a secure future. They are back in large numbers throughout most of their prehistoric range after having been eliminated or greatly reduced in the 1800s. Their natural predators, such as wolves and panthers, are now gone from most of North America. Highly adaptable whitetails can be found living in suburbs and even cities, adjusting their activity patterns to be asynchronous with those of their human neighbors. But there are problems. Both human and deer populations are growing rapidly.

As deer numbers increase unchecked, they soon exceed the carrying capacity of their habitat, relegating many animals to an existence of bare survival or death from disease or starvation. Hungry deer can destroy the natural balance in plant and animal communities by eliminating forage species and reducing the overall diversity of living things. Overabundant deer populations also threaten human interests, causing highway accidents, damaging farmers' crops and homeowners' gardens and spreading disease.

With the elimination of wolves and panthers from most whitetail range, only man remains as a major deer predator, but anti-hunting pressures and the proximity of some deer to urban areas often make hunting difficult and unsafe.

There are ways to increase the effectiveness of human hunters, though. The Quality Deer Management Association advocates the practice of biologically and ethically responsible harvests. These dedicated and knowledgeable hunters voluntarily harvest those deer that need to be removed in order to correct imbalances in herd structure. This usually involves taking an adequate number of females and allowing more males to reach adulthood. In other words, these hunters are selectively harvesting to produce sex ratios, age structures, and other parameters more like those thought to exist when primitive man and other natural predators controlled deer populations. In many cases, because they are trained to be more careful and selective, these hunters can safely harvest those formerly unhuntable deer close to human habitation.

The whitetail's adaptability is changing its

For the deer, farms are a concentrated source of food; for the farmer, deer are a nuisance. Tolerance of the animals varies with their cost to agriculture.

ROBBINS

BIGGS

SMITH

MARCHEL

Gleaning a cornfield helps this herd survive the winter; should these animals return during the summer, they will cause considerable damage to the crop.

status from denizen of the forest to agricultural pest, garden invader, or hooved rat. As people and deer interact in suburban neighborhoods, the antihunting sentiment seems to grow. To the nonhunting, nongardening public, deer are perceived as domestic pets—far removed from the game animals they have been in the past.

Research is under way to develop other methods for controlling deer populations, but so far, the results are not promising. Poisons are generally inhumane and hazardous to humans and other animals, so few people support their use—and rightfully so. One nonlethal method would be birth control drugs for deer; these are theoretically possible but have not proven practical or very effective. Even if a practical, inexpensive way of administering antifertility drugs to large deer populations were to be found, and this appears unlikely, the result could be devastating to the sociobiological life of deer. Does that fail to conceive cycle into estrus for many months. If bucks were made sterile, they would in vain continue to breed these does. In a normal breeding season of about one month, bucks lose up to 25 percent of their body weight; in a breeding season that lasted seven months or more, they could destroy themselves.

Human encroachment into deer habitat will accelerate as our population increases and builds more highways, golf courses, ski resorts, vacation homes, and shopping malls. And where government subsidies encourage the conversion of farmland to, for example, pine plantations, deer will lose valuable food resources. Although deer's natural predators are being reintroduced in certain places, human hunters will remain important for controlling deer populations and maintaining healthy herds. Nevertheless, new methods of population control must be explored.

—R. Larry Marchinton and Joseph Hamilton

References

Abler, W.A., D.F. Buckland, R.L. Kirkpatrick, and P.F. Scanlon. "Plasma Progestins and Puberty in Fawns As Influenced by Energy and Protein." *The Journal of Wildlife Management* 40 (1976): 442–446.

Adams, M.G., and E. Johnson. "Seasonal Changes in the Skin Glands of Roe Deer *(Capreolus capreolus)*." *Journal of Zoology* (London) 191 (1980): 509–520.

Alexander, B.G. "Movements of Deer in Northeast Texas." *The Journal of Wildlife Management* 32 (1968): 618–620.

Anderson, A.E. "Morphological and Physiological Characteristics." In *Mule and Black-tailed Deer of North America,* edited by O.C. Wallmo, 27–97. Lincoln: University of Nebraska Press, 1981.

Anderson, A.E., and D.E. Medin. *Reproductive Studies.* Colorado Game and Fish Department Game Research Report, Federal Aid Project W-105-R-3, Job Completion Report. 1964.

———. *The Breeding Season in Migratory Mule Deer.* Colorado Division of Game, Fish and Parks, Information Leaflet 60. 1967.

Anderson, A.E., D.E. Medin, and D.C. Bowden. "Indices of Carcass Fat in a Colorado Mule Deer Population." *The Journal of Wildlife Management* 36 (1972): 579–594.

———. "Growth and Morphometry of the Carcass, Selected Bones, Organs, and Glands of Mule Deer." *Wildlife Monographs* 39 (1974): 1–122.

Anderson, A.E., and O.C. Wallmo. *Odocoileus hemionus.* American Society of Mammalogists, Mammalian Species, Special Publication No. 219. Shippensburg, Pa.: 1984.

Anderson, R.C. "The Helminth and Arthropod Parasites of the White-tailed Deer *(Odocoileus virginianus):* A General Review." *Transactions of the Royal Canadian Institute* 34, pt. 1 (1962): 57–92.

Anthony, R.G. "Ecological Relationships between Mule Deer and White-tailed Deer in Southeastern Arizona." Ph.D. dissertation, University of Arizona, Tucson, 1972.

Anthony, R.G., and N.S. Smith. "Ecological Relationships between Mule Deer and White-tailed Deer in Southeastern Arizona." *Ecological Monographs* 47 (1977): 255–277.

Arizona Game and Fish Department. *The Arizona*

White-tailed Deer. Arizona Game and Fish Department, Special Report 6. Phoenix: 1977.

Atkeson, T.D. "Aspects of Social Communication in White-tailed Deer." Ph.D. dissertation, University of Georgia, Athens, 1983.

Atkeson, T.D., and R.L. Marchinton. "Forehead Glands in White-tailed Deer." *Journal of Mammalogy* 63 (1982): 613–617.

Atkeson, T.D., R.L. Marchinton, and K.V. Miller. "Vocalizations of White-tailed Deer." *American Midland Naturalist* 120 (1988): 194–200.

Atkeson, T.D., V.F. Nettles, R.L. Marchinton, and W.V. Branan. "Nasal Glands in the Cervidae." *Journal of Mammalogy* 69 (1988): 153–156.

Backhaus, D. "Experimentelle Untersuchungen über die Sehschärfe und das Farbensehen einiger Huftiere." *Zeitschrift für Tierpsychologie* 16, no. 4 (1959): 445–467.

Baker, R.H. "Origin, Classification, and Distribution." In *White-tailed Deer: Ecology and Management,* edited by L.K. Halls, 1–18. Harrisburg: Stackpole Books, 1984.

Bakken, G.S. "How Many Equivalent Black-bodied Temperatures Are There?" *Journal of Thermal Biology* 6 (1980): 59–60.

Ballard, W., and H. Merriam. "The Deer Dilemma." In *Alaska Fish Tale and Game Trails,* 4–5, 20–21.

Banasiak, C.F. *Deer in Maine.* Maine Department of Inland Fisheries and Game, Game Division Bulletin No. 6. Augusta: 1961.

Barber, H.L. " 'Browse' Study Shows Food Availability for Herds." *Kentucky Happy Hunting Ground* 18, no. 5 (1962): 4–6.

———. "Eastern Mixed Forest." In *White-tailed Deer: Ecology and Management,* edited by L.K. Halls, 245–354. Harrisburg: Stackpole Books, 1984.

Barbour, T., and G.M. Allen. "The White-tailed Deer of the United States." *Journal of Mammalogy* 3 (1922): 65–78.

Barick, F.B. "Deer Trapping Coordinated with Weather." *Wildlife in North Carolina* 16, no. 10 (1952): 10–11, 20.

Barrell, G.K. "Melatonin for Early Fawning." *The Deer Farmer* 40 (1987): 41–42.

Bartholow, J. *POP-II Population Model System Docu-*

mentation (IBM-PC Version 7.00). Fossil Creek Software, August 1992.

Bartmann, R.M. "Growth Rates of Mule Deer Fetuses under Different Winter Conditions." *Great Basin Naturalist* 46 (1986): 245–248.

Bartmann, R.M., G.C. White, and L.H. Carpenter. "Compensatory Mortality in a Colorado Mule Deer Population." *Wildlife Monographs* 121 (January 1992): 1–39.

Bartos, L. "Social Status and Antler Development in Red Deer." In *Horns, Pronghorns and Antlers*, edited by G.A. Bubenik and A.B. Bubenik, 442–459. New York: Springer-Verlag, 1990.

Bartush, W.S., and J.C. Lewis. "Behavior of Whitetail Does and Fawns during the Parturition Period." *Proceedings of the Annual Conference of the Southeastern Association of Fish and Wildlife Agencies* 32 (1979): 246–255.

Bashore, T.L., W.M. Tzilkowski, and E.D. Bellis. "Analysis of Deer-Vehicle Collision Sites in Pennsylvania." *The Journal of Wildlife Management* 49, no. 3 (1985): 769–774.

Beasom, S.L. "Intensive Short-term Predator Removal as a Game Management Tool." *Transactions of the North American Wildlife and Natural Resources Conference* 39 (1974): 230–240.

Behrend, D.F. "Behavior of White-tailed Deer in an Adirondack Forest." New York Department of Environmental Conservation, Project W-105-R-7, Job No. V-A, Job Completion Report. Albany: 1966.

Beier, P. "Sex Differences in Quality of White-tailed Deer Diets." *Journal of Mammalogy* 68 (1987): 323–329.

———. "Reanalysis of Data on Sex Differences in White-tailed Deer Diets." *Journal of Mammalogy* 69 (1988): 435.

Beier, P., and D.R. McCullough. "Factors Influencing White-tailed Deer Activity Patterns and Habitat Use." *Wildlife Monographs* 109 (April 1990): 1–51.

Berger, J., and J.D. Wehausen. "Consequences of a Mammalian Predator-prey Disequilibrium in the Great Basin Desert." *Conservation Biology* 5 (1991): 244–248.

Bergerud, A.T. "Antipredator Tactics of Calving Caribou: Dispersion along Shorelines." *Canadian Journal of Zoology* 63 (1985): 1324–1329.

Bergerud, A.T., H.E. Butler, and D.R. Miller. "Antipredator Tactics of Calving Caribou: Dispersion in Mountains." *Canadian Journal of Zoology* 62 (1984): 1566–1575.

Bergstrom, A.S., J.R. Palmateer, and S.L. Free. "Incidence of Maxillary Canine Teeth in White-tailed Deer from New York." *New York Fish and Game Journal* 18 (1971): 66–67.

Bertmar, G. "Variations in Size and Structure of Vomeronasal Organs in Reindeer *Rangifer tarandus* L." *Archives of Biology* (Brussels) 92 (1981): 343–366.

Billingham, R.E., R. Mangold, and W.K. Silvers. "The Neogenesis of Skin in the Antlers of Deer." *Annals of New York Academy of Sciences* 83 (1959): 491–498.

Blair, R.M. "Deer Forage in a Loblolly Pine Plantation." *The Journal of Wildlife Management* 31, no. 3 (1967): 432–437.

———. "Timber Stand Density Influences Food and Cover." In *White-tailed Deer in the Southern Forest Habitat, Proceedings of a Symposium Held in Nacogdoches, Texas*. New Orleans: U.S. Department of Agriculture, Forest Service, Southern Forest Experiment Station, 1969.

Blouch, R.A. "Reproductive Seasonality of the White-tailed Deer on the Colombian Llanos." In *Biology and Management of the Cervidae*, edited by C.M. Wemmer, 339–343. Washington, D.C.: Smithsonian Institution Press, 1987.

Blouch, R.I. "Northern Great Lakes States and Ontario Forests." In *White-tailed Deer: Ecology and Management*, edited by L.K. Halls, 391–410. Harrisburg: Stackpole Books, 1984.

Branan, W.V., and R.L. Marchinton. "Reproductive Ecology of White-tailed and Red Brocket Deer in Suriname." In *Biology and Management of the Cervidae*, edited by C.M. Wemmer, 344–351. Washington, D.C.: Smithsonian Institution Press, 1987.

Braun, E.L. *Deciduous Forests of Eastern North America*. Philadelphia: The Blakiston Co., 1950.

Bridges, R.J. "Individual White-tailed Deer Movement and Related Behavior during the Winter and Spring in Northwest Florida." Master's thesis, University of Georgia, Athens, 1968.

Brokx, P.A. "Age Determination of Venezuelan White-tailed Deer." *The Journal of Wildlife Management* 36 (1972): 1060–1067.

———. "Ovarian Composition and Aspects of the Reproductive Physiology of Venezuelan White-tailed Deer *(Odocoileus virginianus gymnotis)*." *Journal of Mammalogy* 53 (1972): 760–773.

———. "South America." In *White-tailed Deer: Ecology and Management*, edited by L.K. Halls, 525–546. Harrisburg: Stackpole Books, 1984.

Bromley, A.W., and C.W. Severinghaus. "Live-Trapping White-tail Deer." *The New York State Conservationist* (October 1956): 4–5.

Brown, B.A., Jr. "The Annual Behavioral Cycle of Male White-tailed Deer." Master's thesis, Texas A&M University, College Station, 1971.

Brown, B.A., Jr. "Social Organization in Male Groups of White-tailed Deer." In *The Behaviour of Ungulates and Its Relation to Management*, vol. 2, edited by V. Geist and F. Walther, 436–446. Morges, Switzerland: International Union for the Conservation of Nature and Natural Resources, 1974.

Brown, B.A., Jr., and D.H. Hirth. "Breeding Behavior in White-tailed Deer." Proceedings of the Welder Wildlife Foundation Symposium. 1 (1979): 83–95.

Brown, D.E. "In Search of the Bura Deer." In *Deer in the Southwest: A Symposium*, edited by P.R. Krausman and N.S. Smith, 42–44. Tucson: University of Arizona, School of Renewable Natural Resources, 1984.

Brown, E.R. *The Black-tailed Deer of Western Washington*. Washington Department of Game, Bulletin No. 13. 1961.

Brown, R.D. "Some Aspects of the Endocrine Control of Antler Growth in White-tailed Deer *(Odocoileus virginianus)*." Ph.D. dissertation, The Pennsylvania State University, University Park, 1975.

———. "Water Requirements of White-tailed Deer." In *Livestock and Wildlife Management during Drought*, edited by R.D. Brown, 19–26. Kingsville, Tex.: Caesar Kleberg Wildlife Research Institute, 1985.

———. "Nutrition and Antler Development." In *Horns, Pronghorns and Antlers*, edited by G.A. Bubenik and A.B. Bubenik, 426–441. New York: Springer-Verlag, 1990.

Brown, R.D., R.L. Cowan, and K. Kavanaugh.

"Effect of Pinealectomy on Seasonal Androgen Titers, Antler Growth and Feed Intake in White-tailed Deer." *Journal of Animal Science* 47 (1978): 435–440.

———. "Effect of Parathyroidectomy on White-tailed Deer." *The Texas Journal of Science* 33 (1981): 113–120.

Brownlee, R.G., R.M. Silverstein, D. Müller-Schwarze, and A.G. Singer. "Isolation, Identification and Function of the Chief Component of the Male Tarsal Scent in Black-tailed Deer." *Nature* 221 (1969): 284–285.

Brückner, R. "Beiträge zur Biologie des Auges." *Biologie Zentralblatt* 80 (1961): 129–138.

Bubenik, A.B. "Physiology." In *Elk of North America: Ecology and Management,* edited by J.W. Thomas and D.E. Toweill, 125–179. Harrisburg: Stackpole Books, 1982.

———. "The Behavioral Aspects of Antlerogenesis." In *Antler Development in Cervidae,* edited by R.D. Brown, 389–449. Kingsville, Tex.: Caesar Kleberg Wildlife Research Institute, 1983.

———. "Epigenetical, Morphological, Physiological and Behavioral Aspects of Evolution of Horns, Pronghorns and Antlers." In *Horns, Pronghorns and Antlers,* edited by G.A. Bubenik and A.B. Bubenik, 3–113. New York: Springer-Verlag, 1990.

Bubenik, G.A. "Neuroendocrine Regulation of the Antler Cycle." In *Horns, Pronghorns and Antlers,* edited by G.A. Bubenik and A.B. Bubenik, 265–297. New York: Springer-Verlag, 1990.

Bubenik, G.A., and A.B. Bubenik. "Seasonal Variations in Hair Pigmentation of White-tailed Deer and Their Relationship to Sexual Activity and Plasma Testosterone." *The Journal of Experimental Zoology* 235 (1985): 387–395.

Bubenik, G.A., and D. Schams. "Relationship of Age to Seasonal Levels of LH, FSH, Prolactin and Testosterone in Male, White-tailed Deer." *Comparative Biochemistry and Physiology* 83A (1986): 179–183.

Bubenik, G.A., D. Schams, and C. Coenen. "The Effect of Artificial Photoperiodicity and Antiandrogen Treatment on the Antler Growth and Plasma Levels of LH, FSH, Testosterone, Prolactin and Alkaline Phosphatase." *Comparative Biochemistry and Physiology* 83A (1987): 551–559.

Bubenik, G.A., and J.H. Smith. "The Effect of Thyroxine (T$_4$) Administration on Plasma Levels of Tri-iodothyronine (T$_3$) and T$_4$ in Male White-tailed Deer." *Comparative Biochemistry and Physiology* 83A (1986): 185–187.

Bubenik, G.A., P.S. Smith, and D. Schams. "The Effect of Orally Administered Melatonin on the Seasonality of Deer Pelage Exchange, Antler Development, LH, FSH, Prolactin, Testosterone, T$_3$, T$_4$, Cortisol and Alkaline Phosphatase." *Journal of Pineal Research* 3 (1986): 331–349.

Bunnell, F.L., and A.S. Harestad. "Dispersal and Dispersion of Black-tailed Deer: Models and Observations." *Journal of Mammalogy* 64 (1983): 201–209.

Burt, W.H. "Territoriality and Home Range Concepts as Applied to Mammals." *Journal of Mammalogy* 24 (1943): 346–352.

Byers, R.E., D.H. Carbaugh, and C.N. Presley. "Screening of Odor and Taste Repellents for Control of White-tailed Deer Browse to Apples or Apple Shoots." *Journal of Environmental Horticulture* 8 (1989): 185–189.

Byford, J.L. "Movement Responses of White-tailed Deer to Changing Food Supplies." *Proceedings of the Annual Conference of the Southeastern Association of Game and Fish Commissioners* 23 (1969): 63–78.

———. "Movements and Ecology of White-tailed Deer in a Logged Floodplain Habitat." Ph.D. dissertation, Auburn University, Auburn, Alabama, 1970.

Carbaugh, B., J.P. Vaughan, E.D. Bellis, and H.B. Graves. "Distribution and Activity of White-tailed Deer along an Interstate Highway." *The Journal of Wildlife Management* 39 (1975): 570–581.

Carl, G.R., and C.T. Robbins. "The Energetic Cost of Predator Avoidance in Neonatal Ungulates: Hiding versus Following." *Canadian Journal of Zoology* 66 (1988): 239–246.

Carlsen, J.C., and R.E. Farmes. "Movements of White-tailed Deer Tagged in Minnesota." *The Journal of Wildlife Management* 21, no. 4 (1957): 397–401.

Carpenter, L.H. "Nitrogen-Herbicide Effects on Sagebrush Deer Range." Ph.D. dissertation, Colorado State University, Fort Collins, 1976.

Cartwright, M.E. "An Ecological Study of White-tailed Deer in Northwestern Arkansas: Home Range, Activity, and Habitat Utilization." Master's thesis, University of Arkansas, Fayetteville, 1975.

Caton, J.D. *The Antelope and Deer of America.* New York: Forest and Stream Publishing Co., 1877.

Cheatum, E.L., and G.H. Morton. "Breeding Season of White-tailed Deer in New York." *The Journal of Wildlife Management* 10 (1946): 249–263.

Cliff, E.P. "Relationship between Elk and Mule Deer in the Blue Mountains of Oregon." *Transactions of the North American Wildlife Conference* 4 (1939): 560–569.

Clutton-Brock, T.H., F.E. Guinness, and S.D. Albon. *Red Deer: Behavior and Ecology of Two Sexes.* Chicago: University of Chicago Press, 1982.

Clutton-Brock, T.H., G.R. Iason, and F.E. Guinness. "Sexual Segregation and Density-related Changes in Habitat Use in Male and Female Red Deer *(Cervus elaphus).*" *Journal of Zoology* (London) 211 (1987): 275–289.

Coblentz, B.E. "Food Habits of George Reserve Deer." *The Journal of Wildlife Management* 34 (1970): 535–540.

Cogley, T.P. "Effects of *Cephenomyia* spp. (Diptera: Oestridae) on the Nasopharynx of Black-tailed Deer *(Odocoileus hemionus columbianus).*" *Journal of Wildlife Diseases* 23 (1987): 596–605.

Compton, B.B., R.J. Mackie, and G.L. Dusek. "Factors Influencing Distribution of White-tailed Deer in Riparian Habitats." *The Journal of Wildlife Management* 53 (1988): 544–548.

Connolly, G.E. "Predators and Predator Control." In *Big Game of North America: Ecology and Management,* edited by J.L. Schmidt and D.L. Gilbert. Harrisburg: Stackpole Books, 1978.

———. "Assessing Populations." In *Mule and Black-tailed Deer of North America,* edited by O.C. Wallmo, 287–345. Lincoln: University of Nebraska Press, 1981.

———. "Limiting Factors and Population Regulation." In *Mule and Black-tailed Deer of North America,* edited by O.C. Wallmo, 245–285. Lincoln: University of Nebraska Press, 1981.

Cook, R.L. "Management Implications of Heavy

Hunting Pressure on Texas White-tailed Deer on the Kerr Wildlife Management Area." *Proceedings of the Annual Conference of the Southeastern Association of Game and Fish Commissioners* 27 (1973): 114–119.

Cook, R.S., M. White, D.O. Trainer, and W.C. Glazener. "Mortality of Young White-tailed Deer Fawns in South Texas." *The Journal of Wildlife Management* 35 (1971): 47–56.

Cooper, W.E., Jr., and G.M. Burghardt. "Vomerolfaction and Vomodor." *Journal of Chemical Ecology* 16 (1990): 103–105.

Corbett, R.L., R.L. Marchinton, and C.E. Hill. "Preliminary Study of the Effects of Dogs on Radio-equipped Deer in a Mountainous Habitat." *Proceedings of the Annual Conference of the Southeastern Association of Game and Fish Commissioners* 25 (1972): 69–77.

Corty, F.L., and A.C. Main. *Louisiana Forest Industry; Its Economical Importance and Growth.* Louisiana State University, Department of Agricultural Economics, Agri-business Research Report 462. Baton Rouge: 1974.

Cowan, I.M. "Distribution and Variation in Deer (Genus Odocoileus) of the Pacific Coastal Region of North America." *California Fish and Game* 22 (1936): 155–246.

———. "Life and Times of the Coast Black-tailed Deer." In *The Deer of North America,* edited by W.P. Taylor, 523–617. Harrisburg: The Stackpole Co., 1956.

———. "What and Where Are the Mule and Black-tailed Deer?" In *The Deer of North America,* edited by W.P. Taylor, 335–359. Harrisburg: The Stackpole Co., 1956.

Cowan, I.M., and C.J. Guiguet. "The Mammals of British Columbia." In *British Columbia Providence Museum Handbook.* Vol. 11. 1965.

Cowan, I.M., and A.G. Raddi. "Pelage and Molt in the Black-tailed Deer *(Odocoileus hemionus,* Rafinesque)." *Canadian Journal of Zoology* 50 (1972): 639–647.

Cowan, I.M., and A.J. Wood. "The Growth Rate of the Black-tailed Deer *(Odocoileus hemionus columbianus)."* *The Journal of Wildlife Management* 19 (1955): 331–336.

Cowan, R.L., and A.C. Clark. "Nutritional requirements." In *Diseases and Parasites of White-tailed Deer,* edited by W.R. Davidson, F.A. Hayes, V.F. Nettles, and F.E. Kellogg, 73–86. Miscellaneous Publication No. 7. Tallahassee, Fla.: Tall Timbers Research Station, 1981.

Cowan, R.L., E.W. Hartsook, and J.B. Whelan. "Calcium-strontium Metabolism in White-tailed Deer as Related to Age and Antler Growth." *Proceedings of the Society for Experimental Biology and Medicine* 129 (1968): 733–737.

Cowan, R.L., and T.A. Long. *Studies on Antler Growth and Nutrition of White-tailed Deer.* Pennsylvania Cooperative Wildlife Research Unit, Paper No. 107. N.d.

Crawford, G.J. "A Preliminary Investigation of the White-tailed Deer on Crab Orchard National Wildlife Refuge." Master's thesis, Southern Illinois University, 1962.

Cronin, M.A. "Molecular Evolutionary Genetics and Phylogeny of Cervids." Ph.D. dissertation, Yale University, New Haven, Conn., 1989.

Cronin, M.A., M.E. Nelson, and D.F. Pac. "Spatial Heterogeneity of Mitochondrial DNA and Allozynes among Populations of White-tailed Deer and Mule Deer." *Journal of Heredity* 82 (1991): 118–127.

Croyle, R.C. "Nutrient Requirements of Young White-tailed Deer for Growth and Antler Development." Master's thesis, The Pennsylvania State University, University Park, 1969.

Curlewis, J.D., A.S.I. Loudon, J.A. Milne, and A.S. McNeilly. "Effects of Chronic Long-acting Bromocriptine Treatment on Live Weight, Voluntary Food Intake, Coat Growth and Breeding Season in Nonpregnant Red Deer Hinds." *Journal of Endocrinology* 119 (1988): 413–420.

Dahlberg, B.L., and R.C. Guettinger. *The White-tailed Deer in Wisconsin.* Wisconsin Conservation Department, Technical Wildlife Bulletin No. 14. Madison: 1956.

Darling, F.F. *A Herd of Red Deer. A Study in Animal Behavior.* New York: Oxford University Press, 1937.

Dasmann, R.F. "Fluctuations in a Deer Population in California Chaparral." *Transactions of the North American Wildlife Conference* 21 (1956): 487–499.

Dasmann, R.F., and R.D. Taber. "Behavior of Columbian Black-tailed Deer with Reference to Population Ecology." *Journal of Mammalogy* 37 (May 1956): 143–164.

Dasmann, W.P. *If Deer Are to Survive.* Harrisburg: Stackpole Books, 1971.

Davidson, W.R., F.A. Hayes, V.F. Nettles, and F.E. Kellogg, eds. *Diseases and Parasites of White-tailed Deer.* Miscellaneous Publication No. 7. Tallahassee, Fla.: Tall Timbers Research Station, 1981.

Davidson, W.R., and V.F. Nettles. *Field Manual of Wildlife Diseases in the Southeastern United States.* Athens: University of Georgia, College of Veterinary Medicine, Department of Parasitology, Southeastern Cooperative Wildlife Disease Study, 1988.

Davis, R.B., and C.K. Winkler. "Brush vs. Cleared Range as Deer Habitat in Southern Texas." *The Journal of Wildlife Management* 32 (1968): 321–329.

Den Uyl, D. "The Central Region." In *Regional Silviculture of the United States,* edited by J.W. Barrett, 137–177. New York: The Ronald Press Co., 1962.

DeYoung, C.A. "Aging White-tailed Deer on Southern Ranges." *The Journal of Wildlife Management* 53 (1989): 519–523.

Dixon, K.R. "Mountain Lion *(Felis concolor)."* In *Wild Mammals of North America: Biology, Management, and Economics,* edited by J.A. Chapman and G.A. Feldhamer, 711–727. Baltimore: The Johns Hopkins University Press, 1982.

Dobie, D. "Bucks of Many Colors." *North American Whitetail* 9, no. 3 (1990): 53, 54, 56–59.

Dorn, R.D. "White-tailed Deer in Southeastern Minnesota: Winter Observations." *Journal of the Minnesota Academy of Science* 37 (1970–1971): 16–18.

Downing, R.L. "Success Story: White-tailed Deer." In *Restoring America's Wildlife, 1937–1987,* edited by H. Kallman, 44–57. Washington, D.C.: U.S. Department of the Interior, U.S. Fish and Wildlife Service, 1987.

Downing, R.L., and B.S. McGinnes. "Capturing and Marking White-tailed Deer Fawns." *The Journal of Wildlife Management* 33, no. 3 (1969): 711–714.

———. "Movement Patterns of White-tailed Deer in a Virginia Enclosure." *Proceedings of the Annual Conference of the Southeastern Association of Game and Fish Commissioners* 29 (1975–1976): 454–459.

Downing, R.L., B.S. McGinnes, R.L. Petcher, and J.L. Sandt. "Seasonal Changes in Movements of White-tailed Deer." In *White-tailed Deer in the Southern Forest Habitat, Proceedings of a Symposium Held in Nacogdoches, Texas.* New Orleans: U.S. Department of Agriculture, Forest Service, Southern Forest Experiment Station, 1969.

Duke-Elder, S. *The Eye in Evolution.* Vol. 1. *System Ophthalmology.* St. Louis: C.V. Mosby Co., 1958.

Dusek, G.L. *An Inventory of Vegetation, Wildlife, and Recreational Resources of the Long Pines, Montana.* Montana Department of Fish, Wildlife and Parks, Ecological Services Division, Final Report. Helena: 1980.

————. "Ecology of White-tailed Deer in Upland Ponderosa Pine Habitat in Southeastern Montana." *Prairie Naturalist* 19 (1987): 1–17.

Dusek, G.L., R.J. Mackie, J.D. Herriges, Jr., and B.B. Compton "Population Ecology of White-tailed Deer along the Lower Yellowstone River." *Wildlife Monographs* 104 (October 1989): 1–68.

Ellisor, J.E. "Mobility of White-tailed Deer in South Texas." *The Journal of Wildlife Management* 33, no. 1 (1969): 220–222.

Evans, W. "Southern Rocky Mountains." In *White-tailed Deer: Ecology and Management,* edited by L.K. Halls, 505–512. Harrisburg: Stackpole Books, 1984.

Eyre, F.H. *Forest Cover Types of the United States and Canada.* Washington, D.C.: Society of American Foresters, 1980.

Farner, D.S. "Birdbanding in the Study of Population Dynamics." In *Recent Studies in Avian Biology,* edited by A. Wolfson, 397–499. Champaign: University of Illinois Press, 1955.

Fay, R.R. *Hearing in Vertebrates: A Psychophysics Databook* Winnetka, Ill.: Hill-Fay Associates, 1988.

Fenneman, N.M. *Physiography of Eastern United States.* New York: McGraw-Hill, 1938.

Forand, K.J., and R.L. Marchinton. "Patterns of Social Grooming in Adult White-tailed Deer." *American Midland Naturalist* 122 (1989): 357–364.

Forand, K.J., R.L. Marchinton, and K.V. Miller. "Influence of Dominance Rank on the Antler Cycle of White-tailed Deer." *Journal of Mammalogy* 66 (1985): 58–62.

Foreyt, W.J., and W.M. Samuel. "Parasites of White-tailed Deer of the Welder Wildlife Refuge in Southern Texas: A Review." In *Proceedings of the Welder Wildlife Foundation Symposium,* edited by D.L. Drawe, 105–132. Welder Wildlife Contribution B-7. Corpus Christi, Tex.: 1979.

Forrester, D.J. *Parasites and Diseases of Wild Mammals in Florida.* Gainesville: University Press of Florida, 1992.

Freddy, D.J. "Predicting Mule Deer Harvest in Middle Park, Colorado." *The Journal of Wildlife Management* 46 (July 1982): 803–806.

Freddy, D.J., D.L. Baker, R.M. Bartmann, and R.C. Kufeld. *Deer and Elk Management Analysis Guide, 1992-94.* Colorado Division Wildlife Report 17. 1993.

French, C.E., L.C. McEwen, N.D. Magruder, R.H. Ingram, and R.H. Smith. "Nutrient Requirements for Growth and Antler Development in White-tailed Deer." *The Journal of Wildlife Management* 20 (1956): 221–232.

Fudge, J.R., K.V. Miller, R.L. Marchinton, D.C. Collins, and T.R. Rice. "Effects of Exogenous Testosterone on Scent Marking and Agonistic Behaviors of White-tailed Deer." In *Chemical Signals in Vertebrates VI.* In press.

Fyvie, A., and E.M. Addison. *Manual of Common Parasites, Diseases and Anomalies of Wildlife in Ontario.* Ontario, Canada: Ontario Ministry of Natural Resources, 1964.

Gallina, S., E. Maury, and V. Serrano. In *Deer Biology, Habitat Requirements, and Management in Western North America,* edited by P.F. Folliott and S. Gallina, 135–148. Mexico: Instituto de Ecologia, 1981.

Gallizioli, S. Statement. In *Improving Fish and Wildlife Benefits in Range Management,* edited by J.E. Townsend and R.J. Smith, 90–96. Washington, D.C.: U.S. Department of the Interior, U.S. Fish and Wildlife Service, Office of Biological Services, 1977.

Gasaway, W.C., R.D. Boertje, D.V. Grangaard, D.G. Kelleyhouse, R.O. Stephenson, and D.G. Larsen. "The Role of Predation in Limiting Moose at Low Densities in Alaska and Yukon and Implications for Conservation." *Wildlife Monographs* 120 (1992): 1–59.

Gauthier, D., and C. Barrette. "Suckling and Weaning in Captive White-tailed and Fallow Deer." *Behaviour* 94 (1985): 128–149.

Gavitt, J.D., R.L. Downing, and B.S. McGinnes. "Effect of Dogs on Deer Reproduction in Virginia." *Proceedings of the Annual Conference of the Southeastern Association of Game and Fish Commissioners* 28 (1974): 532–539.

Gee, K.L., M.D. Porter, S. Demarais, F.C. Bryant, and G.V. Vreede. *White-tailed Deer and Their Foods and Management in the Cross Timbers.* Ardmore, Okla.: The Samuel Roberts Noble Foundation, Inc., 1991.

Geist, V. "Behavior: Adaptive Strategies in Mule Deer." In *Mule and Black-tailed Deer of North America,* edited by O.C. Wallmo, 157–223. Lincoln: University of Nebraska Press, 1981.

————. "On the Taxonomy of Giant Sheep (*Ovis ammon* Linnaeus, 1766)." *Canadian Journal of Zoology* 69 (1990): 706–723.

Gilbert, D.L. "Evolution and Taxonomy." In *Big Game of North America: Ecology and Management,* edited by J.L. Schmidt and D.L. Gilbert, 1–9. Harrisburg: Stackpole Books, 1978.

Gilbert, F.F. "Aging White-tailed Deer by Annuli in the Cementum of the First Incisor." *The Journal of Wildlife Management* 30 (1966): 200–202.

Gipson, P.S., and J.A. Sealander. "Ecological Relationships of White-tailed Deer and Dogs in Arkansas." In *Proceedings of the 1975 Predator Symposium,* edited by R.L. Phillips and C. Jonkel, 3–16. Missoula: University of Montana, Montana Forest Conservation Experiment Station, 1977.

Gladfelter, H.L. "Midwest Agricultural Region." In *White-tailed Deer: Ecology and Management,* edited by L.K. Halls, 427–440. Harrisburg: Stackpole Books, 1984.

Glass, B.P. *A Key to the Skulls of North American Mammals.* Stillwater: Oklahoma State University of Agriculture and Applied Science, Department of Zoology, 1977.

Goldman, E.A., and R. Kellog. "Ten White-tailed Deer from North and Middle America." *Proceedings of the Biological Society of Washington* 53 (1940): 81–89.

Golley, F.B. "Gestation Period, Breeding and Fawning Behavior of Columbian Black-tailed Deer." *Journal of Mammalogy* 38 (1957): 116–120.

Goodrum, P.D., and V.H. Reid. "Deer Browsing in the Longleaf Pine Belt." *Proceedings of the Society of American Foresters, Salt Lake City, Utah* (1958): 139–143.

Goss, R.J. *Deer Antlers: Regeneration, Function, and Evolution.* New York: Academic Press, 1983.

Griffin, P.F., R.L. Chatham, and R.M. Young. *Anglo-America: A Systematic and Regional Geography.* 2d ed. Palo Alto, Calif.: Fearon, 1968.

Gruell, G.E. *Post-1900 Mule Deer Irruptions in the Intermountain West: Principle Cause and Influences.* U.S. Department of Agriculture, Forest Service, General Technical Report INT-206. May 1986.

Guynn, D.C., J.R. Sweeney, and R.J. Hamilton. "Adult Sex Ratio and Conception Date in a South Carolina Deer Herd." *Proceedings of the Annual Southeastern Deer Study Group Meeting* 9: 13.

Hahn, H.C., Jr., and W.P. Taylor. "Deer Movements in the Edwards Plateau." *Texas Game and Fish* 8, no. 12 (1950): 4–9, 31.

Hall, E.R. "The Deer of California." *California Fish and Game* 13 (1927): 233–256.

———. *The Mammals of North America.* 2d ed. Vol. 2. New York: John Wiley and Sons, 1981.

Hall, E.R., and K.R. Kelson. *The Mammals of North America.* Vol. 2. New York: The Ronald Press Co., 1959.

Halls, L.K. *White-tailed Deer: Ecology and Management.* Harrisburg: Stackpole Books, 1984.

Hamlin, K.C., and R.J. Mackie. "Age-specific Reproduction and Mortality in Female Mule Deer: Implications to Population Dynamics." *Proceedings of the Eighteenth Congress of the International Union of Game Biologists* (1987).

Hamlin, K.L., and R.J. Mackie. *Mule Deer in the Missouri River Breaks, Montana: A Study of Population Dynamics in a Fluctuating Environment.* Montana Department of Fish, Wildlife and Parks, Federal Aid in Wildlife Restoration Project W-120-R-7-18, Final Report. Helena: 1989.

Hanley, T.A., C.T. Robbins, A.E. Hagerman, and C. McArthur. "Predicting Digestible Protein and Digestible Dry Matter in Tannin-containing Forages Consumed by Ruminants." *Ecology* 72 (1992): 537–541.

Hanley, T.A., C.T. Robbins, and D.E. Spalinger. *Forest Habitats and the Nutritional Ecology of Sitka Black-tailed Deer: A Research Synthesis with Implications for Forest Management.* U.S. Department of Agriculture, Forest Service, General Technical Report PNW-GTR-230. Portland, Oreg.: 1989.

Hardin, J.W. "Behavior, Socio-biology, and Reproductive Life History of the Florida Key Deer." Ph.D. dissertation, Southern Illinois University, Carbondale, 1974.

Harlow, R.F., and D.C. Guynn. *Foods, Food Habits and Food Habits Analysis Studies of White-tailed Deer.* Clemson, S.C.: Clemson University, Department of Forestry, 1987.

Harlow, R.F., and W.F. Oliver, Jr. "Natural Factors Affecting Deer Movement." *Quarterly Journal of the Florida Academy of Science* 30 (1967): 221–226.

Harmel, D.E. "Effects of Genetics on Antler Quality and Body Size in White-tailed Deer." In *Antler Development in Cervidae,* edited by R.D. Brown, 339–348. Kingsville, Tex.: Caesar Kleberg Wildlife Research Institute, 1983.

Harrington, R. "Evolution and Distribution of the Cervidae." In *The Biology of Deer Production,* edited by P.F. Fennessy and K.R. Drew, 3–11. Bulletin No. 22. Wellington: The Royal Society of New Zealand, 1985.

Haugen, A.O. "Reproductive Performance of White-tailed Deer in Iowa." *Journal of Mammalogy* 56 (1975): 151–159.

Haugen, A.O., and L.A. Davenport. "Breeding Records of White-tailed Deer in the Upper Peninsula of Michigan." *The Journal of Wildlife Management* 14 (1950): 290–295.

Hawkins, R.E., and W.D. Klimstra. "A Preliminary Study of the Social Organization of White-tailed Deer." *The Journal of Wildlife Management* 34, no. 2 (1970): 407–419.

———. "Deer Trapping Correlated with Weather Factors." *Transactions of the Illinois State Academy of Science* 63 (1970): 198–201.

Hawkins, R.E., W.D. Klimstra, and D.C. Autry. "Dispersal of Deer from Crab Orchard National Wildlife Refuge." *The Journal of Wildlife Management* 35 (1971): 216–220.

Hayes, C.L. "Nocturnal Activity of Female Desert Mule Deer." Master's thesis, University of Arizona, Tucson, 1992.

Heffner, R.S., and H.E. Heffner. "Evolution of Sound Localization in Mammals." In *The Evolutionary Biology of Hearing,* edited by D.B. Webster, R.R. Fay, and A.N. Popper, 691–715. New York: Springer-Verlag, 1992.

Henshaw, J. "Antlers—The Bones of Contention." *Nature* (London) 224 (1969): 1036–1037.

Hershberger, T.V., and C.T. Cushwa. *The Effects of Fasting and Refeeding on White-tailed Deer.* The Pennsylvania State University, College of Agriculture, Agricultural Experiment Station, Bulletin No. 846. University Park: 1984.

Hervert, J.J., and P.R. Krausman. "Desert Mule Deer Use of Water Developments in Arizona." *The Journal of Wildlife Management* 50 (1986): 670–676.

Hesselton, W.T. "The Incredible White Deer Herd." *The Conservationist* (October–November 1969): 18–19.

Hesselton, W.T., C.W. Severinghaus, and J.E. Tanck. "Deer Facts from Seneca Depot." *The Conservationist* (October–November 1965): 28–32.

Hibler, C.P. "Diseases." In *Mule and Black-tailed Deer of North America,* edited by O.C. Wallmo, 129–155. Lincoln: University of Nebraska Press, 1981.

Hirth, D.H. "Social Behavior of White-tailed Deer in Relation to Habitat." Ph.D. dissertation, University of Michigan, Ann Arbor, 1973.

———. "Social Behavior of White-tailed Deer in Relation to Habitat." *Wildlife Monographs* 53 (1977): 1–55.

———. "Mother-Young Behavior in White-tailed Deer, *Odocoileus virginianus.*" *The Southwestern Naturalist* 30 (1985): 297–302.

Hirth, D.H., and D.R. McCullough. "Evolution of Alarm Signals in Ungulates with Special Reference to White-tailed Deer." *The American Naturalist* 111 (1977): 31–42.

Hobbs, N.T. "Linking Energy Balance to Survival in

Mule Deer: Development and Test of a Simulation Model." *Wildlife Monographs* 101 (April 1989): 1–39.

Hoffmeister, D.F. *Mammals of Arizona.* Tucson: The University of Arizona Press and Arizona Game and Fish Department, 1986.

Hofmann, R.R. "Digestive Physiology of Deer—Their Morphophysiological Specialization and Adaptation." In *The Biology of Deer Production,* edited by P.F. Fennessy and K.R. Drew, 393–408. Bulletin No. 22. Wellington: The Royal Society of New Zealand, 1985.

Holter, J.B., H.H. Hayes, and S.H. Smith. "Protein Requirement of Yearling White-tailed Deer." *The Journal of Wildlife Management* 43 (1979): 872–879.

Hölzenbein, S., and R.L. Marchinton. "Emigration and Mortality of Orphaned Male White-tailed Deer." *The Journal of Wildlife Management* 56, no. 1 (1992): 147–153.

———. "Spatial Integration of Maturing-Male White-tailed Deer into the Adult Population." *Journal of Mammalogy* 73 (1992): 326–334.

Hölzenbein, S., and G. Schwede. "Activity and Movement of Female White-tailed Deer during the Rut." *The Journal of Wildlife Management* 53 (1989): 219–223.

Hood, R.E. "Seasonal Variations in Home Range, Diel Movement and Activity Patterns of White-tailed Deer on the Rob and Bessie Welder Wildlife Refuge (San Patricio County, Texas)." Master's thesis, Texas A&M University, College Station, 1971.

Hornocker, M.G. "An Analysis of Mountain Lion Predation upon Mule Deer and Elk in the Idaho Primitive Area." *Wildlife Monographs* 21 (1970): 1–39.

Hoskinson, R.L., and L.D. Mech. "White-tailed Deer Migration and Its Role in Wolf Predation." *The Journal of Wildlife Management* 40, no. 3 (1976): 429–441.

Howard, V.W., Jr. "Behavior of White-tailed Deer within Three Northern Idaho Plant Associations." Ph.D. dissertation, University of Idaho, Moscow, 1969.

Hudson, R.J., D.M. Herbert, and V.C. Brink. "Occupational Patterns of Wildlife on a Major East Kootenay Winter-spring Range." *Journal of Range Management* 29 (1976): 38–43.

Hughes, A. "The Topography of Vision in Mammals of Contrasting Life Style: Comparative Optics and Retinal Organization." In *Handbook of Sensory Physiology: The Visual System in Vertebrates,* VII/5, 704. 1975.

Hyman, H. *Comparative Vertebrate Anatomy.* Chicago: University of Chicago Press, 1956.

Inglis, J.M., R.E. Hood, B.A. Brown, and C.A. De-Young. "Home Range of White-tailed Deer in Texas Coastal Prairie Brushland." *Journal of Mammalogy* 60 (1979): 377–389.

Jackson, R.M., M. White, and F.F. Knowlton. "Activity Patterns of Young White-tailed Deer Fawns in South Texas." *Ecology* 53 (1972): 262–270.

Jacob, J., and E. von Lehmann. "Chemical Composition of the Nasal Gland Secretion from the Marsh Deer *Odocoileus (Dorcelaphus) dichotomus* (Illiger)." *Zeitschrift für Naturforschung* 31 (1976): 496–498.

Jacobsen, N.K. "Physiology, Behavior and Thermal Transactions of White-tailed Deer." Ph.D. dissertation, Cornell University, Ithaca, N.Y., 1973.

Jacobson, H.A. *Investigations of Phosphorus in the Nutritional Ecology of White-tailed Deer.* Federal Aid in Wildlife Restoration Project W-48-31, Study XXIII, Progress Report. 1984.

———. "Deer Condition Response to Changing Harvest Strategy, Davis Island, Mississippi." In *The Biology of Deer,* edited by R.D. Brown, 48–55. New York: Springer-Verlag, 1991.

Jacobson, H.A., and D.A. Darrow. "Effects of Baiting on Deer Movement and Activity." *Proceedings of the Fifteenth Annual Southeastern Deer Study Group Meeting, Annapolis, Maryland* 15 (1992): 23–24.

Jacobson, H.A., D.C. Guynn, R.N. Griffin, and D. Lewis. "Fecundity of White-tailed Deer in Mississippi and Periodicity of Corpora Lutea and Lactation." *Proceedings of the Annual Conference of the Southeastern Association of Fish and Wildlife Agencies* 33 (1979): 30–35.

Jacobson, H.A., and S.J. Waldhalm. "Antler Cycles of a White-tailed Deer with Congenital Anophthalmia." In *The Biology of Deer,* edited by R.D. Brown, 520–524. New York: Springer-Verlag, 1991.

Jaczewski, Z. "The Effect of Changes in Length of Daylight on the Growth of Antlers in the Deer *(Cervus elaphus* L.)." *Folia Bilogie* 2 (1954): 113–143.

———. "The Artificial Induction of Antler Growth in Deer." In *Antler Development in Cervidae,* edited by R.D. Brown, 143–162. Kingsville, Tex.: Caesar Kleberg Wildlife Research Institute, 1983.

Jakimchuk, R.D., S.H. Ferguson, and L.G. Sopuck. "Differential Habitat Use and Sexual Segregation in the Central Arctic Caribou Herd." *Canadian Journal of Zoology* 65 (1987): 534–541.

Jenkins, K.J., and R.G. Wright. "Resource Partitioning and Competition among Cervids in the Northern Rocky Mountains." *Journal of Applied Ecology* 25 (1988): 11–24.

Jeter, L.K., and R.L. Marchinton. "Preliminary Report of Telemetric Study of Deer Movements and Behavior on the Eglin Field Reservation in Northwestern Florida." *Proceedings of the Annual Conference of the Southeastern Association of Game and Fish Commissioners* 18 (1964): 140–152.

Jewell, P.A. "The Concept of Home Range in Mammals." In *Play, Exploration and Territory in Mammals,* edited by P.A. Jewell and C. Loizos, 85–109. New York: Academic Press, 1966.

Johansen, K.L., R.L. Marchinton, K.V. Miller, and R.C. McGuire. "Seasonal Variation in Marking Behavior of White-tailed Deer." Abstract. *Southeast Deer Study Group* 11 (1988): 15.

Johnson, E. "Moulting Cycles." *Mammalogy Reviews* 1 (1972): 198–208.

Johnson, E., and J.T.S. Leask. "Metabolism of Testosterone by Forehead Skin of the Roebuck *(Capreolus capreolus)*." *Journal of Endocrinology* 75 (1977): 363–372.

Kammermeyer, K.E. "Movement-Ecology of White-tailed Deer in Relation to a Refuge and Hunted Area." Master's thesis, University of Georgia, Athens, 1975.

Kammermeyer, K.E., and R.L. Marchinton. "The Dynamic Aspects of Deer Populations Utilizing a Refuge." *Proceedings of the Annual Conference of the Southeastern Association of Game and Fish Commissioners* 29 (1975): 466–475.

———. "Notes on Dispersal of Male White-tailed Deer." *Journal of Mammalogy* 57 (1976): 776–778.

———. "Seasonal Change in Circadian Activity of Radio-monitored Deer." *The Journal of Wildlife Management* 41 (1977): 315–317.

Kamps, G.F. "Whitetail and Mule Deer Relationships in the Snowy Mountains of Central Montana." Master's thesis, Montana State University, Bozeman, 1969.

Karstad, L., ed. *Diseases of the Cervidae: A Partly Annotated Bibliography. Wildlife Disease* 43. 1964. Microcards.

———. *Diseases of the Cervidae: Bibliographic Supplement I. Wildlife Disease* 52. 1969. Microcards.

Kautz, M.V. "Energy Expenditure and Heart Rate of Active Mule Deer Fawns." Master's thesis, Colorado State University, Fort Collins, 1978.

Kay, R.N.B. "The Comparative Anatomy and Physiology of Digestion in Tragulids and Cervids and Its Relation to Food Intake." In *Biology and Management of the Cervidae,* edited by C.M. Wemmer, 214–222. Washington, D.C.: Smithsonian Institution Press, 1987.

Kay, R.N.B., W.V. Engelhardt, and R.G. White. "The Digestive Physiology of Wild Ruminants." In *Digestive Physiology and Metabolism in Ruminants,* edited by Y. Ruckebusch and P. Thivend, 743–758. Westport, Conn.: AVI Publishing Co., 1980.

Kay, R.N.B., and M.L. Ryder. "Coat Growth in Red Deer *(Cervus elaphus)* Exposed to a Day-length Cycle of Six Months Duration." *Journal of Zoology* (London) 191 (1978): 505–510.

Kearney, S.R., and F.F. Gilbert. "Habitat Use by White-tailed Deer and Moose on Sympatric Range." *The Journal of Wildlife Management* 40 (1976): 645–657.

Kellogg, F.E., A.K. Prestwood, and R.E. Noble. "Anthrax Epizootic in White-tailed Deer." *Journal of Wildlife Diseases* 6 (1970): 226–228.

Kelly, R.W., K.P. McNatty, and G.H. Moore. "Hormonal Changes about Oestrus in Female Red Deer." In *The Biology of Deer Production,* edited by P.F. Fennessy and K.R. Drew, 181–184. Bulletin No. 22. Wellington: The Royal Society of New Zealand, 1985.

Kie, J.G., and M. White. "Population Dynamics of White-tailed Deer *(Odocoileus virginianus)* on the Welder Wildlife Refuge, Texas." *The Southwestern Naturalist* 30 (1985): 105–118.

Kie, J.G., M. White, and F.F. Knowlton. "Effects of Coyote Predation on Population Dynamics of White-tailed Deer." In *Proceedings of the Welder Wildlife Foundation Symposium,* edited by D.L. Drawe, 65–82. Welder Wildlife Contribution B-7. Corpus Christi, Tex.: 1979.

Kile, T.L., and R.L. Marchinton. "White-tailed Deer Rubs and Scrapes: Spatial, Temporal and Physical Characteristics and Social Role." *American Midland Naturalist* 97 (1977): 257–266.

Kincer, J.S. "Climate and Weather Data for the United States." In *Climate and Man,* 685–1169. Washington, D.C.: U.S. Government Printing Office, 1941.

Kingston, N. "Protozoan Parasites." In *Diseases and Parasites of White-tailed Deer,* edited by W.R. Davidson, F.A. Hayes, V.F. Nettles, and F.E. Kellogg, 193–236. Miscellaneous Publication No. 7. Tallahassee, Fla.: Tall Timbers Research Station, 1981.

Kleiminger, J. "Untersuchungen uber die Eignung von Freilebenden Wildarten als Bioindikatoren zur Erfassung von Flachenhagten Schwermetallkontamination in Niedersachsen" (Suitability of Wild Animals as Biological Indicators of Environmental Pollution with Heavy Metals in Lower Saxony). Inaugural dissertation, Veterinary School, Hanover, Germany.

Klein, D.R. "Population Ecology: the Interaction between Deer and Their Food Supply." In *The Biology of Deer Production,* edited by P.F. Fennessy and K.R. Drew, 13–22. Bulletin No. 22. Wellington: The Royal Society of New Zealand, 1985.

Klien, E.H. "Phenology of Breeding and Antler Growth in White-tailed Deer in Honduras." *The Journal of Wildlife Management* 56 (1992): 826–829.

Knipe, T. *The Javelina in Arizona.* Arizona Game and Fish Department, Wildlife Bulletin No. 2. 1957.

Knox, W.M., K.V. Miller, and R.L. Marchinton. "Recurrent Estrous Cycles in White-tailed Deer." *Journal of Mammalogy* 69 (1988): 384–386.

Kong, Y.C., and P.P.H. But. "Deer–The Ultimate Medicinal Animal (Antler and Deer parts in medicine)." In *The Biology of Deer Production,* edited by P.F. Fennessy and K.R. Drew, 311–326. Bulletin No. 22. Wellington: The Royal Society of New Zealand, 1985.

Kramer, A. *A Review of the Ecological Relationships between Mule and White-tailed Deer.* Alberta Fish and Wildlife Division, Wildlife Section, Occasional Paper no. 3. Edmonton: 1972.

———. "Interspecific Behavior and Dispersion of Two Sympatric Deer Species." *The Journal of Wildlife Management* 37 (1973): 288–300.

Krausman, P.R., and E.D. Ables. *Ecology of the Carmen Mountains White-tailed Deer.* Science Monograph Series No. 15. Washington, D.C.: U.S. Department of the Interior, National Park Service, 1981.

Krausman, P.R., B.D. Leopold, K.R. Rautenstrauch, J.R. Morgart, and R.C. Etchberger. "Desert Mule Deer Mortality and the Central Arizona Project." In *The Biology of Deer,* edited by R.D. Brown, 43–47. New York: Springer-Verlag, 1991.

Krausman, P.R., B.D. Leopold, R.F. Seegmiller, and S.G. Torres. "Relationships between Desert Bighorn Sheep and Habitat in Western Arizona." *Wildlife Monographs* 102 (July 1989): 1–66.

Krausman, P.R., L.L. Ordway, F.M. Whiting, and W.H. Brown. "Nutritional Composition of Desert Mule Deer Forage in the Picacho Mountains, Arizona." *Desert Plants* 10 (1990): 32–34.

Krefting, L.W., and A.B. Erickson. "Results of Special Deer Hunts on the Mud Lake National Wildlife Refuge, Minnesota." *The Journal of Wildlife Management* 20 (1956): 297–302.

Krefting, L.W., A.B. Erickson, and V.E. Gunvalson. "Results of Controlled Deer Hunts on the Tamarac National Wildlife Refuge." *The Journal of Wildlife Management* 19 (1955): 346–352.

Kroll, J.C. *Study Shows High Breeding Success.* Newsletter. Nacogdoches, Tex.: Stephen F. Austin State University, College of Forestry, Institute for White-tailed Deer Management and Research, 1992.

Kronevi, T., B. Holmberg, and K. Borg. "Lens Lesions in the Elk." *Acta Veterinaria Scandinavica* 18 (1977): 159–167.

Kucera, T.E. "Social Behavior and Breeding System of the Desert Mule Deer." *Journal of Mammalogy* 59 (1978): 463–476.

Kuehn, D.W. "An Evaluation of Tooth Wear as a Criterion for Estimating Age in White-tailed Deer."

Master's thesis, University of Minnesota at Minneapolis St. Paul, 1970.

Kufeld, R.C., D.C. Bowden, and D.L. Schrupp. "Influence of Hunting on Movements of Female Mule Deer." *Journal of Range Management* 41 (January 1988): 70–72.

———. "Distribution and Movement of Female Mule Deer in the Rocky Mountain Foothills." *The Journal of Wildlife Management* 53 (October 1989): 871–877.

Langenau, E.E., and J.M. Lerg. "The Effects of Winter Nutritional Stress on Maternal and Neonatal Behavior in Penned White-tailed Deer." *Applied Animal Ethology* 2 (1976): 207–223.

Lassiter, J.W., and H.M. Edwards, Jr. *Animal Nutrition.* Reston, Va.: Reston Publishing Co., 1982.

Lautier, J.K., T.V. Dailey, and R.D. Brown. "Effect of Water Restriction on Feed Intake in White-tailed Deer." *The Journal of Wildlife Management* 52 (1988): 602–606.

Lent, P.C. "Mother-Infant Relationships in Ungulates." In *The Behaviour of Ungulates and Its Relation to Management,* vol. 1, edited by V. Geist and F. Walther, 14–55. Morges, Switzerland: International Union for the Conservation of Nature and Natural Resources, 1974.

Leopold, A., T. Riney, R. McCain, and L. Tevis, Jr. *The Jawbone Deer Herd.* California Department of Fish and Game, Bulletin No. 4. Sacramento: 1951.

Leopold, B.D., and P.R. Krausman. "Diets of Two Desert Mule Deer Herds in Big Bend National Park, Texas." *The Southwestern Naturalist* 32 (1987): 449–455.

Lewis, D.M. "Telemetry Studies of White-tailed Deer on Red Dirt Game Management Area, Louisiana." Master's thesis, Louisiana State University and A. & M. College, Baton Rouge, 1968.

Lincoln, G.A. "The Role of Deer Antlers in the Behavior of Red Deer." *The Journal of Experimental Zoology* 182 (1970): 233–250.

Lincoln, G.A., R.W. Youngson, and R.W. Short. "The Social and Sexual Behavior of the Red Deer Stag." *Journal of Reproduction and Fertility Supplement* 11 (1970): 71–103.

Lindzey, F. "Mountain Lion." In *Wild Furbearer Management and Conservation in North America,* edited by M. Novak, J.A. Baker, M.E. Obbard, and B. Malloch, 656–668. Ontario, Canada: Ontario Ministry of Natural Resources, 1987.

Lingle, S. "Limit Coordination and Body Configuration in the Fast Gaits of White-tailed Deer, Mule Deer, and Their Hybrids: Adaptive Significance and Management Implications." Master's thesis, University of Calgary, Alberta, Canada, 1989.

Linsdale, J.M., and P.Q. Tomich. *A Herd of Mule Deer: A Record of Observations Made on the Hastings Natural History Reservation.* Berkeley: University of California Press, 1953.

Litchfield, T.R. "Relationships among White-tailed Deer Rubbing, Scraping and Breeding Activities." Master's thesis, University of Georgia, Athens, 1987.

Lojda, Z. "Histogenese Parohu Nasich Cervidu a Jeji Histochemicky Obraz" (Histogenesis of Antlers of Our Cervidae and Its Histochemical Picture). *Ceskoslovenska Morfologie* 4 (1956): 43–66.

Longhurst, W.M., E.O. Garton, H.F. Heady, and G.E. Connolly. *The California Deer Decline and Possibilities for Restoration.* Fresno, Calif.: Western Section of The Wildlife Society, 1976.

Longhurst, W.M., A.L. Lesperanse, M. Morse, R.J. Mackie, O.L. Neal, H. Salwasser, D. Swickland, P.J. Urness, and J.O. Yoakum. "Livestock and Wild Ungulates." In *Proceedings of the Workshop on Livestock and Wildlife-Fisheries Relationships in the Great Basin.* University of California, Division of Agricultural Science, Special Publication 3301. Berkeley: 1983.

Lonner, T.N., and R.J. Mackie. "Interactions between Big Game and Livestock." In *Forestland Grazing, Proceedings of a Symposium,* edited by B.F. Roche, Jr., and D.M. Baumgartner. Pullman: Washington State University, Cooperative Extension Service, 1983.

Loudon, A.S.I., J.A. Milne, J.D. Curlewis, and A.S. McNeilly. "A Comparison of the Seasonal Hormone Changes and Patterns of Growth, Voluntary Food Intake and Reproduction in Juvenile and Adult Red Deer *(Cervus eluphus)* and Père David Deer *(Elaphurus davidianus)." Journal of Endocrinology* 122 (1989): 733–745.

Loveless, C.M. *The Everglades Deer Herd: Life History and Management.* Florida Game and Fresh Water Fish Commission, Technical Bulletin No. 6. Tallahassee, Fla.: 1959.

———. *Ecological Characteristics of a Mule Deer Winter Range.* Colorado Game, Fish and Parks Department, Technical Bulletin No. 20. Denver: 1967.

Low, W.A., and I.M. Cowan. "Age Determination in Deer by Annular Structure of Dental Cementum." *The Journal of Wildlife Management* 27 (1963): 466–471.

Luick, J. "The Velvet Antler Industry." In *Antler Development in Cervidae,* edited by R.D. Brown, 329–338. Kingsville, Tex.: Caesar Kleberg Wildlife Research Institute, 1983.

McArthur, C., C.T. Robbins, A.E. Hagerman, and T.A. Hanley. "Diet Selection by a Ruminant Browser in Relation to Plant Chemistry." In press.

McBeath, D.Y. "Whitetail Traps and Tags." *Michigan Conservation* 10, no. 11 (1941): 6–7, 11.

McCabe, R.E., and T.R. McCabe. "Of Slings and Arrows: An Historical Retrospection." In *Whitetailed Deer: Ecology and Management,* edited by L.K. Halls, 19–72. Harrisburg: Stackpole Books, 1984.

McCaffery, K.R., and W.A. Creed. *Significance of Forest Openings to Deer in Northern Wisconsin.* Wisconsin Department of Natural Resources, Technical Bulletin No. 44. Madison: 1969.

McCulloch, C.Y. "Seasonal Diets of Mule and White-tailed Deer." In *Deer Nutrition in Arizona Chaparral and Desert Habitats,* 1–37. Arizona Game and Fish Department, Special Report 3. 1973.

McCullough, D.R. *The George Reserve Deer Herd: Population Ecology of a K-Selected Species.* Ann Arbor: The University of Michigan Press, 1979.

McCullough, D.R., D.H. Hirth, and S.T. Newhouse. "Resource Partitioning between Sexes in White-tailed Deer." *The Journal of Wildlife Management* 53, no. 2 (1989): 277–283.

McCullough, D.R., D.S. Pine, D.L. Whitmore, T.M. Mansfield, and R.H. Decker. "Linked Sex Harvest Strategy for Big Game Management with a Test Case on Black-tailed Deer." *Wildlife Monographs* 112 (1990).

McDowell, R.D. "Photoperiodism among Breeding

White-tailed Deer *(Odocoileus virginianus).*" In *Trans-actions of the Northeast Section of the Wildlife Society,* 19–38. Bethesda, Md.: Wildlife Society, 1970.

McEwen, L.C., C.E. French, N.D. Magruder, R.W. Swift, and R.H. Ingram. "Nutrient Requirements of the White-tailed Deer." *Transactions of the North American Wildlife Conference* 22 (1957): 119–132.

McGinnes, B.S., and R.L. Downing. "Fawn Mortality in a Confined Virginia Deer Herd." *Proceedings of the Southeastern Association of Game and Fish Commissioners* 23 (1970): 188–191.

———. "Factors Affecting the Peak of White-tailed Deer Fawning in Virginia." *The Journal of Wildlife Management* 41 (1977): 715–719.

McKean, W.T., and R.M. Bartmann. *Deer-Livestock Relations on a Pinyon-Juniper Range in Northwestern Colorado.* Colorado Game, Fish and Parks Department, Federal Aid Project W-101-R, Final Report. Denver: 1971.

Mackie, R.J. "Montana Deer Weights." *Montana Wildlife* (Winter 1964): 9–14.

———. "Range Ecology and Relationships of Mule Deer, Elk, and Cattle in the Missouri River Breaks, Montana." *Wildlife Monographs* 20 (1970).

———. "Interspecific Competition between Mule Deer, Other Game Animals and Livestock." In *Symposium on Mule Deer Decline in the West.* Logan: Utah State University, College of Natural Resources, Agricultural Experiment Station, 1976.

———. "Impacts of Livestock Grazing on Wild Ungulates." *Transactions of the North American Wildlife and Natural Resources Conference* 43 (1978): 462–476.

———. "Interspecific Relations." In *Mule and Black-tailed Deer of North America,* edited by O.C. Wallmo, 487–507. Lincoln: University of Nebraska Press, 1981.

———. "Natural Regulation of Mule Deer Populations." In *Natural Regulation of Wildlife,* edited by D.S. Eastman, F.L. Bunnell, and J.M. Peck. University of Idaho, Forest, Wildlife and Range Experiment Station, Proceedings No. 14. Moscow: 1983.

———. "The Deer-Elk-Cattle Triangle." In *Symposium on Western Elk Management,* edited by G.W. Workman. Logan: Utah State University, 1985.

———. "Mule Deer." In *Restoring America's Wildlife, 1937-1987,* edited by H. Kallman. Washington, D.C.: U.S. Department of the Interior, U.S. Fish and Wildlife Service, 1987.

———. "Big Game Historical Perspective." Abstract. In *Livestock-Big Game Symposium, Reno, Nevada, September 18-20, 1991.*

Mackie, R.J., and G.L. Dusek. "Deer Habitat Relationships and Management in the Northern Rocky Mountains and Great Plains." *Western Wildlands* 18 (1992): 14–90.

Mackie, R.J., K.L. Hamlin, and D.F. Pac. "Census Methods for Mule Deer." In *Census and Inventory Methods for Populations and Habitats,* edited by F.L. Miller and A. Gunn. University of Idaho, Forest, Range, and Wildlife Experiment Station, Contribution 217. 1981.

———. "Mule Deer." In *Wild Mammals of North America: Biology, Management, and Economics,* edited by J.A. Chapman and G.A. Feldhamer. Baltimore: The Johns Hopkins University Press, 1982.

Mackie, R.J., K.L. Hamlin, D.F. Pac, G.L. Dusek, and A.K. Wood. "Compensation in Free-ranging Deer Populations." *Transactions of the North American Wildlife and Natural Resources Conference* 55 (1990): 518–526.

Mackie, R.J., D.F. Pac, and H.E. Jorgensen. *Population Ecology and Habitat Relationships of Mule Deer in the Bridger Mountains, Montana.* Montana Department of Fish and Game, Montana Deer Studies, Federal Aid in Wildlife Restoration Project W-120-R-9, Progress Report. Helena: 1978.

McLean, D.D. "The Deer of California, with Particular Reference to the Rocky Mountain Mule Deer." *California Fish and Game* 26 (1940): 139–166.

McMahan, C.A. "Suitability of Grazing Enclosures for Deer and Livestock Research on the Kerr Wildlife Management Area, Texas." *The Journal of Wildlife Management* 30 (1966): 151–162.

Main, M.B., and B.E. Coblentz. "Sexual Segregation among Ungulates: A Critique." *Wildlife Society Bulletin* 18, no. 2 (1990): 204–210.

Marchinton, R.L. "Activity Cycles and Mobility of Central Florida Deer Based on Telemetric and Observational Data." Master's thesis, University of Florida, Gainesville, 1964.

———. "Telemetric Study of White-tailed Deer Movement–Ecology and Ethology in the Southeast." Ph.D. dissertation, Auburn University, Auburn, Alabama, 1968.

Marchinton, R.L., and T.D. Atkeson. "Plasticity of Socio-spatial Behaviour of White-tailed Deer and the Concept of Facultative Territoriality." In *The Biology of Deer Production,* edited by P.F. Fennessy and K.R. Drew, 375–377. Bulletin No. 22. Wellington: The Royal Society of New Zealand, 1985.

Marchinton, R.L., and D.H. Hirth. "Behavior." In *White-tailed Deer: Ecology and Management,* edited by L.K. Halls, 129–168. Harrisburg: Stackpole Books, 1984.

Marchinton, R.L., and L.K. Jeter. "Telemetric Study of Deer Movement–Ecology in the Southeast." *Proceedings of the Annual Conference of the Southeastern Association of Game and Fish Commissioners* 20 (1966-1967): 189–206.

Marchinton, R.L., K.L. Johansen, and K.V. Miller. "Behavioural Components of White-tailed Deer Scent Marking: Social and Seasonal Effects." In *Chemical Signals in Vertebrates V,* edited by D.W. Macdonald, D. Müller-Schwarze, and S.E. Natynczuk, 295–310. Oxford University Press, 1990.

Marchinton, R.L., K.V. Miller, R.J. Hamilton, and D.C. Guynn. "Quality Deer Management: Biological and Social Impacts on the Herd." In *Proceedings of the Tall Timbers Game Bird Seminar,* edited by C. Kyser, D.C. Sisson, and J.L. Landers, 7–15. Tallahassee, Fla.: Tall Timbers Research Station, 1990.

Marshall, A.D., and R.W. Whittington. "A Telemetric Study of Deer Home Ranges and Behavior of Deer during Managed Hunts." *Proceedings of the Annual Conference of the Southeastern Association of Game and Fish Commissioners* 22 (1969): 30–46.

Martinka, C.J. "Habitat Relationships of White-tailed Deer and Mule Deer in Northern Montana." *The Journal of Wildlife Management* 32 (1968): 558–565.

———. "Ungulate Populations in Relation to Wilderness in Glacier National Park, Montana." *Transactions of the North American Wildlife and Natural Resources Conference* 43 (1978): 351–357.

Masterton, R.B. "Adaptation for Sound Localization in the Ear and Brainstem of Mammals." *Federal Proceedings* 33 (1974): 1904–1910.

Mathews, W.C., and L.L. Glascow. *Deer Preference Ratings of Louisiana Woody Plant Species*. Louisiana State University and A. & M. College, Agricultural Experiment Station, Louisiana State University Forestry Notes No. 133. Baton Rouge: 1981.

Matschke, G.H., K.A. Fagerstone, F.A. Hayes, W. Parker, R.F. Harlow, V.F. Nettles, and D.O. Trainer. "Population Influences." In *White-tailed Deer: Ecology and Management*, edited by L.K. Halls, 169–188. Harrisburg: Stackpole Books, 1984.

Mattfeld, G.F., R.W. Sage, R.D. Masters, and M.J. Tracy. "Deer Movement Patterns in the Adirondacks—A Progress Report." *Transactions of the Northeastern Deer Study Group* 11 (1977): 157–167.

Mattfield, G.F. "Northeastern Hardwood and Spruce/Fir Forests." In *White-tailed Deer: Ecology and Management*, edited by L.K. Halls, 305–330. Harrisburg: Stackpole Books, 1984.

Matthiessen, L. "Ueber den physikalisch-optischen Bau des Auges von *Cervus alces mas*." *Archiv für die gesamte Physiologie des Menschen und der Tiere* 40 (1887): 314–323.

Mautz, W.W., P.J. Pekins, and J.A. Warren. "Cold Temperature Effects on Metabolic Rate of White-tailed, Mule, and Black-tailed Deer in Winter Coat." In *The Biology of Deer Production*, edited by P.F. Fennessy and K.R. Drew, 453–457. Bulletin No. 22. Wellington: The Royal Society of New Zealand, 1985.

Mayr, E. "Ecological Factors in Speciation." *Evolution* 1 (1947): 263–288.

Mech, L.D. *The Wolf: The Ecology and Behavior of an Endangered Species*. Garden City, N.Y.: Natural History Press, 1970.

——. "Predators and Predation." In *White-tailed Deer: Ecology and Management*, edited by L.K. Halls, 189–202. Harrisburg: Stackpole Books, 1984.

Mech, L.D., and P.D. Karns. *Role of the Wolf in a Deer Decline in the Superior National Forest*. U.S. Department of Agriculture, Forest Service, North Central Forest Experiment Station, Research Paper NC-148. St. Paul, Minn.: 1977.

Menzel, K.E. "Central and Southern Plains." In *White-tailed Deer: Ecology and Management*, edited by L.K. Halls, 505–512. Harrisburg: Stackpole Books, 1984.

Meredith, M., and R.J. O'Connel. *Journal of Physiology* (London) 286 (1979): 301–316.

Michael, E.D. "Movements of White-tailed Deer on the Welder Wildlife Refuge." *The Journal of Wildlife Management* 29, no. 1 (1965): 44–52.

——. "Daily and Seasonal Activity Patterns of White-tailed Deer on the Welder Wildlife Refuge." Ph.D. dissertation, Texas A&M University, College Station, 1966.

——. "Playing by Deer in South Texas." *American Midland Naturalist* 80 (1968): 535–537.

——. "Activity Patterns of White-tailed Deer in South Texas." *The Texas Journal of Science* 21 (1970): 417–428.

Miller, F.L. "Distribution Patterns of Black-tailed Deer *(Odocoileus hemionus columbianus)* in Relation to Environment." *Journal of Mammalogy* 51 (1970): 248–260.

Miller, K.V., T.E. Kiser, and R.L. Marchinton. "Melatonin and the Seasonal Cycle of White-tailed Deer." Abstract. *Southeast Deer Study Group* 13 (1990): 22.

Miller, K.V., R.L. Marchinton, and P.B. Bush. "Signpost Communication by White-tailed Deer: Research Since Calgary." *Applied Animal Behavior Science* 29 (1991): 195–204.

Miller, K.V., R.L. Marchinton, K.J. Forand, and K.L. Johansen. "Dominance, Testosterone Levels and Scraping Activity in a Captive Herd of White-tailed Deer." *Journal of Mammalogy* 68 (1987): 812–817.

Miller, K.V., R.L. Marchinton, and W.M. Knox. "White-tailed Deer Signposts and Their Role as a Source of Priming Pheromones: A Hypothesis." *Transactions of the Eighteenth Congress of the International Union of Game Biologists*. In press.

Miller, K.V., O.E. Rhodes, Jr., T.R. Litchfield, M.H. Smith, and R.L. Marchinton. "Reproductive Characteristics of Yearling and Adult Male White-tailed Deer." *Proceedings of the Annual Conference of the Southeastern Association of Fish and Wildlife Agencies* 41 (1987): 378–384.

Milne, J.A., A.S.I. Loudon, A.M. Sibbald, J.D. Curlewis, and A.S. McNeilly. "Effects of Melatonin and Dopamine Agonist and Antagonist on Seasonal Changes in Voluntary Intake, Reproductive Activity and Plasma Concentrations of Prolactin and Triiodothyronine in Red Deer Hinds." *Journal of Endocrinology* 125 (1990): 241–249.

Moen, A.N. "The Critical Thermal Environment: A New Look at an Old Concept." *BioScience* 18, no. 11 (1968): 1041–1043.

——. "Energy Exchange of White-tailed Deer, Western Minnesota." Ecology 49, no. 4 (1968): 676–682.

——. "Surface Temperatures and Radiant Heat Loss from White-tailed Deer." *The Journal of Wildlife Management* 32, no. 2 (1968): 338–344.

——. *Wildlife Ecology: An Analytical Approach*. San Francisco: W.H. Freeman and Co., 1973.

——. "Energy Conservation by White-tailed Deer in the Winter." *Ecology* 57, no. 1 (1976): 192–198.

——. "Seasonal Changes in Heart Rates, Activity, Metabolism, and Forage Intake of White-tailed Deer." *The Journal of Wildlife Management* 42, no. 4 (1978): 715–738.

——. "Deer and the Energy Cycle." *The Conservationist* 35, no. 2 (1980): 38–40.

——. *Deer Management at the Crane Memorial Reservation and Wildlife Refuge*. Ithaca, N.Y.: Educational Software Products, 1984.

——. "Deer Population Dynamics; Survey Results." *Deer & Deer Hunting* 11, no. 2 (1987): 102–109.

Moen, A.N., M.A. DellaFerra, A.L. Hiller, and B.A. Buxton. "Heart Rates of White-tailed Deer Fawns in Response to Recorded Wolf Howls." *Canadian Journal of Zoology* 56, no. 5 (1978): 1207–1210.

Moen, A.N., and R.A. Moen. *Deer Management at the Bernheim Foundation Properties, Clermont, Kentucky*. Ithaca, N.Y.: Educational Software Products, 1985.

Moen, A.N., and S. Scholtz. "Nomographic Estimation of Forage Intake of White-tailed Deer." *Journal of Range Management* 34, no. 1 (1981): 74–76.

Moen, A.N., and C.W. Severinghaus. "Annual Weight Cycle Equations and Survival of White-tailed Deer." *New York Fish and Game Journal* 28, no. 2 (1981): 162–177.

——. "Hair Depths of the Winter Coat of White-tailed Deer." *Journal of Mammalogy* 65, no. 3 (1984): 497–499.

——. "Estimating Numbers with a Universal Key."

New York Fish and Game Journal 32, no. 1 (1985): 89–92.

———. "Estimating Deer Populations from Harvest and Mortality Data." In *Symposium Proceedings: Deer, Forestry, and Agriculture: Interactions and Strategies for Management,* 62–69. Warren, Pa.: Allegheny Society of American Foresters, 1987.

Moen, A.N., C.W. Severinghaus, and R.A. Moen. Deer CAMP (Computer-Assisted Management Program). Ithaca, N.Y.: Educational Software Products, 1986.

Moen, A.N., S. Whittemore, and B. Buxton. "Effects of Disturbance by Snowmobiles on Heart Rate of Captive White-tailed Deer." *New York Fish and Game Journal* 29, no. 2 (1982): 176–183.

Montgomery, G.G. "Nocturnal Movements and Activity Rhythms of White-tailed Deer." *The Journal of Wildlife Management* 27 (1963): 422–427.

Moore, W.G., and R.L. Marchinton. "Marking Behavior and Its Social Function in White-tailed Deer." In *The Behaviour of Ungulates and Its Relation to Management,* vol. 2, edited by V. Geist and F. Walther, 447–456. Morges, Switzerland: International Union for the Conservation of Nature and Natural Resources, 1974.

Mueller, C.C., and R.M.F.S. Sadlier. "Changes in the Nutrient Composition of Milk of Black-tailed Deer during Lactation." *Journal of Mammalogy* 58 (1977): 421–423.

Müller-Schwarze, D. "Complexity and Relative Specificity in a Mammalian Pheromone." *Nature* 223 (1969): 525–526.

———. "Pheromones in Black-tailed Deer *(Odocoileus hemionus columbianus)*." *Animal Behaviour* 19 (1971): 141–152.

———. "Social Significance of Forehead Rubbing in Blacktailed Deer *(Odocoileus hemionus columbianus)*." *Animal Behaviour* 20 (1972): 788–797.

———. "Pheromone Bioassay in Game Mammals." In *Global Trends in Wildlife Management, Proceedings of the Eighteenth Congress of the International Union of Game Biologists, Krakow, Poland, August 1987,* edited by B. Bobek, K. Perzcinowski, and W.L. Regelin. 1991.

Müller-Schwarze, D., R. Altieri, and N. Porter. "Alert Odor from Skin Gland in Deer." *Journal of Chemical Ecology* 10 (1984): 1707–1729.

Müller-Schwarze, D., U. Ravid, A. Claesson, A.G. Singer, R.M. Silverstein, C. Müller-Schwarze, N.J. Volkman, K.F. Zemanek, and R.G. Butler. "The 'Deer Lactone': Source, Chiral Properties, and Responses by Black-tailed Deer." *Journal of Chemical Ecology* 4 (1978): 247–256.

Müller-Schwarze, D., R.M. Silverstein, C. Müller-Schwarze, A.G. Singer, and N.J. Volkman. "Response to a Mammalian Pheromone and Its Geometric Isomer." *Journal of Chemical Ecology* 2 (1976): 389–398.

Müller-Schwarze, D., N.J. Volkman, and K.F. Zemanek. "Osmetrichia: Specialized Scent Hair in Black-tailed Deer." *Journal of Ultrastructure Research* 59 (1977): 223–230.

Murphy, D.A. "Toxicosis." In *Diseases and Parasites of Whitetailed Deer,* edited by W.R. Davidson, F.A. Hayes, V.F. Nettles, and F.E. Kellogg, 43–51. Miscellaneous Publication No. 7. Tallahassee, Fla.: Tall Timbers Research Station, 1981.

Murphy, D.A., and H.S. Crawford. *Wildlife Foods and Understory Vegetation in Missouri's National Forests.* Missouri Department of Conservation, Technical Bulletin No. 4. 1970.

Nagy, J.G., H.W. Steinhoff, and G.M. Ward. "Effects of Essential Oils of Sagebrush on Deer Rumen Microbial Function." *The Journal of Wildlife Management* 28 (1964): 785–790.

Nellis, C.H., J.T. Thiessen, and C.A. Prentice. "Pregnant Fawn and Quintuplet Mule Deer." *The Journal of Wildlife Management* 40 (1976): 795–796.

Nelson, M.E., and L.D. Mech. "Deer Social Organization and Wolf Predation in Northeastern Minnesota." *Wildlife Monographs* 77 (1981).

———. "Home-range Formation and Dispersal of Deer in Northeastern Minnesota." *Journal of Mammalogy* 65, no. 4 (1984): 567–575.

———. "Mortality of White-tailed in Northeastern Minnesota." *The Journal of Wildlife Management* 50, no. 4 (1986): 691–698.

———. "Demes within a Northeastern Minnesota Deer Population." In *Mammalian Dispersal Patterns: The Effects of Social Structure on Population Genetics,* edited by B.D. Chepko-Sade and Z.T. Haplin, 27–40. Chicago: University of Chicago Press, 1987.

Newsom, J.D. "Coastal Plain." In *White-tailed Deer: Ecology and Management,* edited by L.K. Halls, 367–380. Harrisburg: Stackpole Books, 1984.

Newsom, W.M. *Whitetailed Deer.* New York: Scribner's, 1926.

Nielsen, D.G., M.J. Dunlap, and K.V. Miller. "Prerut Rubbing by White-tailed Bucks: Nursery Damage, Social Role, and Management Options." *Wildlife Society Bulletin* 10 (1982): 341–348.

Nixon, C.M., L.P. Hansen, P.A. Brewer, and J.E. Chelsvig. "Ecology of White-tailed Deer in an Intensively Farmed Region of Illinois." *Wildlife Monographs* 118 (1991).

Nordan, H.C., I.M. Cowan, and A.J. Wood. "The Feed Intake and Heat Production of the Young Black-tailed Deer *(Odocoileus hemionus columbianus)*." *Canadian Journal of Zoology* 48 (1970): 275–282.

Nowak, R.M., and J.L. Paradiso. *Walker's Mammals of the World.* Baltimore: The Johns Hopkins University Press, 1983.

Nudds, T.D. "The Prudent Predator: Applying Ecology and Anthropology to Renewable Resources Management." In *Wild Furbearer Management and Conservation in North America,* edited by M. Novak, J.A. Baker, M.E. Obbard, and B. Malloch, 113–118. Ontario, Canada: Ontario Ministry of Natural Resources, 1987.

Odend'hal, S., K.V. Miller, and D.M. Hoffman. "Preputial Glands in the White-tailed Deer *(Odocoileus virginianus)*." *Journal of Mammalogy* 73 (in press).

Odum, E.P. *Fundamentals of Ecology.* 3d ed. Philadelphia: W.B. Saunders Co., 1971.

Oftedal, O.T. "Milk, Protein, and Energy Intakes of Suckling Mammalian Young: A Comparative Study." Ph.D. dissertation, Cornell University, Ithaca, N.Y., 1981.

Ogren, H.A. *Barbary Sheep of New Mexico.* New Mexico Department of Game and Fish, Bulletin No. 11. 1962.

Olson, H.F. "Deer Tagging and Population Studies in Minnesota." *Transactions of the North American Wildlife Conference* 3 (1938): 280–286.

Ordway, L.L., and P.R. Krausman. "Habitat Use by Desert Mule Deer." The *Journal of Wildlife Management* 50 (1986): 677–683.

Ortega, I.M. "Deer and Cattle Foraging Strategies under Different Grazing Systems and Stocking Rates." Ph.D. dissertation, Texas Tech University, Lubbock, 1991.

Ozoga, J.J. "Aggressive Behavior of White-tailed Deer at Winter Cuttings." *The Journal of Wildlife Management* 36, no. 3 (1972): 861–868.

———. "Induced Scraping Activity in White-tailed Deer." *The Journal of Wildlife Management* 53 (1989a): 877–880.

———. "Temporal Pattern of White-tailed Deer Scraping Behavior." *Journal of Mammalogy* 70 (1989b): 633–636.

Ozoga, J.J., and L.W. Gysel. "Response of White-tailed Deer to Winter Weather." *The Journal of Wildlife Management* 36 (1972): 892–896.

Ozoga, J.J., and L.J. Verme. "Reproduction and Physical Characteristics of a Supplementally Fed White-tailed Deer Herd." *The Journal of Wildlife Management* 46 (1982): 281–301.

———. "Effects of Family-Bond Deprivation on Reproductive Performance in Female White-tailed Deer." *The Journal of Wildlife Management* 48, no. 4 (1984): 1326–1334.

———. "Comparative Breeding Behavior and Performance of Yearlings vs. Prime-age White-tailed Bucks." *The Journal of Wildlife Management* 49, no. 2 (1985): 364–372.

———. "Relation of Maternal Age to Fawn-rearing Success of White-tailed Deer." *The Journal of Wildlife Management* 50, no. 3 (1986): 480–486.

Ozoga, J.J., L.J. Verme, and C.S. Bienz. "Parturition Behavior and Territoriality in White-tailed Deer: Impact on Neonatal Mortality." *The Journal of Wildlife Management* 46, no. 1 (1982): 1–11.

Pac, D.R., R.J. Mackie, and H.E. Jorgensen. *Mule Deer Population Organization, Behavior and Dynamics in a Northern Rocky Mountain Environment.* Montana Department of Fish, Wildlife and Parks, Federal Aid in Wildlife Restoration Project, Final Report. Helena: 1991.

Pac, H.I., W.F. Kasworm, L.R. Irby, and R.J. Mackie. "Ecology of the Mule Deer, *Odocoileus hemionus,* along the East Front of the Rocky Mountains, Montana." *Canadian Field-Naturalist* 102 (1988): 227–236.

Palmer, R.S. "The Whitetail Deer of Tomhegan Camps, Maine, with Added Notes on Fecundity." *Journal of Mammalogy* 32 (1951): 267–280.

Parker, K.L. "Effects of Heat, Cold, and Rain on Coastal Blacktailed Deer." *Canadian Journal of Zoology* 66 (1988): 2475–2483.

Parker, K.L., and C.T. Robbins. "Thermoregulation in Mule Deer and Elk." *Canadian Journal of Zoology* 62 (1984): 1409–1422.

———. "Thermoregulation in Ungulates." In *Bioenergetics of Wild Herbivores,* edited by R.J. Hudson and R.G. White, 161–182. Boca Raton, Fla.: CRC Press, 1985.

Parker, K.L., C.T. Robbins, and T.A. Hanley. "Energy Expenditures for Locomotion by Mule Deer and Elk." *The Journal of Wildlife Management* 48 (1984): 474–488.

Pearson, R.W., and L.E. Ensminger. "Southeastern Uplands." In *Soil,* edited by A. Stefferud, 579–594. Washington, D.C.: U.S. Government Printing Office, 1957.

Peek, J.M. "Northern Rocky Mountains." In *Whitetailed Deer: Ecology and Management,* edited by L.K. Halls, 497–504. Harrisburg: Stackpole Books, 1984.

Petersen, L.E. "Northern Plains." In *White-tailed Deer: Ecology and Management,* edited by L.K. Halls, 345–354. Harrisburg: Stackpole Books, 1984.

Pimlott, D.H., J.A. Shannon, and G.B. Kolenosky. *The Ecology of the Timber Wolf in Algonquin Provincial Park.* Toronto, Canada: Ontario Department of Lands and Forests, 1969.

Pledger, J.M. "Activity, Home Range, and Habitat Utilization of White-tailed Deer *(Odocoileus virginianus)* in Southeastern Arkansas." Master's thesis, University of Arkansas, Fayetteville, 1975.

Plotka, E.D. "Morphologic and Metabolic Consequences of Pinealectomy in Deer." In *Pineal Gland,* Vol. 3. *Extra-reproductive Effects,* edited by R. Reiter, 154–170. Boca Raton, Fla.: CRC Press, 1982.

Plotka, E.D., U.S. Seal, M.A. Letellier, L. Verme, and J.J. Ozoga. "Endocrine and Morphologic Effects of Pinealectomy in White-tailed Deer." In *Animal Models for Research on Contraception and Fertility,* edited by N.J. Alexander, 452–466. New York: Harper and Row, Publishers, 1979.

Pojar, T.M. "Use of a Population Model in Big Game Management." *Proceedings of the Western Association of Game and Fish Commissioners* 57 (1977): 82–92.

Prescott, W.H. "Interrelationships of Moose and Deer of the Genus *Odocoileus.*" In *International Symposium on Moose Ecology.* 1973.

Prins, H.H.T., and G.R. Iason. "Dangerous Lions and Nonchalant Buffalo." *Behaviour* 108, no. 3 (1989).

Progulske, D.R., and T.S. Baskett. "Mobility of Missouri Deer and Their Harassment by Dogs." *The Journal of Wildlife Management* 22, no. 2 (1958): 184–192.

Progulske, D.R., and D.C. Duerre. "Factors Influencing Spotlighting Counts of Deer." *The Journal of Wildlife Management* 28 (1964): 27–34.

Pruitt, W.O., Jr. "Rutting Behavior of the White-tailed Deer." *Journal of Mammalogy* 35 (1954): 129–130.

Putman, R. *Grazing in Temperate Ecosystems: Large Herbivores and the Ecology of the New Forest.* Beckenham, England: Croom Helm, 1986.

———. *The Natural History of Deer.* London: Christopher Helm, and Ithaca, N.Y.: Comstock Publishing Associates, 1989.

Pybus, M.J., and W.M. Samuel. "Lesions Caused by *Parelaphostrongylus odocoilei* (Nematoda: Metastrongyloidea) in Two Cervid Hosts." *Veterinary Pathology* 21 (1984): 425–431.

Quay, W.B. "Microscopic Structure and Variation in the Cutaneous Glands of the Deer, *Odocoileus virginianus.*" *Journal of Mammalogy* 40 (1959): 114–128.

Quay, W.B., and D. Müller-Schwarze. "Functional Histology of Integumentary Glandular Regions in Black-tailed Deer *(Odocoileus hemionus columbianus).*" *Journal of Mammalogy* 51 (1970): 675–693.

———. "Relationship of Age and Sex to Integumentary Glandular Regions in Rocky Mountain Mule Deer *(Odocoileus hemionus hemionus).*" *Journal of Mammalogy* 52 (1970–1971): 670–685.

Radwan, M.A., and G.L. Crouch. "Plant Characteristics Related to Feeding Preference by Black-tailed Deer." *The Journal of Wildlife Management* 38 (1974): 32–34.

Raisz, E. *Land Forms of the United States. Physiographic Divisions.* Modified from *Goode's School Atlas.* 1957.

Ransom, A.B. "Determining Age of White-tailed Deer from Layers in Cementum in Molars." *The Journal of Wildlife Management* 30 (1966): 197–199.

Rautenstrauch, K.R., and P.R. Krausman. "Influences of Water Availability and Rainfall on Movements of Desert Mule Deer." *Journal of Mammalogy* 70 (1989): 197–201.

———. "Preventing Mule Deer Drownings in the Mohawk Canal, Arizona." *Wildlife Society Bulletin* 17 (1989): 280–286.

Rautenstrauch, K.R., P.R. Krausman, F.M. Whiting, and W.H. Brown. "Nutritional Quality of Desert Mule Deer Forage in King Valley, Arizona." *Desert Plants* 8 (1980): 172–174.

Rees, J.W., R.A. Kainer, and R.W. Davis. "Chronology of Mineralization and Eruption of Mandibular Teeth in Mule Deer." *The Journal of Wildlife Management* 30 (1966): 629–631.

Reimers, E. "Growth in Domestic and Wild Reindeer in Norway." *The Journal of Wildlife Management* 36 (1972): 612–619.

Reiter, R.J. "Pineal Gland: Interface between the Photoperiodic Environment and the Endocrine System." *Trends in Endocrinology and Metabolism* 2 (1991): 13–19.

Richardson, L.W., H.A. Jacobson, R.J. Muncy, and C.J. Perkins. "Acoustics of White-tailed Deer *(Odocoileus virginianus).*" *Journal of Mammalogy* 64 (1983): 245–252.

Richardson, L.W., W.A. Mitchell, H.A. Jacobson, and C.J. Perkins. "Behavior of Captive White-tailed Does and Their Fawns." *Proceedings of the Annual Southeastern Deer Study Group Meeting* 3 (1980): 24–25.

Richter, A.R., and R.F. Labisky. "Reproductive Dynamics among Disjunct White-tailed Deer Herds in Florida." *The Journal of Wildlife Management* 49 (1985): 964–971.

Riney, T. "Standard Terminology for Deer Teeth." *The Journal of Wildlife Management* 15 (1951): 99–101.

Robbins, C.R., A.E. Hagerman, P.J. Austin, C. McArthur, and T.A. Hanley. "Variation in Mammalian Physiological Responses to a Condensed Tannin and Its Ecological Implications." *Journal of Mammalogy* 72 (1991): 480–486.

Robbins, C.T. *Wildlife Feeding and Nutrition.* New York: Academic Press, 1983.

Robbins, C.T., T.A. Hanley, A.E. Hagerman, O. Hjeljord, D.L. Baker, C.C. Schwartz, and W.W. Mautz. "Role of Tannins in Defending Plants against Ruminants: Reduction in Protein Availability." *Ecology* 68 (1987): 98–107.

Robbins, C.T., and A.N. Moen. "Milk Consumption and Weight Gain of White-tailed Deer." *The Journal of Wildlife Management* 39, no. 2 (1975): 355–360.

———. "Uterine Composition and Growth in Pregnant White-tailed Deer." *The Journal of Wildlife Management* 39, no. 4 (1975): 684–691.

Robbins, C.T., A.N. Moen, and J.T. Reid. "Body Composition of White-tailed Deer." *Journal of Animal Science* 38, no. 4 (1974): 871–876.

Robbins, C.T., S. Mole, A.E. Hagerman, and T.A. Hanley. "Role of Tannins in Defending Plants against Ruminants: Reduction in Dry Matter Digestion?" *Ecology* 68 (1987): 1606–1615.

Robbins, C.T., R.L. Prior, A.N. Moen, and W.J. Visek. "Nitrogen Metabolism of White-tailed Deer." *Journal of Animal Science* 38, no. 1 (1974): 186–191.

Robbins, C.T., P.J. Van Soest, W.W. Mautz, and A.N. Moen. "Feed Analyses and Digestion with Reference to White-tailed Deer." *The Journal of Wildlife Management* 39, no. 1 (1975): 67–79.

Robbins, R.L. "1973 Progress Report on the National Elk Refuge." Jackson, Wyo.: 1973. Unpublished.

Robinette, D.L., and M.K. Causey. "Preliminary Report on White-tailed Deer Movements in River-Swamp and Flatwoods Areas in Sumter County, Alabama." *Journal of the Alabama Academy of Science* 41 (1970): 151–152.

Robinette, W.L. "Mule Deer Home Range and Dispersal In Utah." *The Journal of Wildlife Management* 30 (April 1966): 335–349.

Robinette, W.L., C.H. Baer, R.E. Pillmore, and C.E. Knittle. "Effects of Nutritional Change on Captive Mule Deer." *The Journal of Wildlife Management* 37 (1973): 312–326.

Robinette, W.L., J.S. Gashwiler, D.A. Jones, and H.S. Crane. "Fertility of Mule Deer in Utah." *The Journal of Wildlife Management* 19 (1955): 115–136.

Robinette, W.L., J.S. Gashwiler, J.B. Low, and D.A. Jones. "Differential Mortality by Sex and Age among Mule Deer." *The Journal of Wildlife Management* 21 (1957): 1–16.

Robinette, W.L., J.S. Gashwiler, and O.W. Morris. "Food Habits of the Cougar in Utah and Nevada." *The Journal of Wildlife Management* 23 (1959): 261–273.

Robinette, W.L., N.V. Hancock, and D.A. Jones. *The Oak Creek Mule Deer Herd in Utah.* Utah State Division of Wildlife Resources, Publication 77–15. Salt Lake City: 1977.

Robinette, W.L., D.A. Jones, G. Rogers, and J.S. Gashwiler. "Notes on Tooth Development and Wear for Rocky Mountain Mule Deer." *The Journal of Wildlife Management* 21 (1957): 134–153.

Rogers, K.J., P.F. Folliott, and D.R. Patton. *Home Range and Movement of Five Mule Deer in a Semidesert Grass-Shrub Community.* U.S. Department of Agriculture, Forest Service, Research Paper RM-355. 1978.

Rongstad, O.J., and J.R. Tester. "Movements and Habitat Use of White-tailed Deer in Minnesota." *The Journal of Wildlife Management* 33, no. 2 (1969): 366–379.

Roseberry, J.L., and W.D. Klimstra. "Differential Vulnerability during a Controlled Deer Harvest." *The Journal of Wildlife Management* 38 (1974): 499–507.

Ruff, F.J. "Trapping Deer on the Pisgah National Game Preserve, North Carolina." *The Journal of Wildlife Management* 2 (1938): 151–161.

Russell, C.P. "Seasonal Migration of Mule Deer." *Ecological Monographs* 2 (1932): 1–46.

Russo, J.P. *The Kaibab North Deer Herd, Its History, Problems, and Management.* State of Arizona Game and Fish Department, Wildlife Bulletin No. 7. 1964.

Ryder, M.L. "Moulting and Hair Replacement." In *Progress in the Biological Sciences in Relation to Dermatology,* vol. 2, edited by A. Rook and R.H. Champion, 325–335. Cambridge, England: Cambridge University Press, 1964.

——. "Seasonal Coat Changes in Grazing Red Deer (*Cervus elaphus*)." *Journal of Zoology* (London) 181 (1977): 137–143.

Ryder, M.J., and R.N.B. Kay. "Structure of and Seasonal Change in the Coat of Red Deer (*Cervus elaphus*)." *Journal of Zoology* (London) 170 (1973): 69–77.

Ryel, L.A., L.D. Fay, and R.C. Van Etten. "Validity of age determination in Michigan deer." *Papers of the Michigan Academy of Science, Arts and Letters* 46 (1961): 289–316.

Sacks, J.J., D.G. Delgado, H.O. Lobel, and R.L. Parker. "Toxoplasmosis Infection Associated with Eating Undercooked Venison." *American Journal of Epidemiology* 118 (1983): 832–838.

Sadlier, R.M.F.S. *The Ecology of Reproduction in Wild and Domestic Mammals*. London: Methuen and Co. Ltd., 1969.

——. "Energy and Protein Intake in Relation to Growth of Suckling Black-tailed Deer Fawns." *Canadian Journal of Zoology* 58 (1980): 1347–1354.

Samuel, W.M. "Internal Parasites of Alberta's Wild Ruminants." In *Focus on a New Industry. Proceedings of the First Alberta Game Growers' Association Conference*, edited by L.A. Renecker, 71–78. Alberta, Canada: 1987.

——. "What's Bugging Your Deer." *Deer & Deer Hunting* 12, no. 69 (December 1988): 39–45.

——. "A Partially Annotated Bibliography of Meningeal Worm, *Parelaphostrongylus tenuis* (Nematoda), and Its Close Relatives." In *Synopses of the Parasites of Vertebrates*, edited by M.J. Kennedy. Edmonton, Alberta, Canada: Queen's Printer, 1991.

Sanderson, G.C. "The Study of Mammal Movements—A Review." *The Journal of Wildlife Management* 30 (1966): 215–235.

Sauer, P.R. "Physical Characteristics." In *White-tailed Deer: Ecology and Management*, edited by L.K. Halls, 73–90. Harrisburg: Stackpole Books, 1984.

Saunders, B.P. "Meningeal Worm in White-tailed Deer in Northwestern Ontario and Moose Population Densities." *The Journal of Wildlife Management* 37 (1973): 327–330.

Sawyer, T.G. "Behavior of Female White-tailed Deer with Emphasis on Pheromonal Communication." Master's thesis, University of Georgia, Athens, 1981.

Sawyer, T.G., R.L. Marchinton, and C.W. Berisford. "Scraping Behavior in Female White-tailed Deer." *Journal of Mammalogy* 63 (1982): 696–697.

Sawyer, T.G., R.L. Marchinton, and K.V. Miller. "Response of Female White-tailed Deer to Scrapes and Antler Rubs." *Journal of Mammalogy* 70 (1989): 431–433.

Sawyer, T.G., K.V. Miller, and R.L. Marchinton. "Patterns of Urination and Rub-Urination in Female White-tailed Deer." *Journal of Mammalogy* 74 (1993): 477–479.

Schoen, J.W., and O.C. Wallmo. "Timber Management and Deer in Southeast Alaska: Current Problems and Research Direction." In *Sitka Black-tailed Deer: Proceedings of a Conference in Juneau, Alaska*, edited by O.C. Wallmo and J.W. Schoen, 69–85. Juneau: U.S. Department of Agriculture, Forest Service, Alaska Region, and Alaska Department of Fish and Game, 1978.

Schwartz, C.C., W.L. Regelin, and J.G. Nagy. "Deer Preference for Juniper Forage and Volatile Oil Treated Foods." *The Journal of Wildlife Management* 44 (1980): 114–120.

Schwede, G., H. Hendrichs, and C. Wemmer. "Activity and Movement Patterns of Young White-tailed Deer Fawns." In *The Biology of Deer*, edited by R.D. Brown, 56–62. New York: Springer-Verlag, 1991.

Scott, M.D. "Fluorescent Orange Discrimination by Wapiti." *Wildlife Society Bulletin* 9 (1981): 256–260.

Semeyn, R.D. "An Investigation of the Influence of Weather on the Movements of White-tailed Deer in Winter." Master's thesis, Michigan State University, East Lansing, 1963.

Seton, E.T. *Lives of Game Animals*. Part 1. Vol. 3. Garden City, N.Y.: Doubleday, Doren and Co., 1927.

——. *Lives of Game Animals*. New York: Literary Guild of America, 1937.

Severinghaus, C.A. "The Willingness of Nursing Deer to Adopt Strange Fawns." *Journal of Mammalogy* 30 (1949): 75–76.

Severinghaus, C.W. "Tooth Development and Wear as Criteria of Age in White-tailed Deer." *The Journal of Wildlife Management* 13 (1949): 195–216.

——. "Seneca Ordinance Deer—Part II." *The Conservationist* (February–March 1958): 19.

——. "Deer Management." *The Conservationist* (April–May 1975): 35–37.

Severinghaus, C.W., and E.L. Cheatum. "Life and Times of the White-tailed Deer." In *The Deer of North America*, edited by W.P. Taylor, 57–186. Harrisburg: The Stackpole Co., 1956.

Severinghaus, C.W., and A.N. Moen. "Prediction of Weight and Reproductive Rates of a White-tailed Deer Population from Records of Antler Beam Diameter among Yearling Males." *New York Fish and Game Journal* 30, no. 1 (1983): 30–38.

Severson, K.E., and A.V. Carter. "Movements and Habitat Use by Mule Deer in the Northern Great Plains South Dakota." *Proceedings of the First International Rangelands Congress, Society for Range Management, Denver, Colorado* (1978): 466–468.

Shick, C. *Deer Management on Private Lands*. Michigan State University, Cooperative Extension Service, Extension Bulletin E-427. East Lansing: 1967.

Shields, W.M. *Philopatry, Inbreeding and the Evolution of Sex*. Albany: State University of New York Press, 1982.

Shiras, G., III. *Hunting Wildlife with Camera and Flashlight*. Vol. 1. Washington, D.C.: National Geographic Society, 1935.

Short, H.L. "Food Habits of Mule Deer in a Semidesert Grassland Habitat." *Journal of Range Management* 30 (1977): 206–209.

——. "Nutrition and Metabolism." In *Mule and Black-tailed Deer of North America*, edited by O.C. Wallmo, 99–127. Lincoln: University of Nebraska Press, 1981.

Short, H.L., J.D. Newsom, G.L. McCoy, and J.F. Fowler. "Effects of Nutrition and Climate on Southern Deer." *Transactions of the North American Wildlife and Natural Resources Conference* 34 (1969): 137–146.

Shrauder, P.A. "Appalachian Mountains." In *White-tailed Deer: Ecology and Management*, edited by L.K. Halls, 331–344. Harrisburg: Stackpole Books, 1984.

Siglin, R.J. *Movements and Capture Techniques/A Literature Review of Mule Deer*. Colorado Department of

Game, Fish and Parks, Game Research Division and Cooperative Wildlife Research Unit, Special Report 4. Denver: 1965.

Silverstein, R.M. "Some Collaborative Pheromone Investigations." *Twenty-third International Congress of Pure and Applied Chemistry* 3 (1971): 3–15.

Smith, B.L., D.J. Skotko, W. Owen, and R.J. McDaniel. "Color Vision in the White-tailed Deer." *The Psychological Record* 39 (1989): 195–202.

Smith, F.H., Jr. "Daily and Seasonal Variation in Movements of White-tailed Deer on Eglin Air Force Base, Florida." Master's thesis, University of Georgia, Athens, 1970.

Smith, T.D., and C.W. Fowler. "An Overview of the Study of the Population Dynamics of Large Mammals." In *Dynamics of Large Mammal Populations,* edited by C.W. Fowler and T.D. Smith, 1–18. New York: John Wiley and Sons, 1981.

Smith, W.P. "Maternal Defense in Columbian White-tailed Deer: When Is It Worth It?" *The American Naturalist* 130 (1987): 310–316.

———. *Odocoileus virginianus.* American Society of Mammalogists, Mammalian Species, Special Publication No. 388. Shippensburg, Pa.: 1991.

Sohn, R., and T.M. Yuill. "Bluetongue and Epizootic Hemorrhagic Disease in Wild Ruminants." *Bulletin of the Society for Vector Ecology* 16 (1991): 17–24.

Spalinger, D.E., T.A. Hanley, and C.T. Robbins. "Analysis of the Functional Response in Foraging in the Sitka Black-tailed Deer." *Ecology* 69 (1988): 1166–1175.

Spalinger, D.E., C.T. Robbins, and T.A. Hanley. "The Assessment of Handling Time in Ruminants: The Effect of Plant Chemical and Physical Structure on the Rate of Breakdown of Plant Particles in the Rumen of Mule Deer and Elk." *Canadian Journal of Zoology* 64 (1986): 312–321.

Sparrowe, R.D., and P.F. Springer. "Seasonal Activity Patterns of White-tailed Deer in Eastern South Dakota." *The Journal of Wildlife Management* 34, no. 2 (1970): 420–431.

Staines, B.W. "A Review of Factors Affecting Deer Dispersion and Their Relevance to Management." *Mammalian Review* 4 (1974): 79–91.

Staknis, M.A., and D.M. Simmons. "Ultrastructure of the Eastern Whitetail Deer Retina for Color Perception." *Pennsylvania Academy of Science* 64 (1990): 8–10.

Steerey, W.F. "Distribution, Range Use, and Population Characteristics of Mule Deer Associated with the Schafer Creek Winter Range, Bridger Mountains, Montana." Master's thesis, Montana State University, Bozeman, 1979.

Stock, T.M. "Gastro-intestinal Helminths in White-tailed Deer *(Odocoileus virginianus)* and Mule Deer *(Odocoileus hemionus)* of Alberta: A Community Approach." Master's thesis, University of Alberta, Edmonton, Canada, 1978.

Stonehouse, B. "Thermoregulatory Function of Growing Antlers." Nature (London) 218 (1968): 870–872.

Stumpf, W.A., and C.O. Mohr. "Linearity of Home Ranges of California Mice and Other Animals." *The Journal of Wildlife Management* 26, no. 2 (1962): 149–154.

Suttie, J.M., and P.F. Fennessy. "Recent Advances in the Physiological Control of Velvet Antler Growth." In *The Biology of Deer,* edited by R.D. Brown, 471–486. New York: Springer-Verlag, 1991.

Swank, W.G. *The Mule Deer in Arizona Chaparral.* Arizona Game and Fish Department, Wildlife Bulletin No. 3. 1958.

Sweeney, J.R. "The Effects of Harassment by Hunting Dogs on the Movement Patterns of White-tailed Deer on the Savannah River Plant, South Carolina." Master's thesis, University of Georgia, Athens, 1970.

Sweeney, J.R., R.L. Marchinton, and J.M. Sweeney. "Responses of Radio-monitored White-tailed Deer Chased by Hunting Dogs." *The Journal of Wildlife Management* 35, no. 4 (1971): 707–716.

Swenson, J.E. "Effects of Hunting on Habitat Use by Mule Deer on Mixed-grass Prairie in Montana." *Wildlife Society Bulletin* 10 (Summer 1982): 115–120.

Swenson, J.E., S.J. Knapp, and H.J. Wentland. "Winter Distribution and Habitat Use by Mule Deer and White-tailed Deer in Southeastern Montana." *Prairie Naturalist* 15 (1983): 97–112.

Swenson, J.E., and S.T. Stewart. "On the Use of Population Condition Indices in Deer Management." In *Practical Application of Recent Research Findings, Proceedings of the Wildlife Society, Montana Chapter,* edited by C.D. Eustace, 28–35. Billings: Wildlife Society, Montana Chapter, 1982.

Taber, R.D. "Deer Nutrition and Population Dynamics in the North Coast Range of California." *Transactions of the North American Wildlife Conference* 21 (1956): 159–172.

Taber, R.D., and R.F. Dasmann. *The Black-tailed Deer of the Chaparral; Its Life History and Management in the North Coast Range of California.* California Department of Fish and Game, Bulletin No. 8. Sacramento: 1958.

Telfer, E.S. "Winter Habitat Selection by Moose and White-tailed Deer." *The Journal of Wildlife Management* 34 (1970): 553–559.

Thomas, D.C., and I.M. Cowan. "The Patterns of Reproduction in Female Columbian Black-tailed Deer, *Odocoileus hemionus columbianus*." *Journal of Reproduction and Fertility* 44 (1975): 261–272.

Thomas, J.W., R.M. Robinson, and R.G. Marburger. "Social Behavior in a White-tailed Deer Herd Containing Hypogonadal Males." *Journal of Mammalogy* 46 (1965): 314–327.

Thomas, J.W., J.G. Teer, and E.A. Walker. "Mobility and Home Range of White-tailed Deer on the Edwards Plateau in Texas." *The Journal of Wildlife Management* 28, no. 3 (1964): 463–473.

Thomas, K.P. "Nocturnal Activities of the White-tailed Deer on Crab Orchard National Wildlife Refuge." Master's thesis, Southern Illinois University, 1966.

Thompson, C.B., J.B. Holter, H.H. Hayes, H. Silver, and W.E. Urban, Jr. "Nutrition of White-tailed Deer. I. Energy Requirements of Fawns." *The Journal of Wildlife Management* 37 (1973): 301–311.

Thorne, E.T. "Normal Body Temperature of Pronghorn Antelope and Mule Deer." *Journal of Mammalogy* 56 (1975): 697–698.

———. "Bacteria." In *Diseases of Wildlife in Wyoming,* 2d ed., edited by E.R. Thorne, N. Kingston, W.R. Jolley, and R.C. Bergstrom, 29–106. Cheyenne: Wyoming Game and Fish Department, 1982.

Thorne, E.T., E.S. Williams, T.R. Spraker, W. Helms, and T. Segerstrom. "Bluetongue in Free-ranging Pronghorn Antelope *(Antilocapra americana)* in Wyoming: 1976 and 1984." *Journal of Wildlife Diseases* 24: 113–119.

Tibbs, A.L. "Summer Behavior of White-tailed Deer and the Effects of Weather." Master's thesis, The Pennsylvania State University, University Park, 1967.

Torgerson, O., and W.R. Porath. "Midwest Oak/Hickory Forest." In *White-tailed Deer: Ecology and Management,* edited by L.K. Halls, 411–426. Harrisburg: Stackpole Books, 1984.

Townsend, T.W. "Factors Affecting Individual Rank in the Social Hierarchy of Penned White-tailed Deer *(Odocoileus virginianus borealis)*." Ph.D. dissertation, University of Guelph, Ontario, Canada, 1973.

Townsend, T.W., and F.D. Bailey. "Effects of Age, Sex and Weight on Social Rank in Penned White-tailed Deer." *American Midland Naturalist* 106 (1981): 92–101.

Trainer, C.E. "Direct Causes of Mortality in Mule Deer Fawns during Summer and Winter Periods on Steens Mountain, Oregon." *Proceedings of the Annual Meeting of the Western Association of Game and Fish Commissioners* 55 (1975): 163–170.

Ullrey, D.E. "Nutrition and Antler Development in White-tailed Deer." In *Antler Development in Cervidae,* edited by R.D. Brown. Kingsville, Tex.: Caesar Kleberg Wildlife Research Institute, 1983.

Ullrey, D.E., W.G. Youatt, H.E. Johnson, L.D. Fay, and B.L. Bradley. "Protein Requirements of White-tailed Deer Fawns." *The Journal of Wildlife Management* 31 (1967): 679–685.

Ullrey, D.E., W.G. Youatt, H.E. Johnson, L.D. Fay, B.L. Schoepke, and W.T. Magee. "Digestible and Metabolizable Energy Requirements for Winter Maintenance of Michigan White-tailed Does." *The Journal of Wildlife Management* 34 (1970): 863–869.

Urbston, D.F. "Herd Dynamics of a Pioneer-like Deer Population." *Proceedings of the Annual Conference of the Southeastern Association of Game and Fish Commissioners* 21 (1967): 42–50.

U.S. Department of Agriculture. *Climate and Man.* Washington, D.C.: U.S. Government Printing Office, 1941.

Vacek, Z. "Innervace Lyci Rostoucich Parohu u Cervidu" (Innervation of the Velvet of Growing Antlers in Cervidae). *Ceskoslovenska Morfologie* 3 (1955): 249–270.

Van der Eems, K.L., R.D. Brown, and C.M. Gundburg. "Circulating Levels of 1,25 Dihydroxy Vitamin D, Alkaline Phosphatase, Hydroxyproline, and Osteocalcin Associated with Antler Growth in White-tailed Deer." *Acta Endocrinologica* (Copenhagen) 118 (1988): 407–414.

Van Gelder, R.G., and D.F. Hoffmeister. "Canine Teeth in White-tailed Deer." *The Journal of Wildlife Management* 17 (1953): 100.

Van Hoven, W., and E.A. Boomker. "Digestion." in *Bioenergetics of Wild Herbivores,* edited by R.J. Hudson and R.G. White, 103–120. Boca Raton, Fla.: CRC Press, 1985.

Van Ness, G.B. "Anthrax." In *Diseases and Parasites of Whitetailed Deer,* edited by W.R. Davidson, F.A. Hayes, V.F. Nettles, and F.E. Kellogg, 161–167. Miscellaneous Publication No. 7. Tallahassee, Fla.: Tall Timbers Research Station, 1981.

Van Soest, P.J. *Nutritional Ecology of the Ruminant.* Corvallis, Oreg.: O&B Books, 1982.

Vaughan, T.A. *Mammalogy.* 2d ed. Philadelphia: W.B. Saunders Co., 1978.

Verme, L.J. "Swamp Conifer Deeryards in Northern Michigan, Their Ecology and Management." *Journal of Forestry* 63, no. 7 (1965): 523–529.

———. "Reproductive Patterns of White-tailed Deer Related to Nutritional Plane." *The Journal of Wildlife Management* 33 (1969): 881–887.

———. "Movements of White-tailed Deer in Upper Michigan." *The Journal of Wildlife Management* 37, no. 4 (1973): 545–552.

———. "Assessment of Natal Mortality in Upper Michigan Deer." *The Journal of Wildlife Management* 41, no. 4 (1977): 700–708.

———. "Sex Ratio Variations in *Odocoileus*: A Critical Review." *The Journal of Wildlife Management* 47, no. 3 (1983): 573–582.

———. "Progeny Sex Ratio Relationships in Deer: Theoretical vs. Observed." *The Journal of Wildlife Management* 49 (1985): 134–136.

———. "Decline in Doe Fertility in Southern Michigan Deer." *Canadian Journal of Zoology* 69 (1991): 25–28.

Verme, L.J., and J.J. Ozoga. "Influence of Winter Weather on White-tailed Deer in Upper Michigan." In *Proceedings of Snow and Ice in Relation to Wildlife and Recreation Symposium,* edited by A.O. Haugen, 16–28. Ames: Iowa State University, Iowa Cooperative Wildlife Research Unit, 1971.

———. "Sex Ratio of White-tailed Deer and the Estrus Cycle." *The Journal of Wildlife Management* 45 (1981): 710–715.

Verme, L.J., and D.E. Ullrey. "Physiology and Nutrition." In *White-tailed Deer: Ecology and Management,* edited by L.K. Halls, 91–118. Harrisburg: Stackpole Books, 1984.

Walker, M.L., and W.W. Becklund. *Checklist of the Internal and External Parasites of Deer,* Odocoileus hemionus *and* O. virginianus, *in the United States and Canada.* Index-Catalogue of Medical and Veterinary Zoology, Special Publication No. 1. Washington, D.C.: U.S. Government Printing Office, 1970.

Wallmo, O.C. "Mule and Black-tailed Deer *(Odocoileus hemionus)*." In *Big Game of North America: Ecology and Management,* edited by J.L. Schmidt and D.L. Gilbert, 31–42. Harrisburg: Stackpole Books, 1978.

———. "Mule and Black-tailed Deer Distribution and Habitats." In *Mule and Black-tailed Deer of North America,* edited by O.C. Wallmo, 1–25. Lincoln: University of Nebraska Press, 1981.

———. ed. *Mule and Black-tailed Deer of North America.* Lincoln: University of Nebraska Press, 1981.

Wallmo, O.C., L.H. Carpenter, W.L. Regelin, R.B. Gill, and D.L. Baker. "Evaluation of Deer Habitat on a Nutritional Basis." *Journal of Range Management* 30 (1977): 122–127.

Walls, G.L. *The Vertebrate Eye and Its Adaptive Radiation.* Cranbrook Institute of Science, Bulletin No. 19. Bloomfield Hills, Mich.: 1942.

Walther, F.R. "Territorial Behavior in Certain Horned Ungulates with Special Reference to the Examples of Thomson's and Grant's Gazelles." *Zoologica Africana* 7 (1972): 303–307.

Warren, R.J., R.W. Vogelsang, R.L. Kirkpatrick, and P.F. Scanlon. "Reproductive Behavior of Captive

White-tailed Deer." *Animal Behaviour* 26 (1978): 179–183.

Weigand, J.P. "Canine Teeth in Two Nebraska Mule Deer." *Journal of Mammalogy* 46 (1965): 528.

Welch, J.M. "A Study of Seasonal Movements of White-tailed Deer *(Odocoileus virginianus couesi)* in the Cave Creek Basin of the Chiricahua Mountains." Master's thesis, University of Arizona, Tucson, 1960.

West, N.O., and H.C. Nordan. "Hormonal Regulation of Reproduction and the Antler Cycle in the Male Columbian Black-tailed Deer *(Odocoileus hemionus columbianus).* Part I. Seasonal Changes in the Histology of the Reproductive Organs, Serum Testosterone, Sperm Production, and the Antler Cycle." *Canadian Journal of Zoology* 54 (1976): 1617–1636.

White, K.L. "Differential Range Use by Mule Deer in the Spruce-Fir Zone." *Northwest Science* 34 (1960): 118–126.

Whitehead, G.K. *Deer of the World.* New York: Viking Press, 1972.

Whitney, M.D., D.L. Forster, K.V. Miller, and R.L. Marchinton. "Sexual Attraction in White-tailed Deer." In *The Biology of Deer,* edited by R.D. Brown. New York: Springer-Verlag, 1991.

Whittemore, S., and A.N. Moen. "Composition and in vitro Digestibilities of Various Summer Foods of White-tailed Deer." *Canadian Journal of Animal Science* 60 (1980): 189–192.

Whittington, R.W. "Piedmont Plateau." In *White-tailed Deer: Ecology and Management,* edited by L.K. Halls, 355–366. Harrisburg: Stackpole Books, 1984.

Wiggers, E.P., and S.L. Beasom. "Characterization of Sympatric or Adjacent Habitats of Two Deer Species in West Texas." *The Journal of Wildlife Management* 50 (1986): 129–134.

Williams, E.S., and S. Young. "Chronic Wasting Disease of Captive Mule Deer: A Spongiform Encephalopathy." *Journal of Wildlife Diseases* 16 (1980): 89–98.

Witzel, D.A., M.D. Springer, and H.H. Mollenhauer. "Cone and Rod Photoreceptors in the White-tailed Deer *Odocoileus virginianus.*" *American Journal of Veterinary Research* 39 (1978): 699–701.

Wobeser, G., W. Runge, and D. Noble. "Necrobacillosis in Deer and Pronghorn Antelope in Saskatchewan." *Canadian Veterinary Journal* 16 (1975): 3–9.

Wood, A.K. "Ecology of a Prairie Mule Deer Population." Ph.D. dissertation, Montana State University, Bozeman, 1987.

———. "Use of Shelter by Mule Deer during Winter." *Prairie Naturalist* 20 (1988): 15–22.

———. "Comparative Distribution and Habitat Use by Pronghorn Antelope and Mule Deer." *Journal of Mammalogy* 70 (1989): 335–340.

Wood, A.K., R.J. Mackie, and K.L. Hamlin. *Ecology of Sympatric Mule and White-tailed Deer Populations in a Prairie Environment.* Montana Department of Fish, Wildlife and Parks, Technical Bulletin. Helena: 1989.

Woods, G.R., D.C. Guynn, R.L. Marchinton, and K.V. Miller. "Rub Research: An Update." *Deer & Deer Hunting* 15, no. 3 (1991): 104–106.

Woods, G.R., and L.W. Robbins. "Scrape Behavior in Female White-tailed Deer." Abstract. *Annual Meeting of the American Society of Mammalogists* 67 (1987): 556.

Woodson, D.L., E.T. Reed, R.L. Downing, and B.S. McGinnes. "Effects of Fall Orphaning on White-tailed Deer Fawns and Yearlings." *The Journal of Wildlife Management* 44 (1980): 249–252.

———. "Effect of Fall Orphaning on White-tailed Deer Fawns and Yearlings." Unpublished.

Youatt, W.G., D.E. Ullrey, and W.T. Magee. "Vitamin A Concentrations in the Livers of White-tailed Deer." *The Journal of Wildlife Management* 40 (1976): 172–173.

Youmans, H.B. "Habitat Utilization by Mule Deer of the Armstrong Winter Range, Bridger Mountains, Montana." Master's thesis, Montana State University, Bozeman, 1979.

Zagata, M.D., and A.O. Haugen. "Influence of Light and Weather on Observability of Iowa Deer." *The Journal of Wildlife Management* 38 (1974): 220–228.

Zagata, M.D., and A.N. Moen. "Antler Shedding by White-tailed Deer in the Midwest." *Journal of Mammalogy* 55, no. 3 (1974): 656–659.

Index
